Aristocratic SPLENDOUR

MONEY & THE WORLD OF
THOMAS COKE
EARL OF LEICESTER

D.P. MORTLOCK

SUTTON PUBLISHING

First published in the United Kingdom in 2007 by
Sutton Publishing Limited · Phoenix Mill
Thrupp · Stroud · Gloucestershire · GL5 2BU

British Library Cataloguing in Publication Data
A catalogue record for this book is available from the British Library.

Hardback ISBN 978-0-7509-4370-3
Paperback ISBN 978-0-7509-4371-0

For Edward Coke, 7th Earl of Leicester, who for nearly a
quarter of a century has given me constant support and
encouragement. The countless happy hours that I have
enjoyed under his eye in one of the finest private libraries
in the world have been a blessing beyond compare.

Typeset in Photina MT.
Typesetting and origination by
Sutton Publishing Limited.
Printed and bound in England.

CONTENTS

List of Illustrations		iv
Foreword		v
Acknowledgements		vii
Map		viii
	Introduction	1
1.	The Marriage	7
2.	The Great Estate	15
3.	On Home Ground	51
4.	The Town House and its Parish	61
5.	Money Matters	72
6.	The Family	84
7.	The Social Creature	105
8.	The Arts, Culture and Taste	131
9.	Sport	147
10.	Food, Drink and Household Supplies	160
11.	Travel and Stable Matters	184
12.	Servants	191
13.	What of the Future?	212

Appendices

1.	A List of Manors and Properties Purchased by Sir Edward Coke	218
2.	Individual Manors of the Great Estate in the 1720s	220
3.	Advowsons in the Gift of Thomas Coke	244
4.	Household and other Account Books Consulted	245
	Notes	247
	Bibliography	259
	Index	265

LIST OF ILLUSTRATIONS

1. Thomas Coke, miniature by Christian Zincke
2. Lady Margaret, miniature by Christian Zincke
3. Minster Lovell, engraving by Nathaniel and Samuel Buck
4. Thanet House, Great Russell Street
5. William Kent's drawing of his layout of the south lawn up to the Great Wood
6. Eighteenth-century map of Norfolk showing Holkham's position relative to Raynham and Houghton
7. Engraving of Thomas Coke and one of his esquires in John Pine's *The Procession and Ceremonies Observed at the Time of the Installation of the Companions of the Bath*
8. Hogarth's South Sea Bubble engraving, 1724
9. Hogarth's Cockpit engraving [1760s?]
10. Sir Edward Coke, the Chief Justice, portrait by Cornelius Johnson
11. Thomas Coke just returned from the Grand Tour, by Francesco Trevisani
12. Holkham, an aerial view of the house and park

FOREWORD

Over the years the history of Holkham, the estate and the family who have lived in the house has been well documented. However, almost everything written about Holkham has been with a 'broad sweep of the brush'. Sam Mortlock, the Holkham librarian, has chosen to examine, in fascinating detail, the ten years from Thomas Coke's return from the Grand Tour in 1718 to his elevation to the peerage in 1728, and thus before the start on building the great house in 1734 that was to be his life's passion.

Immediately on his return from the Continent, Thomas Coke married an heiress, Margaret Tufton, and it was expected that he would then press on with the house. But it was not to be. Coke rashly invested in South Sea Stock at the very top of the market. The bubble burst in 1720, and he lost the equivalent in present-day money of nearly £3 million. The result was a delay of fourteen years, during which he rebuilt his finances, and that delay has always seemed to me to be a tragedy, as on his death in 1759 the house had still not been completed. The statutory, books, manuscripts, drawings and paintings that still decorate the house were collected by him or at his direction, and it is particularly poignant that he did not live to see it all in situ, or indeed the completed house, the design of which owed so much to his inspiration.

However, Mr Mortlock shows that those years were not wasted. During Coke's younger years, his estates were competently managed by his trustees, but after his marriage he directed his attention to increasing the return from his land. In the early eighteenth century English farming was still set in the rigid manorial mould that had existed for centuries. Coke set about transforming farming by practices we would recognise today, thus increasing the profits of his tenants and his own rental income. This, combined with the close direction of his non-agricultural properties, produced a 17½ per cent increase in income between 1722 and 1728.

Coke's energy was prodigious. In 1720 work on a large new kitchen garden was begun; a thorn nursery was established to provide plants for the proposed new hedges. At the same time a huge operation to enhance the landscape to the south of the proposed new house was started. Several thousand tons of soil were removed; thousands of trees were brought in, many semi-mature and some from as far away as Yorkshire. Almost as a diversion, he reclaimed 560 acres of marsh from the sea. In 1725, anticipating the building of his new house, he bought a nearby brickyard. By the time the foundations had been dug in 1734, the prospects of all sides were now far removed from the 'open and barren' estate Coke had returned to in 1718.

Mr Mortlock has unearthed fascinating snippets. Coke spent the staggering sum of £5,409 on clothes, jewellery, horses and presents during preparations for his wedding, including £50 on a gold tweezer case for his fiancée. Later, despite the vast gap in their social positions, Coke surprisingly borrowed £60 from Tomley, the hall porter, and £200 from his library, admittedly during the South Sea debacle. Handkerchiefs were bought by the dozen at 4*s* 6*d*, which is considerably more, if translated into today's money, than we pay for handkerchiefs now. In 1728 duty of £1 5*s* 6*d* was paid on the importation of 307 drawings, plus half a crown to the Customs Officer to keep him sweet.

Hogarth's view of the gluttonous Englishman is confirmed when we read in the accounts for February 1727 that everyone in the household was given a daily meat allowance of 2½lb. We are mildly astonished to read of fifty coconuts bought for the kitchen. What were they used for? Total expenditure on food for the household in 1725 was £952, with £526 spent on wine, beer and other alcoholic drinks, perhaps confirming Trevelyan's observation that 'Drunkedness is the vice of Englishmen of all classes'. Nothing much has changed!

No doubt, in another 300 years, historians may be as fascinated by life in all its aspects in the Holkham of the early twenty-first century as I have been reading about life in the early eighteenth century. I would not be the least surprised to hear the same names feature in the twenty-fourth century as they do now. We have a Frary, a Futter and a Mallet working here now, as their forebears did in 1720. Perhaps that says something for the stability and continuity of life on at least one of the great estates of England.

Last of all, my very great thanks go to Sam Mortlock for his dedication in producing quite the most informative and enchanting record of perhaps the most interesting decade in the history of Holkham.

Earl of Leicester

Acknowledgements

*M*y first thanks are to Lord Leicester and the Trustees of the Holkham Estate, for permission to transcribe and make use of the Holkham archival materials listed in Appendix 4, which form the bedrock of this book. I am grateful also for their permission to reproduce the subjects of Plates 1–5, 7, 10, 11, taken from pictures, Old Master Drawings and books in the house. The text would never have reached its final state had it not been for the guiding hand of Michael Daley MBE, Holkham's House Administrator, particularly in IT matters. All the photography (with the exception of the aerial view) is his work, and I could ask for no better.

No project spread over twenty years thrives without a generous measure of tea and sympathy, perceptive criticism, doubtful jokes and encouragement when the impulse is to throw everything in the lake and retreat to the pub. Dr Suzanne Reynolds and Michael are in my debt on all counts, and deserve my deep appreciation.

I was fortunate in being able to call upon Raymond Frostick's knowledge of maps and local surveyors, and he generously provided the reproduction of a section of the eighteenth-century map that appears as Plate 6.

My indebtedness to my publishers is profound. It was commissioning editor Christopher Feeney's infectious enthusiasm that gave me heart to look more critically at the original text, and sent me on my way with a light heart. Since that happy day, my copy-editor Elizabeth Stone and project editor Hilary Walford have been invaluable in guiding me gently towards the finishing tape. I can only hope that their confidence is justified.

No ancient eccentric has ever been blessed with a more sympathetic wife. Barbara has endured weeks of isolation in Norwich over the years, while I disappeared in search of enlightenment in labyrinthine Holkham and numerous libraries – great fun for me but not for her, and I am deeply grateful.

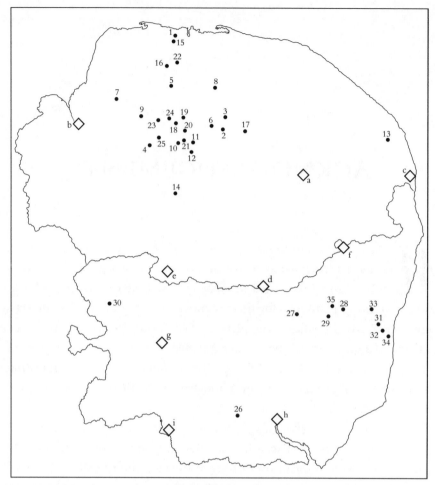

An outline map showing the disposition of the Norfolk and Suffolk manors of the Great Estate in 1720, and the principal towns of the two counties.

KEY

NORFOLK

1. Holkham
2. Billingford
3. Bintree
4. Castle Acre
5. Dunton and Doughton
6. North Elmham
7. Flitcham
8. Fulmodeston
9. Great Massingham
10. Kempstone
11. Longham
12. Wendling
13. Martham
14. Panworth Hall
15. Quarles
16. South Creake
17. Sparham
18. Tittleshall
19. Godwick
20. Mileham
21. Beeston
22. Waterden
23. Weasenham
24. Wellingham
25. West Lexham

SUFFOLK

26. Aldham
27. Horham Thorpehall, Thorpehall Wood
28. Huntingfield Park, Huntingfield Manor
29. Laxfield, Laxfield Rectory, Laxfield Roadstreet
30. Mildenhall, Lambsholme
31. Scotshall
32. Westleton
33. Thorington
34. Candelent, Falkenham
35. Cratfield

a. Norwich
b. King's Lynn
c. Great Yarmouth
d. Diss
e. Thetford
f. Bungay
g. Bury St Edmunds
h. Ipswich
i. Sudbury

INTRODUCTION

*D*uring the years in which I was preparing a new catalogue of Holkham's printed books I often had occasion to search the volumes of the household accounts in the archives for information about the house, its contents and the history of the Coke family. As I did so, I came to realise that a mass of fascinating material lay hidden in their pages. Not unnaturally, many before me had made good use of these records. One has only to read any of Dr Hassall's books and papers, or those of Charles W. James, to find innumerable references to the accounts. Without exception, however, my predecessors had been content to quote individual entries in order to illustrate or validate a point, and I came to believe that only by producing a full transcript could one extract the full measure of the quality of these records. Seeking to keep my enthusiasm within reasonable bounds, I decided that one decade of the eighteenth century should be the limit. The majority of studies so far have focused on the period 1712 to 1718, which covers Thomas Coke's Grand Tour, and on the great span between 1734, when the house was begun, to its completion after his death in 1759. The gap between invited exploration, lying neatly between Coke's marriage on his return from the Continent in 1718 and his elevation to the peerage in 1728. As I became more familiar with the material, I realised that it could be used to illuminate a part of his life that not only had been neglected but was of great importance in his development.

My principal source material is the accounts dealing with the years 1718 to 1730, contained in a series of vellum-bound folio volumes in the Holkham archive repository. Not wholly uniform in content or layout, they record the expenses of the household at Holkham and in London, the management of the home farm, details of the economy of the estate lands scattered across England, and income derived from a number of sources. Records of expenditure were kept at three levels if not four, from the hall porter's notebook up to the land steward's quarterly and annual summaries. Coverage is not complete, and the scraps of paper that probably formed the lowest level of record have virtually all disappeared, along with nearly all receipted bills.

The volumes contain records kept by land stewards, house stewards and senior servants such as the butler, housekeeper and valet. Supervision and control were exercised at the intermediate level by checking the subordinates and correcting them where necessary before writing up a consolidated version for the house or land steward. Quarterly summaries were then prepared for submission to the master of the house.

In the wider world of the estate, the bailiff of each manor was responsible for preparing accounts of income and expenditure relating to the tenants, to be presented to the land steward or his representative at the manor's annual court meeting. Finally, the land steward journeyed to London for a meeting with the family's auditor, where he was joined by the bailiffs from Oxfordshire and Dorset. These definitive audits lasted for ten days or so, in which all the year's accounts were examined and approved (or amended) for presentation to the owner.

Fifteen account books and three audit books survive from the chosen period, and in most cases the cover title or an internal heading identifies the person who prepared the record (although, confusingly, the phrase 'this accountant' is often used in place of the servant's formal title). In several cases the periods covered overlap, and the same transaction is sometimes noted in more than one place; three of the ledgers contain accounts prepared by more than one person, having been bound up together for convenience of handling. A summary list of these volumes is provided in Appendix 4.

A typical household account book sets out purchases in groups according to the department for which they were made – kitchen, still room, cellar, stables and so on, or by the commodities that were shared requirements, such as fuel. All outgoings were totalled week by numbered week, and at the end of each quarter (Lady Day, Midsummer, Michaelmas and Christmas) the account was submitted for payment. The servants regularly dispensed gratuities on behalf of the master and kept him supplied with spending money, entering the amount 'for My Master's Pockett'. Often the hall porter would be sent for a flask of spirits or a paper and then recoup the cost from the house steward at the end of the week. Cash was drawn regularly by the stewards from Peniston Lamb, the family's attorney and man of business, and a balance was drawn in that respect at the year's end. Thomas Coke sometimes signed off household accounts, and his signature is paired with his wife's here and there.

The system of accounting was one that had been used by landowners since the Middle Ages. Its main purpose was not to establish profit or loss but to monitor the probity of the servant involved, and the estate audit books employ a standard format based on this principle. For each year, under the individual manor's heading, the first section headed 'The Charge' records in detail all the sums for which the compiler was responsible and lists rents and casual profits before finishing with a 'Total Charge' figure. Then follows 'The Discharge', comprising an equally exhaustive list of payments and expenses including quit rents paid, Land Tax payments, expenditure on repairs, allowances for 'Improvements' and 'Neat Money'. Outstanding tenants' debts are listed before a 'Total Discharge' figure is calculated, which allows a balance to be struck. After all the properties are dealt with comes the heading: 'The Abstract of the foregoing Audit Accompt of the sev.ll Estates for the year 17..'. Under this, the totals of income and expenditure for each manor are tabulated using twelve categories, including 'Old Arrears', 'Deficiencies' and 'Arrears Returned'. In conclusion, there is always the written proviso that the accounts are passed subject to the possibility of errors. Overall, this accounting formula made it difficult if not impossible to assess relative productivity, but at least it gave the owner a clear picture of who owed what to whom. The absence of realistic forecasts of income – the absence of any apparent concern to *determine* real income – is a reminder of how remote from today's practice the accounting procedures of eighteenth-century landowners remained. Even Edward Laurence's *Duty of a Steward to his Lord* (London, 1727), which spelled out proper methods for making estate surveys, valuing individual farms and accounting with tenants, nevertheless omitted any mention of how to calculate the real return on the owner's land.[1]

Thomas Coke's role as prime mover in the creation of Holkham Hall has been largely understated: a typical example is John Summerson's comment on the building in his chapter 'The Palladian Phase 1710–1750': 'Holkham Hall, Norfolk may well owe as much to Burlington as to Kent', and the relevant plates carry the legend: 'William Kent, Holkham Hall'.[2] However, a phrase of Christopher Hussey's acts as a useful corrective: 'It is possible that Kent was then [in 1733] advising on what Lord Lovel called the "pictoresk" and that *the actual designing of the house should be assigned to those years preceding the digging of the foundations in 1734*' (emphasis added)[3] – in other words my chosen period. In the latest comprehensive overview of the house, its architecture, construction and contents, Prof. Leo Schmidt has this to say: 'Unique in its combination of magnificent architecture, landscape design and decoration, it forms – along with its priceless collections – a single, complex work of art. Principally the achievement of one man, Thomas Coke, Earl of Leicester.'[4] The accounts of the 1720s have a good deal to tell us about the way in which Thomas Coke approached the project that was to become his consuming and lifelong interest, and, while analysing the entries dealing with the preliminary work in advance of building, I was aware that other aspects of his life and times could be explored. Indeed, it seemed unrealistic to consider the preparations for the building in isolation, and I was encouraged by the example provided by Parker's survey of farming at Holkham.[5]

In the course of transcribing the audit books in particular I realised (with some surprise) that the old ways and practices of manorial life in English villages were still firmly in place in the early 1700s – a fact often taken for granted by historians and assumed as common knowledge. To me it was a revelation and encouraged a long look at the day-to-day details of village life on the Coke manors. Curiosity fuelled by ignorance must be held responsible for much of the explanatory matter in Chapter 2. Without this information, I could make no sense of what I found, nor succeed in expressing an understanding of what was going on in, say, Hindolveston in 1723. For those with interests in particular village communities, in Appendix 2 I have given brief details of every Coke manor in East Anglia, listing the principal tenants and craftsmen.

Another and more cogent reason for looking in detail at the landed estate during the 1720s is the fact that Thomas Coke's contribution to the development of agriculture, particularly in Norfolk, has been seriously undervalued. Most commentators have focused on the achievements of his great-nephew Thomas William Coke, known to all as 'Coke of Norfolk'. The latter's reputation in his own day was unrivalled, and his fame and patriarchal benevolence, coupled with an aptitude for publicity, have assured his place in history. His admirers established the tradition that he had inherited a sandy waste that he duly transformed. A reading of Arthur Young's survey published five years before Thomas William assumed control at Holkham is all that is needed by way of correction[6] – the crucial changes were effected through the 1st Earl's management, foresight and determination. The popular image of 'Coke of Norfolk' endures, despite one of my predecessors' efforts to redress the balance:

> The yeomen of Norfolk erected no column to commemorate the agricultural efforts of the 1st Earl, as they did in the case of his successor. But had they erected a monument to the man under whose rule the sheepwalks had been changed into a country which gave tenant-farmers £1,300 to £3,000 a year, besides building the house which is one of the stateliest in England, they would have been amply justified in so doing.[7]

If quality of mind, firmness of purpose and a genius for not only creating the finest Palladian mansion in England but at the same time invigorating a great estate are to be taken into account, then Thomas Coke should stand equal in public esteem with his better-known successor.

In the chapters that follow, I present a picture of life in the Coke household and across his estate under a series of general headings, with the aim of recreating 'a landscape with figures'. Dame Veronica Wedgwood once wrote that she found the behaviour of men as individuals more interesting than their behaviour as groups or classes,[7] and, while agreeing with that sentiment, I have found that in Thomas Coke's case the behaviour marks a character that is obstinately elusive. Even in his own day he was seen as an odd mixture, combining a fanatical love of field sports with a level of classical learning that commanded respect. His character appears both harsh and compassionate, and the fact that he remains an enigma does not lessen the attraction.

Financial records are sometimes assumed to be dull and mundane, but those I have explored are anything but that. A whole eighteenth-century vocabulary comes into play with dozens of specialised terms for trades, commodities, weights, measures and hundreds of articles in everyday use – lasts of wheat and chaldrons of coal jostle with ankers of brandy and ells of cloth throughout, all priced in pounds, shillings and pence. For those unfamiliar with pre-decimal currency, an aide memoir may be helpful:

There was no pound coin in the eighteenth century, but there were twenty silver shillings in the pound, twelve copper pennies in the shilling, and the pennies were subdivided into two halfpennies and four farthings. Three other silver coins were common: the two-shilling florin (2s), the two-shillings-and-sixpence half a crown (2s 6d), and the crown (5s). After an erratic history, the golden guinea stabilised in the late seventeenth century at twenty-one shillings and was used for professional fees, gambling, at auction and to confuse the multitude until the twentieth century.

These pages illuminate for an instant the individuals among the hundreds of ordinary folk going about their daily lives, whose only other memorials lie unheeded in the parish registers – Tom Manning, whose job it was to 'fright the crows from the seeds in the Great Wood'; Ann Blinkhorn, the charwoman who found herself transformed into the emergency cook in the London house on a shilling a day and did the job for three months; old Charlie Hodsby, whose mare was seized for a heriot when he died at Portbury; and Henry Carter, who, with his wife and son, spent a week thatching Robert Parker's barn at Minster Lovell. They come into focus for a moment and then vanish, but together they create a powerful impression of what it was like to 'live and have one's living' (Acts of the Apostles 17: 28) under the hand and eye of Thomas Coke.

In a work such as this there is always a temptation to flesh out the picture in order to make it more attractive. 'Perhaps', 'presumably' and 'no doubt' are seductive, but I have tried to use such terms sparingly and to anchor each statement or statistic on sound evidence found in the archives or in identified secondary sources.

Chapter 1

THE MARRIAGE

O n Tuesday 13 May 1718, Thomas Coke landed at Dover with his entourage, having spent 'near 6 years Travails in France, Italy, Sicily, Germany, Malta, Holland and Flanders'. He was met by Edward Smith, the household's master of horse, who that day began a new journal in which he recorded all payments made covering his master's

> Expenses in London from that Time to ye 17th of June following which day ye sd. Mr Coke Attain.d to ye Age of 21 Years. And upon Thursday ye 3d of July following was Marryed to ye Rt. Hon.ble ye Lady Margaret Tufton 3d. Daughter to Thomas Earl of Thanet, a Lady of Great Beauty, Singular Virtue & Goodness, being 18 years of Age, 16th of June 1718. These Acct.s also Contain ye Charges of Mr Cokes Equipping himself for ye said Wedding, And for Liveries, Coaches, Horses, Furniture, presents to his said Lady and Gratuities &c.[1]

It was to be a busy seven weeks and there was much to be done.

It is very unlikely that Thomas had met Lady Margaret before his return, but negotiations concerning a possible alliance had been going on for some time between his guardians and the Earl of Thanet. It would seem that things went forward smoothly and the lawyers for both sides had begun work on drafting the marriage settlement papers. When the young traveller arrived at Dover, his luggage was cleared through the Customs House, a coach and six was hired for the journey to London and arrangements were made for the two berlins* that had been bought abroad to be taken up to town. They probably carried most of the baggage and were guarded during the two overnight stops. On arrival, the whole party went into lodgings with a Mrs Cooley and a Mrs Ireland, and there were tavern bills and bills for wood, candles, washing and sheets. Edward Smith's father, Humphrey, the land steward, joined him, and, together with three footmen, a coachman, two grooms, a postilion, a stable boy and two helpers, they were all on board wages for eight weeks.

Thomas Coke's coming of age on 17 June was the signal for the details of the marriage settlement to be finalised, and copies of the documents involved are collected in one volume entitled *Copys of the Deed to Lead the Use of the Recoveries, of the Marriage Settlement, and of the Settlement of the house in London made by Sir Thomas Coke*.[2] The first seven pages are taken up with a detailed list and description of all the properties that comprised the Coke estate in Norfolk and elsewhere, and, after every possible legal synonym, alternative usage and eventuality had been exhausted, it was agreed between the parties (Thomas himself, Sir Edward Coke and John Coke, two of his guardians) that everything was to be 'to the use and behoof of the said Thomas Coke, his heirs and assigns for ever'. The next indenture was drawn up between Coke and a long list of other parties headed by Thomas, Earl of Thanet and the Lady Margaret Tufton, recording that 'a marriage is intended shortly to be had and solempnized [sic] between the said Thomas Coke and Lady Margaret Tufton'. It stipulated that £5,000 be passed to Coke immediately as part of Lady Margaret's marriage portion, the remaining £10,000 to be paid later by agreement. There followed the jointure provisions that were to be available for Lady Margaret's maintenance should she outlive her husband. A dozen Norfolk manors were

---

* A four-wheeled covered carriage with a seat behind fitted with a hood.

selected that yielded £3,354 a year in rent, thus providing her with a tax-free income of £1,600. Within this seemingly interminable list of property details is embedded the more interesting matter of the young wife-to-be's 'pin money'. During the lifetime of Coke's grandmother, Lady Anne Walpole, Lady Margaret was to have £400 a year in equal quarterly instalments from the income of the estate, rising to £500 on the death of Lady Anne. Four other Norfolk manors, yielding £922 a year, were picked to cover the cost, and the first payment was duly made to her in March 1719, covering the preceding three quarters. As with all 'settled estates', the questions of sucession and entail were gone into in great detail, and provision was made for the education of any younger children and the maintenance and dowries of any daughters the couple might have. The final indenture in this collection dealt with the Earl of Thanet's house in Bloomsbury, the freehold of which was owned by Lady Russell. It specified that, 'in consideration of the intended marriage and of the summe of two thousand pounds . . . to be paid to him the said Thomas Earl of Thanet by the said Thomas Coke', the residue of the lease of Thanet House would pass to Coke, including the stables, coach houses and other accommodation in Blue Boar Yard. Moreover, the entire contents of the property were similarly assigned. Almost as an afterthought, below the signatures and seals of the various parties there is a separate memorandum that records an agreement that the Earl of Thanet should enjoy the use of an apartment of his choice in the house for the rest of his life.

On the young man's arrival in London, one of the first requirements was transport, and the following were bought in short order – eight coach horses, four saddle horses for servants, a grey gelding, a 'managed cropped' gelding, and a pad* for Lady Margaret, costing £440 in all. Stable, shoeing, bitting and feed expenses followed as a matter of course and amounted to over £70 for the first seven weeks. By then, Coke had moved into Thanet House, confirmed by the cost of feeding the four dogs there being entered in the accounts for the first time. Having made his first exploratory journey down to Hothfield Place, the Earl of Thanet's house near Ashford in Kent, he made a second visit towards the end of June, accompanied by his guardians and this time using his new custom-built 'chariot' lined with fine scarlet cloth drawn

---

* A docile, easy-paced horse suitable as a mount for ladies and the inexperienced.

by his new team of horses in the hands of Francis Riggs, the coachman. He had spent £50 on a gold tweezer case for his fiancée, and this may have been his opportunity of presenting it to her.

There is no doubt that for all concerned this dynastic wedding was of supreme importance, and no effort or expense was to be spared in ensuring that the bridegroom's contribution matched that of the noble family to which he was to be allied. That first present was but a small part of a great flurry of spending that was packed into a few weeks prior to the wedding. For the man himself, the primary consideration was his clothes, his linen and his accessories. Over fifty yards of fine cloth, five of scarlet drab, paduasoy silk and nearly sixty pounds worth of gold and silver lace from Mr Henry Hicks went into making six suits. They were made up by William Haines the family tailor, and Mrs Mary Gameron earned £87 for embroidering two of them. There were stockings from Mrs Twamlow, shoes from John Verdon and hats with feathers from John Leek. Shirts, handkerchiefs and linen were all made to order, and another £101 went on lace. Two periwigs, six pairs of gloves and a sword belt completed the list of apparel, but there was more to come. Coke then bought a gold watch, chain and swivel from George Graham, as well as an agate snuffbox, a ring and shoe buckles set with diamonds; pearl tassels enlivened by diamonds and rubies were chosen to adorn his new suits. His silver barber's basin along with six razors, strops and sundry toiletries, all in a shagreen case, completed Coke's personal inventory, and two new hair trunks were ordered in which to pack the clothes. His 14-year-old brother, Robert, was kitted out with two suits of clothes trimmed with lace to be worn over a brocade waistcoat, plus stockings, boots and shoes, and a new periwig. Because it was probably his first entry into society, the boy required a sword, a seal and a new setting for his diamond ring, plus seven guineas in pocket money. Both brothers took fencing and dancing lessons under a Mr Bostwick.

The servants who were to travel with the party were newly dressed overall, headed by Humphrey Smith, the steward, who was provided with a suit of fine cloth fringed with gold, together with a hat, stockings, boots and shoes. His son Edward, the gentleman of the horse, had the slightly superior gold lace on his suit, as did Edward Jarrett, the valet-de-chambre. Ten lower servants all had swords and greatcoats to go with their new liveries trimmed with silver lace, and there were twelve pairs of buckskin breeches and velvet caps for the coachmen and grooms.

All the horses that had been bought were furnished with new trappings. Coke's own horse had a 'Rich Red Velvet Embroider'd Saddle Royal with Crimson Cloth & other Matters Compleat'. There was also a slightly less expensive set upholstered in blue Genoa velvet enlivened with gold lace and fringe that had a caparison cloth to go with it, which was probably for Robert Coke. Both saddles were fitted with a case of fine pistols supplied with powder and ball. The gentleman of the horse's new saddle also came with pistol cases and saddle cloth all embroidered. Yet more saddles were needed for the livery servants and the postilion, and a full set of harness for the team of six carriage horses.

By far the largest outlay in this riot of spending was for jewellery and other presents to give to Lady Margaret. The list was headed by a diamond necklace of forty-eight stones, followed by earrings, stay buckles and tags, a sprig for the hair, a gold watch and chain, and a gold seal, and there were wedding rings for both of them. For her new horse she was to have a side-saddle in green embroidered velvet with gold lace and fringes, together with a set of harness. An intriguing item is the £108 of 'old gold for an Endowing purse', which was presumably to be presented to the bride. The totals are noted below:

	£	s	d
Thomas Coke's clothing	504	1	11
Thomas Coke's jewellery &c.	574	15	0
Robert Coke's clothing	105	12	0
Servants' clothing	328	7	4
Horses	440	1	0
The chariot & harness	179	0	6
Saddlery & harness	199	17	4
Lady Margaret's presents	3,077	15	4
	5,409	10	5[3]

One further small matter had to be attended to. It was apparently required of the young bridegroom that he produce his birth certificate, and the incumbent of St James's Piccadilly charged half a guinea for providing evidence of his birth and christening.

Those members of his family who had been invited to attend the wedding were gathering, and Sir Edward Coke travelled from Longford in Derbyshire to

Sandway,* where servants met him with fresh horses to bring him up to London. Sir John Newton had already gone ahead to Hothfield, but Mr Newton was fetched by coach from Barr's Court in Gloucestershire, and John Coke came down from Baggrave in Leicestershire. Lady Anne Walpole, Thomas's grandmother, was of the party, and used her own coach with five servants, and his principal man of affairs, Peniston Lamb, was invited, bringing with him not only his nephew but a clerk in case there was business to transact (his bill for 'drawing the wedding writings & other business' was £493 4s, with a further £25 for one of the Masters in Chancery). Humphrey Smith was naturally in attendance, and Mr Haines, the tailor, sent his foreman down to ensure that final touches to the wedding finery were professionally managed. Wedding favours for Mr Coke's party were provided by a Mr Cooley for £85, and John Casey, the house steward, entered 13s 6d expenses for taking them down.

The scene moves to Hothfield Place, the seat of the Earls of Thanet, where the Tufton family had resided since the time of Henry VIII. The official receipt books record that Lord Tufton paid £5,000 into the Treasury in 1625 for his peerage, but that would hardly have been a suitable topic on which to dwell in 1718, except, perhaps, as a private reminder that 'money was embracing money'. Of the house itself very little is known, and, although no illustration of it has been traced, it is shown symbolically on John Seller's map of Kent 'newly corrected and amended' of 1710. It was demolished in the 1790s and replaced by a severe stone mansion by James Wyatt, which in its turn was torn down when the estate passed into other hands. All that remains, apart from a fine view to the south across the extensive park, are the original stables and long stretches of mellow red brick walls. The church of St Margaret stands close by, with its substantial shingled spike above a sturdy early fourteenth-century tower. The nave was devasted by a lightning strike in 1598, but restored by Sir John Tufton in 1603. The simple three-bay arcade has exceptionally wide arches leading to a short chancel, which was rebuilt in the late eighteenth century; the rood screen and other medieval woodwork no doubt perished in the fire. The one thing that must have caught the eye of the wedding party still stands just to the left of the chancel entrance. It is the magnificent tomb of the Sir John who restored St Margaret's, which is quite

* Probably Sandy in Bedfordshire.

the best of its period in the county. The recumbent alabaster figures of Sir John and his second wife, Christian, are in pristine condition, with their many children kneeling as weepers below, and the splendid array of heraldic shields in full colour is in remarkable condition. Apart from the evidence of the parish register, which is now in the care of the Kent County Archive Service, nothing can be discovered about the ceremony itself save that it took place on Thursday 3 July 1718, and the chances are that the day was fine. The bride's father was Thomas Tufton, Baron Clifford and 6th Earl of Thanet. He had been born at the London house in 1644, and, having married Lady Catherine, daughter of the Earl of Newcastle, he was for ten years Member of Parliament for Appleby and, briefly, Lord Lieutenant of Westmorland and Cumberland. He had been a Privy Councillor between 1702 and 1707, but his Tory allegiance lost him his place on the accession of George I in 1714.

As soon as Coke arrived, there had been duty vails (or gratuities) to be handed out to the house staff. Mrs Baker, Lady Margaret's woman, was given ten guineas, Mrs Price, the housekeeper, five guineas, and a further fifteen guineas were distributed to the rest of the servants. That was but a foretaste of what they received on the day of the wedding, when Mrs Baker received a further twenty guineas, Mrs Price and Mr Drut, the house steward, ten guineas each, and so on down through a total of over thirty servants to a couple of guineas for the 'helpers in ye House'. Then there were vails for all the relatives' servants, nineteen guineas for the quintet of musicians who provided the house entertainment, and brother Robert's obligations to fourteen of Lord Thanet's servants amounted to another eleven guineas. At the church, as was customary, the parson, his clerk, the doorkeeper and the ringers were all rewarded, and the heart warms to Thomas for giving five guineas to a poor man 'to keep him out of Goal [sic]'. The sum total of this charitable giving lightened his pocket by £249 18s, and adds substance to the contemporary complaints by the well-to-do that they were being held to ransom by servants everywhere.

After the wedding, most of the family returned to London, but on 25 July Thomas took a trip in his smart new chariot to Tunbridge Wells. Guided by the old Hothfield huntsman and served by Humphrey Smith, his valet, coachman, postilion and a helper, he stopped overnight at Goudhurst, where the ringers got half a guinea for their welcome and the poor gained half-a-crown. He went shopping in Tunbridge for 'golden toys' and managed to lose five guineas at basset, a card game rather like faro. Shortly after, he made a trip to Maidstone with the same entourage, but there is no mention of Lady Margaret on either occasion. However, another family wedding was imminent. On 16 August, Lady Margaret's sister, Lady Catherine, married Lord Sondes, son and heir of the Earl of Rockingham, and the Cokes were naturally invited to stay. Just before that occasion they had called on Lady Fairfax and Sir Robert Furnish, and by 18 August they were on the road back to London, staying overnight at the Bull at Rochester. The chariot was used to transport the maids, while the rest of the party continued the journey by hired coach. Carriers moved over a ton of goods up from Kent to Mr Gibson's yard, and it took four cart-loads to transfer everything to Thanet House. Meanwhile, the young couple's arrival in Bloomsbury was greeted by the drummers of the three foot regiments, augmented by six trumpeters, a kettle drummer, the Grenadiers' trumpeter and the odd hautbois player. Such was possible because, unlike today's concentration of troops in barracks, at that time the 1st Guards with its two battalions had nine companies spread about Holborn, two in Clerkenwell, two in St Giles's Cripplegate and eight elsewhere about the city.[4] The (unspecified) 'parish music' joined in, and St Giles's ringers added to the welcome. Before the end of the month Thomas Coke had been invited to dine with George I at Hampton Court: it must have seemed that good fortune was his indeed.

Chapter 2

THE GREAT ESTATE

S ir Edward Coke, like many of his generation of thrusting middle-class
Elizabethans, had been eager for land. It was his wish to establish a
patrimony based on solid foundations, and on the lordship of manors in
particular. A Holkham manuscript familiarly known as 'The Great Book of
Conveyances' gives details of seventy-seven manors.[1] The list is headed by
Tittleshall Austens, bought for £5 from yeoman Robert Austen in 1576, soon
after Coke's admission to Clifford's Inn and the Inner Temple. Adjacent
Godwick, the house that was to be his family home in Norfolk, came four years
later, from the Drewry family, purchased at the much higher price of £3,600.
In 1580 Thorington Hall, the first of Coke's Suffolk manors, was bought from
Edward Moulton, a relative of Coke's wife-to-be, Bridget Paston. In 1596 the
net was spread wider to include a manor in Buckinghamshire, and, before the
century was out, Stoke Poges, the house in which he was to spend his final
years, was bought from the Countess of Huntingdon for £4,000. Properties in
Oxfordshire, Dorset, Cambridgeshire, Somerset, Derbyshire, Essex, Staffordshire
and London followed. Perhaps sentiment was involved in the purchase of
Paston House in Norwich, just across the street from the church of St Peter

Parmentergate, where his parents had been married, although it might have been a reminder to his wife's family of his growing power and influence. His last acquisition was Cookley in Suffolk, which must have given him considerable satisfaction – remembering that he and Bridget had been married there in the church of St Michael thirty-six years before. In all, Sir Edward laid out well over £100,000 between 1570 and 1618.[2]

These properties formed the foundation for the fortune that the Chief Justice bequeathed to his descendants, and there were very few changes in the land holdings by the time that Thomas Coke's guardians took over the responsibilities of the estate, when total acreage stood at 40,499.[3] The guardians' principal concern was to maintain the situation until the reins could be handed over to the new owner, but some purchases were made, principally in the Holkham manor in order to bring more of it under direct control. The holding known as Withersby's was bought from John Thatcher, and various parcels of land that made up the small farm known thereafter as 'Mansor's' were bought from Robert Mansor's heirs in 1717. The first decade of Thomas Coke's rule was to be one of transition in the countryside from the known and accepted ways based firmly on manorial precedent and custom, to new and sometimes speculative practices that were inherent in a capitalistic approach to property management.

As a generalisation, throughout southern, midland and eastern counties in the eighteenth century, the land, other than wastes and forests, was ploughland and in very large fields, with a concentration of the population in villages, and little or no evidence of farmhouses and steadings built upon the land outside them. In these areas 'the ancient system of land tenure based on communal cultivation obtained'.[4] The village supported itself by cultivating large open fields in which the people held small strips of land, which were allocated evenly according to their quality. Because each man's strips were scattered, all had to conform to a common cropping pattern. This worked well for over a thousand years, but, when new crops and improved techniques made farming for profit a reality, the common field system could not hold out against the benefits of enclosure.[5] Farms that had been given names such as 'Hall farm', 'Grange farm' and so on had in the main been consolidated and enclosed from an early date, but it is notable that a detailed map of the Holkham manor based on a 1720s survey shows the 'East Field' clearly marked and unenclosed. A gathering momentum in the process of enclosing land is noticeable in the seventeenth century, and by the early years of the eighteenth century it was focused on the common arable fields, but it was not until the late 1700s, when the majority had been dealt with, that 'the growth of population and the great technical improvements in agriculture caused men to turn their attention more and more to the possibilities of improvement in the technical efficiency of farming'.[6] Thomas Coke was one of the first great landowners to promote this particular form of development, followed at the turn of the century by his successor, Thomas William Coke, whose personality and skill in promoting agricultural experiment have enhanced his reputation in this respect and diverted attention from the innovative activities of his great-uncle.

Almost all the information contained in this chapter has been gleaned from the series of audit account books.[7] The arrangement is standardised throughout, set out quarter by quarter through the year, with a section for each manor or separate property. There are two divisions, 'The Charge', which details all items of income, and the 'Discharge', which lists outgoings. On the charge side there are subdivisions for outstanding debts, rents and casual profits (the latter covering non-recurring items such as Leet Court fines and sales of materials); on the discharge side the subdivisions cover taxes, repairs, allowances, deficiencies (that is, allowed variations in charges and payments) and debts outstanding at the end of the period. With the exception of Kingsdown, Kent, where there was a minor variation, the estate paid all national and local taxes, and met the cost of all repairs to premises, whether carried out by the landlord or the tenant. The term 'repairs' was applied quite loosely – as at Knightley, Staffordshire, where the tenant of the Park farm was allowed £9 7s 9d under that head to 'enlarge his dairy and make a new parlour over it'; similarly, at Panworth Hall, Norfolk, the conversion of one end of the hall into a brewhouse and malthouse for £166 was treated as a repair, and, as the amount was too high to allow the manor's accounts to be balanced, it was entered under the land steward's general 'Accompt Current' for that year. Under 'Allowances' payments are listed for improvements made by tenants, of which more will be said later. The typical cottage in Norfolk and Suffolk was built of clay lump, roughly plastered, with a roof thatched with straw, and a typical 'deficiency' was entered when one of these at Massingham collapsed (as they often did). In that case the entry ran: 'To be allowed, a defalcation in Mr Carr's farm by the fall of a cottage.' Each year's entries are rounded off by an abstract of the manorial accounts and an 'Accompt Current' in which the land steward set out all his accounts, covering not only the properties but also the house budgets, staff costs, finance arrangements and so on.

A decisive change in the administration and control of the estate was confirmed by the appointment of a new land steward. Humphrey Smith had held that position for some considerable time, and it was to be expected that his son Edward, the 'Gentleman of the Horse', would take over when his father retired. Over the years, Smith had established something of a cosy relationship with the guardians, judging by an extract from his letter to Sir John Newton in 1710: 'My wife has by ye same waggon sent my Good Lady Newton a harvest Goose and a Turkey which she beggs may be accepted of with her humble duty, and thanks for ye Noble present my Lady was pleased to make her.'[8] Things had been left very much in Smith's hands, but one of the guardians at least had begun to have reservations. In June 1711 Sir Edward Coke voiced his opinion: 'I think it would doe well to be out of Debt & to have a Command of money, & to put these Norfolk repairs under some restriction, & not to leave them so absolutely to the pleasure of the Steward.' He suggested paying 'some person who understands building & countrey affairs' to survey and report back.[9]

Change was in the air, and a new man was brought in from outside, possibly from Longford in Derbyshire, the home of Thomas's guardian Sir Edward Coke. George Appleyard's name first appears as land steward in the audit accounts for 1722 on a salary of £200 a year. Smith had been paid £30, the same rate as his son and the house steward, John Casey, so the introduction of a replacement as the senior servant of the estate on a salary that equalled the income of many a minor gentleman must have come as a distinct shock, not only to the household but to the county at large. Appleyard's first annual accounts disclose that his predecessor was in debt to the estate. Until Michaelmas 1722, Humphrey Smith was still renting Hill Hall farm, Wellands farm, various marshes in Holkham, lands in Tittleshall and Godwick, and one of the Huntingfield manors in Suffolk. He was living in Hill Hall house on a lease that required him to keep it in repair, for which he was allowed £26 5s in 1717, the year when he finally got round to rebuilding the 15ft-high garden wall that had been blown down by the 'great wind' three years previously. By the end of 1722 he was £337 15s 8d in arrears, and by 1725 the debt had grown to £1,298 0s 11d, as more and more deficiencies were uncovered that had to be laid at his door. A number of these concerned the West Country properties, where, for example, from Donyatt in

Somerset, Smith had collected £610 8s 9¾d in fines but had omitted to enter them. By 1728 his indebtedness had dropped to £1,098 0s 11d – 'part being forgiven and the other part secured to be paid', with no clue as to what was allowed and what had been secured. Coke's informed interest in the estate from the moment he assumed control may well have made him aware of Smith's lack of ability, but the need to recruit a land steward of higher calibre overrode his undoubted respect for an old family servant.

Once he had taken over the running of the estate, Coke set out to farm on the best known principles, growing wheat, clover, turnips and lucerne, fertilised with marl in the approved fashion, in common with his Walpole and Townshend neighbours. From this time forward, leases bound tenants to a course of cropping that included turnips and a clover ley of two years or longer; tenants were encouraged to marl, either at their expense or with financial assistance from the landlord.[10] Enclosure and the four-shift rotation bore down on the open-field foldcourses, making the close-folding of sheep in north-west Norfolk anachronistic. In this situation, the keynote of animal husbandry in our period was the beef trade. Because in-wintering was the essence of the new system, the muck cart became as important as the marl cart. The accounts refer to stock bought after the harvest, fatted and sold the following year, and it was possible to make a gross profit of £100 on some fifty bullocks, but feed costs at about eight shillings a beast over six months meant that no great fortunes were to be made that way.[11]

To some extent, Coke and his new steward were fortunate, at least in Norfolk, in the quality of their labour force. At the end of the century William Marshall had this to say:

In respect of day labourers, two remarkable circumstances are united; namely, hard work and low wages. A Norfolk farm labourer will do as much work for one shilling, as some two men, in many other places, will do for eighteenpence each. There is an honesty, I had almost said an honour, about them, when working by the day, which I have not been able to discover in the day labourers of any other country.

On working practices he commented:

The Norfolk practice of going what are called two journeys a day, with the plow teams starting at 6 or 7 am., the men reach home by dinner time, and having refreshed themselves and their horses, are ready to start again at 1 or 2 o'clock for the afternoon journey until 6 or 7 pm. They employ five-horse teams, with one horse at rest, two used in the morning and two used after dinner. Whether on the road or on the farm, the common practice is to trot with empty carriages [thus improving the turn-round time significantly].[12]

The land steward spent some time once a year in London presenting his accounts to the auditor; they were then presumably placed before Thomas Coke for signature, but he did this only once in the decade and that was in 1725, when they were countersigned by Appleyard, Peniston Lamb and John Coke, one of his old guardians. In 1728 Thomas himself attended a manorial audit at Huntingfield, when £2 was expended on wine to do him honour.

In the period under review, the accounts for an estate such as this provide a great deal of interest in historical, social and economic terms. Agriculture was buoyant between the Treaty of Utrecht in 1714 and the war with Spain in 1727, although the Land Tax, introduced in 1692 and which favoured Tory landlords in the west rather than the mainly Whig landlords in the east of the country, featured significantly in the estate's outgoings. It was the earliest and longest-lasting form of direct taxation in the realm and was applied without exception throughout the eighteenth century whenever Great Britain fought a major war; it was particularly convenient for the Treasury to know that, by increasing the tax rate by a shilling, an extra £500,000 could be raised. There was a yearly quota for each county, and it was left to the local administration to decide how to assess and collect the tax. During Marlborough's campaigns it stood at four shillings; with the coming of peace in 1714 it dropped to two shillings and continued at that rate until 1727, when it doubled for a short period to finance the Spanish war before dropping to three shillings in the latter half of the following year. For all leased properties the estate met the charge rather than the tenant, and, because the assessment was linked with parishes, the tax paid in respect of tenants who held land in more than one parish had to be broken down into separate returns (a tedious complication). There was, however, a variation at Kingsdown in Kent, where the tenants paid a shilling for every pound of their rent, the landlord paying the remainder. For example, the tax for Heverplace farm, the woods and Clark's farm (total rent £122 17s 11d) was £9 18s, of which the tenants Samuel and Richard Hill paid £5 19s. In one instance, at

Portbury in Somerset, the land steward had been paying Land Tax for copyhold tenants, but there is an auditor's marginal note: 'Q[uery]. Why pay the Copy hold taxes. The tenants themselves generally paying the same.' In 1722, the Land Tax soaked up 9.3 per cent of the gross income from Coke rents in Norfolk.

Nearly all the properties were still subject to age-old manorial customs, with Courts Leet being held regularly. This was true of manors in Norfolk and of those in other counties, although there were many variations in detail. The auditor was not always happy about the ongoing situation, and left a marginal comment against the Tittleshall, Norfolk, entry of 1717, which records a 'Charge of a Court' costing 19s: 'Note to enquire whether the courts of Norfolk can be put on [a] better foot.' Courts were normally convened twice a year, and their costs varied appreciably. At Laxfield, in Suffolk, two successive courts cost £4 2s 9d, but in other cases it was a matter of shillings only. It may well have been the auditor's concern that prompted a change of policy in Norfolk. Christopher Bedingfeld was lord of the manor of Wighton, adjacent to Holkham, and there is a fine touchstone slab for him, his wife and daughters in the chancel floor of All Saints' church there. He was a practising attorney, handling business for Thomas Coke from time to time, and in the 1720s he took over the administration of a number of the estate's manorial courts; by 1725 he was dealing with those for Tittleshall, Weasenham, Wendling, Longham and Bintry, charging a small fee for each. Each manorial audit was a matter for the Court Leet, and at Holkham a 1722 entry shows that a jury was empanelled for the occasion. The formal proceedings were followed by an audit feast that was the expected corollary to painful demands for money or recriminations over misdeeds, and the essential element seems to have been an anchor or half-anchor of brandy, plus sugar and lemons to make punch. The brandy often came from Richard Porter, the Newdigates tenant, or William Pickford, the hare huntsman, who was a cottage tenant – and was undoubtedly smuggled. Catherine Loines, the housemaid, provided bread, butter, cheese and milk, and the mutton came fresh from the Hall farm. The annual cost ran to just over £10.

One can sympathise with the auditor's puzzlement over the Huntingfield accounts where an entry reads: 'Paid 2 men at the Brundish Turne 2s. at the Courthouse.' His marginal note was: 'Q[uery] the meaning of this line.' Brundish lies a couple of miles west of Huntingfield, and similar entries occur in the accounts of other manors close by, possibly referring to a militia levy.

Courts Leet had a foreman of the leet, and the man at Laxfield received one shilling for each sitting, with the same amount being paid to the woman who prepared the village Court House. In some cases the fee was paid to another official of the manor; at Knightley in Staffordshire, Edward Moore, the woodward or keeper of the woods, received £1 5s for 'court expenses as usual', but at the same time a Mr Green (who was possibly a local attorney) took a guinea for 'keeping a Court'. Costs there took account of messenger journeys and horse hire to deliver summonses to the tenants, requiring them to attend the court. Although courts in most manors were held at least yearly, there were exceptions. At West Lexham, Norfolk, in 1727 there were ten years of Constable's Leet fees outstanding at 3s 4d a time, but the auditor ruled that the £1 13s 4d in question should be listed as a 'deficiency' and not paid, because it became payable only when a Court Leet was held – indicating that there had not been a court in the manor for at least a decade.

A tenants' dinner was sometimes provided by the lord of the manor at modest expense when a Court Leet was convened. Thomas Coke visited the West Country in 1724, taking the opportunity to attend a Michaelmas Court at Portbury on 13 October. The arrangements matched the occasion: Mrs Ann Luttrell dressed the dinner and supplied the drink for £1 12s 10d, while the parish bell-ringers were given ten shillings for their trouble 'when the Hon.ble Mr Coke was at the Court'. On that occasion the Court Foreman Joseph Edwards was paid £4 for 'Court keeping as usual' – a good deal more than the normal rate.

Most of the routine business of the Courts Leet concerned the recovery of customary charges from the tenants. These were largely fines levied when a property within the manor changed hands following the death of the tenant, or when an exchange took place, or when the area of land held was altered by agreement. In the case of a death, the relative who inherited an interest in the property, or assumed the tenancy, was charged a 'descent fine' or a 'purchase fine' (sometimes called 'entry' or 'admittance' fines), and, although most were for small sums, some were considerable. The highest amount noted was a descent fine of £107 at Cratfield in Suffolk for eight messuages and 86 acres, but the average was much less. At a Huntingfield Court, Mark Snelling paid a descent fine of only £23 10s for admission to 'two Messuages, twenty-seven acres, two roods of Land after the death of Bury Snelling', and a purchase fine of eleven guineas was levied on Stephen Aldous for his 'admission to fifteen acres of land of the surrender of Richd. Gowing'. At

Laxfield in Suffolk, William Brampton had to pay a descent fine of £24 for his and his wife's admission to 13 acres, one rood of land by the will of (his mother-in-law?) Sara Mynne. However, John Dresser's descent fine at the same court for his admission to two roods of land after the death of his father was only ten shillings, an indication that the level of charge was largely determined by the extent of the property and possibly by precedent. The surrender of a property was sometimes the occasion for celebration, as at Donyatt in Somerset, when two shillings was 'Paid for drink for the Tenants at the taking of James Butt's surrender' (Butt's holding had passed to another tenant). There are very few references to Courts Leet in the Holkham Manor, but a descent fine was recorded under the 'Casual Profits' heading in the accounts for 1727, when Bridget Carter, a widow, was charged fifteen shillings for her admission to a cottage. An illustration of the trifling transactions that were often on court agendas is the case of John Butcher at Laxfield, who had to pay a purchase fine of five shillings for a piece of land that was only 15 yards long and 10 yards wide.

On the outlying manors in particular, there were many copyhold tenancies that were held for one, two or three 'lives' (reminiscent of Giles Winterborne's predicament in Thomas Hardy's *The Woodlanders*). These provided a steady income in the form of fines charged when the tenant or his successor wished to extend the tenure. At Minster Lovell in Oxfordshire there was a twelve-guinea fine for extending the lease by 'two lives after one' on a cottage and 1¼ acres, and another of £32 15s for two lives in reversion of the tenant's own lease, in consideration of the surrender of his own life by copy in a cottage.

On two manors a little income came from regular fairs. At Castle Acre in Norfolk the tolls and profits of the St James's, St Bartholomew's and St Mark's fairs came to £3, while at Laxfield the profits in each year were about ten shillings. Riparian rights were another minor source of income. At Minster Lovell, Dr Wheeler (a dilatory payer), followed by Mr Peacock, was granted the fishery and 'the Royalty of the River' for two guineas a year, and at Durweston in Dorset, William Dominey had the same privilege, until he reneged on the rent when it was raised to four guineas and was arrested by the bailiff.

In some manors the old custom of charging heriots was still maintained. Originally, the heriot was a feudal service consisting of the restoration of weapons or horses to the lord on the death of his tenant. Over time it became the surrender of the best live beast or most valuable possession to the lord, and the imposition remained both customary and legal as long as the manorial system lasted. Within the Coke estate, only the tenants of the manors in the south and west of the country were subject to heriot – Durweston and Shillington in Dorset, Donyatt and Portbury in Somerset, and Knightley in Staffordshire. By the 1720s nearly all the heriots were quoted in monetary terms, and as a unit charge. For each tenant's death, from one to ten heriots were demanded, and the cost ranged from three shillings for a '1 heriot' at Knightley to ten guineas for an '8 heriot' at Portbury. Two Donyatt cases show that the charge was linked to property. In the first, 'A Heriot charged upon Mary Mandry's death, her Tenement being a Copyhold Overland and not heriotable', £1 6s 8d was therefore allowed as a deficiency. In the second, a heriot that had been charged the previous year was allowed as a deficiency in 1725: 'his cottage not being heriotable'. At Portbury, the old custom of claiming a beast was applied twice. In the case of Charles Hodsby's heriot, 'a Mare seized & delivered to Sir Thomas Coke's stables at £9 of which deduct 15s. paid to a farrier for curing her of a farcy and £1.9.9d. for keeping her at that time, the remis as neat profit £6.16.0d.'. From this it is clear that the executors redeemed the horse (with 9d gone astray in the accounting). In the following year, a £7 heriot was taken by the same means, and John Rutter charged 7s 6d for 'farrying a colt that was taken for Ballard's heriot'. There was undoubted discontent among tenants over this type of levy. In Donyatt a man had to be paid the cost of his horse hire to collect an eight-guinea heriot, and the bailiff charged 15s 6d expenses on the same account. At Knightley £18 10s was taken in heriots, but Edward Moore, the woodward, was given an extra £1 for 'the extraordinary trouble in seizing heriots'. When goods were seized to meet a heriot, a court was summoned to agree a valuation, and at Donyatt on one occasion the tenants 'prized [i.e. appraised] the goods taken for Mr Hunt's heriots'. As in the case of rents and other charges, allowance was sometimes made on behalf of the indigent, and at Donyatt, heriots on the deaths of Sarah Marks, Mary Trench and the widow Hayball were waived 'by reason of their poverty'.

Courts Leet were summoned on occasion to determine the outcome of disputes by empanelling a jury. Trees were often used as landmarks to define a manorial, parish or common boundary, and at Knightley a dispute required two men to be called to give evidence about particular trees. A Mr Cotton (possibly an attorney) attended the arbitration, and the jury were plied with drink while carrying out a site visit. Messengers were dispatched to Stafford and Burton for 'writings', which they then carried to Derby, and the wrangle was made an excuse for a court dinner washed down with three quarts of wine. Going to law in this case had cost the estate £22, but no doubt the tenants thought it well worth the money. At Minster Lovell, there was a variant of the more common 'beating the bounds of the parish': under 'Court expenses' £2 5s is entered as the 'expenses of the processioners going about the bounds of this Mannor'.

A land survey in a manor sometimes required a court to be convened. When John Vaston carried out a survey of Donyatt, with the bailiff Henry King acting as his assistant for fifteen days, four guineas was entered as the cost of entertaining the land steward at a Court of Survey. The tenants went along to view the boundaries of the common, and their entertainment was considered a legitimate court expense. Activities such as these will have created something of a stir in the placid life of the village, and custom naturally required that they be marked by some local celebration.

The Court Leet's affairs combined with those of the parish on occasion. At a Donyatt court Stephen Burridge was paid two guineas for taking 'the poor apprentice which was put upon Mandry's tenement', and ten shillings went 'to the Mother of the apprentice for keeping her some time and £2.18.9d. for two suits of cloaths for her'. The placing of apprentices and the costs involved were normally the responsibility of the parish, and this case may be an example of a strictly local practice. It is also notable for the fact that it was a girl rather than a boy and that she was put to a specific property. Similarly, in the same manor a tenant was paid a guinea for serving as 'a tythingman for Butt's tenement', and John Woodward received ten shillings for serving as 'Overseer for Osborne's tenement'. At Portbury, the widow Delamore was paid five shillings 'for serving the tythingship' and nine pence 'for the Sherif's Turn common fine' (echoing the 'Brundish Turne' in Suffolk). Both were normally parish rather than manorial offices, and were linked with particular holdings, reinforcing the suggestion that this was a standard local practice.

Parish taxes of various sorts were a charge on the landlord rather than the tenant. 'Poors', church and constable's rates (levied on woodland as well as farms) were common to all manors, with a number of local variations. 'Trophy money', a tax levied to cover incidental militia expenses, was paid on behalf of tenants in the Norfolk manors of Billingford, Sparham, Hastings and Bintree, at Knightley, Staffordshire, in the Bevis Marks property in London, and at Minster

Lovell, where an extra 13s 4d was added for a militia horse. That manor also paid ten shillings a year 'for keeping Windle a lunatic'. Farnham Royal in Buckinghamshire was assessed for highway maintenance and had also to pay £1 13s 'gaol money', with £1 7s 4½d 'allowed more for building the County Goal [sic]' at Aylesbury in 1722. An unusual entry in the Sparham accounts reads: 'Repair of the Partible Bridge £2.8.0d.', which probably refers to an upkeep responsibility shared between two manors. It is no surprise to find that the Candelent and Falkenham manor near the Suffolk coast had to meet '18 levies for repairing the sea banks', and a causeway rate was levied in the Norfolk manor of Martham. Parishes often provided pounds for the detention of stray animals, but there were also manorial pounds in a few cases. They were normally built of brick or stone, and the new one at Farnham Royal built for the manor by a tenant cost £7 10s. At Horham and Cratfield in Suffolk, however, tenants were reimbursed for hedging their pounds.

Some minor payments were made in the contrary direction, from manor to parish, such as the ten shillings charged by the Suffolk Scotshall and Westleton manor for gravel supplied to the Overseers of the Highways of Feverton, and two old Holkham cottages had their rents paid by the parish overseers. Another cottage rent at Holkham was charged to Great Ryburgh, a parish 20 miles away, presumably because the tenant could not claim a settlement in Holkham under the Poor Law regulations.

By custom, on all the manors each tenant was bound to pay an annual assize rent to the lord, and, as they were not subject to revision, the amounts in some cases were quite small. Even then there was some backsliding: in 1717 it was noted that at Candelent and Falkenham 'The Rents of Assize are £3.15.2d. but have not been paid for many years'. Some idea of the scale is given by the total for Tittleshall, Mileham and Beeston combined, which was only £6 12s 2½d, and for Kingsdown it was £3 13s 11½d; at Laxfield, however, £46 12s 6½d was collected.

Those tenants with land holdings of more than the average 1¼ acres that normally went with a cottage had their rents assessed and listed separately, varying from a few pounds to over £300 a year. The method is known as rack renting – a system of agreed rents that gave the landlord an economic return on his investment and left the tenant with a reasonable reward for his labour. 'The level at which the rent was set needed to be carefully determined if it were to act as an incentive to the tenant without potentially either bankrupting him, or forcing him to farm (or try to farm) in a manner designed to produce the greatest possible revenue with the least attention to the long-term good of the soil.'[13] Over the estate as a whole there was a historic situation of under-renting, and one feature of the new regime under Thomas Coke and George Appleyard was a rigorous re-evaluation of rentals. Between 1722 and 1728 many of the manors were subjected to new surveys, and virtually all the separately itemised rents were increased. An analysis of increases applied during that period on sixty-nine properties, from large farms down to individual cottages, reveals that rents went up by an average of 32.57 per cent. Two extreme instances have been excluded from the calculation: the rent of Little Wicken farm and foldcourse at Godwick, which had been £29 a year, rose to £150 – an increase of 417 per cent (also notable for the fact that the tenant was Thomas Morecroft, the estate master carpenter) – and a piece of marshland at Thorington in Suffolk, which had been £2 10s a year, was revalued at £10, a 300 per cent increase.

The value set on land in different areas varied a great deal, depending on its quality, whether it was grassland or arable, and on local standards of value in each county. Rent was therefore 'a capricious thing, often regulated by the character of the landlord or his agent, and the custom of the neighbourhood than by the value of the soil or the commodities it produced'.[14] Even in a single manor there was often inconsistency, as at Sparham, where two tenants were charged the same rent of £42 10s, although one farmed 108 acres and the other 129 acres. The variations in cost per acre were extreme in some cases: at Castle Acre, George Archer's 697-acre farm was assessed at just over five shillings per acre, while his neighbour at the Wicken farm of 247 acres paid 9s 6d per acre – nearly twice as much. In Suffolk the whole hundred of Blithing was let at £30 a year, while Widow Howlett at Mildenhall over in the west of the county paid as much for 66 acres. For small areas the rent was equally variable. Even though some of the increases can be linked to a new survey having been completed, many were applied on the basis of old surveys. There is a significant number of instances, however, where a change in the level of rent is linked with the tenant being offered a long lease (which in all cases was for twenty-one years). The first of these was for the West Lexham farm and foldcourse in 1724, where the rent had been £40 but was raised to £81 (an increase of 102 per cent) when a new tenant moved in. Sometimes one reassessment was followed rapidly by another, as at Massingham, where the farm and foldcourse had its rent raised from £135 to £170 in 1724, and then to £190 the following year – an 11.7 per cent following hard on the heels of a 25.9 per cent increase. On the Staffordshire manor, incoming tenants were charged 'aforehand rents' in some instances to allow for a change taking place in mid-quarter.

Inspections of the outlying manors revealed that in three of them, over the years, squatters had been building on the commons. At Knightley there were fifteen houses with gardens 'on the Lord's Wast[e]', and from then on £1 14s in rents was collected from them. Amounts collected in Durweston and Donyatt were at the same level, suggesting that the cottages were no more than rude bothies.

Originally, most rents were paid in kind, and even in the eighteenth century vestiges of the old practice survived. At Cratfield in Suffolk, 5s 1d was received 'for the rent eggs as usual'; at Minster Lovell, 'a year's rents of hens and capons' was charged at eleven shillings, and in the Portbury accounts entries include: 'for the price of 9 hens and 8 capons 14s.'. In Norfolk, the tenant at Panworth Hall had an allowance 'for the loss of 11 Comb 2 Bushels in the barly rents at 5s. per Comb for 3 years, £8.12.6d.'; prior to that, the farm was charged a rent of '82 stone, 2 bushels & 2 pecks of barley'; at Kempstone, an increase was expressed as 'ten combs of rye at market price'.

In the majority of his manors, there were properties owned by landlords other than Coke himself. Similarly, the estate had land that lay in manors adjoining its own. One of the most extensive groups was in Suffolk, where the Scotshall manor accounts list lands held in the manors of Darsham-cum-Yoxford, Westleton Cliffs, Westleton Grange, Westleton-cum-Membris, Hinton, Kelsale and Bramford. Parishes often contained more than one manor, and some lordships extended across parish boundaries. In all such cases it was the custom for a quit rent to be demanded or paid. Originally this was a payment made in lieu of services that might be required of the occupier of the property, and was normally a very small amount (although Viscount Townshend received £27 4s 6d for the Showering foldcourse in Flitcham, and at Farnham Royal the Earl of Sandwich was paid £46 4s 0½d annually). There is a certain piquancy in the fact that, twenty years before he himself assumed the title, Thomas Coke's Kentish manor of Kingsdown paid quit rents to the then Lord Leicester's manors of Shoreham and Kemsing & Seele, when John Sydney lived in state at Penshurst as the 6th Earl. 'Fee farm' and 'free suit' money were similar levies across manorial boundaries, and in a few instances the payment was made to someone other than the lord of the manor. At Sparham, a backlog of sixteen years' quit rents at 3s 6d a year were paid to Sir Jacob Astley as lord of the hundred of Eynsford; similarly, at Durweston, free suit money was paid to the Earl of Salisbury as lord of the hundred of Pimpern, and in neighbouring Shillington the Earl claimed it wearing the hat of 'Lord Paramount of the Honour of Gloucester and Manour of Cranbourn'. Nearer home, Dunton and Doughton made a payment called 'a year's Certainty' to the sheriff of the county, which before the Reformation had been paid to the monks of Pontefract. Similar rents survived in Suffolk, where the bailiff of the eight manors in Huntingfield, Horham, Laxfield and Cratfield was paid to collect 'the Castleguard and Chantry rents belonging to the Honour of Eye' and the 'Wardsilver Rents', all of which went to the Crown.

At Holkham itself, the following entries are typical: 'Paid Mr Bedingfeld severall small [Quit] Rents due to his Manor of Wighton for one year ended at Mich.as 1717, none of which amount to a £ – £2.16.1½d.'; 'Paid to Mr Lombard one years Quitrent to his manor of [Burnham] Thorpe due at Mich.as 1717 1s.0½d. & for Mansors [farm] 14s.'; 'Paid Mr Carlton . . . a Years Fee farm rent for lands in Holkham due at Mich.as 1717, £1.3.4d.'. To these sums a further small charge called an acquittance was added, and an even smaller deduction was made to allow for Land Tax paid by the estate. The Quarles manor, now just outside the park, was in a slightly different category in that the tenant had a twenty-one-year lease, but the estate paid an annual rent of £31 1s to the Master and Fellows of Christ's College Cambridge, which rose to £35 15s in 1725; two years later the college charged £144 for renewing the lease for another twenty-one years. Otherwise, normal customs were followed there: courts were held, assize rents were collected and, in 1724, fourteen quit rents were listed as unpaid, including three years owing from Viscount Townshend.

There is abundant evidence that by the early eighteenth century quit rents had become a source of irritation and quiet rebellion among tenants in general, from wealthy landlords down to cottagers. This is particularly marked in some manors, suggesting that neighbours had a common grievance and acted accordingly. Bintry was an extreme example, where Sir Jacob Astley owed thirty-nine years of quit rents, and ten other tenants' debts under this head amounted to over £18. In 1727 an effort was made to clear this impasse when a deficiency was entered for nineteen of Sir Jacob's thirty-nine years, and 14s 6d was collected for the remainder. Another defaulter was allowed eight out of thirteen oustanding years, but the total recovered that year was only £2 7s 7d, with four hard cases still holding out. At Fulmodeston in Norfolk, the fifteen years of combined quit rents outstanding amounted to only fifteen shillings, and a Billingford tenant, also fifteen years in arrears, owed 5s 7½d, 'which he denied'. In cases like these it must have cost the estate more in collection costs than the quit rents were worth.

The local administration of the various parts of the estate was largely in the hands of bailiffs, who were in many cases tenants, and it was with them that the annual accounts were drawn up by the land steward. Some were responsible for more than one manor. Charles Hutchinson covered the Huntingfield, Laxfield and Cratfield manors, and by 1724 all the four manors in Dorset and Somerset were under Henry King, who travelled up to London yearly to agree the accounts with the land steward and the auditor. The Minster Lovell bailiff also made a yearly trip to London to settle the manor accounts, and on one occasion he travelled over to Holkham on business. All the bailiffs received annual fees relating to their responsibilities, ranging from John Baker's 3s 4d at Wellingham for collecting quit rents, to £30 for Henry King in the West Country working in two counties. His predecessor at Portbury had enjoyed a salary of £10 for the one manor, but this was challenged by the auditor's note in 1717: 'Q[uery] it may be received of a bailiff', and the £2 paid that year to the bailiff of the hundred was also vetoed: 'It being no profit to the Court keeper of ye manor I ought to allow nothing.' Nevertheless, the Knightley bailiff's salary remained at £10. Each manor's relationship with its parish or parishes was not always straightforward, and it was the bailiff's responsibility to ensure that local taxes were correctly assessed, as at Portbury when Henry King contested the taxing of Burchill copse and warren with the parishes in which they lay. In the Holkham manor, Richard Porter, the tenant of Newdigates, was reimbursed for collecting taxes from all the farms, and John Halsey, the surveyor, collected the assize rents for most of the manors in Norfolk, receiving £21 5s 1d in fees on top of his salary.

As will be seen later, the estate contained a large woodland acreage, and all the West Country and shire manors employed a woodward or a woodreeve to keep an eye on the timber. At Farnham Royal and Knightley the two roles of bailiff and woodward were combined, and at Minster Lovell the bailiff was paid £16 5s for 'keeping the Chase, woods and walls' and doubling as gamekeeper with a livery allowance.

The land steward paid occasional visits to outlying manors, and spent time regularly in London on estate business. In 1717 Humphrey Smith took nine weeks there to pass his accounts and lodged an expenses claim for £18 (John Rodgers, the auditor, stayed in town six weeks himself and his gloss on Smith's claim was: 'Q[uery] whether yt may n't be abated his lodging with me'). In 1722, early in his career as Smith's successor, George Appleyard inspected the estates, receiving an additional £52 10s 'for his trouble'; his annual travelling expenses were normally over £50.

Another senior servant who travelled extensively was the master carpenter. Until 1717 John Baker had doubled as master carpenter and bailiff for the Tittleshall group of manors, with another carpenter to help him, but the auditor noted: '1 carpenter enough for the future'. Nevertheless, under Appleyard's new management Thomas Morecroft was recruited in 1722 on a salary of £30 a year. He was paid five guineas 'expenses with his wife & family from Longford to Tittleshall in Nov. 1722', so the appointment was doubtless on the recommendation of Sir Edward Coke once more. Woodland management, exploitation and control of timber resources and building maintenance were to prove important, and this was a key appointment. Coupled with Appleyard's rigorous approach and the enquiring eye of their master, the change was to have a salutory effect, particularly on the outlying manors, where Humphrey Smith's hand had lain lightly on the tenantry.

Apart from his work as a carpenter, Morecroft established a kiln at Tittleshall and supplied bricks and tiles for local work, from which the estate drew a modest profit. In 1725 he was granted a twenty-one-year lease for the Little Wicken farm at Godwick, along with part of Godwick Hall farm, and a year later he moved into the Little Wicken farmhouse and added a new parlour with a chamber and garret above. In 1728 he was still improving the property, sinking a 102ft well. The Tittleshall woods were worth £40 a year, and in 1724 the estate took them in hand; from that time Morecroft assumed control of all timber matters in Norfolk and Suffolk, extracting timber from the woods at Fulmodeston, Billingford and elsewhere, negotiating coppicing agreements and sales of bark, and controlling 'covenant wood' agreements with tenants. Apart from felling, he superintended the working-up of timber in the woods for making gates, fold hurdles, bank hurdles and the carrying-out of repairs on farm buildings. In doing so, he very quickly became as much a clerk of works as master carpenter. His presented accounts covered not only woodwork, but painting, ironmongery and the provision of other materials. He normally reserved certain work for his personal attention, and specialised in roof construction. When the barn at Flitcham Abbey farm was rebuilt, he constructed the roof and put out the rest of the carpentry to the local builder who was doing the brickwork. His remit extended well beyond Norfolk, and at Park farm, Huntingfield, he carried out extensive repairs when George Appleyard assumed the tenancy, and worked in the Suffolk manors of Scotshall and Westleton in the same year. In 1724 he submitted bills of £45 12s 6½d for erecting a new barn at Farnham Royal in Buckinghamshire, together with repairs to the house and stables there. Again, he dealt with the roof himself and recruited other workmen locally. The tenant was paid for lending his own men 'in raising the barn'. This phrase, still current in the United States, is a reminder that it was standard practice for all the components of a barn frame to be cut, jointed, bored for mortice-pegging, numbered and stacked on site before any construction was begun; when that point was reached the master carpenter directed the work of erection. In this case Morecroft and his horse were boarded for eleven weeks by the farmer while the work was in progress. On these 'out-county' trips he took the opportunity to deal with other work that needed doing, as at Farnham, where he carried out repairs at the mill. He paid a visit to Minster Lovell in 1726, and his claim for £30 expenses was linked with the heavy programme of timber extraction there, of which more will be said later. In 1727 he began entering his accounts in 'a Book of Repairs', which has not survived, so that after that time much less detail about specific jobs appears in the audit accounts. Nevertheless, there is mention in the following year that he built a new house and barn at Longlands on the Holkham manor for £328 7s 4½d, another house on the Marsh for £20 16s 1¾d, and converted Nettleton's farmhouse into cottages for £2 15s 8d. It is noticeable in the Norfolk manors that craftsmen moved about from village to village; John Layton, a bricklayer, worked at Holkham, Dunton and South Creake, while John Baker, a carpenter, worked at both Dunton and Flitcham.

Under the Trustees between 1707 and 1717 a considerable quantity of timber had been sold, and minor woodland lettings agreed, but the pace had slackened. At the end of that period, the auditor pencilled in a query against a sale of coppice wood at Farnham Royal: 'How often sold?', and one of the results of Appleyard's and Morecroft's assessments over the next five years was a significant increase in felling within an overall tightening of control. Large-scale falls started in 1723 when thirty-eight oaks were extracted from

Elmham Park, and in the following year there was a massive sale of timber at Minster Lovell. In Posson's Copse it cost £6 15s to fell 500 oaks and took two men six days to draw the timber out of the wood using horses lent by tenants. The trees were sold for £336 17s 5d in parcels ranging from thirty-nine trees to William Townshend of Woodstock with free delivery, down to single oaks. Even old and decayed trees went to tenants for ten shillings to £1 each, and £112 was gained from the sale of coppice wood. For the latter, fifty buyers were involved, and the method used is interesting. The copse was divided into named furlongs, and from each the coppicing was gathered in 'braids' priced between one shilling and 2s 6d each. The tops and small stuff left after felling were made up into 5,500 faggots, which sold for between twelve and fifteen shillings a hundred. Wherever oak was felled on the estate the bark was sold separately. It was 'pilled' (i.e. peeled off) on site, stacked to dry, and, at 1s 9d or so a yard, there was a ready sale to tanneries, for whom bark was an essential source of tannin. This particular sale of timber realised an extra £75 for the bark. During that year Minster and Astall woods were taken in hand, and Posson's Copse was enclosed within new hedges after the timber fall; the new chained and locked gates that were installed were a sign that the estate was taking its timber resources seriously. Two years later another of the Minster woods was the scene of a major fall, when 473 oaks were taken out of Crawley Coppice raising £490, and the remaining 540 trees were topped to make an additional £80. As at Posson's Copse, the twelve-year undergrowth from 53 acres was made up into 2,133 braids, which sold for £274. All the timber was taken from named furlongs, and the copse was 'furlonged' again after the felling. Each buyer had to leave 'samplers' behind, which were marked with red lead and oil, and in some cases they were reimbursed for leaving more than had been agreed. During 1727 the other half of Crawley Coppice was cleared, yielding a further 257 oaks. It is notable that, a year after that, Morecroft claimed £7 6s 1d travelling expenses when he went to Minster Lovell 'to fell the underwood' and at the same time ordered wheelwright's tools for the manor at a cost of £11 18s 4d – a considerable sum. Under his direction over 200 oaks from 50 acres of Queen's Standing coppice, together with the underwood, realised another £500.

At Farnham Royal, the woods were taken in hand in 1724, and within two years Morecroft had supervised the extraction of forty-six oaks and the underwood from 15 acres, with nineteen more trees felled in 1728. Down in

Kent, the Kingsdown manor yielded thirty-one oaks and eighty-nine elms in 1725, followed by fifty-two oaks and eight ash trees in 1728. Nearer home, 112 more trees were sold from Elmham and 101 oaks (followed shortly by another sixty-two) were taken from Horham woods, plus coppice timber; sixty-eight oaks were felled on the Mildenhall land prior to its being sold in 1725, and John Clark had paid £138 6s 6d for them, 'of which £8.16.6d. was allowed him by order of the Hon.ble Mr Coke in consideration of the badness of the bargain'.

There are numerous examples of Morecroft's ability to secure small sums on timber that tenants had previously taken without leave. At Fulmodeston, even firewood cut from an old hedge was priced at £1 10s; at Minster Lovell, 'an old hedgerow' cost £4 plus a further £1 for the gates in it; in Dorset the Durweston tenants were charged a few shillings for cutting timber on their own tenements; at North Elmham, Morecroft charged £1 5s for 'two old pieces of timber', and, in an extreme case, a tree 'that had laid in the mote near twenty yrs.' cost a Horham man five shillings. At Knightley, two men and a woman were charged £3 'for the fern on the Common', which they had surely taken for nothing under the old regime. Some tenants quietly got their own back by entering the string of minor claims that followed, particularly in the outlying manors where the yoke had lain lightest. At Donyatt, for example, two shillings was claimed for a well bucket shortly after a charge had been made for firewood.

There are in the accounts one or two entries concerning 'pump trees' – three were sold at Sparham for £3 10s in 1725, for example. Although few people now would understand its significance, until the 1870s the term was common currency in country areas. From the earliest days until the advent of lead and iron pipes, every pump that drew water from a well was made of wood, and each area had a 'pump doctor' whose skill it was to select the timber, fashion and install the pump. At Holkham, Mr Frary supplied the Hall with two pump trees in 1727, and the old ones were repaired: 'For carrying, boring & setting down 2 new pumps at Holkham Hall £6.18.0d.' He will have been out looking for prime elm trees free of knots and blemishes. Once felled they were used 'green' with the sap still in them; two lengths were needed for a pump, each 12ft long and 18in square. A 5in-diameter hole was bored from end to end in both of them by two men using a 15ft auger – a task that took a full week. The average well was 20ft deep, and the two sections were sealed together in situ with hot mutton fat before the wrought-iron handle and shaft were added. After Frary had finished his work, the Hall would then have had reliable pumps that would never freeze during their long life. Full details of the remarkable skills involved and the qualities of the craftsmen who employed them are to be found in a splendid book by Walter Rose.[15]

Apart from its use in pump construction, green timber was often used for other work rather than being stacked for seasoning. An entry for Minster Lovell reads: 'Paid for felling 19 trees for repairs at several tenements.' Thomas Morecroft used timber in this way from the Tittleshall woods, but for the Holkham area the demand could not be satisfied from the estate's own resources, particularly for softwood. Richard Porter, who farmed Newdigates, also acted as a timber merchant, charging £150 for deals used in repairs at a number of Holkham farms in 1726. Most estates further inland had to rely wholly on home-grown hardwoods, whereas Scandinavian softwood was readily available in north Norfolk through ports such as Wells. Tittleshall woods were also able to supply Hill Hall house with charcoal for cooking, and Andrew Griffiths the butler took delivery of sixty sacks during 1726. By that time the woods were in hand and were showing a small yearly profit of just over £100.

There are references to 'Covenant woods' at Billingford and Sparham, an indication that some leases included covenants that granted tenants certain timber rights; Thomas Morecroft charged expenses on one occasion for 'setting out Covenant wood', and it is noticeable that in these cases the bark was always accounted for separately as the landlord's income. Similarly, some leases had 'firing' clauses, and in 1727 a South Creake tenant claimed four chaldrons of coal in lieu of firewood 'by agreement'.

Thomas Coke's visit to the West Country in 1724 prompted two interesting developments. First, the Portbury accounts include the entries: 'Colepit timber sold from Burch Hill £6.18.0d.', referring to pit-props supplied to a local coal mine, and 'Stones raised on Portishead Down 14s.', which may have been part of the same transaction. In addition, John Atherton, the bailiff, was paid for entertaining a Mr Hutchinson, his servant and their horses for thirteen days. He was a surveyor and, having charged 6s 4d for tools, he was eventually paid his travel expenses to Somerset 'to give his opinion concerning the mines'. It is likely that Coke wanted to see if the local coal seams extended under his property. The second matter illustrates his awakening interest in the development of landscape. During his visit to the

Staffordshire property he ordered that trees should be planted on Knightley Hill and that they should be adequately protected by using 'stulps' and rails.

The entries in the accounts on the 'Discharge' side under the sub-heading 'Improvements' are of particular importance in that they provide evidence to show how Coke and his senior staff engineered the vital transformation of an estate set in the rigid manorial mould of ancient custom and precedent into one geared to a progressive capitalist economy. The overhaul of the rental structure, as detailed above, produced a 17.5 per cent increase in income from that source between 1722 and 1728, and equally important was the move, over time, to improve the quality of the land holdings. This was achieved principally, on the Norfolk farms, by beginning a programme of soil enrichment, and with a series of piecemeal enclosure projects in a number of other counties.

A distinctive practice that increased the productivity of the land, particularly where the soil was light, was the use of a wide variety of fertilisers, especially clay and marl. The latter is a subsoil mixture of clay and chalk containing calcareous earth found at various depths, and its use dated back at least to Roman times and continued down the centuries.[16] The effects of application could last up to a century, and the amounts used varied. Arthur Young was of the opinion that fertilisers were the most important factor in Norfolk husbandry and named nineteen varieties from sticklebacks to soot, but the most important was marl.[17] It had been used by Coke's neighbours the Townshends at Raynham in the seventeenth century,[18] and Coke tenants began to be encouraged to adopt the practice by having the costs met by the estate, although it has to be said that, at the time, the chemical factors of marling were only vaguely guessed at. Pits were dug wherever the mixture could be found, and many remain today as small ponds scattered across farmland. The first reference is in 1722, when John Money was paid for spreading 600 loads at 3½d a load. When William Dewsing took a tenancy in South Creake in 1726, he agreed to spread 5,000 loads within three years at 3¼d each, and a similar bargain was struck at Billingford. On the Holkham farms there was a different arrangement whereby the estate carried out the marling and increased the tenant's rent accordingly.

The amount of animal manure used at that time can be gauged from 'change of tenancy' agreements. When Edward Creamer vacated the Lushers farm at Holkham, he was allowed fifteen guineas for the muck in the yards and £2 18s 6d for carrying and spreading fifty-four loads on the land. A

Weasenham tenant was allowed £24 for the 400 loads he left behind, and there is an interesting distinction at Billingford, where the Beck Hall tenant was paid for 170 loads of yard muck and two more of 'dove muck' from the dovecote. Pigeon keeping became popular after the Restoration, and numerous dovecotes were built or rebuilt in the latter years of the seventeenth century. Birds were good for the table, and the dung was highly prized for bringing on special crops, such as the Portuguese onions that John Cockburn urged his gardener to grow in 1735 in Scotland.[19]

In the 1720s the improvements brought about by enclosures were not the result of private Acts, but were the beginning of a series of rationalisations in land use that created fields of suitable size and, in some cases, took in land from commons, wastes and downs. Small closes were amalgamated, and some measure of improvement in strip holdings was achieved by transfers. Nearly. all the changes relate to Norfolk, and the evidence lies in the number of entries recording reimbursements for the purchase of 'layers' (blackthorn setts planted to create hedges), for 'bank hurdles' to provide a barrier against livestock damage while the hedges were growing, and for ditching to establish efficient drainage for the fields being created. On the Holkham Honclecrondale (Rectory) farm, William Leeds was allowed the cost of ditching and the purchase of 4,920 layers 'for which his farm [rent] is advanced 5s.6d. a year'. At South Creake, 40 acres were enclosed 'by agreement', which involved seventy rods of new ditching, thirty-two rods of old ditching scoured out, 4,000 layers planted, and the provision of fourteen dozen new hurdles, at 5s 6d a dozen. In 1728 a further 10,200 layers, thirty-three dozen hurdles and 110 rods of new ditching were called for in enclosing part of the Brecks. More breck ground or heath was taken in at West Lexham, where two tenants planted 6,000 layers and used ten dozen hurdles to protect them. Between 1722 and 1728 three Sparham farms used 24,360 thorn setts between them, and in one year 25,300 were planted on five Tittleshall farms, followed by another 45,000 on three farms three years later. The latter example is a little unusual in that the cost of weeding was allowed in one case, and, in another, 10,000 whin (gorse or furze) layers were included; at Massingham, a thorn hedge was interspersed with 100 oak saplings. The initial scheme on Henry Knott's Holkham farm took 5,500 layers, ninety-five rods of new ditching and nine dozen hurdles, but perhaps the most ambitious development so far was in 1726 on Thomas Haylet's farm at Godwick, where 117,250 layers were planted and 1,062 rods of new ditching dug. All the hurdles were supplied by Thomas Morecroft from the Tittleshall woods, and, when he sent five loads to Nicholas Anger's Holkham farm before the hedges were established, the eighty-six dozen cost £15 (3s 5d per dozen). In 1728 Morecroft also supplied eighty-three dozen bank hurdles at about the same price 'for the new inclosure at Longlands', where 15,500 layers had been planted. A 'layer' nursery was established at Holkham, and between 1722 and 1728 in Norfolk well over a quarter of a million were planted; during the same period more than 5 miles of new ditches were dug in the initiative to make individual farms more effective and more profitable. At Southmill in Dunton manor, one enclosure created a particular knock-on effect: the rent arrears listed against three tenants between 1723 and 1727 were justified because they were 'by reason of the Common being enclosed'.

The only other Coke manors where similar developments began at this time were in the West Country. At Durweston an acre of ground was enclosed on the down and rented out at ten shillings a year, and at Donyatt banks were 'thrown up' for quicksets* to be planted on them between small fields. At Shillington the operation is described in some detail, probably because it was one of the first of its kind in the area: '3½ days work for 2 men and 5 horses with a Waggon in carrying Thorns &c. for making an Hedge to inclose a Piece of Ground upon the Down near Elcomb Copps £1.10.0d.'; 'For ditching, planting with Quicksets and hedging 82 rods for enclosing the said Ground at 15d. p. rod £2.5.0d. [sic] and for cutting 72 lugs [sic] of Underwood at 1d. p. lug for making the said Hedge 6s.'. A year later, fifty-six rods of hedging were needed 'to keep the cattle from the layers planted on the side of the down 4 days team work carrying thorns for this'. The following year, the rent for that piece of downland was increased by 66 per cent.

A reasonable and justifiable level of rents could be determined only on the basis of accurate surveys, but for many of the Coke manors in the early 1720s assessments had to be made using old maps. For this reason, the other senior servant who travelled extensively in Norfolk and beyond was John Halsey, the surveyor. He had been employed by the estate since 1713, and in 1714 produced his first map, a survey of Waterden, an elaborate piece of work intended, perhaps, to impress the steward. By the 1720s he was earning £30

---

* Quicksets are live slips or cuttings of plants, especially hawthorn, set in the ground to grow into a hedge.

rising to £40 a year, which is an indication of the value set on his work by his
employer. During that period he surveyed the Norfolk manors of Tittleshall,
Beeston, Kempstone, Fulmodeston, Flitcham and Panworth Hall; in Suffolk he
dealt with Huntingfield, Horham (where he boarded with Samuel Pulham) and
Mildenhall. For the survey of Knightley he went equipped for measuring
timber as well, having bought a book, line, nails and paper specifically for this
purpose. When he worked at Portbury, his box went via London and Bristol,
and for the ten days he was there Absalom Williams, the woodward, acted as
his assistant.[20] Halsey also acted as bailiff for the Dunton and Doughton
manor, and collected assize rents in thirteen other Norfolk properties. Later on
he also worked for other employers, including the Duke of Bedford, whose
Thorney estate he surveyed in 1731. Interestingly, Halsey trained his son in his
own profession, and the boy made a 'casting' or field book when he was only
10 years old, which survives in the Holkham archives.[21]

Other surveyors were used on occasion: in 1719 Mr Bateson was paid
fifteen guineas for 'viewing the [Holkham] salt marshes'; George Collet
surveyed Donyatt in 1723 for ten guineas, and John Vaston mapped and
surveyed the same manor again three years later for £15, with Henry King
the bailiff assisting him during the nine days he was there; Solomon Goff
received £1 for surveying Crawley Coppice on the Minster Lovell manor, prior
to the felling in 1727.

Building maintenance had not been neglected under the Trustees, and the
work continued in the 1720s, with the accounts providing useful detail and
examples of new projects. Morecroft employed estate workers in some cases,
and in others subcontracted to local craftsmen.[22] Labourers were normally
hired from the tenant who was having the work done, although there are two
instances where the tenant's lease required him to meet part of the labour
costs: at Flitcham Abbey farm, £3 (5 per cent) was deducted from the sum
allowed the tenant for repairs for 'Covenant days work', and at Martham
there was a sixteen shillings (25 per cent) deduction 'for Covenant work'.

A large barn was essential for an arable farm, not only for storage but for
threshing corn, and was the most expensive building on the homestead. At
Massingham the cost of a 94ft by 31ft barn, complete with two hangerells
(open lean-to sheds built onto the sides) and a porch, was £130, while
William Kent's new barn at Weasenham was even more expensive at £172.
On the Oxfordshire manor, the gamekeeper needed a small barn, which was
built by Edward Lock & Partners; they repaired his house at the same time for

an all-in cost of £4 4s 6d, so the barn must indeed have been very small. A hardwood threshing-floor was always laid between the two large doors of a barn, one in each long wall, so that a through-draught would blow the husks away from the grain as it was being threshed with flails. These floors needed renewing regularly; the two replaced at Waterden in 1724 cost £2 10s. When the floor at Longham Hall was done, the walls of the barn were re-boarded at the same time at a total cost of £4 4s 6d. It is worth noting that Marshall acknowledges the superiority of plank floors, but says that, in the east of the county at least, clay was more common. There, the farmers realised that corn threshed on a clay floor became slightly soiled and did not, therefore, settle so close in the bushel measure as that which had been threshed on a clean wooden floor – the latter practice thereby increased its sale value.[23] A reference to 'dove muck' at Billingford has been noted earlier, and at South Creake the size of the dove-house called for £21 8s 5½d to be spent on carpentry and £6 12s on brickwork in a virtual rebuilding.

Wage-rates were relatively stable in the 1720s, and a sufficient number of individual examples are found to provide comparisons between various types of manual labour and to shed some light on the amount of effort needed by a labourer to earn a living. Most of the data relates to Norfolk and Suffolk, simply because most of the work involved was on arable land, whereas in most of the outlying manors a pastoral economy predominated. By no means all types of work can be assessed, because in many cases one or more factors in the equation are missing – piece-work carried out by a group for a given price will not yield a wage-return figure for one man unless the size of the group is quoted, even though the work itself is measurable. Nevertheless, it is worth considering those categories where some conclusions may be drawn, of which thatching is one. The first distinction to be made is that in the eastern counties all thatched buildings, with the exception of most churches and houses in large villages or towns, were covered with straw and not reed, simply because the former was freely available close to hand; it was normally provided by the tenant of the farm, and it was always cheaper than reed. The operation was standardised and functioned with a team of three: the thatcher himself, who laid the thatch on the roof and was responsible for the quality of the work, his yealmer and his server. The yealmer's task was to wet a mound of straw, draw handfuls of stalks out and align them into a bundle called a yealm, so that the server could pick it up within a straw band and carry it up the ladder for his master to lay. Apart from the straw, all that was needed was a supply of broaches (or brotches), the slim sticks of wood that were used in conjunction with rough wooden hooks to secure the yealms of straw onto the roof. In Norfolk the farmer normally supplied broaches and hooks made of prickwood, the local name for the wood of a spindle tree, which was tough enough to make the spindles from which it gained its name. Over at Minster Lovell there was a family team, Henry Carter thatching, his wife yealming and his son serving. Together they re-roofed Robert Parker's barn for 16s 9d, and, as the daily rate was about half-a-crown (2s 6d), it represented a full week's work. East Anglian churches were often thatched (those at Sisland, Theberton and a number of other places still are), and in the 1720s some roofs in north Norfolk, such as that of Castle Acre, were probably the work of Henry May from Holkham, who cut his reed in the Burrow and New Marsh channels for 1s 6d a day. Terms naturally varied county to county, and the '40 stitch of billeys' provided for a Somerset thatcher at Donyatt no doubt matched the bundles of broaches served to Henry May. In Somerset, however, all thatching was in reed, there being no great acreage of corn to provide straw. It is a matter of record that the method of thatching and the rough materials it required did not change in any way on small Norfolk and Suffolk farms until the Second World War, except that the straw came from an outside stack after it had been mechanically threshed, rather than from a barn where the grain had been beaten out with a flail.

Another specialism that involved teamwork was the care of sheep. Although the shepherd was pre-eminent and worked largely on his own with only a 'page' or boy, at shearing and lambing times he had to have assistance. Most of the shearing was taken on by small gangs, so that at Holkham John Nobbs & Partners sheared the Longlands flock of 900 at 4s 6d a hundred, and dealt with 544 ewes and crones for sixpence less. Prices fluctuated a little, and, a few years later, wethers were being sheared and washed for five shillings and ewes for four shillings a hundred. In 1724 nine men clipped and washed 394 sheep for £1 8s, meaning that one man earned 1s 10d for shearing forty-four of them, at a halfpenny each. The price per hundred on that basis would have been 4s 2d, against the six to seven shillings a hundred paid to a shearer working on his own. The gangs were therefore competitive, but, unlike the single man, they had no food and drink supplied. The labourer received a penny each for greasing lambs, and, again, his basic meals were provided.

In the mainly arable counties, the harvest was regarded as the most important season in the farming calendar and the labour required was regulated differently. Workers were engaged to work for the whole of the harvest period (however long that might be) for an agreed sum, which for most of the men was the only insurance they had against the inevitable short working hours of winter. As with shearing, it was common for eight or ten of them to band together, and at Holkham a typical 1720s harvest wage was £3 12s, with the boys earning £1 10s 6d (the average labourer's weekly wage was six shillings, so he was anxious to see the harvest over in not much over eight weeks). In one instance the bargain struck was £3 for six weeks, and the men must have kept an anxious eye on the sky. Food and drink were supplied, and a horkey or 'harvest home' could be expected, but the hours were as long as the daylight and loads often came in by moonlight. One or two examples of rates for single men as opposed to gangs contradict the suggestion that gangwork was necessarily cheaper for the employer. On a Holkham farm a man mowed 15 acres for 2½d an acre, whereas Andrew Leather & Partners had an agreed price that was more than double that figure.

In his eulogy of the farming revolution carried out by Coke of Norfolk, R.N. Bacon credits him with the introduction of wheat as a main crop: 'When Mr Coke came to Holkham [in 1776] very little if any wheat grew between that place and Lynn.' No attempt has been made here to analyse the cropping patterns of the 1720s, but the audit books make it quite plain that wheat was grown in quantity at Holkham from the very beginning of Thomas Coke's time there – another example of the reputation of Coke of Norfolk being inflated at the expense of his predecessor.

Before the harvest, there was the haysel, when the fodder crops were mowed. This was noticeably better paid at a shilling per acre for both grass and clover – crops such as hay and sanfoin are heavier work and need much more care in the handling, which explains the higher figure. Similarly, threshing grass seed took much time and care with the primitive winnowing machines and hair sieves then in use, a fact reflected in the one-shilling comb rate.

It has been seen that the programme of enclosures involved a vast amount of ditching, the cost of which is often itemised in the accounts. The average price for new ditches was one shilling per rod (5½ yds), with little variation between counties. Sometimes, if the land was light, it was less – eight pence per rod in west Norfolk, for example, and less still if an old ditch were being scoured out ready for its new role. Gang labour was common in all manors for this particular work.

The drive for better soil quality involved a massive amount of hand labour, and the 2¾d a load was minimal for a two-man team filling a tumbril with muck that weighed, on average, a ton, and then spreading the contents on the field. Another example quotes three shillings as the weekly labour charge for this work, so that they would have to load, cart and spread thirteen loads to equal the piece-work price. This is easy to state, but there is a need to visualise a field in which heaps were dropped in rows at 7yd intervals and one ton was spread over 2 acres by the labourer swinging a loaded fork. Again, the practice survived until the 1940s. A teamsman could earn 2s 6d an acre for ploughing and harrowing prior to sowing, and when turnips were fit for hoeing the rate was anything between 2s 2d and five shillings per acre, depending on the stage and age of the crop, with gangs normally making about four shillings.

The records of building work do not yield so much information on wage-rates. The average journeyman carpenter could expect to earn between ten and twelve shillings a week, and, lower down the scale, brick-kiln labourers (again in a gang) in one instance earned fifteen shillings for unloading and stacking 53,700 bricks from the kiln (which were then sold for 10s 6d per thousand). Assuming a gang of no more than eight, the overhead cost related to the selling price was little enough. Painting (or daubing as it was called) and plastering was charged at a halfpenny a foot run, but that gives no idea of what a wall cost to cover. More interesting is the fact that earth was dug at Donyatt to be mixed with the plaster, and in Norfolk quantities of animal hair and smithy dust were bought for the same purpose.

The one Norfolk manor that differed from the rest in its make-up was North Elmham, in that it was a deer park. There had been deer parks in England since before the Conquest, and apart from the royal parks they were all controlled by lords of the manor; by the end of the Middle Ages, there were over fifty in Norfolk and they were operated under royal licence.[24] Elmham manor had been bought by Sir Edward Coke in 1598, and the park, which lay to the west of the village, can still be located by a 'Park House' on the north side of the Brisley road. It was well established by the end of the seventeenth century, equipped with two substantial lodges, and in the 1720s was managed by Andrew Pigg. Pigg was also the tenant of the 300-acre Park farm, for which he paid a rent of £100, sometimes accommodating grazing bullocks for the estate. His office of park keeper required him to supply five and a half brace of bucks (the first five of which were to go to Thomas Coke and his guardians), and a brace of does. The rest of the bucks were distributed mainly among Coke's relatives and friends: a tally of the 1717 distribution will be found in Appendix 2. Pigg was entitled to a guinea for each buck, but no fee was allowed for does. At the end of that year he found himself in debt and entered a plea: 'This arrear of £200 the Keeper craves to be forgiven him for that he rented the parke at a high price. And had had two great Losses of Deer Vizt. in Spring 1710 he lost 70 head of Male Deer and in the hard Winter before 60 head of Deer. So that for 5 Years last past he has not sold any and through his care & good management he has now raised a full stock of 500.' As keeper, Pigg earned £3 6s 8d a year and was a liveried servant, receiving a hat, breeches, stockings, boots and shoes. These items cost £2 10s, but in 1725 he took £6 13s 4d in lieu, and in the following year his salary and livery allowance were merged at £10. He claimed for a number of recurring expenses in the running of the park, including the mowing, making and stacking of hay for the deer, and growing turnips for their feed in the winter. In one year he needed to buy in ten additional loads of hay, but this does not seem to have been a regular requirement. In 1726 there is also a charge for 'feining in the park', which probably referred to care exercised during the fawning season, and the keeper claimed fifteen shillings for seven and a half dozen moles caught in the park. He arranged for all the venison destined for London to be taken to Norwich, where it was dispatched via the regular coach service.

A deer park was a valuable property, since venison consumption was a sign of status, and a gift of game was one of the more delicate means by which the gentry expressed influence and solicited favour.[25] A good haunch served as a centre-piece to a small dinner party – Jonathan Swift noted in his *Journal to Stella* when writing of attendance at the Court at Windsor in 1711: 'We had for dinner the fellow of that haunch of venison I sent to London; 'twas mighty fat and good, and eight people at dinner, that was bad.'[26] In 1722 the price of a haunch was between £3 and £5, and other parts of the carcass made the venison patties that were in demand for select fork suppers; the skin, offal and sometimes the rest of the beast were often the perquisites of the under-keepers.[27] The Elmham deer park was an inheritance, but in the eighteenth century many gentry for the first time formed parks contiguous with their seats, walled or fenced them, and employed a staff of keepers.[28] Pigg was also Thomas Coke's swan-upper, the 'swan nupper' of the accounts, and was paid £1 a year for looking after the stock on the upper Wensum. The 1728 profit and loss account contains no mention of Pigg, or the Park lodges, nor is there any record of venison sales, but later audit account volumes show that the park continued to function as before in the 1730s.

One of the Huntingfield manors in Suffolk was also a deer park, but there is no recorded activity on that score in the 1720s, although there is at Minster Lovell. There, the bailiff was paid for 'keeping the Chase, woods & walls', and in 1724, when Thomas Coke stayed there, his eight days of buck hunting added £4 to the manor's expenses.

Although it does not feature in the audit books, one other property warrants a brief mention here. When Thomas Coke's grandmother Lady Anne Walpole died in 1722, she left him an estate at Conisbrough in Yorkshire, for which one would have expected to find entries. The single reference that has been traced is in the household accounts for 1728, where Thomas Morecroft is reimbursed his expenses incurred in a trip to Yorkshire and Derbyshire with John Aram, the Holkham under-gardener. They visited Chatsworth, Chesterfield and Conisbrough, and were almost certainly buying trees for the Holkham Park development described in Chapter 4.

The Coke estate was almost wholly agricultural, but a handful of London properties also brought in rents. In the ledgers they are listed collectively under 'Bevis Marks' and were in the parish of All Hallows-in-the-Wall. A dozen houses stood on Camomile Street and in the eponymous Coke's Court, and their rents varied from £5 10s to £18. The Saracen's Head Inn was the most substantial, and the tenant, Mrs Whitwich, paid £100 a year. The inn, at 7 Camomile Street (on the south side), was one of the older inns of the city and can be identified on Ogilby and Morgan's map of 1677. A daily coach plied from there to Eltham, and the inn was still in existence in 1851. By 1918 the site was taken by a passage leading to Coke's Court (renamed Bishopgate Avenue), and the whole area was laid waste by the air raids of the Second World War. A substantial rent of £17 10s was paid by Mr Charles Highmore of Peckham, a city merchant, either for himself or for one of his staff. A Mr Needham rented three houses, one for himself and two others to sub-let. Of the other tenants, John Highmore was a linen draper, and Mrs Dashwood ran a coal merchant's business in Spitalfields Market. Trophy money was paid for all of them. It is notable that, although one rent was collected from the Bank of England, others were paid at inns, the Dolphin and the Blackamoore's Head in Cheapside, and the Hand & Pen in Houndsditch. Both Bevis Marks and Camomile Street survive as street names and are part of the traffic artery that connects London Wall with the Minories.

Thomas Coke rarely went to Norwich, but the family had owned a town house there since 1613, when the Chief Justice purchased Paston House in Conisford Street from Sir William Cope of Hardwick for £800; the house is the oldest surviving domestic building in the city today, dating from the twelfth century. The street had been the centre of the Jewish community in the Middle Ages, but by the eighteenth century it was a busy mixture of substantial town houses and commercial premises lying between the Wensum waterfront and the castle. However, when Coke attended the assizes, he tended to stay with Dr Humphrey Prideaux at the Deanery, so in 1723 the house was sold for £400 to a Mr Gobbet. Known for long as 'The Music House', 'Wensum Lodge' is now a county council further education complex, with a little green plaque on the wall to remind passers-by of the Coke family connection. Once he had disposed of the big town house, there seems to be no logical reason why Coke paid £46 in 'consideration money' for another and much more modest dwelling 'over the water' on Pit Street in St Augustine's parish. He would never have used it himself, and it was promptly let to a William Lindsey for £4 a year, taxes being paid and repairs carried out.

Apart from the Norwich house mentioned above, only two other properties were discarded in the 1720s. There were 66 acres called Lambsholme at Mildenhall on the western edge of Suffolk that formed part of Sir Thomas Hanmer's manor (its isolation from other Coke properties may have prompted the sale for an unspecified amount in 1725), and a 60-acre farm at Chediston in the east of the county, which was sold for £525 in the same year.

At Holkham, two houses, two cottages and a barn were bought for a total of £200, and the interest on £245 'consideration money' was paid for land belonging to Henry Knotts, the tenant of Mansers. About the same time some land lying in the manor of Wells cost £921 to add to the estate; an instalment was paid but the residue was held over. A good deal more was invested in the outlying manors, largely in the purchase of 'lives' (see above), which had a value dependent on the annual income derived from the property. The possibility of buying in these 'lives' was mooted by the auditor in 1717 when he added a marginal gloss to an entry about a Minster Lovell farm: 'To purchase these two lives. Whether it be advantageous, the owner being in low circumstances', the inference being that a shrewd bargain was possible. In the Donyatt entries for 1726, there is a group of these transactions: the assignment of two lives bought for £50; one life on a 5-acre copyhold for £22; a widowhood life, plus her under-age son's life on 5 acres plus their tenement for £120; a tenement taken in hand and purchased for £180. At Portbury, a widow's rights in two tenements were bought for £100, and three lives in another tenement cost £175. In all these cases, part of the purchase price was handed over straight away, while the balance was held over for a year or so to ease the cash-flow situation, requiring interest to be paid out on it in consequence. In 1728 Thomas Coke had the opportunity to buy the Tittleshall rectory manor and the manor of Bintry, in both of which he already owned land. The price is not recorded, but £13 17s 8½d in fines and fees, plus an outstanding twenty years of a five-shilling suit fine had to be handed over to His Majesty's Honour of Clare – one of those payments that remained embedded like fossils in manorial finances long after the Reformation.

In every part of the estate the affairs of the Church were closely interwoven with the life of the manor, nowhere more so than in matters of patronage, and it is important to recognise the effect of this particular power as exercised by the Coke family. From the very beginning an advowson was regarded, not only as a responsibility exercised by the Crown or by the lord of the manor, but as a particular form of property that could be transferred by gift or sale. The owner (known as the patron) could not present his nominee with the spiritual or even legal possession of the office, but his authority and control in the affairs of the parish via such patronage were substantial, even in the eighteenth century and later. He held the freehold of the entire church but had no control over the nave, aisles or the tower if it had one, although in many instances he met the upkeep and repair costs and paid for extensions. The chancel, however, was his alone, and there he undertook all the maintenance. He had the right to the principal seat and could instal pews for himself and his family, and the family's tombs, memorials and ledger slabs are not to be found elsewhere in the church unless there was no more room. Even then (as at Tittleshall for the Coke memorials) chancel windows and doors could be blocked at will to make wall space for additions. When the floor was completely taken up, coffins might be housed in a mausoleum, either as a separate building or attached to the chancel (again, as at Tittleshall). As lay rector (or impropriator) the patron claimed the greater tithes from the parishioners, but that particular levy was sometimes hidden within rentals.

In the early eighteenth century, 53 per cent of 'livings', as they are often called, were controlled by landed gentry, and 10 per cent by the Crown, with the remainder in the hands of the Church. In his day, Sir Edward had collected quite a number and bequeathed them to his posterity, so that Thomas Coke found himself possessed of a round score.[29] A third of the tythes came to him as the lay impropriator, but there were variations in practice concerning clergical stipends: in some parishes, the estate paid a curate an annual stipend – for example, £20 to Mr Rice (followed by Mr Money) at Flitcham; £12 to Mr Hardy at Bylaugh; in 1717 a Mr Lane was serving the cures at Longham and Wendling, but six years later 'John Lane, Clerk' (the rector) was charged £28 16s for the profits of Wendling rectory, which were then used as the stipend of the Wendling and Longham curate. The Tittleshall rector, Mr Budworth, held the rectory manor, and the estate paid him a quit rent for land within it (until Thomas Coke bought the manor), but at the same time he rented a third of Fisher's tenement for £10 a year in a Coke Tittleshall manor and was allowed his Land Tax. At Castle Acre, 'Abraham Pimlow, Clerk' was the vicar and was allowed £14 for 'a year's augmentations and composition money', but he too was a tenant, paying an assize rent and having his Land Tax paid for him.

Chancel repairs are recorded a number of times. At Weasenham, the tenant of Tythe farm dealt with them in 1717, more work being done in 1722, and in 1724 Will Rice was paid 14s 9½d for glazing the chancel, and went back to do more in 1727 (this may have been a 'small boys throwing stones' problem – in desperation, Tunstead in east Norfolk bricked up the entire east window of its chancel at about this time for that very reason!). More glazing was carried out at Holkham in 1726 and at Laxfield in 1728. When Thomas Morecroft supervised the chancel 'new reeding' at Castle Acre, he costed it at £12, with a ladder being supplied by Mr Glover, a local builder. This was not a complete re-roofing, for only two loads of reed were taken over to Castle Acre from Holkham, one by Edward Creamer, the tenant of Lushers, and the other by Anne Nicholls of Peterston. The Tittleshall mausoleum mentioned earlier is a large and rather gaunt accretion in red brick on the north side of the chancel, and repairs were carried out 'at the Burial Place in the Church' in 1727. Apart from that, the parish had to be content with 'to the church and poor as usual at Xmas £1.10.0d'.

There is one instance in the 1720s when Thomas Coke took the opportunity to purchase an advowson. It was for the living at Cratfield, one of the family manors in Suffolk. Its owner was John Middleton of Wisbech, the price was £120 and negotiations were handled by Mr Bedingfeld, Coke's Wighton neighbour and local attorney. His clerk was paid for his trouble in drawing up the papers, and Humphrey Smith went over to Wisbech in company with Charles Hutchinson, the Cratfield manor bailiff, to complete the formalities and pay the money.

When all the routine steps had been taken to secure payment of rents, fines and other charges from tenants, there was an inevitable residue involving the unfortunate, the feckless and the intransigent upon which the weight of the law descended; and Thomas Coke was not averse to court proceedings. On the Holkham Manor, Nathaniel Kendarly rented the Clint and in 1722 took over 'the newly inclosed marshes' on a rent of £400. This led him into debt over the next few years, and by 1727 his liability had risen to £824. The matter went to law, but relief came the following year when the residual debt of £230 2s 10d was 'forgiven by my Lord'. At Panworth Hall near Watton a dispute over foldcourse rights was taken to court in the same year. At Dunton, Peter Tubbing had the main farm on a rent of £223 a year, but became so tangled up in a dispute with the estate in 1723 that his Land Tax was not allowed, and he finished the year £173 in debt 'for which he hath been arrested'. For three years his name disappears from the accounts, and then normal relations are resumed with his agreement to pay off his £300 debt at £100 a year. At Fulmodeston John Money's taxes were not allowed, 'he being absconded and his effects seized upon'. The manor bailiff charged a fee for distraining his goods for non-payment of rent to the tune of £73 18s 7¼d. At Horham, John Moulton owed £23 5s 3d 'for the security of which his effects are seized upon, but not yet sold'. Under the faintly improbable heading of 'Improvements', the Farnham Royal accounts record that Joseph Hearne, who was both tenant farmer and bailiff-cum-woodward combined, was allowed eleven shillings expenses 'in seizing and whipping three Broom men that were found cutting birch in Seer Green Wood' (birch was always the preferred wood for making broom heads). For that little exercise he claimed a £4 fee. At Portbury the bailiffs were paid fifteen shillings for distraining Widow Delamore's goods, and a lawyer's clerk attended the court for the case, drawing ten shillings subsistence for his journey. The resistance to Leet Court fees has already been noted, and at Donyatt a £55 fine was withheld for two years by John Baker before he was finally arrested and sent for trial at Bridgewater Assizes. When Coke visited Shillington in 1724, he tipped Thomas Gillingham £1 for 'shewing the Lands and in seizing the Timber by Mr Coke's order', and tenants were prosecuted there for felling trees without authority. At Knightley in the same year Mr Haynes, a Derby attorney, visited with a servant to deal with 'the trees in dispute', and the Park farm tenant went to Derby later to see him about them and was paid to fell them some months later. These matters perhaps had a salutory effect upon the tenantry at large, but at a cost. The legal charges arising from this handful of cases totalled well over £200.

Now and then charity or common sense prevailed, as in the cancellation of the debt of £12 10s owed by Will Gray, a Huntingfield tenant described as 'desparate'. At Shillington, Widow Gosney was allowed her three shillings arrear, 'she not being in a capacity of paying'. A Minster Lovell tenant was excused a firewood bill of twelve shillings, which had been outstanding for two years, 'he being poor and not in a capacity of paying it'. Rather more was involved when Donyatt Bailiff John Marks died owing £169 1s 9¾d, but no action against his executors is recorded (although this does not necessarily mean that none was taken).

In this chapter I have attempted a survey of the estate that Thomas Coke had inherited, spread across England from East Anglia to Somerset. He set about managing it effectively, but the focus must now be on the core of his activity in the 1720s – the development of Holkham and the setting for his life's work.

Chapter 3

ON HOME GROUND

*T*he young man of fortune comes of age, enters into his inheritance and marries an heiress. He has just spent six years travelling on the Continent, spending much of his time having his artistic senses sharpened by the delights of statuary, pictures, Old Master drawings and, above all, splendid architecture set in landscapes that fashioned his lifelong devotion to the paintings of Claude Lorrain. What next? He was fortunate enough to have been presented with a fine London town house, but his wealth and lineage required a country property that could become the centre of family life when not enjoying the fashionable city life during the season – and where he could indulge in his passion for cockfighting and hunting.

There is little doubt that Thomas Coke considered the possibilities open to him, reviewing in his mind the properties he had known as a boy and perhaps others that had been suggested. Longford in Derbyshire was not an option, with his guardian Sir Edward Coke long established there. However, there was Huntingfield in Suffolk with its manor and deer park, and Minster Lovell, one of the great aristocratic houses of Oxfordshire; its mellow medieval buildings, set delectably beside the Windrush, had been used occasionally by his illustrious ancestor, the Chief Justice. But he was fresh from the spacious settings of the Veneto and the Roman campagna, and Huntingfield was perhaps too confined, too small in scale. His full-blooded enthusiasm for the architecture of Palladio would hardly be compatible with the Gothic mustiness of Minster Lovell, a supposition confirmed when he dismantled the house in 1747 and used the ruins for farm buildings. Another possibility was the Stoke Poges house where Sir Edward Coke had spent his final years, and it would seem that Thomas Coke thought seriously about it. It had been bought by the Chief Justice in 1599 for £4,000 from Katherine, Countess of Huntingdon, but in 1656 his son-in-law leased both the manor and the house to John Gayer, and the reversionary interest in the property was sold later. In 1723 Gayer's son Robert refused to abide by the terms attached to the purchase, and, after a legal tussle in Chancery, there was a forced sale and the property went to Edmund Halsey for £12,000. Prior to that, in 1719, Thomas Coke had sent the architect Colen Campbell, accompanied by the steward, a carpenter and a bricklayer, down from London to survey the property: the object of the visit was specifically 'about buying Stoke'. Coke himself visited at least twice, but nothing came of it. There is an intriguing ledger entry in May 1721 that records a three-day outing 'when his Hon'r went with Mr Kent to Mr Tallmans'. William Kent, Coke's friend and artistic collaborator, had journeyed with John Talman to Rome a decade earlier when the latter was already an established architect, and this visit may have been part of the decision-making process in Coke's mind – he had paid Talman ten guineas for a drawing two months earlier.

Be that as it may, it is a reasonable assumption that by that time he had already begun to treat Holkham as the chosen site for his new country home. The family connection had begun in 1600 when Sir Edward Coke acquired the manor of Wheatley in the parish; and, in 1612, when his son John married Meriel Wheatley, the old Elizabethan manor house known as Hill Hall became the family home. Colen Campbell had briefly appeared on the Norfolk scene in 1719 when he came up by coach to Lynn with Humphrey Smith, and his object can only have been to survey the Holkham site with a view to building. He was at that time involved in preparing the first (and abortive) designs for Robert Walpole's Houghton, and the two projects may well have gone hand in hand, to judge by the 'four tower' concept for the Walpole house and the similarities of the eventual layout at Holkham. Coke's uncle Michael wrote to his father Sir John Newton about Holkham in November

1721: 'Mr Coke likes this place so well now that I believe if he ever builds it will be here, and he will find it necessary to add something, for there is not a convenient room for the company he usually has with him.'[1] It is not known why 'Campbell the surveyor' was paid sixteen guineas in 1725, but the first positive evidence of the project that was to absorb most of Coke's energies for the rest of his life appears as a single line in the household accounts for March 1726 under 'Gratuities': 'To Mr Breckingham by Sr. Thomas's order for drawing a Plan for a New House £10.10.0.' The product of this commission was almost certainly the seven drawings in Brettingham's hand with notes and measurements added by Coke, which are now in the British Museum collections,[2] the importance of which was recognised by Dr Leo Schmidt in 1980.[3] Thus Matthew Brettingham, senior, known affectionately by Coke over the years simply as 'Bret', set the ball rolling that did not come to rest for another forty years.

However, long before that, there was a great deal of activity on the Holkham manor in three main areas, the home farm, the kitchen gardens and the Great Lawn with its crowning wood. Here was a site that horrified many of its fashionable visitors, who thought it an idiotic choice – barren and unfertile, bleakly open to the cutting north wind from the sea, and totally uncongenial to a man of taste and sensibility. There was a belief held locally, but with no corroboration, that Coke's first choice of site was where the obelisk now stands, but that this was discarded because there was no adequate water supply. Even after ten years the comments were uncomplimentary. John, Lord Hervey, went with a party in 1731 to dine at Hill Hall and reported to the Prince of Wales: 'It is at present a most unpleasant place, but he [Lord Lovel] comforts himself with a park in embryo, and a Burlington house with four pavilions – on paper.'[4] At about the same time, Sir Thomas Robertson was taken to see Lord Lovel in his 'exceedingly bad old house' and was pessimistic about 'so much to be compassed only by art, time, and expense'. Nevertheless Hill Hall still had a vital role to play in providing kitchens and rooms for guests during the long gestation of the new house, and it was not finally demolished until 1757. This old Elizabethan manor house, with its thirty-four hearths and wainscotted rooms, had been the home of the Norfolk branch of the family continuously for generations and was familiar to Thomas, who had spent time there as a boy; one should remember, too, that his father's 1707 bookplate bore the legend: 'Edward Coke of Norfolk Esqr.'. The audit books give the lie to claims made by Edward Rigby and R.N. Bacon in Coke of Norfolk's day that the estate was still 'a barren wilderness' as late as the 1860s. The phrase in the inscription placed above the entrance to the Marble Hall by the Dowager Countess reads 'an open, barren estate', but the phrase described Holkham as it was when Thomas Coke took it in hand in 1718. For him it had the potential that he sought, space to fashion a setting that would be worthy of the great house he had in mind. The Chief Justice's manor house at Godwick, too, was not far away, and the fact that a box was sent there from London via the Lynn coach in January 1720 shows that it was still being used by the family. This was home ground.

In 1717 Humphrey Smith, the land steward, rented 829 acres including the home farm and was responsible for the upkeep of Hill Hall. He may have had rooms there, although in the marriage settlement papers his address is given as Burnham Overy. His removal from office is detailed in Chapter 2: at Michaelmas 1722 his holding was divided up. Coke took 63 per cent in hand, comprising the whole area within the new park boundary, at a ledger rent of £267 13s 3d, Nicholas Anger, the tenant of Neals, took 7 per cent, and the rest was split between seven other tenants. At the same time Coke took 40 per cent of the Godwick manor in hand, for which he was charged a further £34, with the remainder divided between Thomas Morecroft, the master carpenter (who also took the Little Wicken farm), Thomas Haylett and Pomfret Flaxmore. The Clint marsh had been reclaimed from the sea by the guardians some years before, and in 1719 a Mr Bateson was paid fifteen guineas for advising on a further enclosure of salt marshes; Coke tipped the labourers a guinea when he went to view the area. Shortly after, Nathaniel Kendarly (or Kindersley), who rented the Clint, was paid the first half of £2,000 for 'inbanking Holkham marshes' – 560 acres near Holkham Staithe, known thereafter as the New Marsh.

At this stage, the major Holkham landowners and tenants were Nicholas Anger with Neals farm, and part of the home farm; Henry Knotts with Mansers farm, the upper side of the feeding marsh and the smithy; James Bircham with Thoroughgoods farm; Richard Porter with Newdigates farm (the Holkham Staithe farm, which included the Clint marsh), Nettletons farm and the lower side of the feeding marsh (Newdigates also included a 'Coney House' on the Merum (*sic*) Hills with about 100 acres lying next to the sea 'stockt with conies' and William Wegg had the rabbits for £4 a year); Edward Creamer with Lushers farm, Shepherds marsh and part of Mansers farm; Mrs Ann Nicholls with Peterston farm; William Leeds with Honclecronkdale farm ('the parsonage, well built of stone and brick'), Dalehole marsh and part of Mansers farm; and Nathaniel Kendarly with the recently enclosed New Marsh.

It could perhaps be safely assumed that the Holkham manorial rights included control of the foreshore of Holkham Bay and all jetsam stranded on it, but it is interesting that, when a ship was wrecked there, a Richard Swanton was paid £11 0s 6d. Subsequently the gang known as Ben Wright & Partners earned £1 12s 6d for breaking it up so that the timbers could be used for farm repairs.

Over the next five years Coke gradually added to his holding. In 1725 he purchased a small part of land belonging to Henry Knott's father, and took in the Clint; two years later some fields were bought in Wells parish, and when by 1728 Nathaniel Kendarly had fallen deeply in debt, the new marshes that he had drained and imbanked were taken in hand, the cost of the gates reimbursed and the ditches scoured out. The nearest brickyard had been bought from a Mr Wells in 1725 and let to William Mellenton for £10 a year, but by 1727 his widow owed nearly that sum, so Coke took it over, knowing that he would be needing a reliable and productive source of good bricks in the years ahead.

Having assumed control, Coke soon began to restock and equip the farm up to his and Appleyard's standards. During 1723 ten carthorses, fifty-six bullocks and a sufficiency of swine and turkeys cost £261, a figure that included their being driven from fairs at Thornham, North Elmham and Thorney. A total of 542 ewes and 561 wether sheep were bought from a number of tenants for £484. Later in the year a further 1,129 wether sheep and forty-one bullocks were bought at market and cost £492. At the same time, the farm's equipment was enhanced with one new and one second-hand cart, three ploughs, a set of harrows and three pairs of traces. William Might the horse-collarmaker's two bills came to £18 3s, and £45 in all was invested, with a further £20 spent on seed corn and ploughing. The latter was done by Morecroft's men, and Richard Springall the vicar supplied twelve loads of dung from his glebe, with Nicholas Anger called on for seed corn. Even William Jolly the carpenter contributed by lending a cart for harvest.

Thomas Haylett was mentioned earlier as farming part of Godwick, and he was appointed to manage the husbandry as farm bailiff; he drew a not inconsiderable salary of £74 13s 4d the following year. In the year that began at Michaelmas 1722, the husbandry labourers were paid £42 16s 2d for their work between Lady Day (25 March) and 3 August, and for the six weeks of harvest that followed they earned £45 12s 9d. Turnip hoeing and other 'back-end' work up to Michaelmas cost £12 3s 1d, and the 'Taskers' took on the threshing in the barns for £10 7s 7d, followed by the sheep shearing and washing for £5 19s 2d. They were treated to 'an earnest' for drink before they started, and again before they began muck carting. In all, the year's labour cost £116 18s 9d, including the two shepherds' wages and the husbandman's board. As part of his overall scheme of soil enrichment, Coke paid £7 10s for 500 loads of marl from John Money.

On the other side of the account, fifty-six bullocks were sold for £214 18s 6d and 576 sheep plus ten pigs for £284 1s 7d.[5] Wheat, rye, oats, barley and peas brought in a further £155, and £50 was credited for hay and straw delivered to the stables. By 1725 the home farm was able to supply eighty of the 116 loads of hay needed, but, until more land was put under the plough, only a third of the straw. Hides from the fatstock slaughtered for the kitchens were sold direct to the local breeches makers, George and Edmund Rix. Taking the valuation of the stock in hand into account, and including minor items in the outgoings such as 'barly and milk for Old Mary's pigs' and 'tarr & grease for the sheep', Appleyard calculated that they had recorded a net profit of £103 18s 6¼d on the year's work at Holkham and Godwick, and the following year there was a healthy increase to £990 9s 1½d. However, consistently large gains were not to be expected at the beginning of the new regime, and Coke will surely have felt satisfied in having brought mismanagement to an end and placed himself in firm control of the crucial centre of his estate, his own home ground.

As a manor house of some substance, Hill Hall had gardens close by to keep it supplied with vegetables and fruit, and, while an eighteenth-century surveyor's map of the manor does not provide a precise location, there are outlines to the east of the buildings that may be significant.[6] In the new scheme of things it was obvious that there would need to be changes, knowing that building work would shortly call for a total clearance near the old house, and that the much larger establishment would need a more generous provision of supplies. That being so, plans were made to site an entirely new and expanded kitchen garden west of the lake athwart the obliterated old road to Burnham. As early as 1720 work had begun, and John Creed the head gardener was paid £38 for 'making the new ground'. Trees were being bought, labourers were 'busy about the gardens and ponds', and a fish pond was stocked. Two years on, a team of women was weeding in the garden, and the labourers' wages bill was £116 – three times the cost of the farm equivalent. A nursery was established for hedge 'layers' (see Chapter 2), and in December 1722 a separate cost is quoted for the labourers working there. The nurseryman was Henry Cooke, who, a little later, made use of his professional contacts to get 1½ pecks of horse chestnuts from his opposite number at Raynham, and some garden trees came from Sir Charles Turner's at Warham. The following year Thomas Morecroft built a greenhouse for John Creed, who was perhaps anxious to make progress in advance of the permanent buildings that came later. Soon after, James Framingham had his rent abated by £1 because some of his land had been enclosed 'in the gardens'.

John Creed gained an assistant in December 1723 when John Aram was appointed as under-gardener, having been recruited from Nottinghamshire. He undoubtedly had good contacts with seedsmen and nurserymen generally, and was soon being sent on buying expeditions. He made a trip to London and the Home Counties in April 1725, buying forest trees from Mr Arslett of New Brentford and seeds from a Mr Fuller. He went back to his old county in 1724, and two years later he was in York buying trees for the new kitchen garden, where twenty-three old trees had been felled and stubbed out (which shows that the site was not completely barren). Trees from Yorkshire were freighted from the Humber, and Aram made the return journey with them in Will Denham's vessel and had them offloaded at Wells. For the fruit trees, baskets were made to protect and strengthen the roots when they were planted. In 1728 Thomas Morecroft went along with the under-gardener on a round of buying that took in the Conisbrough property, Chesterfield and the Duke of Devonshire's Chatsworth estate. By that time a great deal of progress had been made in the establishment of the new gardens. The garden walls were being built with the 100,000 bricks made by John Parker in the estate kiln, and the labour force was hard at work sinking three ponds, making slopes, carting muck, ploughing, trenching and cutting reed to protect the new hot beds that they had completed. James Lee, one of the Fulmodeston tenants, supplied 560 holly 'layers' at this stage, which were probably planted to form internal divisions within the various parts of the garden.

While all this was going on, a much larger operation was in progress elsewhere. In their plans for the mansion and its environs, Thomas Coke and William Kent had settled on a north–south axis that would stretch 2½ miles, from a triumphal arch at its southernmost point, through lodge gates up to an eminence on which an obelisk would rise, continuing down a broad swathe of lawn flanked by ranks of trees to a barrier canal, beyond which the house would command the scene. What the existing landscape was like in detail can only be a matter of guesswork, but the ground rose helpfully in a transverse ridge at about the right place. The principal requirements were to clear and grade the 53 acres or so that would constitute the 'Great Lawn' between the obelisk and the house, to clear and plant the 'Great Wood' that would crown the gentle hill, and to close a couple of inconvenient roads and create substitutes. The legal processes involved in that particular problem had been handled by Nathaniel Athill, who was paid £15 10s 'in part of his bill in 1722 in relacion of turning the roads at Holkham to make a park'.

After some preliminary skirmishing, work began in earnest in 1724, when labourers were at work 'improving the Lawn'. This involved stubbing out 1,452 yards of old fencing, and six days of felling and removing all the old trees. In that year the widow Carter was compensated for loss of ground that was to be taken into the lawn, and for the turnips she was growing on it. A massive earth-moving operation followed, which was carried out in phases. First, more than 1,000 tons of earth were removed, and a new ditch was dug all round and lined with paled fencing supplied by Morecroft from Tittleshall. In May 1725, Natt Wilkinson and Henry May dug the transverse canal or basin (see Plate 5) across the south frontage of the house site, and, between June and the following March, 6,133 loads of topsoil were carted in. Old walls were taken down by John Towl, and Henry Walker's gang dug up the old road. John Howman planted 6,500 birch, holly and hornbeam setts on the boundaries, and ten dozen bank hurdles were delivered from Tittleshall to protect them. Between May 1726 and the following February, 4,361 loads of earth were moved (that is, not less than 2,180 tons) in the process of grading slopes over 200 and 187 yards; 300 faggots were used at the bottom of the lawn, probably to strengthen the outer bank of the new canal. Work on clearing the way and marking out the new road took place in the winter, and there was to be a further two years spent on levelling the Great Lawn, culminating in a final 2,319 loads of earth being moved in 1728. Just under a hundred trees were planted, railed round and stayed with lines, and these will have been those shown standing in parallel ranks flanking the vista up to the obelisk (see Plate 6).[7]

While the Great Lawn was being prepared, a similar development was going ahead on the brow of the hill behind it. The site for the obelisk that was to command the axis between the triumphal arch and the house would be the centre of a polygonal wood covering the ridge of high ground. Bearing in mind that Coke was a member of the Craft, both the shape of the wood and its central obelisk may have had masonic significance. In the late seventeenth and early eighteenth centuries woods were sometimes shaped deliberately on that account – Blenheim and West Wycombe may be cited as examples. The land for the wood was taken from two farms: Nicholas Anger had his rent for Neals and part of the Hall farm reduced by twelve guineas, while James Bircham's rent for Thoroughgoods and another part of the old Hall farm was cut by £10, partly in compensation for a lost barley crop. In all, 26 acres were released, and Bircham took on the contract for ploughing in the Great Wood. When he had finished he carted prickwood posts and pales from Fulmodeston and Mileham to mark the boundaries, and supplied the turnip seed for sowing there as a cleansing crop. From October 1727 to the following March work went ahead preparing the ground 'in the New Wood', and whin faggots were brought from the heath to protect the young turnips in the spring. There was a neat economy in their re-use to fire the brick kiln when the young plants were sturdy enough to stand free. The lawn had been sown with hayseed the previous spring, and now it was time for Tom Futter to spend seven weeks driving his teams over the ground. Crows were a problem, and so Edward Creamer supplied gunpowder for Tom Manning 'to fright the crows from the seeds in the wood' while Sam Gidney was hoeing weeds there.

One of Holkham's unusual features is the large number of ilex trees (the *Quercus Ilex*, sometimes called evergreen or holm oaks), planted in groups on either side of the south drive, in the obelisk wood, and scattered throughout the park to the north of the house. It has been suggested, but without sound evidence, that they sprang originally from branches used as packing for statues that were shipped from Italy – but it is remarkable that there is not a single mention of them being bought or planted in the 1720s. However, by the mid-nineteenth century they had become famous: 'The most remarkable trees here, and for which this park has become celebrated all over England, are the evergreen oak, some of their trunks having attained to the unusual dimensions of twelve feet and a half in circumference.'[8] Trees and seeds of all sorts came in considerable quantities from a variety of sources, but only rarely is a specific location for them identified. Those bought from the Brentford nursery in 1721 were specifically 'forest trees' and were destined for

'the Holkham plantations', which could mean anywhere on the periphery of
the park. In 1724, 2,250 beech saplings, 2,700 birch and holly and 5,000
filberts were planted, along with a bushel of Spanish chestnuts, but they are
more likely to have been integrated with hedges. The Great Wood was ready
for planting by 1728, and there is one specific reference just before then to a
'parcel of walnuts' being sown there and beech mast being received from Sir
John Hobart at Blickling and from Ashe Windham at Felbrigg. Another comb
of beech mast came up from Joseph Langton's estate farm at Farnham Court
in Buckinghamshire, Suffolk acorns were sent from Huntingfield, and more
horse chestnuts were provided by Viscount Townshend's gardener at
Raynham. The 2,000 cherry stocks from Yorkshire were for hedgerow
planting, as perhaps were the 5,500 walnuts or, alternatively, for siting in the
plantations or the Great Wood. The two sacks of fir seeds from Blickling were
perhaps destined for shelter belts on the seaward side of the park. Towards
the end of 1728 yet more trees were shipped down from Yorkshire, and there
were gifts of trees from Sir Robert Walpole's garden at Houghton and Sir
Henry Bedingfeld's at Oxbrough; as in all similar cases, their gardeners were
tipped 'by order of Sr. Thomas in consideracon of Trees'. It is too late to be
certain just what was established in the Great Wood initially, except for the
strong negative evidence that ilex trees were not included. The year 1728 saw
what was perhaps the first tentative step to occupancy and use of the Great
Lawn, as eighteen chairs and two settees were painted and put in use, and
charged to the garden account. Moles too were obviously enjoying all that
friable, sweet soil: Absalon Griffin, the official molecatcher, trapped nineteen
dozen in the wood, the garden and the lawn. Another side effect was the need
for the 'great plow' and the hand-pushed ploughs to be repaired or renewed
repeatedly during this period.

By the time the first foundations were dug for the Family Wing in 1734,
the prospect on every side had changed and would continue to do so. To the
north, some of the scattered houses of the old village would make way for
builders' yards, to the west the kitchen gardens would flourish, and to the
south a noble prospect was emerging, with smoothed lawns across the canal
basin taking the eye up to the proud obelisk already in place at the centre of
the Great Wood.

With the estate firmly under control and his great house about to rise at its
heart, the young head of the family can have had few regrets over his choice
of Holkham for his home ground.

Chapter 4

THE TOWN HOUSE AND ITS PARISH

*U*nder the terms of their marriage settlement, the young couple were to have the use of Thanet House as their London residence, with the proviso that there should be rooms reserved for the use of Lady Margaret's father for as long as he required them. The earliest lease for the property in the Woburn archives is dated 1686, but it is not known exactly when or by whom the house was built. The Earl of Thanet was living there by the mid-1680s, and in 1693 he took a sixty-two-year lease on the property from Lady Russell, so that by the 1720s it had been the Tufton family's town house for forty years, at a ground rent of £26 a year. It stood in Great Russell Street, which by the early eighteenth century had become a popular site for the homes of the wealthy. It was a time of rapid development, astonishing Daniel Defoe: 'Westminster is in a fair way to shake hands with Chelsea, as St. Gyles's is with Marybone [*sic*]; and Great Russel Street by Montague House, with Tottenham-Court . . . whither will this monstrous city then extend?'[1] In the same year, John Strype describes Great Russell Street, which was within the parish of St Giles, as 'a very handsome, large and well built street, and the best inhabited by the nobility and gentry (especially on the north side, as having gardens behind the houses and the prospect of pleasant fields up to Hampstead and Highgate), insomuch as this place is esteemed the most healthful in London. In its passage it saluteth Southampton House, Montague House, and Thanet House; all these seats of noblemen.'[2] Despite the fact that Thanet House is mentioned, the map published in Strype's edition of *A Survey of the Cities of London and Westminster*, while depicting Montague House and Southampton House with their gardens, shows the site of Thanet House covered by a terrace that was certainly not there. Samuel Parker's *Plan of the City of London . . . with the New Additional Buildings* of 1720 is similarly inaccurate in showing the same terrace. Henry St John in Thackeray's *Henry Esmond* remarks: 'Why Bloomsbury is the very height of the mode. 'Tis rus in urbe. You have gardens all the way to Hampstead, and palaces round about you.' In the early seventeenth century the fields to the north were called Cowles Field and Cowles Pasture, becoming 'Long Fields' or 'the Southampton Fields' a century later, a place where, according to Strype, 'robberies and murders had been committed – the scene of depravity and wickedness the most hideous for centuries'. Francis Place records that in the 1770s there were several large ponds in the Long Fields and the amusements were duck hunting and badger baiting. By way of variety the boys would throw a cat in the water and set their dogs on it.[3]

Thanet House stood at the south-east corner of a plot between Charlotte Street and Caroline Street, the site presently occupied by Nos 100–103. James Elmes in his life of Sir Christopher Wren says that the architect designed a fine mansion on this street that was afterwards occupied by his son, and this has led some to assume that this referred to Thanet House; but there is no evidence to support this, as Stephen Wren was in fact living on the *other* side of the street in 1751.[4] Thomas Coke's lease was renewed for a short period in 1753, but after a few years the house passed into other hands, and in 1787 it was divided in two. In 1823 the façade was removed and Thomas Cubitt refaced the building and subdivided it into three.[5]

In its original form the house was substantial, with a frontage of 72ft. Above a basement with areas in front, there were three floors, with attic rooms lit by dormer windows. An early nineteenth-century history of the parish has a lithograph by George Scharf showing it after it had been divided (see Plate 4), and the original façade probably had five windows on the left and three on the right of the front door.[6] However, the alterations and eastward extension carried out soon after Coke took over the house make it difficult to be certain. The number of rooms cannot be calculated accurately, but in 1727 £1 10s was paid in window tax; for houses of more than twenty rooms the rate was one shilling per window, giving Thanet House a total of thirty. Between thirty and forty might be a reasonable estimate, judging by the number of flues swept regularly: in 1718 thirty-three were swept for eleven shillings, and in 1722 Ann Merrit was paid eighteen shillings for dealing with twenty-seven chimneys.

The accounts provide detailed information on the various taxes, local assessments and recurring overheads in relation to the house. The King's Tax of £5 12s 6d was collected once a quarter by a Mr Bavand and the window tax was paid yearly. The Commissioners of Sewers' rate for repairing and cleaning sewers in Southampton Square, Great Russell Street and several streets in St Giles was four pence in the pound, and the annual payment of £2 10s shows that the house was assessed at £150. Until the Westminster Paving Act of 1762, all the eighteenth-century London acts dealing with highways had merely been attempts to enforce the old personal obligation of each householder to pave his own frontage and keep it in repair. There was, however, a parish maintenance charge, which for Thanet House was £2 10s in 1721 (four pence in the pound, on the rateable value of £150). This was undoubtedly used to pay Mary Scarth, the raker of St Giles-in-the-fields parish from 1705 until 1723. She was paid £400 by the parish and employed 'twenty horses, four carts and five men',[7] though whether she valued them in that order is a matter of conjecture. Such external security as there was at night was provided by the parish watch at a yearly cost of ten shillings per household. Apart from the standing army, London's defence against riot or tumult lay in the hands of the trainbands, and a Mr Ragland collected eleven shillings a quarter – the cost of two men from the parish to parade with the trainband plus the mustermaster's charge. In 1725, over and above the parish poor rate of £2 6s a quarter collected by Mr Mills the Overseer, Coke donated £50 to the St Giles workhouse; other examples of his charitable giving are to be found in Chapter 7.

Another standing charge relating to the house was for water. A century earlier, Hugh Middleton, a London goldsmith, had seen the need for safe drinking water in London, at least for those who could afford to pay for it. He channelled springs in Hertfordshire and brought the water via a 38-mile cut to a resevoir in Clerkenwell, from which the city and its immediate suburbs were supplied by gravity. Known as 'the New River', it supplied fresh water three times a week via an underground network of pipes; individual houses stored the water in lead cisterns. In March 1718, a Mr Seymour collected £1 15s for half a year's supply of 'New River' water to the house. Daniel Defoe commented in 1724:

> No city in the world is so well furnished for the extinguishing of fires when they happen: by the great convenience of water which being everywhere laid in the streets in large timber pipes, as well as from the Thames as the New-River, those pipes are furnished with a fire plug, which the parish officers have the key of, and when opened, let out not a pipe, but a river of water into the streets, so that making but a dam in the kennel [gutter], the whole street is immediately under water to supply the engines . . . the New-River, brought by an aqueduct or artificial stream from Ware, continues to supply the greater part of the city with water.[8]

The availability of 'New River' water made a crucial difference to the standard of cleanliness attainable in the kitchen and still room, and for floors throughout the house; clothes could be laundered more effectively and more often, and it was now possible to supply water in bedrooms and bathrooms.

Behind the house a large garden stretched back over 200ft to Caroline Mews, with stables and coach houses ranged on the east side. These included living accommodation for staff – a 'double sacking bedstead' was purchased for the stable room in March 1719, and in September a bedstead, blankets, feathers and tick were bought for the coachman's room. This accommodation was not, however, sufficient for the family's needs, and, like some of his neighbours, Coke rented additional stabling in Blue Boar Yard further along the street on the same side, consisting of two stables, coach houses and a chamber. There was no inn on this site, and the yard may have had to do with the celebrated Blue Boar on the south side of Holborn.

A fire insurance was taken out on the house in 1720 with 'The Amicable Insurers'. The cover was for £1,500 over seven years, with an annual premium of £6 7s 6d, and five shillings to the clerk for his trouble. Seven years later the surveyor and two clerks from the 'Hand & Hand Fire Office' (the Hand in Hand Fire Office) were tipped, but no entries have been traced for premiums to this company. Defoe is again informative (if notably over-optimistic):

The several ensurance offices . . . have each of them a certain sett of men, who they keep in constant pay, and who they furnish with tools proper for the work . . . these men make it their business to be ready at call, all hours . . . Almost every parish has an admirable [fire engine], and some private citizens have them of their own, so that no sooner does a fire break out, but the house is surrounded with engines, and a flood of water poured upon it, 'till the fire is, as it were, not extinguished only, but drowned.[9]

Thanet House had its own fire engine, possibly a two- or four-manual model, but in 1729 a Mr Newsham was paid £38 to exchange it for a chain pump, presumably because the latter was more efficient.

Security at night was principally the responsibility of John Purden, the house's nightwatchman, and Sultan, the crop-eared mastiff, was on hand to ward off intruders, wearing during the day 'a fine collar and muzzel'. The family's frequent absences from town were always covered by one or more servants being paid to stay in the house. Purden was on board wages while they were away, but he received an extra guinea 'for his care in lying in the House during the winter'. Occasionally, outside help was recruited, as when Richard Idle, a sedan chairman, was paid £43 6s 8d in 1723 for watching the house for twelve weeks and two days – a case of rewarding probity with a very high weekly rate.

Among other regular payments relating to the property was the half guinea a quarter paid to a Mr Lee for watering the street in summer in order to lay the dust, and the £2 a year to the scavenger who may have kept the frontage tidy as well; at the bottom of the labour market were Mary Scarth's dustmen, who had to be content with four shillings a year for carting away the household rubbish.

The City of London attempted to improve street lighting in 1716 by requiring all householders to hang out lights in the winter months from six o'clock until eleven 'on dark nights', and before that an Act of William and Mary provided for street lighting in London from Michaelmas to Lady Day from dark until midnight. It was not very effective, however, and it was not until 1736 that an Act gave power to parishes to levy a rate so that streets could be lit all the year round. Whenever Thomas Coke or Lady Margaret went out at night, they did not employ the common linkmen but were lit on their way by their own footmen carrying *flambeaus*, which cost a guinea a dozen. The main entrance of the house will have had inverted iron extinguisher cones on either side of the main entrance for use after an outing, examples of which can still be found in front of a few London houses of the period.

In 1718 the first steps were taken to improve Thanet House. It is a little surprising that Coke chose James Gibbs, who was both a Tory and a Catholic, for his architect, but he was an essentially pragmatic young man, and his friend Lord Burlington had chosen Gibbs as the first architect to work on Burlington House in 1716. The architect's enduring reputation rests on his design for St Mary-le-Strand, which he had completed the year before, and for St Martin-in-the-Fields, which was built in 1726, but he was not above the small commission that might lead to greater things. Thus, he is found picking up a three-guinea fee for designing a new staircase for Thanet House, and the joiners were given ten shillings 'at their putting up the stairs and to Encourage their going forward wth. their work'. Straw was bought specifically to lay on the stair 'when the fretwork was cleaning' (i.e. the balusters). More extensive alterations under Gibbs's supervision were put in hand in the autumn of that year when the house was extended eastwards, with Samuel Cun, the surveyor, being paid seven guineas for a week's measuring and casting up joiners' and carpenters' work. The family took the opportunity to visit Sir Edward Coke at Longford while this was going on, and a shilling was given to the parish watch 'for their care during the time the Scaffolding was up'; as usual, the family's own nightwatchman was paid extra for sleeping in while they were away. In the December, men working for Mr Pattison, the smith, were given half-a-crown for drink, with a shilling for the bricklayers and stone-cutters 'at the weighing of the rails', when the new railings were set in along the frontage. It is a commonplace that house owners inevitably find that alterations take longer and cost more than they bargained for, and a month later Coke is found writing to his grandfather: 'My house in town has taken up much more time in altering than I at first expected, which makes me make a longer stay here.'[10] The substantial nature of the extension to the house is borne out by the increased ground rent, £13 against the previous £6 10s. John Casey, the house steward, was given a £21 gratuity in recognition of the extra work involved and James Gibbs received the same. Some measure of the extent of the alterations is shown by the £1,554 2s spent in employing all the carpenters, stone-cutters, smiths, plumbers, braziers, glaziers and painters. In 1730 there were extensive repairs to 'ye great new room' when Davis the carpenter was paid £80, John Bosen a carver £43, John Cleaver a smith £11 2s and Elizabeth Sharpe the plumber £16 9s 6d. This is likely to have been the room designed as a library to house all the books that Coke had acquired abroad, and it was spacious enough to require forty-one yards of crimson bed damask to curtain the windows in 1743. In 1731 a 'car' and two chairmen with a barrow were recruited to move pictures and books from Sir John Newton's house in Soho Square (he was Coke's grandfather and one of his guardians). Three 'deal presses for books' had already been made by the joiner Laurence Andrews, possibly to supplement cases already in the house, and, under Dr Ferrari the librarian's charge, the stock began to be arranged by subject to a scheme that was eventually followed at Holkham. Very early on, in November 1718, there was a resident problem that had to be dealt with by buying 'a Couple of Mous-Traps to set among the books 1s.'.

John Rocques's 1745 map of London shows that there was by that time a building intervening between Thanet House and Montague House, but their gardens had a common boundary some distance back from the street. Capper, the gardener's son, was given half a guinea in 1719 for a key to the gate at the end of the Duke of Montague's wall, from which it may be assumed that the Cokes had an invitation to make use of his large and elaborate garden (admired by John Strype for its 'curious layout' in his 1720 edition of Stow's *Survey of the Cities of London and Westminster*; an engraving by James Simon of 1724 provides a handsome illustration).[11] In 1722 Benjamin Townshend, a landscape gardener, was paid five guineas for drawing a plan of the Earl of Peterborough's garden at Parsons Green and for copying a print of Greenwich Park, commissions more likely to have been in connection with Great Russell Street rather than Holkham, where development had not yet begun. Improvements had already been carried out three years earlier when Capper was paid £3 14s for mould and gravel, and for removing rubbish; the nurseryman Thomas Proverb provided roots and trees, and £4 worth of seeds were bought from a Mr Fuller. In 1721 two joiners were paid £13 10s for work in the garden – enough to suggest that arbours or gazebos were installed.

The family also had an interest in another house in the neighbourhood. In the accounts for 16 September 1718 (that is, two months after the marriage) entries refer to the carriage of pewter, brass and other things into Brownlow Street, on the north side of High Holborn. There are no rate books surviving to check for evidence, and it is possible that this was merely the removal of effects belonging to the Tufton family into another house.

Great Russell Street lay within the parish of St Giles-in-the-Fields, Holborn, which in the seventeenth century was London's 'West End' and one of the fashionable places to live. It reached as far as Lincoln's Inn: Soho had not yet arisen and what is now Oxford Street was a country lane. By the early years of the next century, however, it had taken on a depressing reputation, and the place became a byword for poverty, squalor and crime. Between the church and Great Russell Street, 'St Giles's Rookery' was an area notorious throughout England for its beggars and rogues. The Great Plague of 1665 began in the parish and it was there that it extracted its highest toll in percentage terms. From its 2,000 houses over 3,000 died, and 1,361 were buried in the churchyard in July of that year.[12] Dorothy George calls Hogarth's print *Gin Lane* 'an historic document whose essential truth is confirmed in numberless details incidentally recorded in the Old Bailey Session Papers'.[13] It is set in St Giles's parish where a quarter of the houses sold gin 'besides about eighty-two twopenny houses of the greatest infamy where gin was the liquor drunk'.[14] These 'twopenny houses' were common lodging houses, some of which doubled as brothels and safe houses for criminals and were caches for all manner of stolen goods. Improvement was a very slow process, but a new workhouse, hospital and burying ground were established in Vinegar Yard in 1725, and a new infirmary was built in 1727. At that time there were some 160 paupers over the age of 70, 126 parents overburdened with children, 183 orphans, 70 sick and 300 lame, blind or mad. Not far to the east of Great Russell Street, Turnmill Street and Cow Cross were known collectively as 'Jack Ketch's Warren', and lived up to their reputation. The eighteenth-century reformer Jonas Hanway described St Giles's parish as 'the greatest sink of mortality in these kingdoms, if not the face of the whole earth'.[15] It was one of the centres for Irish immigrants, who, when they were not reduced to begging, took mainly to costermongering and street selling (in Ireland, St Giles had the reputation of being generous in matters of poor relief). In mid-century Dr John Shebbeare contrasted the 'good order, sobriety and honesty' of the poor in the country with the poor in London: 'among the lower class all is anarchy, drunkedness [*sic*] and thievery.'[16] Thomas Coke may well have come to the same conclusion, alternating as he did between the rural quiet of Holkham and Bloomsbury, with its disreputable neighbours. With his peers he seems to have accepted with equanimity the paradox of vast and ostentatious wealth existing side by side with abject poverty.

The parish of St Giles-in-the-Fields came into being in 1101, when Queen Matilda founded a monastery for lepers in the fields to the west of the city. Its chapel served not only the inmates but the people of the village that grew up around it. The hospital was dissolved in 1539, and the chapel became wholly a parish church in 1547.[17] Rebuilt in 1625, it was this building that the Coke family and their servants worshipped in between 1718 and 1728. By that time it was in poor repair and suffering heavily from the effect of innumerable burials both within the church and in the churchyard, which was now much higher than the inside. Henry Flitcroft (an architectural protégé of Lord Burlington whom Coke may well have known) was contracted to demolish it and design and build the replacement that was opened in 1734.[18] Meanwhile, part of St Giles's parish became the new parish of St George's Bloomsbury, and its new church, designed by Nicholas Hawksmoor, was built in 1724 and consecrated in 1730. Its spire, topped by the figure of George II and called 'a masterpiece of absurdity' by Horace Walpole, can be seen on the skyline of Hogarth's *Gin Lane* engraving. The family lived well within the new parish, so one would expect them to have used this elegant classical building from its opening, situated as it was in more salubrious surroundings, but neither the household accounts nor the church records offer any evidence that this was so. There is, however, a good deal to be learned from both sources about the Cokes' connection with St Giles-in-the-Fields, and about the church itself. The rector was Dr William Baker, but he held the living in plurality, being at the same time Bishop of Bangor. He was translated to Norwich in 1727 and seems to have hung on to the London living. This is why the payments in the accounts are usually to 'the St Giles Minister'. Nevertheless, the £4 Easter offering went to the rector, and on occasion he acted a a conduit for charity – in October 1718, for example, he was paid six guineas 'as a gift from my Master to the poor'; the curate Dr Mills also received an Easter offering of £1. The seventeenth-century parliamentary practice of appointing lecturers to individual parishes seems to have continued here. These lecturers were bitterly resisted by the beneficed clergy from the outset – originally they were all nonconformist; their duty was to lecture on the Christian faith in churches, supported by voluntary contributions from the parishioners. 'The St Giles Lecturer' was Dr Knags (or Nags), and the family contributed £1 to his expenses in February 1721.

Household prayers were a regular feature at Thanet House, with the Revd Batchelor (or Batcheldor) officiating: 'Sept. 19, 1719 Given to Mr Batcheldor the Minister for his attending to Read Prayers near half a Year ten guineas', to which Lady Margaret added a five-guinea gratuity. He also collected the quarterly payment of £2 10s for the local charity school; indeed, this may have been his main concern. In 1722 his place at prayers was taken on the same terms by Mr Linnet, but neither appears in the clergy lists for the parish, although, as will be seen below, Mr Linnet officiated on occasion at St Giles. Between 1718 and 1728, John Arden, Thomas Powell and Daniel Bolton all took fees in succession as vestry clerks at the parish church; George Hopkins was the sexton, collecting the family's pew rent of £8 a year. Vails were given to the door-keeper and to the stair-keeper, so the pew, which was used both by the family and by their servants, was in one of the galleries of the church. In May 1720, one of Coke's generosities was 'A Charity to John How the Pewkeepr. by paying his Debt and for his Discharge out of Prison − £2.19.7d.'. The December account entries for each year include lists of 'Christmas Boxes', and the St Giles ringers duly received their sovereign.

The first increase to the Coke family came in June 1719 when Lady Margaret was brought to bed of a son, Edward. He was christened at St Giles on 3 July by Mr Batchelor, with fees of two guineas for the parson and half a guinea for Arden the Clerk. Edward was destined to be an only child, for his parents had their hopes dashed a number of times in the early years of the marriage. Baby Elizabeth was stillborn and buried at St Giles on 5 April 1720, with Mr Barron being paid £2 for 'a child's coffin covered with velvet, shroud, sheet &c.', and George Hopkins the sexton took his fee of £2 three days later 'for depositing an abortive child in the church'; the gravedigger '& the woman who attends in St Giles' were given three shillings between them. In January 1721: 'To Mr Batchelor for Chrisning little Master Thomas Coke who dye'd immediately after £2.2.0d.' The sum of £3 13s 4d was paid 'to ye Parish of St Giles's for the Burial of Mast. Thos. Coke altho' he was sent to Tittleshall to be inter'd there; given to Dr Baker on that Account a £1'; Mr Barron the undertaker again supplied the velvet-lined coffin, shroud and winding sheet, this time for £2 12s 6d, and a week or so later the Tittleshall parish clerk had five shillings for the burying. On 1 August 1722 another 'Master Thomas Coke' was christened by the Minister, Mr Linnet, involving a two-guinea fee, and this is likely to have been a private ceremony, possibly even an emergency baptism. The infant did not survive and the church registers contain no entry for his burial. Lady Margaret was 'churched' (the ceremony of thanksgiving after childbirth) in the early months of 1724, not long after another shroud had been bought; so once again she had lost an infant.

Some of the family's servants were buried in the parish during our period, but they warranted a full entry in the register only if they were in a senior position. Thomas Johnson, Coke's farrier, was buried on 29 May 1722, but the register entry on 17 May merely gives 'Martha of Thos. Coke', and on 31 August of the same year the entry reads: 'Jno. of Edward Coke' (a servant of Thomas's younger brother).

Although Thanet House passed into other hands after Thomas Coke's time, it played a crucial role in his social life and that of his family, particularly in the early days of his marriage. It was against that background that most of his financial adventures were played out, and it is to them that we must now turn.

Chapter 5

MONEY MATTERS

*T*he financial affairs of Thomas Coke have to be seen against the monetary climate of the early eighteenth century; and, if they are to be fully understood, his family background and the attitudes of his social class have to be taken into account. In addition, there is always the underlying difficulty of equating the money values of the period with those of the twenty-first century. In the Quarterly Bulletin of the Bank of England for May 1994, MacFarlane and Mortimer-Lee of the Bank's economic division sum up the problem succinctly: 'Calculating how much prices have risen during the last 300 years is a difficult task. Part of the reason for this is that the bundle of goods and services that was available in 1694 and the bundle consumed now show some important differences.'[1] Some elements are, of course, common to both – for example, basic foodstuffs such as eggs, lamb and bread – so their prices can be compared (the price of a quarten loaf of bread in London in the early 1700s was 5½*d* as against roughly £1 for two sliced loaves today. Coal in London cost six shillings a ton in 1700; the early twenty-first-century price is £145). But it is more difficult to find seventeenth-century (and eighteenth-century) analogues of other elements in today's Retail Price Index.

Although we might be able to discover the relation between the ticket prices for a concert of Purcell's music now and in 1694, we cannot compare the prices of digital compact disc recordings of his music. Similarly, the cost of Lady Margaret's sedan chair bought in 1718 bears no relation to the cost of the Countess of Leicester's second-hand Mercedes coupé of 1999.

The early eighteenth century in England was a time when wealth was increasing faster than at any other period in the country's history, and faster than in any other country, despite the extremes of poverty and wealth, luxury and want, elegance and filth. People were, on average, better off than people in the developing countries of today, and better off than their neighbours and rivals, the French and the Dutch. The country was well above subsistence level for most of the century, and the substantial agricultural and industrial surpluses for export rose from £6.5 million to £40.8 million between 1700 and 1800.

Prices remained remarkably stable: the cost of an average 'basket' of essential articles varied little between 1700 and 1739. According to Helen MacFarlane, 'The first half of the century might well be called a "golden age" for labour, when all staple foods were cheap and plentiful. In the previous century meat had been 5d.–6d. a lb.; now it was 2d.–3d. a lb, and a rabbit could be had for 4d. If he was in work a labourer could eat meat three or four times a week, and the great London markets were the cheapest and best supplied.'[2]

In terms of inflation, the 2006 estimate from the Office for National Statistics quotes a percentage change since the middle of the eighteenth century of 15,192.2 per cent (£1 × (May 2006 index/1750 index) = £1 × 779.9/5.1 = £152.92). However, the history of the last three centuries is not one of an unbroken rise in prices, but rather of some periods in which prices increased, and others where they fell (tea, for example, halved in price between 1700 and 1750), with little tendency for sustained rises or falls. Indeed, prices rose more quickly in the last half of the twentieth century than in any similar period since 1694.[3] In pure cash terms, the Bank of England estimates that £1 in 1720 was equal to £75 at the end of the twentieth century.

Wages and salaries are extremely difficult to equate, but the nominal wage index shows a 400-fold rise since 1694, so that a £50 salary then would suggest a figure of £20,000 in the 1990s. However, the uncertain validity of comparisons over extended time needs to be stressed.[4] Lorna Weatherall concluded that, in the 1730s, £40 a year was enough for a middle-class tradesman's family to live on, provided they confined themselves to plain fare and indulged in but few extras.[5] A contemporary estimate of average income puts it at £8 to £9 per annum in 1700, rising to £12 to £13 in 1750. By Roy Porter's calculation, a family could survive on ten shillings a week.[6] A general labourer in the London building trade earned only 1s 8d a day, but journeymen bricklayers and carpenters could make between 2s 6d and 3s 4d.

It may be helpful in understanding Thomas Coke's attitude to property, capital, debts and money generally if we look first at the affairs of his parents. Edward and Cary Coke married in 1696 when he was 20 and she was 16. He had inherited an estate that comprised twenty-two properties in Norfolk and fourteen in Suffolk, besides land in Buckinghamshire, Oxfordshire, Somerset, Gloucestershire, Essex, Lancashire, Kent, Dorset and Staffordshire. The annual revenue from the land stood at £6,271, to which they might expect to add his mother's jointure, giving a total of £7,759. His steward promised to increase the rents by £3,390, so that the total annual value of Edward's estate was expected to be just over £11,000. There was a net income of £4,105, which, after outgoings of £2,030, left him with £2,075 for his pocket, clothes, housekeeping and stable necessaries. Cary was a £40,000 heiress, bringing £3,000 in cash to the marriage, together with land in Yorkshire and elsewhere. The marriage settlement stipulated a jointure of £2,500 for her should she be widowed, as well as pin money, and lands to the value of £6,000 a year for the heir, with smaller sums for any other children.

The young couple leased 5 and then 8 St James's Square, where they lived in considerable style. They were looked after by fourteen male and eleven female servants, all well paid, and by the turn of the century they were spending over £6,000 a year, well above Edward's surplus income of £2,075. In 1700 they had to raise more than £2,000 to meet overdue tradesmen's bills, and two years later Edward borrowed £2,000, while Cary asked her father to lend her another £1,000. In addition, there were some old debts outstanding, since in 1705 Thomas Coke's great-grandfather, the Duke of Leeds, asked for the overdue interest on a mortgage of £6,000 that had been taken out in 1673.

This level of extravagance might have been tempered over time had the couple survived, but Edward died in April 1707 when he was only 31, and Cary followed him four months later, leaving a young family of three sons and two daughters, whose trustees and guardians had to deal with a debt of

£22,000. This was largely met by Edward's personal estate, valued at £15,000, but over the next two years they sold £5,500 worth of timber from the estates, and the St James's Square household contents; the seven assorted carriages and eight horses were also disposed of.[7]

One could not, perhaps, expect a youngster bereft of parents and accustomed to a life of luxury and indulgence to be in any way concerned about money. During the six years that Thomas was on the Grand Tour, encouraged by his tutor Dr Hobart, he spent lavishly, particularly on books and manuscripts. In asking for additional funds and by way of excuse, he was careful to point out to Sir John Newton, his guardian and grandfather, that nothing so became a gentleman as a fine library. Soon after he came of age, his wedding provoked the flurry of high spending described in Chapter 1.

His lifestyle, and particularly his approach to money matters and indebtedness, was in many ways typical of the very rich, that tiny proportion of the population who controlled the nation and owned a quarter of it:

> For all the criticism levelled by historians, aristocratic spending does not seem to have deprived the economy of capital, and contemporaries do not appear to have considered their contributions inadequate; indeed, it is arguable that their expensive lifestyle was *expected*, and that any cutback in spending to facilitate economic development would merely have harmed their prestige.[8]

A particular phenomenon was the attitude of the wealthy to debt. For those like Thomas Coke who had inherited huge estates in the eighteenth century there was no shortage of people anxious (or at least willing) to advance them money.

> The majority of money was borrowed privately, either from members of the family or from friends and acquaintances. Attornies often acted as brokers. In Lancashire for example, attornies dominated the county's mortgage market as a result of their knowledge of local society and their ability to tap resevoirs of savings. Interest on mortages fell during the century and money could often be borrowed at 4%.[9]

Peniston Lamb, the Derbyshire attorney, figures frequently in Coke's financial affairs, not least as one of his largest creditors. In the early eighteenth century Peniston with his brother Matthew formed a partnership in which they acted as men of affairs for families in financial difficulties. Judging by the number of estates for which these men acted, there was a scarcity of this type of ability. The two brothers were born in Southwell and became attorneys, founding the fortunes of the Lamb family (and that of the future Prime Minister Lord Melbourne). Peniston was a celebrated conveyancer and was land agent for the (other and unrelated) Coke family of Melbourne, Derbyshire. He died in 1768 worth £500,000 in real estate and as much again in personal possessions.[10]

> Debt . . . was a near-universal feature of the finances of landowners. Stoked by personal extravagance, sometimes by immoderate building ventures and big land purchases, but above all, by the increasingly generous provision for their families within the framework of settled land arrangements, aristocratic and gentry debt mounted across the period as incomes to service it grew. It was fuelled by low interest rates and by the supply of funds landowners could tap with increasing ease . . . Yet debt seldom reached breaking-point, even for the the most profligate landowners.[11]

Benjamin Disraeli made the point in his *Reminiscences*: 'It is difficult if not impossible to ruin a family well rooted in the land,' and a contemporary was even more forthright: 'Landed property is the basis on which every other species of material property rests; on it alone, mankind can be said to live, to move, and to have their being.'[12] Coke cannot be accused of *immoderate* building ventures or big land purchases, for, although Holkham is vast, its building was slow and controlled, and he only (and sensibly) increased the acreage of the estate within Norfolk.

Nevertheless, with an inheritance worth almost £10,000 a year, by 1720 he had overspent by £15,000. Parker found it difficult to know how he had done this, but puts the value of the Paul de Lamarie silver bought at that time at only £2,210, whereas it was in fact £7,372.[13] If the £4,126 for jewellery is added, and £1,000 for drainage of marshes at Holkham, there is little left to explain. That amount of £15,000 would have concerned neither Coke nor his creditors, but worse was to come in the following year. The year 1721 was a milestone in the financial history of the country; it was the year of the South Sea Bubble.[14]

The South Sea Company had been founded by Robert Harley in 1711 and was always called by his flatterers 'the Earl of Oxford's masterpiece'.[15] Conceived as a Tory rival to the Whig-dominated Bank of England, it was essentially a finance corporation designed to consolidate £9 million of public debt that was not secured against taxation. A promotion by the company in 1720 brought about a significant reduction in the costs of servicing the National Debt. Public creditors could exchange their government stock for South Sea stock. This dealt with the problem of very costly irredeemable annuities. But the scheme was then extended to cover all government stock, and, crucially, the company was allowed to increase its stock at a ratio that was not fixed and was thus encouraged to inflate the price. It was able to sell large amounts of stock on its own account and in fact made two issues even before the first exchange. As a result of this scheme, and the absence of proper controls on the company, speculation was rife in the opening months of 1720, with the price of stock escalating from 128 (par 100) in January, to a peak of 1,050 on 24 June. It seemed at the time as if the whole nation had turned stock-jobbers. Exchange Alley was blocked up by crowds and, as a street ballad went:

> Then stars and garters did appear
> Among the meaner rabble;
> To buy and sell, to see and hear
> The Jews and Gentiles squabble.
>
> The greatest ladies thither came,
> And plied in chariots daily,
> Or pawned their jewels for a sum
> To venture in the Alley.[16]

In April someone asked Sir Isaac Newton what he thought of the stock and received the reply that he could calculate the motions of the heavenly bodies but not the madness of the people. He practised what he preached, for on the 20th of that month he signed a power of attorney disposing of his £7,000 stock at 100 per cent profit. In this heady period, the punter's aim, often achieved, was to part with his subscription, as soon as it was bought, to someone else who had the same idea. A typically satiric passage from Defoe points this up:

The city ladies buy South Sea jewels, hire South Sea maids, and take new country South Sea houses; the gentlemen set up South Sea coaches and buy South Sea estates. The hurry of our stock-jobbing bubblers has been so great this week that it has exceeded all that was ever known. There has been nothing but running about from one coffee-house to another and from one tavern to another to subscribe without examining what the proposals were. The general cry has been 'For God's sake let us subscribe to something, we don't care what it is.'[17]

This was the central tragedy of the South Sea year. Whatever promise of material progress there was in human ingenuity, it was blighted by the determination not to invest but to make capital gains.[18]

In August public confidence wavered, the bubble burst and the price plummeted to 290 on 1 October. About 30,000 creditors were affected, and although a few had been astute enough to dispose of their holdings before the crash – including Coke's Norfolk neighbour Sir Robert Walpole, who had sold out his considerable holdings eight months previously – the majority were not so lucky, and for many the crash was a disaster. The Duke of Portland took a colonial governorship and spent the rest of his life in Jamaica; Lord Lonsdale tried to assassinate one of the company directors; and Joseph Pennington of Muncaster in Cumberland was said to be 'going from church to church praying for better times'. Sir Wilfrid Lawson's 'head was turned', Lord Carlisle was 'undone' and the Duke of Chandos wrote that 'the distress mankind was in was inconceivable and a general bancruptcy [sic] was apprehended'. In the words of one historian:

The repercussions of the crash were considerable, not only for individual families, but also for the price of land. Those [like Walpole] who had made windfall profits looked to land purchase as a secure haven for their money. With so much money around, prices soared, only falling as impoverished owners put property on the market and the estates of the company's directors were put up for sale.[19]

And what of Thomas Coke's involvement? At 24, newly married, mildly in debt, he became involved in chasing the exciting will-o'-the-wisp of easy money on 'Change'. An entry in John Casey's (the house steward's) book (p. 244) for June 1720 gives a taste of his master's progress:

Moneys receive'd on Account of Stocks	£	s	d	£	s	d
June 24 Received of My Master by Mr Martins Note	645	0	0			
Receiv'd more by a Bank Note	25	0	0			
Receiv'd more of Ditto in Cash	20	0	0	690	0	0
Paid more than Receiv'd £10 is allow'd						
Mr Casey in page 134				37	12	0

Moneys paid on Account of Stocks						
May 24 Paid to my Lady Margaret	300	0	0	300	0	0
To my Masters Pocket to buy Stock	16	16	0			
More on the same account	31	10	0			
June 7 To Mr Portmans steward	1	1	0			
Paid towards ye purchase of £1000 South						
Sea first Subscription at 510. Advance	100	0	0			
To Jos: Machado for buying it	5	0	0			
9 To My Master on Account of Stocks	21	0	0			
To My Master to pay for the Loan of £1000						
to pay upon the third Subscription	20	0	0			
22 To Sr Henry Bedingfeld, Master lost by Stock	5	0	0	200	07	0
this 200.7.0 placed in ye generall						
account but deducted out of ye general						
discharge as appears page 116						
July 2 To Mr Cunningham for ye Loan of £1000						
for a week	21	0	0			
4 To Mr Hayden a gift	10	10	0			
7 To Mr Drax for Greenland [Company Stock]	100	0	0			
23 To Mr Robe for 20 Shares in Copper Stock	20	0	0			
Given to Mr Headen [Hayden] upon Acct.						
of Stocks & Allow'd to Mr Jarrett as						
Charg'd on his Account	10	10	0			
Sep 22 To Ditto by My Masters Order	5	5	0			
Too [*sic*] pay the difference in Ram [?], and						
Allow'd Mr Jarrett in his account	60	0	0	227	5	0
				727	12	0
Remains due to me to Ballance upon						
Account of Stock and Enter'd in the Day						
Book Page 34	37	12	0			

There are a number of significant points that arise from this sample entry. Coke's loan from his wife was properly acknowledged, and his friend Sir Henry Bedingfeld's involvement in a small loss was put right. Douceurs to the brokers Machado and Haydon were necessary, and £1,000 was raised for as short a time as a week in the hope of a swift if risky profit. Not only was Coke speculating in South Sea shares but also the Greenland Company via Mr Drax and in an unidentified copper mine via Mr Robe. The entry also confirms that John Casey did his best to keep track of the transactions, despite the fact that they were sometimes put through the accounts of Edward Jarrett, the assistant house steward, whose book betrays a certain waywardness in accounting. In the volume of General Accounts covering the years 1718–29, there are a number of entries confirming Coke's methods of raising money and his interest in a variety of shares. In June 1720, for example, he paid Mr Snow £120 for the use of £3,000 for a month at 4 per cent, and in November he paid him £135 for £2,257 10s for two months at 3 per cent. It must be remembered that both the 4 per cent and the 3 per cent were *per month*. The payment to 'Mr Portman's steward' is linked with a loan of £6,000 at 5 per cent from Henry Portman on mortgage. John Casey, his house steward, advanced him £380 to buy five shares in 'the Gold & Silver', and another £1,420 10s to pay for shares in 'London Insurance' bought via Mr Whitworth and Mr Haydon.

Coke had chosen the worst possible time to invest in South Sea stock and borrowed heavily to do so, from, among others, Daniel Lord Finch, one of his wife's relatives Sackville Tufton Esq., Mr Waller, Mr Snow and Dr Hugh Chamberlain, the fashionable obstetrician who attended Lady Margaret. Most of Coke's buying was done at the top of the market in August and September 1721. The price fell catastrophically even before payment was made, and he had to borrow again to meet his debts. There is a certain irony in the account book entry for 20 October: 'Paid to Mr Sherwin for Mr Freke's Paper of the price of Stocks, being for 5 quarters – £1.00.6'; Mr Freke's intelligence had been of little help to the beleaguered investor. It was surely a mark of Coke's magnanimity that he should give a guinea to a Mr Pittone 'of the Clarks of the South Sea' in 1722 when all was lost. Lord Egmont's diary (26 April 1737) says of Coke: 'he was near undone in the South Sea Year by that vile scheme.' In all, the young man had ventured £59,730 in stock generally, of which £58,300 was South Sea; this was reduced by agreement with creditors to £48,900. Total sales amounted to £10,971, so that he lost

£37,928 in all on the South Sea venture. A detailed listing of all the South Sea transactions is to be found on the last four leaves of the volume of General Accounts for 1718–29, and a penetrating analysis of the whole affair is to be found in Parker.[20]

This national scandal was the subject of William Hogarth's first surviving print, *The South Sea Scheme*, probably made in 1721 but not published until three years later. The artist's most recent biographer, Jenny Uglow, has considered the work in detail:

> A beginner's work, it shared many images of the Bubble prints – Dutch, French and English – that had poured out in the past year, but although Hogarth was using a common language, the energy he gave it was all his own. [. . . It] has the fairground hysteria and cruelty of St Bartholomew's Eve: the devil carving flesh from blindfolded Fortune and hurling chunks to the crowd; the nobles and bawds and bankers riding their merry-go-round, the truncated horses' heads like pricks and balls. Like contemporary journalists, he linked the crisis to others that had convulsed the city, like the Plague or the Fire of London, whose monument he adapts . . . Above all, though, Hogarth attacked the loss of principle. In his allegorical figures in the foreground, Self Interest breaks Honesty on the wheel; Villainy flogs Honour.[21]

The young investor was doubtless swept along by the general hysteria, particularly among his peers, but his shade must accept the incisive analysis of a moral sickness on which the episode was based and the artist's mordant reaction.

By the following year Coke was having to pay £2,565 in interest on loans and mortgages out of an income of £10,501. In 1726, by which time he had been honoured with the Order of the Bath and had become Sir Thomas, his creditors are listed in the accounts thus:

Gabriel Roberts (his sister's father-in-law)	£7,000
Dr Hugh Chamberlain	£8,750
Mr Snow	£6,400
John Tufton, Esq. (a relative of his wife)	£14,000
Peniston Lamb (his attorney and man of affairs)	£20,000
Edward Coke (his younger brother)	£2,000

Mr Waller	£2,400
Mr Plummer	£6,000
Mr Budworth (coachmaker)	£705
Mr Wright (corn chandler)	£200
Mr Hains (tailor)	£336
Total	£67,791

In addition, he was paying interest to Peniston Lamb on the annual difference between income and expenditure, currently running at about £1,800. He was so strapped for cash that he was driven to pawn his Bath jewel, and in the following year he was reduced to mortgaging the family plate to an attorney for £1,600 and having it lodged in the Bank of England. There are a number of instances in the household accounts where sums were borrowed from his staff and from tradesmen, and some were not inconsiderable. In 1729 he borrowed £200 from Dr Ferrari, his librarian, and a further £60 from Wlliam Tomley, the hall porter; the year before, Andrew Griffith, the butler, was paid a year's interest of £100 on a promissory note. In minor matters, like royalty it seems, the rich young man did not necessarily have loose change about him, and often turned to the nearest source of supply. In 1718 a porter lent him a shilling – this turned out to be a good investment when later he was tipped half-a-crown.

His whole attitude seems to have been one of insouciance, which echoes that of his neighbour Sir Robert Walpole, described by J.H. Plumb:

Bonds were easy to sign and money not hard to come by. The riches and extravagances of London life intoxicated him. He determined to live as if money were of no importance to him – open-handed, generous, extravagant, he pinned his hope on the future, for an office of profit could quickly reduce a mountain of debt. Each month the demands from his creditors for payment became louder and more insistent.[22]

Unlike Walpole, however, Sir Thomas had to wait some time for that 'office of profit', the joint Postmaster-Generalship that came his way later, and the lucrative Dungeness light fees, which were to be his as part of his wife's dowry, were not yet his to command. Despite that, however, throughout the 1720s he was making steady progress on the transformation of the Holkham site, and he made no effort to restrict his personal or household expenditure.

He was, moreover, a successful gambler on occasion, and in 1723 at least the problem of cash flow was eased by his skill or luck at the tables. In that year he won £2,592 8s 6d (largely from Lord Finch, who was listed above as one of his creditors) and lost a mere £146 10s.

Richard Wilson and Alan Mackley maintain that 'Most landowners . . . were also not good accountants even by the standards of their day.'[23] Whereas merchants needed to employ double-entry book-keeping, this was well beyond the capabilities of the average landowner or his agent; indeed, they often failed to achieve a balance at the year's end. This was not the case with Coke, at least on the surface, and he had little excuse to be unaware of his current financial situation. Between 1707 and 1717 his guardians had instituted an efficient system of accounting for the estate by using an annual audit account, a year-by-year statement of income and expenditure for each parish or group of parishes containing Coke property. Arrears, profits, rents paid out, taxes, costs of improvements and repairs, fees and court expenses – all were meticulously kept. Both Thomas Coke's and Lady Margaret's initials appear regularly in the household accounts as evidence that they at least looked them over before authorising payment; on some he signed his full name, with: 'Examined and allowed this account (Errors excepted)', and there were quarterly and yearly summaries to ponder over, if either of them were so minded. It might have been in the first flush of enthusiasm, but in May 1719 Edward Jarrett entered £2 4s 5d as the cost of dinner and wine at an inn when the accounts were passed, although it is not known if Coke himself was present.

The conclusion seems inescapable that Coke accepted his level of indebtedness with something like equanimity and got on with his life, concentrating his energies on those things that he enjoyed – his properties, his architectural ambitions, good living, hunting and cockfighting. This philosophy never changed materially, and, despite selling land from the outlying estates for £60,000 between 1749 and 1756, at his death in 1759 his debts totalled £90,974 (£60,357 on mortgage, £30,617 on bond).[24]

Chapter 6

THE FAMILY

A preoccupation with the need to ensure a stable succession and a sound inheritance was ever a commonplace among the great landed families, and the rules of primogeniture have survived intact into the twenty-first century, at least within the royal family; until the mid-nineteenth century, the problem was exacerbated by the high rate of infant mortality, although the ability of the rich to command the best medical attention placed them a little above the average percentage of risk for all classes of society. Despite this advantage, such were the dangers associated with primitive hygiene, puerperal fever and the common scourges of smallpox and the like that no family, however well endowed, could be confident of seeing their children survive to maturity. The application of the cynical 'heir and a spare' principle was never more necessary than in the eighteenth century.

In this, the Coke family was no exception, although previous generations had been more than usually fortunate – all the five children of Thomas's parents, for example, lived to be over 30. Even so, Thomas himself was not robust as a boy. His uncle Charles Bertie, in writing to Sir John Newton in 1708, was anxious about his health: 'I was sorry to hear a Post or two agoe that my Nephew Coke was indisposed with an aguish distemper & was glad you were in Town to be advisd & consulted wth about him.'[1] It was on these grounds that, in 1711, his guardian Sir Edward Coke suggested that he should be moved from Mr Ellis's school at Isleworth to Longford. On his arrival he reported: 'As to his health I find him very thin, but I hope from following the Doctor's prescriptions and observing of a proper Kitching Diet, and suitable exercise, his Constitution may be restor'd.' Six months later Sir Edward was able to report to Sir John Newton: 'He grows tall, is plump, and looks fresh and vigorous.'[2]

Unlike the previous generation, Thomas, in his own marriage, had to be content with just the one son, Edward, who was born on 22 June 1719 at 8.30 a.m. There was naturally great rejoicing, and the German footman, Abraham Blauner, was sent down with the good news to Lady Margaret's parents at Hothfield. In the five years that followed, the young mother lost three more babies by miscarriages, and thereafter the accounts show no evidence of any more confinements. The record of medical care begins on 21 March 1719, when Sir Hans Sloane received a guinea 'for attending My Lady'. Sloane was an Irishman who, after studies in Paris and Montpellier, graduated at Orange before returning to London, where he built up a successful and highly lucrative practice. He attended Queen Anne during her final illness, and George II appointed him his first physician in 1727, the same year in which he became President of the Royal Society. He was in charge of Christ's Hospital and later founded the Chelsea Botanic Garden. He lived on the north side of Great Russell Street, east of Southampton House, no more than a stone's throw from Thanet House, although he invariably arrived by coach.[3] A contemporary gloss on this runs:

> The carriage marks the peer's degree,
> And almost tells the doctor's fee.

In common with other physicians and surgeons, Sloane's standard fee was a guinea, and his first visits were marked by vails being given to his coachman and footman. Sir Hans made several visits in July, and, the baby having been christened on 3 July, Mrs Dotchen the midwife was given ten guineas 'by My Lady's order'; Nurse Smith (an old Hothfield servant enjoying a £10 a year pension[4]) was in attendance, receiving the same amount, with Nurse Pharah (or Pharoe) to help her.[5] A wet-nurse had already been engaged and given some thread satin and a satin lining as a present, and Mrs Chandler acted as the night nurse, sitting up for seven weeks. The nursery had been furnished, and Bathsheba Gill supplied lace and linen for it to the tune of £130 6s. Quilts, cradles and other necessaries from Mrs Ashcroft cost a further £48, and a few months later hangings of 'blue Hareton' were bought for the room. Following the birth, Lady Margaret's health seems to have given cause for concern, for in the autumn there were frequent visits from medical men. Sloane called in September accompanied by two surgeons, and made another five visits in the following month, with two on the same day. From 10 to 16 November he visited daily, accompanied by Sir David Hamilton, who had been Queen Anne's first physician and later attended Caroline, Princess of Wales. Hamilton was London's leading practitioner in midwifery and was shortly to lose £80,000 in the South Sea debacle in concert with Thomas Coke. From 13 July until 11 September 'Little Master' (as he was already called) was under the care of Sergeant Dickens, the surgeon. One of the prescriptions ordered for him from the apothecary, Mr Garrard, was for a 'Courall' (cureall), which, at £2 7s 6d, was at the expensive end of the range of hopeful but largely useless panaceas. The baby was obviously not making good progress because on that day his father set off for Kent with him via Dartford and Rochester to see if country air would effect an improvement. Mrs Smith went with them and stayed with the baby at Hothfield, while Thomas went back to London the following month. As with every baby, there was a need for nappies, but they did not all have 'a dozen damask clouts' supplied by Mrs Hill at ten guineas. His mother stayed in London rather than go with her baby into Kent, either because she was not fit enough to go with him or, which is more likely, because her concern for her two-month-old baby reflected the prevailing attitude of parents to young children – their survival was a matter of hope rather than a certainty and too much concern was unwise. But the baby returned to London in the care of Lord Thanet's servants, and from late October until mid-November Sir Hans Sloane and Sir David Hamilton were in constant attendance. Meanwhile, the parents had gone down to stay as usual at Holkham. They were not wholly without concern for their infant though, for Thomas wrote in these terms to Sloane:

I am very much obliged for the care you are so kind as to take of my son, and it is a great satisfaction to me that he is under your eye. I am mighty sorry to hear this distemper still continues upon him. They write me word from London that you was so obliging as to offer to lett another Physician be sent for to consult with you . . . we are both very sure he can be in no better hands than yours, but if you wish further advice, I beg you will make choice of who you will (Dr. Chamberlain only excepted). My wife is desirous of mentioning to you whether it would not be proper to wean the child, but that we leave to you.[6]

Kensington's country air was highly praised for invalids and, as the child was still sickly, he, with Nurse Smith and Nurse Key, removed to lodgings with a Mr White in the village, using Uncle Wyvil's coach. Mrs Thompson, the housekeeper, Mrs Jenny and Jenny, the laundry-maid, went to and fro in hackney coaches carrying the necessaries, and John Casey, the house steward, made a visit to see that all was well. Sloane made four calls there in December. It was to be a stay of thirteen weeks, during which time Nurse Smith took charge, paying out £18 8s 11½d on provisions, washing, sundries and additional doctors' fees. Just before they went, Mr Garrard, the jeweller, was paid £2 7s 6d for a 'correll for Little Master' (a toy of polished coral given to teething infants), and on his return home he was given an 'anodyne necklace' for the same reason. The Cokes returned to town after Christmas, and Sloane made Lady Margaret eight visits in January 1720. It was a commonly held belief that asses' milk was a sovereign remedy for any form of debility;[7] it was supplied to the house by a Mr Walker throughout the autumn, and again at Holkham, where a Mr Jones was paid £5 8s for 'an ass for My Lady's use'. Three years later, Richard Springall, the Holkham parson, sold the family a milch ass for five guineas, and in 1724 a local oysterman supplied two more very cheaply. Lady Margaret was still drinking the milk at the end of the decade. It was prescribed for Little Master when he was lodged at Kensington, presumably after the wet-nurse had been dismissed, and later in the year, when the family were at Hothfield, an ass was hired for a month, and another was brought over from the Isle of Thanet.

During the spring of 1720 Lady Margaret spent some £40 on buying 'things for Little Master's use', but she was pregnant again, and was delivered of a stillborn daughter in April, who was to have been called Elizabeth. The house steward was ordered to give her old servant Nurse Smith ten guineas for attending her during her lying in, and Mrs Newesham was the midwife with Mrs Dotchen assisting her; another midwife 'who came to attend My Lady but was not admitted' was given half a guinea for her trouble. In January 1721 a baby boy was born, but lived only long enough to be christened Thomas, with Mrs Dotchen, 'My Lady's midwife and Nurse', receiving twenty guineas, and in August 1722 another Thomas's brief existence is recorded; in both cases large quantities of child-bed linen had come from the drapers Mrs Gill and Mrs Hill. In the spring of 1724, following another stillbirth, Lady Margaret was churched, and the quarter's medical bills were particularly heavy:

	£	s	d
Mr Gilkes	3	16	0
Mr Wisdom surgeon	2	19	0
Mrs Walters midwife	3	3	0
Dr Mead	40	19	0
Dr Woodward	10	10	0
Dr Chamberlain	2	2	0
Surgeons	10	10	0
Midwife	10	10	0
Nurse Smith	10	10	0
Mr Graham apothecary	20	7	7
Mr Hodgson apothecary	24	0	3
	£141	8	10

At this stage Dr Richard Mead took over as principal physician. His position in the profession was quite as eminent as that of Sir Hans Sloane; they both served on the first general committee of the Foundling Hospital. He too was a court physician and became famous for his great private library, being active in the book world and taking, incidentally, a six-guinea subscription from Coke for a history of Tunis in 1729. Other aspects of his life were notably of interest to his contemporaries: his sex life was the subject of a pamphlet entitled *The Cornutor of 75, being a Genuine narrative of the Life, Adventures, and Amours of Don Ricardo Honeywater*. He once fought a duel with a fellow physician, John Woodward, and, having disarmed him, he said 'Take your life', to which the response was 'Anything but your physic!' Samuel Johnson thought well enough of him to affirm that he 'lived more in the broad sunshine of life than almost any man'. With his practice bringing in £7,000 a year, one can appreciate the comment. The long wig and the gold-headed cane were the indispensible props of the fashionable physician, and Richard Mead's cane can still be found on display at the Royal College of Physicians.[8]

After 1724 there is no evidence of further confinements, but meanwhile the health of the young heir was still delicate. Sgt Dickens presented a bill of twenty guineas in April 1720, and a month later Mr Amey charged half a guinea for 'cupping [that is, bleeding] Little Master' – the commonest of all eighteenth-century medical techniques applied here to a baby less than a year old. He was taken down to Hothfield Place again in the summer, and even there Mr Barnard, the Ashford surgeon, was called to attend him. In 1723, when he was 4 years old, the child was again at his grandparents' house being looked after by Nurse Smith, who travelled with him down to Bristol for a course of treatment at the hot wells, coinciding with the visit his parents were making to the West Country. In a diary entry of 1738 John Loveday includes a little vignette of the hot wells: 'In the Pump Room is a good picture of an old man who had been Pump here; as to the public Rooms, below Stairs is a Billiard-Table Room and another Room; above, the Grand Room of 30 feet by 80, much superior to either of those at Bath, but wainscotted in a poor manner, unworthy of so noble an appartment.'[9] The following year Edward was with the family when they stayed at Bristol and Bath, where he had a Bath Ring bought for him to keep him afloat. In 1725 he was again at Bristol, and by that time he had acquired the beginnings of a personal establishment with a valet-de-chambre called Ruth being paid £30 a year, although Betty Lloyd, the nursery maid, was still with him. As at Kensington, Mrs Smith dealt with the payment of expenses there amounting to £94 13s 6d. During these early years Edward's mother bought things for him now and then, spending £29 17s on one occasion and fifteen guineas on another. Like her husband, she did not always have cash to hand: the house steward once lent her half-a-crown in sixpences to give to Little Master, and as a 4-year-old he was given five shillings to dispense in vails. By that time, he had his own 'knife, fork & spoon & other conveniencies', and for his fifth birthday there were special (but unspecified) 'eatables'.

In Edward's sixth year there is a single payment to 'James Brereton Scholemaster' and by the time he was 7, his education was being taken in hand. Mr Disbrowe, with a salary of £40 a year, was his tutor, and he was placed with Mr Dennis Delaplace, whose fees were £43 a quarter, with a mathematical master being paid separately for instructing him in geography. The following year Monsieur Perrin, 'mathematique', received £21 for eight months' tuition, and a Mr Hawgood (or Hogwood) was paid £32 14s 6d during one quarter of 1728 for 'teaching Mr Coke to write'. Possibly with a view to preparing him for Westminster School (where he was entered in 1730), a Mr Bennett succeeded as the boy's tutor, and began buying books for him in some quantity. He bought a copy of Moll's pocket maps of England and spent over £10 in the last quarter of 1727; the following year's accounts include specific bills for Willimott's *Cartalio*, Bowdon's *Geographical Dictionary*, a translation of Herodotus, and the *Construction of the Westminster Grammar*. The drawing master Mr Elliott gave him some lessons for a while, and Captain Bedford (who schooled horses for the family) was his riding instructor. The four-guinea charge 'for Mr Coke's entrance to ride' is likely to have been an access fee to St James's Park. By way of light relief his tutor took the boy 'to the play', but the record is silent on what they saw.

The cost of his upkeep and incidental expenses were now being entered separately in the household accounts, with a yearly total of just under £400. He had his own liveried footman, John Marguerat, on a wage of £8 a year, who, in common with Thomas Coke's servants, paid out various sums on behalf of his master. The boy's suits came from his father's tailor, Mr Haynes, who charged £1 10s 5d for a frock and waistcoat made of Duroy, a good quality worsted cloth that was often glazed. Mr Gow, the hatter, supplied a hat decorated with 'pointe d'espagne', from Mr Griffiths came spatterdashes, and twenty-eight pairs of gloves were bought from Mr Cherriton – one of a number of multiple purchases from various glovers. Ten pairs of shoes at a time were made for him by Mr Littlejohn, and Mrs Ann Spencer (who also worked for his father) charged a pound for making him a dozen shirts. Having bought himself a new watch, Thomas Coke ordered its maker, Mr Purden, to mend and clean his old silver one so that his son might have the use of it.

Edward's miniature 'household within a household' had its own supplies of groceries such as green tea, double-refined sugar and chocolate, and Mr Audley, the pewterer, charged £10 for a dozen plates, a basin and a chamberpot, all engraved with the family crest. It seems precocious that a boy not yet 10 years old should have his own supplies of wine, but the records admit no other interpretation. Four gallons of Mountain (a variety of Malaga wine) and two quarts of red port were bought for him in 1726, and a further nine gallons of Mountain came from Mrs Smith in the following year, with seven more in the year after that. The squirrel and his house that cost only four shillings is more easily understood, along with a pair of drumbattledores and six cocks for 3s 6d and some bows and arrows.

Still not particuarly robust, Edward was nursed for three weeks in 1728, with the occasional visit from Dr Mead and Mr Randby or the surgeon Mr Williams to bleed him. Bristol water was bought in quantity, and in one quarter of that year the boy drank nearly fifty pints of asses' milk. Thomas Coke had his teeth attended to by Mr Delescourt, and in 1727 the dentist charged £15 for cleaning Edward's teeth and for drawing some of them – a high price for a painful experience, even by the standards of the day.

At the end of 1728 Edward's tutor, Mr Bennett, was discharged; by chance a fragment of one of his last letters to his employer survived within the account book for that year: 'I have given Mr Graham the 5 guineas wch Your Lordsh.p order'd for his attendance upon Mr Coke. The Drawing Master's Q.r will be up the 29th of this Instant, and then I will not fail to discharge him. Mr Coke is exceeding well, and if he continues to be as diligent as he has been with me To Day I hope . . .'.

The future promised well for a boy blessed with every material advantage, and, although Richardson's 1727 portrait of him with his mother is rather insipid, the later pastel by Rosalba Carriera has him sumptuously dressed and decidedly good-looking.[10] Mr Bennett's hopes, however, and those of the boy's parents were not to be fulfilled in the dissolute life that was to come.

Coke was the eldest in a family of five children, and while his sister Cary features only in the accounts of the 1720s as Mrs Wyvill and his sister Anne does not appear at all, the younger brothers Edward ('Neddy', born 1702) and Robert ('Bobby', born 1704) are glimpsed briefly. From an early age Thomas was genuinely concerned for their well-being and generous in his support. On 1 March 1716, while he was still on his Grand Tour, he wrote from Messina to Sir John Newton, one of his guardians:

I fear to be thought too presumptuous in daring [to] put in a word concerning the education of my brothers, there is certainly no body a better than you, & the Great love which you have always been pleased to show my family must make you place them to the best. But I don't doubt forgiveness when you see that my forwardness in medling with what don't belong to me, & of which I am no kind of judge, only proceeds from the great love I bear my brothers, & not doubt your goodness as to placing them for the best. It is certain they are in extreamly good hands, & that my family will always have great obligations to Mr Casey [the house steward] for the great care he has of them, & it is to be wished that if they are removed that Mr Casey was able to be still with them; but would you not think it better Sr. that at their age [13 and 12 respectively] they were to go rather to Isleworth, or some free school than continue at London – Being lodged & always continuing amongst so many of their young equals as in a school is a kind of introduction towards living in the world & will teach them how to shift for themselves in different companys. I could wish you were of that opinion, & if perchance their Chancery allowance is not able to do it, if you'll permit me, I offer willingly to bear the charge, & am sure of my other Guardian's consent for it. You will say it is extravagent [sic] to make such an offer when I myself exceed my allowance, but I have taken care in a will to indemnify my Guardians from all loss. Forgive me Hond. Sr. the liberty I take & be assured yt nothing but the concern for my Brothers's wellfare could have given me this boldness.[11]

Towards the end of the Grand Tour, Edward went out to join him, and Thomas wrote to Sir John from Paris saying that, as his brother could not speak the language very well, it prevented his being introduced to the best society. In consequence, he had arranged for the boy to go to Lorraine and had made sure that the Duke would pay him attention. The move worked well, and a subsequent letter to Sir John from Edward shows that his talents matched those of his elder brother:

I am very well satisfied with the Academy and the Civilitys I have met with from the Duke, who often invites me to dine with him, and sometimes makes me partaker of his Diversion of Hunting. Every day I learn double exercises, for whereas others ride but three horses, I ride four, and fence and dance twice, and Learn Mathematics, french, and to play on the Flute, besides which I read with Mr Ferrari [who was to be Coke's librarian], which takes me up to six o'clock, after which I generally go to Court.[12]

The reference to the boys' 'Chancery allowance' is a reminder that they had been comfortably endowed with income from their parents' estate, Neddy with an annual income of over £800 and Bobby of £200. The latter duly went to Isleworth, and the splendour with which he was fitted out for his brother's wedding, as detailed in Chapter 1, shows that Thomas was determined not to be mean. After they returned from Derbyshire, having visited the Peak together in 1721, Coke took the boys down with him to stay with their grandfather at Hothfield Place. Lord Thanet's coach ferried them back as far as Rochester.

As the second son, Edward was destined to succeed to Longford, and in fact did so in 1727 on the death of Sir Edward Coke (although he was not to enjoy it for more than six years). Robert, on the other hand, needed to be settled. Thomas's solution was to buy him a cornetcy in the Duke of Bolton's Regiment of Life Guards. The arrangements were rehearsed in a lawyer's letter to Sir John Newton:

> Hon.d Sir, I have discoursed [with] Mr Coke about the management of his Brother Mr Robert Coke; his pay is about £270 a year, the subsistence money payable every month is £17, which is £4.5.0. a week, which Mr Coke has ordered to be paid instantly into Mr Casey's hands, out of which he is to pay Mr Robt. Coke a guinea a week for his pockett expenses, and the remainder to be kept apart for the payment of his Master's Cloaths and other necessaryes, so that it is intended he shall wholly live within the compass of his pay – and not break into his annuity . . .[13]

Such an intention was no doubt unrealistic, particularly in a crack regiment, and Bobby was soon showing that he shared his elder brother's casual attitude to debt. The account entry of 1719 – 'Given to Mr Robert Coke by my Master's Order – 1 guinea' – was to be repeated at regular intervals, so that their grandfather was provoked into a decidedly testy response to yet another plea for funds:

> To Captain Coke at his quarters at Southampton. July 13, 1723
> Captain, I had yours of ye 8th instant, and am sorry you should apply to me for money, it is what I can't justify to the Court of Chancery, and it is what yr. brother agreed when your Commission was bought that you should live out of the profits of your Commission, your brother can best judge what Occasions you may have had for money, and if he is satisfied that you want any he can furnish you out of my Lady Ann's legacy [Lady Walpole his grandmother], I recommend you to suit your expenses to your comings in. You have that benefit which a Great many Gent. has not, that when you are in town, your lodging and dyet costs you nothing, and you should then save money to bear the extraordinary expenses in the country.
>   Yr. affect. Grandfather J. Newton[14]

Any effect this might have had did not last: there was a flurry of entries in 1726:

		£	s	d
Oct. 12	Paid Mr Robert Coke ½ a year's Annuity	100		
Nov. 9	Paid Mr Robert Coke *on Acct* of his ½ yrs			
	Annuity due 13 Apr. 1727	21		
Feb. 2	Ditto in further part	31	10	0
	Harry the Saddler for Ditto more	6	13	6
Mar. 6	Ditto more in full to Ap. 1727	10	16	6

It must have been some consolation to Thomas to see Bobby marry well in later life, and settle down to being a country gentleman, having inherited Longford and the Reddish estate following his brother Edward's death.

Almost by chance, the future of the Coke inheritance was affected by a romance. Thomas's sister Anne eloped with a neighbour, Philip Roberts, when she was 17, and it was their son Wenman who eventually succeeded to the estate. Anne herself does not feature in the Holkham archives, but her husband's family are mentioned here and there. Her brother was incensed when news of the marriage reached him on his Grand Tour, and he wrote to his grandfather from Sicily:

On my arrival to this place about four hours ago, I met with a letter from my Aunt Newton [announcing] the most unwelcome and surprising news of my Sister Ann's folly and miscarriage. She is certainly unworthy of any of her relations for the future ever looking upon or having anything to do with her, but I can't but be extremely concern'd at what is done having had the ill luck of her having been of my family. At least for my own sake it is some consolation to find that she is with a gentleman & I hope in an honourable family. I have a great deal of uneasiness till I know the circumstances & affairs of the gentleman, not that I shall be ever reconciled with her way of management, but it would be a pleasure to think that my sister is not allied to a man unworthy of her family & I must confess that the former esteem & love that I have had for her would make me wish she was tolerably well-placed, not yt I think of forgiving her, or doing anything for her after this treatment. However she finds herself well or bad I'll have nothing more to say to her, wherefore she must continue as she is, but I confess I have a great concern and apprehension concerning that marriage whether it is done as to hold good by law & I doubt much whether things are done in the true form . . .[15]

His affectionate good nature soon reasserted itself, however, although in a later letter he expressed his disappointment that Anne's father-in-law had not been as generous as he should have been in the matter of settlements. This was Gabriel, known as 'Governor Roberts', a nabob returned from India, where, as Governor of Madras, he had been spectacularly incompetent but had 'shaken the pagoda tree' to good effect. He had a house at Ampthill in Bedfordshire, and the Cokes on one of their early trips to Longford called to see him and used two of his servants to guide them to St Albans. Coke had given his sister a present of 200 guineas, possibly as a belated wedding present, and Philip Roberts was paid interest on 'his Lady's portion' of £5,000 shortly after. The business of the marriage settlement lingered on throughout the 1720s, with a Chancery solicitor, Mr Perkins, being paid his bill 'about settling Mrs Roberts's fortune' in 1725, and six months' interest on £7,000 was paid out to either Gabriel or Philip in 1729. There is irony in the reflection that a runaway marriage that upset the Coke family led in the end to the saving of the great estate, by providing an heir (in the couple's son Wenman, who changed his name to Coke) when the direct succession failed on the death of Thomas's son Edward.

It is often assumed that dress in the eighteenth century was very much more formal and regulated than it is today. In reality, it was much less so, and a great variety was allowed, dictated by individual taste.[16] Fashion affected only the rich, and the high cost of materials ensured that the division between them and the burgeoning middle class remained, although the latter were becoming much more conscious of dress as a social indicator. The servants of great families when off duty made a point of aping their masters, who (unconsciously perhaps) encouraged this by giving them their cast-offs.

Men's coats were knee-length, with large cuffs that were sometimes heavily embroidered, and the tails were buttoned back, becoming purely ornamental as time went by. Lapels were formalised as part of the decoration of the coat, thus making the wider opening at the front a permanent feature. Colours tended to be sombre, with embroidery reserved for the decoration of the waistcoat, which, reaching to the hip, was often the most expensive and eye-catching part of the costume. A typical outfit was completed by breeches and stockings to the knee.

Nothing was more typical of the century's fashion than the tricorne hat, garnished with lace and plume, which cost a good deal more than the hat itself. Peers and Knights of the Garter and Bath wore their decorations even in the street so that their rank might be recognised, and diamonds were fashionably employed in profusion on buttons and shoebuckles. Until about 1725 a bunch of ribbons was worn on the right shoulder, a relic of the fastening that secured the sword belt in the previous century.

Throughout the decade Mr Haynes (or Haines) made most of Coke's clothes, and, although for the most part the archive entries say nothing more than 'for My Lord's apparel', there are occasional snippets of detail such as: 'a silk waistcoat & a pr. large denim breeches – £5.1.7d.', and 'for faceing the Red Coat Sleeves with black – 14s.'. Mr Halborow was paid £1 17s 'for making a Coat & pair of Breeches, lineing the same, with all Furniture', and Coke ordered that his foreman be given half-a-crown. There is more detail concerning materials that were bought separately:

Mr King, Draper. 22 yds fine drab from Mr James Clark of Shepton Mallet
at 15s. per yd. [note that the West Country maker is specified]
Mr Bingham. 3 yds fine calico. 6s.9d.
Mr Powell. A piece of Firret 36 yds for stomachers* £3.10.0d.

Because so much time was spent on horseback, riding cloaks, which were circular and long enough to cover the rider's boot-tops, were a necessity; Coke had a leathern cloak bag made for sixteen shillings so that his cloak could be neatly strapped behind his saddle until it was needed.

The drapers sometimes had to wait a while for their money judging by a two-year-old bill for £60 3s 2d that was presented in 1728 by Messrs Man & Day. Huddleston & Co., who had made Coke a nightgown and cap in blue damask for £8 some years before, were owed £49 in the same quarter. Coke's shirts were always made of holland, a bleached linen that was bought in

---

* Stomacher was the common name for a long waistcoat, which was sometimes made of dimity, a stout cotton woven with raised stripes or fancy figures; firret was stout silk or cotton.

quantity by the yard or the ell (1 ell = 45ins). Twenty-nine ells of gulick holland, at 4s 10d the ell, were used for a dozen hunting shirts, the making of which cost only 4s 6d. They were made by milliners such as Mrs Gill a dozen at a time, and the pair of fine lace ruffles that she applied to each of the best shirts made them very costly, at £6 10s each – one of her bills for materials and labour in 1721 was for £82. For the everyday, the ruffles were of cambric. Mrs Wyse charged only £1 6s for making and ruffling a dozen shirts; similarly, Mrs Edwards charged eighteen shillings for making four shirts and trimming six in cambric. Thomas's stockings were normally of silk, costing between fourteen shillings and a guinea a pair, and one pair in superfine black silk from Mr Reeve was priced at nineteen shillings; the only instance noted of anything cheaper was a pair of 'Doncaster' stockings at 4s 6d. Silk garters to keep them in place were two shillings a pair. Handkerchiefs were bought by the dozen at 4s 6d, but silk handkerchiefs normally cost six shillings each. Gloves of various types were bought in quantity – six pairs from Hemmings for six shillings, two pairs of doeskin from Osborne the breeches maker for seven shillings, four pairs of beaver-skin at twelve shillings, and seven pairs of hunting gloves from Mr Stallard for 10s 6d; a more mundane purchase was six pairs of thread mittens costing four shillings.

Only some half-dozen purchases of hats are listed in the 1720s and all of them from two hatters. Mr Yew made one for £1 and added 1s 6d for the buckle and band, and three more for £3 3s 6d including a mourning band, while Mr Leeke supplied two 'fine beaver hats & tabby lining' for £2 12s. There were also times when Coke had clothes made for him at Holkham: in 1728 John Blyford, the woollen draper, provided the material for a mourning 'frock' and a velvet cap, both made up by the tailor Mr Stoakes.

Most of Coke's shoes were made by Mr Verdon and were quite often bought in batches. Four pairs of 'strong shoes' cost two guineas, with a further eight pairs for £3 0s 6d, all in 1728.

Reference has just been made to a 'mourning frock', and the accounts shed some light on the contemporary conventions that were observed when a family suffered a bereavement. It was not uncommon for a funeral to take place without any of the close relatives being present, and in well-to-do families their place was taken by servants, so that the respectability of the cortège might be maintained. This is well illustrated later in the century in James Woodforde's diary:[17] when Squire Custance's infant son died in 1785, he was carried from Weston Longville Hall to the church in a coach and four accompanied only by two servant maids in very deep mourning and long black hoods: 'Mr Press Custance [the squire's brother] was the Chief Mourner, none of their Relations attended besides. Neither Mr nor Mrs Custance there.' The entry also illustrates the established custom of distributing tokens of mourning to those involved: 'The Drivers and other servants had hatbands and gloves. I also had a fine black silk Hatband tied with white Love-Ribband and a pair of white Gloves.'

In the 1720s accounts, the first relevant entry relates in March 1722 to the death of Lord Sondes, eldest son of the Earl of Rockingham and husband of Lady Margaret's eldest sister, Catherine. Although it is possible that members of the family attended the funeral, there is no evidence of this, but there is a detailed bill for mourning clothes provided for two female servants, Mrs Smith and Fanny Lucas:

Servants Mourning for Ld. Sonds	£ s d
For 28 yds Norwich crepe for Mrs Smith at 2s.2d.	3 0 8
For 26 do. for Fanny at 18d. a yard	1 19 0
For 12½ yds Black Yard wide Stuff at 14d.	0 13 5
For 9¾ yds of Mantua Silk at 4s.6d.	2 0 6
For 2 yds of Muslin	0 9 6
For two Mourning Fans	0 2 3
For 2 pr. Mourning Gloves for Mrs Smith & Fanny	0 4 8
as also for 2 Girdles for ye same	0 2 4
For 2 pair of Shoes for Ditto	0 10 0
For Making Fanny's Mourning & Materials	0 7 0
	9 9 4

In the following August came the death of Thomas Coke's grandmother, Lady Ann Walpole, when a similar entry was made:

Mourning for Lady Ann Walpole	£ s d
To Mr Casey a Suit of Mourning	10 0 0
Nurse Smiths Mourning £5.5.6. Making 6s.10d.	5 12 4
Mourning for ye 2 house maids, one Landry Maid,	
the Cook's Maid, & one house maid at Holkham	19 8 2
	35 0 6

The only other example occurs in 1723 under the heading of 'Liveries':

Paid for 6pr. Stockings for Servants Mourning	1 11 6
Paid for 6 Hatts for Ditto at 8s.6d. A Hatt	2 11 0

For whom the mourning was worn is not revealed, but about the same time, under 'Apparel for his Hon.r', there is an entry that suggests that Coke himself might have been involved:

Paid ye Taylors Bill for faceing ye Red Coat Sleeves wth. black &c.	0 14 0

The choice of servants in the first example may have been dictated by a possible previous connection with the Tufton household, and the second group offers more than one possibility – Casey as a senior servant will have had much to do with the arrangements for Lady Ann's funeral (Thomas Coke was an executor), and the junior servants may well have been on the staff of her London house, but the odd one out is the Holkham housemaid. She cannot have been a member of the official mourning group under Casey, and the only explanation that comes to mind is that she had worked for Lady Ann when she and Col. Walpole lived at Beck Hall.

During this period wigs, or perukes as they were often called, were worn by the upper and middle classes and by liveried servants on all outdoor occasions, normally on cropped or shaven heads. There was considerable variety in styles and qualities. The earliest reference to wigs found in the family papers is a letter of October 1708 from Charles Bertie to Sir John Newton, which shows that Thomas Coke started to wear a wig when he was only 11 years old and highlights the prevailing fashion: 'I hear that I shall find him improved both in his Learning & dancing, & that hee is gott into a Perriwigg Like a Young Beau.'[18] In all his portraits Coke is shown wearing a long wig. Two were bought from the perruquier Mr Morrin for eighteen guineas; another sent over from Paris cost the same, but the common bob periwig was cheaper, and two could be had for five guineas. With the latter, the bottom locks were turned up into bobs or short curls and they had buckles for adjustment; tie wigs were also bought and were similar, except that they were worn over long hair, which was gathered at the back and tied with a knot of ribbon – as in the Rosalba portrait of young Edward Coke; a quality version could cost up to twelve guineas. Another variation was the bob hunting wig, as provided by Mr Bentley of Uttoxeter when Thomas was staying at Longford. While he was there he had a partitioned box made to house his collection. The liveried servants wore bag wigs with which the back hair was enclosed in an ornamental bag, normally of silk, costing five guineas. To cut the cost of a batch of footmen's wigs, Mrs Smith made the bags for them in-house. To keep them in good condition and to effect any necessary repairs, wigs needed occasionally to be 'dressed', and on a visit to Norwich in 1722 Coke had his dealt with by a local barber. Powder for the wigs came in three grades and was bought in quantity – 25lb of tenpenny, 14lb of eightpenny, and 24lb of sixpenny was a typical order in 1720. It was normally stored in the 'powder room', where the whole household's wigs would be dealt with.

The vital accessories for men and women of fashion were snuffboxes and fans respectively; the latter do not feature in the accounts, but Coke bought a number of the former. The finest were in gold, one from Mr Deards at £21, and another set with agate by Mr Ayscough, the toyman, for £12. A pair in silver were much cheaper, those of tortoiseshell cheaper still at six shillings, and a japanned snuffbox was a mere shilling. Custom-made watches were individually numbered by their makers, and when Coke passed his old one to his son, Mr Purden marked his new silver model No. 167 and charged him £7 15s. His combs, their cases and his toothpick case were all made of tortoiseshell; two 'pickers' of the same material cost thirteen shillings, but common wooden toothpicks were bought by the hundred. Along with his swords, his set of razors were ground regularly, and most of the time he was shaved by either his valet, the hall porter or a barber, who charged a shilling. Mr Livard, the perfumier, supplied the household with washballs and the orange-flower water that was commonly used as an after-shave lotion. Naples soap was reputed to be the finest available; supplies came from Mr and Mrs Cortacelli.

In the 1720s ladies' fashions were marked by the increasing popularity of the contouche, which was the equivalent of a twentieth-century peignoir. At first it was worn only in the house as a morning dress, but soon it was to be seen even in the street. It was made of wool, silk or taffeta, and when lighter materials such as gauze or muslin were used it was backed by an under-dress of contrasting colour – Lady Margaret wears one in the Richardson portrait. Corsets still played an essential role, but drawers were not normally worn and stockings came only to the knee, held in place by garters. Unfortunately, virtually nothing can be gleaned from the household accounts concerning Lady Margaret's dress simply because she used her pin money to buy her clothes. In his character assassination of Coke,[19] the Earl of Egmont claimed that she never received such monies, but the accounts prove otherwise. Under the wedding agreement, her yearly allowance was £400, with rents earmarked to cover it, and during the first year two small advances were made 'by My Master's Order'. The amount was increased to £500 in 1721, but by 1725 the quarterly payments were disrupted for lack of money. She drew the summer quarter in advance in June but had only £25 at Michaelmas, with the remainder at Christmas. Late and part payments persisted until 1727, when things were back to normal. In the course of the decade there are only two millinery items linked directly to Lady Margaret – in 1719 Mr Kubleston supplied £17's worth of 'Sattin and Taffity for Embroidery', which was probably for her own handwork, and in the same year Mrs Gameron was paid £101 for 'an Embroidered Quilt, pillows &c. for my Ladys Bed'.

Details have already been given of the attention Lady Margaret and her son received from doctors and surgeons. Some of the same practitioners were on call for the rest of the family and the servants. When his coach overturned at Holkham, Coke had his damaged shoulder attended to by Mr Tubbing, the Burnham surgeon, and his son Edward was inoculated against smallpox when he was 9 years old by Mr Amiance for a fee of twenty guineas – treatment in its experimental stage was by no means cheap. Jack Large, the stable helper, was badly bitten by a dog and was attended by Mr Barnet, the surgeon, who also treated the postilion when he took a fall from the coach. Large then developed what was thought to be chickenpox and was looked after by Nurse Forster for three weeks. The medical fraternity prescribed remedies and dealt with blood-letting, but all the drugs were supplied by apothecaries and druggists, whose bills were far higher than those of the doctors and surgeons. It was generally acknowledged that an apprenticeship to an apothecary carried with it the prospect of a lucrative career. All drugs were entered on the still house account and were dispensed to the household generally. For the females, 'Hysteric water' was bought by the bottle and the gallon, in the belief that 'the vapours' were in some way connected with diseases of the womb. In 1727 Chambers's *Cyclopædia* described hysteric waters as 'those proper to strengthen the matrix or womb and remedy the disorders that befall it' without saying just what the ingredients were. It had been popular in the family for some time. In January 1707 Thomas Coke's great-grandmother's note to her son Sir John Newton shows that individual recipes prevailed: 'I found more good in my daughter Newton's Hesterical water against ye spleen than all the doctors ever gave me.'[20] Another cordial that came by the gallon was treacle water, which was distilled with a spirituous menstruum from a mixture of Venice treacle and various drugs. A rosemary-flavoured brandy known as 'Queen of Hungary water' was a popular tonic; understandably so, given that the usual prescription was 'a spoonful to be taken when feeling run down, night or day, ad libitum'. Hartshorn drops and shavings were used as smelling salts, and there is a single reference to sal volatile for the same purpose. With a diet that encouraged costiveness and a medical regime that tried to cure almost anything either by letting blood or by purging, laxatives were in demand. A favourite was manna, a sweet substance extracted from the bark of the manna ash, and an alternative was hierapickra, a compound of aloes and canella bark, sometimes blended with honey. Fevers and the 'ague' were countered by the use of 'Jesuits' bark', bought by the ounce or by the pound (the bark of the Peruvian Chinchona tree, the sole natural source of quinine). An intriguing item occurs in the 1728 Holkham entries when Mr Lynes is paid £3 18s 4d 'for My Lds. Diddimus', plus postage both ways and half a guinea for his trouble. This was probably a medical preparation disguised by a cover name to conceal its nature and purpose. Dr Stephen Cherry of the Wellcome Unit for the History of Medicine hazards a guess that it is a corruption of 'epididimus', a testicular gland – which might explain the careful obfuscation.

When the family were at Holkham, Dr Hepburn and Dr Holland were the family doctors, and Mr Tubbing of Burnham the surgeon. George Hepburn of King's Lynn had a very high reputation, and his practice extended right across the north of the county as far as Felbrigg, where he attended the Windham family.[21] At £1,000 a year, his income was three times that of the average country physician, and his reputation was still high in the 1750s when Dr Charles Burney, in describing the charms of Lynn to his wife, wrote:

> If 'tis meet to fee or bribe
> A leech of th' Aesculapian tribe,
> We Hepburn have, who's wise as Socrates,
> And deep in physic as Hippocrates.

Most of the family's drugs came from Mr Jones, the Fakenham apothecary, although Mr Framing of Swaffham had a share. As an indication of the comparitive costs, in 1719 Dr Hepburn's fees were ten guineas, Mr Tubbing's were £2, while Mr Jones's came to £52. It is no wonder that an apprenticeship to an apothecary was rated a sound opening for a young man.

In 1719 Mr Skenton, the toyman, was paid six guineas for a pair of ebony backgammon tables with ivory dice boxes, together with a chessboard and its set of ivory and ebony men. Other cheaper sets and a draughtsboard were bought later, along with counters and 'fish' for playing loo. A print of 'The Game of the Goose' cost only two shillings and was, perhaps, a board game. In London there were sometimes visits from itinerant entertainers – 'a woman with a dancing dog' was given half-a-crown, while 'the man that shows slight of hand tricks' did rather better with two guineas. At Holkham 'a Show Man' was given a guinea, and although his man had five shillings for dancing, just what he himself did has to be guessed at.

Over the period the family had a number of pets. The stock of resident house dogs was augmented by gifts from time to time. Lady Gower's porter brought two mastiff whelps to Great Russell Street in 1720, and Mr Archer presented a terrier in 1721; the following year the Minister of St Giles gave them another mastiff whelp, and in 1727 Dr Mead's gift was a Dutch mastiff. A nine-weeks-old tame fox was another present, and a man was given half-a-crown for bringing a monkey. Mr Nettleton gave Little Master a pet squirrel, for which a cage had to be made. There were caged birds in quantity at Thanet House, beginning with two small birds costing eleven guineas the pair and a macaw that promptly escaped; 'five shillings' went on crying the mackaw in the neighbourhood before it was found by the Duke of Montagu's gardener next door. A few years later a cockatoo cost nine guineas, and more birds were bought in at Lady Ann Walpole's sale in 1722 – 'a fine parrot with two cages' for two guineas and 'a little bird in a fine cage' for ten shillings. The dogs and the birds were all fed a great deal of milk, with the macaw having sixty-seven quarts over a quarter. At Holkham an aviary was established (normally referred to as the menagerie), which housed a variety of birds. Early on, a guinea was paid for an eagle, and later there were oyster catchers to tame, a clutch of singing birds, and a man from Wells brought a seabird of some sort that was definitely not for the kitchen. In 1728 Giles Blackman and his wife had their travelling expenses paid from London 'and for the fowles &c.' when they came down to take charge of the aviary, and in that year Peter Lewis supplied twenty-eight young wild ducks for stock.

Communications between the town house and Holkham, and contact with the various manors of the estate scattered across England, relied heavily on the postal service; it is unfortunate that very little of what must have been a heavy postbag survives. At Holkham the letters were delivered by the Burnham postwoman, and outgoing mail was taken to Burnham, either by her or by a servant. In 1725 the Wells postman was on the Christmas box list, so some letters must have gone that way. In 1728 three letters for London and one for Downham Market went for 7d, but for urgent items it was not uncommon to deploy a running footman or a local lad; in 1722, for example, a boy was given four shillings to take a letter to Norwich, a journey of nearly 40 miles each way. In London the penny post was operating within the city: the family lawyer and man of business Peniston Lamb used it to send Coke a £20 bank note in 1725.

It is perhaps appropriate now to look beyond the family and examine the social milieu into which Coke was inevitably drawn.

Chapter 7

THE SOCIAL CREATURE

*I*n 1718, as a young and newly married man of considerable fortune, Thomas Coke was poised to take his destined place among the rich and powerful oligarchy that controlled the affairs of the country and its emerging empire. He was to become a member of a tiny group headed by the first of the Hanoverian Georges whose sovereign power was only a little less than absolute and in whose court lay the key to social advancement. The innermost circle comprised those German courtiers who had followed the king from Hanover, but the rest of the company came almost exclusively from the ranks of the peerage, which was tiny by today's standard – in 1710 there were only 167 members of the House of Lords, and George I showed a distinct reluctance to increase the number. Although the king had the right and the ability to choose his ministers, the control of the House of Commons was another matter, and in 1718 Stanhope and Sunderland were finding Robert Walpole in opposition a subtle adversary. The beginning of Walpole's long supremacy in office was still a few years away, but Thomas Coke must have been very well aware of his Norfolk neighbour's power and influence in the Whig party with which he himself was naturally aligned.

With so much to see, to learn and to enjoy, with commodious houses in town and country, and with the ability to travel freely, the young couple naturally saw their early years together as a time for extending hospitality to friends and relatives and for getting to know many people of their own rank, and higher, in society. George I used Hampton Court on occasion as an alternative 'out of town' residence, and the Cokes were invited there to dinner in August 1718, shortly after their wedding. The following month saw them there again when they called on their way to Longford. The palace is not mentioned specifically again until 1728, when there was a flurry of three visits within a short space of time, with the king's groom being given a handsome two guineas on each occasion. However, there are numerous references in the intervening years to Richmond, with servants putting up at the Green Man Inn and horses being stabled at the Lyon and Lamb, and it is likely that at least some of these relate to calls at Hampton Court.

Nottingham House had been bought by William and Mary in 1689 and then extended to become Kensington Palace. With a large German retinue to house, George I enlarged the building again and added three new state rooms, the King's Drawing Room, the Cube Room and the Privy Chamber. The court was often in residence there, and the numerous Holkham account entries dealing with travelling and incidental expenses for journeys to and from Thanet House to Kensington, by both Coke and Lady Margaret, undoubtedly relate to visits to the palace. The king's groom of the chambers was tipped half a guinea on one occasion; and among the other minor indications of contact with the court are purchases of wine from the royal cellars.

Both the Coke and the Thanet families were firmly established in the higher reaches of society, and the pattern of their visits reflects their standing, each of them making their own contacts. Lady Salisbury had been a guest of Lord Thanet at Hothfield Place, and, when the Coke entourage travelled down to Bath in April 1720, they stayed at Hatfield with the Salisburys for three days before moving on; Thomas called again two months later, giving half a guinea 'to my Lord's Keeper coming thro ye pk.' and distributing ten guineas among the house staff. In June 1722 Lady Margaret hired a coach to pay a visit and, having paid turnpike fees and given 'something to a poor boy' on the way, she handed out vails to Lord Salisbury's servants on her departure. They went to Lord Burlington's ball at Chiswick on 4 May 1721 and later that month they dined with the Henry St Johns – very well it seems, because Coke tipped the cook. Lady Margaret paid regular visits to the Duke of

Kingston's, going by coach to dine there on her own in 1723. The Duke was the Whig Lord of the Bedchamber, and Macky had this to say of him: 'He hath a good estate, is a fine gentleman of good sense, well bred and a lover of the ladies.'[1] It was by all accounts a lively household; his daughter grew up to be the celebrated bluestocking Lady Mary Wortley Montague.

Both Lady Margaret and her husband regularly used sedan chairs to make visits during the day and in the evening. Lady Margaret was sometimes abroad six nights in a week in her own chair, with her footman lighting the way; Coke, on the other hand, hired both chair and chairmen, and used them just as heavily. As he moved about the country visiting his manors, he often took the opportunity to pay social visits; while staying at Minster Lovell he called on Lord Abingdon and Lord Paulett, both men of substance and position in Oxfordshire with close connections with the royal household (Lady Abingdon had been Queen Anne's Lady of the Bedchamber and John, Earl Paulet had served as her Lord Steward of the Household); during other trips he made calls on the Tankervilles at Uppark and the Duke of Richmond at Goodwood. During one of the early stays at Longford he went over to see Mr Curzon at Kedleston (this was before James Paine had begun the great house for Lord Scarsdale), and a couple of years later he dined at Bretby with Philip Stanhope, Lord Chesterfield, coming away with a fat buck as a present. The general enthusiasm among genteel tourists for the 'awful grandeur' of the Lake District had not yet been awakened, but Coke took the opportunity to spend a few days in the Peak District, which he had first seen with his tutor when he was a lad at Longford. The ledger entry shows that he stood one-third of the cost of the trip and, more interestingly, that his companions, his two young brothers, Mr Edward and Mr Robert, must have contributed the remaining £8.

The hospitality that the couple enjoyed in London was naturally matched by entertainments at home. Guests were invited to two parties at Thanet House in the spring of 1721, and it is noticeable that a good deal of extra fish and poultry was ordered in advance and that the pastry cook provided special apple pies. A month or so later they held a ball, and the musicians who were hired played again for them at a second ball in May. There was a need to increase the lighting for these affairs, and in the early days sconces were hired from Mr Pugh, the glass man, to accommodate additional candles. To ensure that he acquitted himself well, Thomas took dancing lessons for three months in 1720 from Monsieur Seris, paying £7 1s for the whole course. At least two of the functions the couple attended in 1719 and 1720 called for fancy dress – these may well have been the masquerades staged at the Haymarket to promote the success of the Royal Academy of Music. For each they hired 'masquerade dresses' and bought masks to go with them, which were supplied by Mr Morn: one entry calls them 'domineys', the traditional Venetian domino costume. Some years later Coke had a 'Turkish dress' made by Mr Maurer, the costumier, to wear at similar parties.

Londoners were fond of excursions to the pretty villages that lay just beyond the growing suburbs, and, although it had a reputation as the haunt of highwaymen, Blackheath was well thought of. A popular poet apostrophised it as 'Blackheath, with wintry woods assail'd'.[2] The Cokes resorted there twice in the summer of 1722. On 14 June they drove down with Lady Margaret's sister and her husband, the Earl of Harold, to dine at the Green Man and, perhaps because they so enjoyed themselves, they went again a week later. This time it was a more elaborate affair, and they began by journeying down the Thames to Greenwich in three barges, each with a crew of six. The family butcher had sent meat there to await their arrival, and John Gundaymore, their chef, then bought more provisions and enlisted an assistant cook to help him. Andrew Griffiths, the butler, had sent on a dozen bottles of Rhenish and bought a good deal more. Six musicians joined the party and together they travelled on to Mrs Tosier's at Blackheath – she may have been the landlady at the Green Man but the record does not actually say so. By the time the musicians had been given seven guineas, the bargees had been paid £7 for their efforts and their craft, £5 10s 3d had been laid out on additional entertainment and all the other bills had been settled, the outing had cost £37 4s 9½d. And without doubt it was well worth the expense.

The eighteenth century saw the development and systematic organisation in England of freemasonry, which enjoyed an extraordinary success very quickly. The movement was characterised in the 1720s by the aristocratic credentials of its highest officials, which conferred upon the Craft a much greater degree of respectability than it had previously enjoyed. In 1717 the London lodges affiliated to form the Grand Lodge of England, of which Thomas Coke's friend the Duke of Richmond became Grand Master in 1723. Coke was a mason as early as 1722, for on 31 May that year members of his lodge were his guests, possibly at the Goose & Gridiron alehouse in St Paul's churchyard, with Mr Richard Turbey being paid £52 10s for 'ye Entertainment on acct. of free masons'. However, it was not until 1731 that

Coke himself was installed as Grand Master: 'A grand Lodge was held at the Devil Tavern, Temple Bar on 17 March, 1730/1. Lord Lovel and the Officers of 29 Lodges were present. Deputy Grand Master Blakerby in the chair proposed (in the Grand Master's name) for Successor, the Lord Lovel, Master of a Lodge, who was saluted as Grand Master Elect.'[3] At an assembly and feast at Mercer's Hall on 27 March 1731:

> The procession of March was very splendid, many Noblemen and Gentlemen (being masons) all clothed in white aprons and gloves, proceeded in coaches, with music from Lord Lovel's house in Great Russell Street Bloomsbury, in the west, eastwards to the Hall where the Deputy Grand Master in the absence of the most noble Thomas Duke of Norfolk, Grand Master, proposed the Right Honourable Thomas Coke Lord Lovel to succeed his Grace in Solomon's Chair for the year ensuing. But Lord Lovel being ill of an Ague, return'd home and left Lord Colerane his Proxy for the day.[4]

By that time Coke had also become involved in Norfolk freemasonry. The minute book 1743–89 of the Maid's Head Lodge (the earliest in Norfolk) has in its first entry:

> Several remarkable distinctions have been paid to this Lodge by ye many Honble & Right Worshipfull Brethren who have visited it very frequently . . . But as an extraordinary Instance of the great regard shown to this Lodge, the Right Honble ye Lord Lovel, when he was Grand Master summoned ye Master and Brethren to hold a Lodge at Houghton Hall. There were present the Grand Master, his Royal Highness ye Duke of Lorrain, and many other noble Brethren, & when all was put in due form, ye Grand Master presented His Grace ye Duke of Newcastle, ye Right Hon. ye Earl of Essex, Major-General Churchill and his own Chaplain who were unanimously accepted of and made Masons by the Right Worshipful Thomas Johnson the then Master of this Lodge.[5]

This illustrates the aristocratic networking that freemasonry employed in its upper reaches. Roy Porter neatly summarises the interesting social dimension of the Craft at that time, when he points out that, although the lodge created a useful context in which constitutionalism and charity could flourish, it was full of tensions; deference to hierarchy vied with egalitarianism under a cloak of mystery and ritual.[6]

At Holkham, life was quieter, and the tally of guests and round of visits hold no surprises. Country neighbours and friends such as Lord Townshend, Sir Robert Walpole, Sir Jacob Astley, Ashe Windham, Sir Ralph Hare and Sir Nicholas Le Strange all feature. Sir Harry Bedingfeld of Oxborough was a hunting companion whom Coke visited and who stayed as a guest at Hill Hall; the New Year party of 1722/3 drew in Lord Lichfield, Lord Gower, Mr Levison Gower and Uncle John Newton. Coke stayed with the Duke of Grafton at Euston in Suffolk in the August of 1723, and at the end of the decade one finds the names of Sir Andrew Fountaine of Narford and Lady Oxford cropping up.

There has never been a time when mankind has not been concerned, even preoccupied or obsessed, with its state of bodily health, and the eighteenth century was not immune. The rich were well nourished and particularly inclined both to overeat and to drink more than was good for them. While the medical profession could only call on a limited range of treatment, physicians had no hesitation in recommending 'a course of the waters' for a whole variety of ailments; accordingly, since the 1670s spas had become fashionable, ranging from the lowly chalybeate spring at Thetford to the renowned hot waters at Bath. At that time the city still had the appearance of a small walled town surrounded by meadows and orchards, and there was only one bridge – the old bridge – spanning the river to the south. The city's popularity was ensured after the visit by Queen Anne and her consort Prince George of Denmark in 1702. Racked by rheumatism for most of her life, the Queen was not noticeably enthusiastic and called it 'a stinking place', and some years later her erstwhile close friend Sarah, Duchess of Marlborough, thought that 'of all the places on earth 'tis the most despicable'. In those early days it was neither very comfortable nor was there much evidence of style. Oliver Goldsmith remarked that 'gentlemen and ladies appear in a disrespectful manner at public entertainments in aprons and spurred and muddy boots', and the city itself he denounced as 'mean and contemptible; no elegant buildings, no open streets, no uniform squares'. Nevertheless, by the 1720s opinions were more favourable: 'The streets though narrow have many handsome shops which are well accustomed by the great resort of nobility & Gentry to this place . . . the Chief walk for the Ladyes and Gentlemen, is one pav'd with freestone reaching from the east end of the

Abbey . . . on one side are Limes planted, on the other very handsome Toy shops like those in London.'[7] Even so, in 1726 the Duke of Chandos, whose great house, Cannons, was a byword for luxury and conspicuous display, was not noticeably impressed with the lodgings: 'to a person of fashion because they did not afford a dressing room & dining room beyond the room, he lyes in, especially if he has his lady with him.' There were no card tables or screens, 'there is not two screens in any one house in Bath except the Great Abbey House'.[8] Apart from the favour it found with the doctors, one man may be credited with turning this dismal provincial city into a magnet for fashionable society. Richard (Beau) Nash had made little progress in either the army or the law and was intent on gambling until he discovered his talent as master of ceremonies. Within a decade he had prodded the city fathers into paving, cleaning and lighting the streets, he had tempted a little orchestra down from London and he had organised the Pump Room; and so, by the time that Thomas Harrison's Assembly Rooms opened in 1715, 8,000 people a year were on their way to Bath in search of health and polite society. In the formative years duels and street brawls were common, but Nash's dominance was such that his *Rules to be observed at Bath* (which incidentally banned the wearing of swords) were displayed in the Pump Room and accepted by the clientele.

It was natural, therefore, that the Cokes and their friends would wish to enjoy this agreeable resort, and in April 1721 Lady Margaret, together with her sister Lady Isabella Tufton, set out for the West Country. They had with them Mrs Thompson, the housekeeper, and their personal maids, with Abraham Thomas, the valet-de-chambre, Francis Riggs, the coachman, one of the postilions and a boy. It took them three days on the road to reach Bath, and, after a day's breather, the coach and six, three saddle horses and four of the servants made their way back to London. Having hired a coach to use in the interval, Coke reverted to his own and followed his wife down to Bath. Queen's Square, the Circus and John Wood's other fine buildings that immediately come to mind when one thinks of the city would not be built for some years yet; the family took modest rooms with a Mrs Atwood at £3 a week, increased to £3 15s when Thomas joined the party. There was apparently some concern about security, which led to locks being mended and new keys cut. They bought some cups and a kettle, but cutlery and glasses were hired from the local grocer. Such was the pressure on the limited accommodation available that Lady Bristol was glad to find a room: 'I must submit to necessity till I can better myself, for at present there is not a room to be got if I would give £5 for it . . . our company increases daily, so that people of fashion is forc'd to be content with garrets.'[9] John Gundaymore, Coke's chef, had remained in London, and so Mrs Atwood was paid for preparing meals, but all the food was bought by their servants, using Hoskins the butcher, Clement the baker, Brown the grocer and other Bath tradesmen. The fare of meat, fish, poultry, vegetables and fruit was quite as varied as in London, with one or two items, such as mackerel, spinach and a pigeon pie, that do not occur elsewhere. The herb man and sundry basket women called at the door, and flummery, tarts and cheesecakes featured on the menu. A gallon of port, quarts of Rhenish, sherry and other wines were bought in, with plenty of beer from a Mrs Purlevent; the family had to find their own candles, wood and coal, and Lady Margaret's footmen needed a supply of flambeaus to light her way when she went out using a sedan chair in the evening. Care of the horses was, as usual, a fairly expensive business. The cost of their standing at livery amounted to £21 4s 2½d, the farrier charged eight shillings, and repairs and replacement of saddlery came to £1 9s 4d; in addition, a sorrel pad mare was acquired for seven guineas.

The social round was a full one. A typical day might begin with an early morning bath in the mineral waters, between six and nine o'clock, followed by a visit to the Pump Room to drink the waters and listen to the band. A morning meal might be taken at a coffee house or at the lodgings, and the Abbey held a daily service at noon for the more devout. Dinner was eaten between two and three, after which it was time to walk about to view and be viewed in turn. The evening could be filled with visiting, gambling or going to the play, and balls were held every Tuesday and Friday at the Pump Room for those who took up a two-guinea subscription.[10] Such was likely to have been the framework of the Cokes' activities during their eight-week stay, with one or two highlights that show up in the ledgers. Mr Harrison provided an entertainment at his Assembly Rooms for £27, with a half a guinea for his servants, and Dame Lindsey provided 'an entertainment & supper' for £18 16s, with the music costing three guineas and a further three for the hire of the room. Another visitor remarked during those summer weeks that Lady Margaret's other sister, Lady Mary, was at Bath, and the Tufton trio will surely have spent much of their time together: 'Now I must tell the devertion [sic] of this place. Last Thursday we came here, that night a play was bespoke by Lady Harold, so we did not see anybody.'[11] Under Nash's direction, those new arrivals who came in their own coach were well advertised; he normally called on them personally and there was a welcome by the Abbey ringers who usually expected half a guinea, but Coke gave them twice that, and the city waits' normal half-a-crown was raised to match.

The holiday at Bath gave an opportunity for a side trip to the rival hot wells at Bristol. John Casey had come down from London by stagecoach, bringing Coke's two younger brothers with him, and they journeyed on with Mrs Thompson and Mrs Jenny in a hired coach to Bristol, where the family had gone to take lodgings with a Mrs Reece for a week or so. Thomas was there again for his health in June 1724, sending a somewhat tetchy letter to his grandfather: 'this being the worst place I was ever at for Provisions . . . I can't say but I am mended since I came hither, tho' I mend but very slowly, so I fear I shall make a longer stay here than I intended at first.'[12] From Bristol the party made their way over to Badminton, again using a hired coach and extra saddle horses to carry the extended party. It would seem that they paused only to view the house before travelling on to stay with Sir Edward Coke at Longford, from whence the extra coach was returned to William Simkin, its owner, in Bristol, who charged fifteen guineas for the nine-day hire. It is worth noting that, as the boys had their own establishments and allowances by then, Edward was debited with half the cost of the extra coach and a horse for his man, and both he and Robert paid their own stable expenses at Bath.

Members of the Coke family had represented Norfolk in the House of Commons since Sir Edward the Chief Justice's day, and it was natural that, once Thomas had become established at Holkham and known to his neighbours, he would be expected to support the Whig interest and play his part in the government of the country. Accordingly, he travelled down from London to Norwich in April 1722 to be present at his election as a Knight of the Shire. There was a good deal of coming and going between Holkham and Norwich, with the house steward staying in the city for three nights, and George Appleyard the land steward entering an account for £53 16s 7d expenses. In all, the election cost the new member £103 1s 10d. That year, the door-keepers and messengers at the House of Commons all received Christmas boxes – which may be viewed either as a typical example of the man's generosity, or a thoughtful ploy on the part of a new boy. Coke continued to serve as an MP until 1728, when he went to the House of Lords, but there is very little evidence of political activity in the intervening years, although copies of Acts of Parliament were brought by messenger occasionally to Thanet House, and the services of the door-keepers and messengers at the House of Commons continued to be acknowledged. Just before he moved to the House of Lords as Baron Lovel, he was in Norwich staying with his fellow MP for Norfolk, Sir John Hobart, who was to be similarly honoured. He went about treating ringers and musicians and giving half a guinea to the city waits in support of the new members Sir Edmund Bacon and Colonel Harbord. At that time a Mr Le Neve was paid £36 as 'the residue of his expenses', which was probably a political payment, and the three guineas dispensed 'to the freeholders of Walsingham' the following year looks like a political douceur. During the 1720s Coke also served as a Justice of the Peace. In this role he will have administered justice conveniently at home for the most part, but in 1724 he attended the Norwich Sessions over four days, accompanied only, it seems, by John Mountain the stable boy, who stood in for a groom. The following year he was summoned by a bailiff to Grand Jury Service at Norwich Assizes and was there for six days. He also attended the Holt Petty Sessions occasionally, staying for a couple of days at the Feathers Inn with just a groom in attendance.

In 1725 George I established the Most Honourable Order of the Bath as a new order of chivalry, claiming it as a revival of an order of Henry IV's time that had never, in fact, existed. Determined to limit the growth of the peerage, he found this a convenient and economical method of rewarding his supporters, with the membership being limited to the sovereign, the Great Master and thirty-six knights companions. Horace Walpole cynically described it as 'an artful bank of thirty-six ribands to supply a fund of favours', but it took its place among those signs of royal favour that carried considerable weight in polite society. The process began at St James's Palace on 27 May 1725 when the King knighted Prince William, his grandson, the Duke of Montagu, as Great Master, those selected as officers of the Order, and all the intended recipients, including Thomas Coke. Then, on Thursday 17 June, Sir Thomas joined his brethren in the Speaker's Chamber of the House of Commons to don the red surcoat and mantle adorned with the ensign of the Order and put on the tall hat with its waving white plumes. Preceded by their esquires, the Abbey prebendaries and the Pursuivants, the Knights Companions processed two by two to the west door of Westminster Abbey by way of a specially prepared boarded walk. Inside, they continued eastward until they reached Henry VII's chapel, where they took up the stalls

assigned to them (Coke was paired with Sir William Morgan), and were seated
under their banners. Each in turn was given his copy of the Order's Statutes
by the Great Master; the Dean of Westminster administered the oath
individually, and the collar of the Order was then bestowed. After the service
they processed out, each pausing at the west door to allow the sovereign's
master cook holding a cleaver to declaim: 'Sir, you know what great oath you
have taken, which if you keep, it will be great honour to you; but if you break
it, I shall be compelled by my office to hack off your spurs from your heels.'
Then came dinner for the new Knights Companions in the Court of Requests
at a table 96ft long laden with 218 dishes – pyramids of sweetmeats
alternating with such delicacies as Geese Alaroyal, potted lampreys, haunches
of venison, stewed pike and veal papiettes. At about nine o'clock the same
evening the knights, their esquires and some 700 nobility and gentry of both
sexes were entertained with a splendid collation prepared and set out on a
huge horseshoe table by Mr Heydigger at the Opera House in the Haymarket.
Sir Thomas rounded off this day of ceremonial enoblement and feasting by
attending a gala ball with his peers. His personal copy of the Order's statutes,
bound in crimson morocco and stamped with the Bath insignia, was carried
home and can still be found in the Long Library at Holkham.[13] Five years
later the engraver John Pine issued a lavish folio description of the founding
and ceremonial of the Order to subscribers, with double-spread plates of the
procession, the service and the dinner. The title page states that the portraits
of most of the Knights Companions and Officers of the Order were done from
original pictures painted for that purpose; and the plates record that the artist
was John Highmore. There is a touch of portraiture-by-rote about them, but
Thomas is shown to advantage in his splendid robes, and his three esquires
can be identified as Ralph Wilbraham, Worcester Wilson and Jean Raworth
(see Plate 7).[14] Pine received two guineas in 1726 for twenty prints of the
knights. The subscription list is instructive in that it illustrates some of the
interconnecting lines of Coke's circle. The Great Master of the Order was the
Duke of Montagu, his next-door neighbour in Great Russell Street, and his
friends the Duke of Richmond and Lord Pomfret were knighted with him.
Among others who took up copies of Pine's book were Sir Robert Walpole, his
political chief and near neighbour (who bought four), his close friend and
artistic collaborator William Kent, and his wife's brother the Hon. Thomas
Tufton. Two proxies had been involved in the original ceremony; one was for
the Duke of Richmond, who was recovering from smallpox, and the other was

Sir Andrew Fountaine, who stood proxy for Prince William and was granted the winged lion supporters that feature in the family arms in recognition of his role in the ceremony. Living at Narford, he was another of Thomas's Norfolk neighbours with whom he had some social contact, but the way in which his father had mulcted John Coke of many thousands of pounds while managing his estates years before must still have been sharp in the family's memory.

This advancement in society naturally brought with it significant attendant costs:

	£	s	d
The Fees of the Knighthood	113	3	2
The Fees of Instalment	410	6	8
The Herald's Fees	40	0	4
The Fees for the Collar	24	17	0
Charges at the Ball	30	9	0
Webster Starr's Fees for making the Order of the Bath	2	2	0
Mr Gibson the Jeweller's charge for the Order	26	0	0
Mrs Thomas the milliner's charges	4	7	6
Total	651	5	8

Sir Thomas's stall plate can still be seen in Westminster Abbey, but his Bath insignia has not survived (as far as is known). So straitened were his financial affairs at the time that, within a year of his knighthood, he was driven to pawn the Bath jewel to provide himself with some ready cash. However, his advancement had brought him a little closer to the centre of influence at court, and in May 1726 he was appointed as one of the eight Sergeants-at-Arms in Ordinary. These officers performed ceremonial duties in the Presence Chamber, waiting quarterly in pairs on Sundays and festival days, and were mace-bearers whose main duty seems to have been to form part of the sovereign's escort to chapel, carrying their maces before him.

It was possible to purchase the appointment through the good offices of the Lord Chamberlain, a post occupied between 1724 and 1757 by the Duke of Grafton, a close friend of Thomas Coke. Such a post was open only to those whose attendance upon the king in public 'added to the dignity and splendour of the monarchy'. In most cases the small salary paid to members of the household was only a part of their income. There were further benefits of several kinds, which could include board wages, diet at court, lodgings (or money in lieu) and travelling expenses. To set against the advantages, court employees had to pay Land Tax and Civil List Tax, which amounted to anything between 12 per cent and 20 per cent of the salary depending on the level of the post. This was levied on the fixed salary, and, the better off the official was, the more was made in fees and perquisites. Expenses of living at court were increased by the social life – what Lord Hervey called 'the necessary expenses incurred by dangling after a court'.[15] By 1722 men's court dress was becoming extremely ornate. Mrs Sarah Osborne described to her brother the celebration at court of the King's birthday: 'Munday last was a great Court at James's,' she wrote, 'and most people very fine, but I believe the gentlemen will wear petty-cotes very soon, for many of their Coats were like our Mantuas. Ld Essex had a silver tissue Coat, and pink colour lutestring wascote, and several had pink colour and pale blue padeswoy [paduasoy] Coats which looked prodigiously effeminate.'[16]

Although his duties included 'attending upon His Majesty's person', Sir Thomas was not with the King when he set out on what was to be his last trip to Hanover in June 1727. George left behind him a country largely content under a strong government whose first minister, Walpole, must have hoped that his sovereign would follow the example of his mother, the Princess Sophia, Electress of Hanover, and live to be 84. But it was not to be, and, seemingly in vigorous health, the King suffered a stroke near Osnabrück. Carried to the castle there, he died in the very room in which he had been born. Despite George II's ambivalence towards Sir Robert, Queen Caroline's overriding influence ensured that he continued in office, to the chagrin of his enemies and the relief of his friends. Coke certainly had reason to be sanguine; conscious of his lineage and comfortable in the position he had gained at court, secure in the friendship of Walpole and other prominent Whigs, he believed that his wealth, based on the security of his great estate, must surely entitle him to expect further advancement. In this he was not disappointed, for on 28 May 1728 he was created Baron Lovel of Minster Lovell in the county of Oxford. Once again, custom demanded the payment of the necessary fees, the purchase of the appropriate trappings and the ceremonies of induction. Mr Tench of the Lord Chancellor's office received £297 14s 8d for the 'fees of hon'r for my Lord's patent', and a Mr Turner was paid ten guineas, being 'the expense of My Lord's Introduction to house of peers'; beyond that, 'the [Earl] Marshall's

Men' were given a guinea to share between them. There was a fee of two guineas for the carrying of the Sword of State, and the same for 'the Order of the House of Lords'. Lord Gower's servant was tipped a guinea 'for bringing robes' that may have been used as a pattern for those made for Sir Thomas by Mrs Roundiel. She charged only £3 13s, but the ermine for them cost £14, and the bill for the gold and silver lace came to £56 12s 6d. Portraits of the Baron and Lady Margaret in their new robes by Andrea Casali still hang in the Chapel Wing at Holkham. Ten years before, Coke and his young wife had been greeted on their return to London by a martial display with music, and to celebrate his new dignity as Lord Lovel there was a repeat performance on a somewhat larger scale – vails were distributed among three regiments of Guards, two troops of Grenadiers, the royal hautboys with the household drums, the militia drums, and the parish waits. The six turtle doves that came as a present from Sir Andrew Fountaine in the autumn perhaps show that the relationship between the two families had quickened following Lord Lovel's move to the House of Lords. Further advancement at court came in 1733 when King George II appointed him Captain of the Band of Pensioners with a salary of £1,000 a year – another largely ceremonial position, but one that was a strictly royal appointment with considerably more social standing.

At this point in his social career it is perhaps appropriate to consider what can be learned about Thomas Coke's personality. Previous studies of the man have focused largely on two aspects of his life: his Grand Tour (which, by the chance survival of the account books kept by Edward Jarrett, his valet, and Dr Hobart, his tutor, provide the most detailed description of a young dilettante's acquisitions and activities abroad), and his creation of Holkham Hall, considered by many to be the finest example of Palladian architecture on a large scale in Britain. Extensive research on both these topics by a number of scholars has given but little indication of the extraordinary range of his character, which seems to have been enlivened by a number of contradictions and paradoxes. The unusual combination of an obsession with cockfighting and a deep love of classical literature, and the sharp contrast between his obviously charitable nature and the harsh treatment of his daughter-in-law are but two examples of this. As a young man, flexing his intellectual muscles, he could not but be influenced by the effect that the 'English Enlightenment' movement, led by members of the Lunar Society, was having on his generation. There was no doubt in the Earl of Shaftesbury's mind that the aristocracy had a decisive role to play in the country's intellectual development: 'To Philosophise, in a Just Signification, is but To carry Good-Breeding a step higher.'[17]

Contemporary assessments of his character are hard to come by, but the correspondence of his guardians when he was a young teenager provides a few pointers to the sort of man he was to become. His first tutor, Mr Wilkins, described him as 'a Gentleman of extraordinary good natural parts, of a great capacity, who has applied himself extreamly much in reading some of ye best Classick Authors & Latin as well as English Poets, and is nothing at all wanting but a continuance of ye same for some time 'till his flattering age be a little more settled'.[18] Despite the difference in their ages, Sir Edward Coke of Longford called him 'the young Gentleman who is the head of my family' and had this to say: 'My Cosen . . . has a spirit and understanding (if they have a happy bent) to make him an Accomplish'd Gentleman.'[19] In another letter he says, 'he has a quick apprehension, a faithful memory, and a good understanding', but he was seen to be wilful, particularly when crossed, and 'his sanguin complexion will not let him act a moderate part'.[20] A brief but telling description of Thomas as a teenager is to be found in a letter from M. Gullmann, the King's Resident in Frankfurt, to the Secretary of State in London,[21] who reported the arrival of this young English gentleman for a three weeks' stay, with a modest entourage and accompanied only by his governor Dr Hobart and two servants. Writing in French, he described him as personable and well built, with light-brown hair, and he took him to be about 23 rather than his 17 years. It was noticeable that he spoke coldly and scornfully about the King, Lord Marlborough and certain government ministers. This public airing of views prompted a warning from one of Gullmann's friends that the Captain General was seen as a liberator in Germany and Coke should watch his tongue.

In the 1720s it would seem that he was very much the young blade and 'man about town', for, as Lord Hervey described him, he was 'at present the darling idol of the professed wits of this good city'.[22] John Percival (later Lord Egmont in the Irish peerage) was related by marriage to the Cokes, and some years later entered an acid comment in his diary concerning the marriage:

Apr. 26 1737. I went this morning to Charlton and dined with my son and daughter Percival. I was not pleased with the account of my Lord Lovel, her uncle, as that my Lady Clifford his wife (who is a very agreeable and good lady) brought him £80,000, and when he was near undone in the South Sea year by that vile scheme recovered his affairs . . . half a year after her marriage he resumed his debaucheries and continues them with several ladies of quality and fashion.[23]

C.W. James, a pre-war Holkham librarian, in his account of the family considered this to be ill-natured and unfounded gossip, but there is some reason to consider its validity.[24] Having entered into an arranged marriage and succeeded in producing an heir, and Lady Margaret having suffered a series of miscarriages, it is not at all unlikely that Coke should look beyond the confines of the conjugal bed for his pleasure. There are, indeed, one or two account entries that support this thesis:

1720.	Paid for his Honour's bathing at the Bagnio	10s 6d
	Given to the waiter	2s 6d
1721. 15th April	Gave ye waiter last night at ye Bagnio	5s 0d
	To a barber there.	2s 6d
1721. 14th Oct.	Paid my Masters and Mr Edward Cokes charges at ye Bagnio	3 guineas
1722. 8th Aug.	Quart of Lavender water from ye Bagnio.	6s 0d

The first bagnio opened as a genuine bath house in the Covent Garden Piazza in 1681, and was an immediate success. By the turn of the century, however, such establishments had evolved into houses of assignation. The brothel on the continental model was introduced into England only in the eighteenth century, and while they catered mainly for the upper classes, the bagnio was a distinctly superior establishment, run by such queens of the profession as Molly King, Mother Douglas, Mrs Gould and Mrs 'Hellfire' Stanhope. The crucial difference lay in the fact that there were no girls in the establishment. The client was free either to send out for the prostitute of his choice or to use the premises as a house of assignation. Those exhausted by more rigorous pleasures could relax quietly in an atmosphere of luxury and, when sufficiently revived, sample some quiet and discreet debauchery.[25] Later in the century, a foreign visitor provided a detailed description:

In London there is a certain kind of house, called bagnios, which are supposed to be baths; their real purpose, however, is to provide persons of

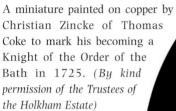

A miniature painted on copper by Christian Zincke of Thomas Coke to mark his becoming a Knight of the Order of the Bath in 1725. *(By kind permission of the Trustees of the Holkham Estate)*

The matching 1725 miniature of Sir Thomas Coke's wife, Lady Margaret, Baroness Clifford. *(By kind permission of the Trustees of the Holkham Estate)*

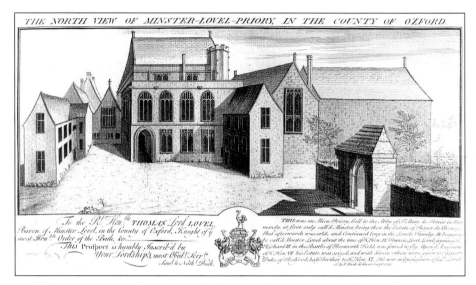

A 1730s engraving by the brothers Nathaniel and Samuel Buck of the only Oxfordshire manor house in the Coke's Great Estate, dedicated to the recently ennobled Thomas as Lord Lovel. *(By kind permission of the Trustees of the Holkham Estate)*

A reproduction of an early nineteenth-century lithograph by George Scharf of Thanet House in Great Russell Street used originally in a contemporary history of St Giles Parish. *(Taken from C.W. James,* Chief Justice Coke. His Family and Descendants at Holkham, Country Life, *1929)*

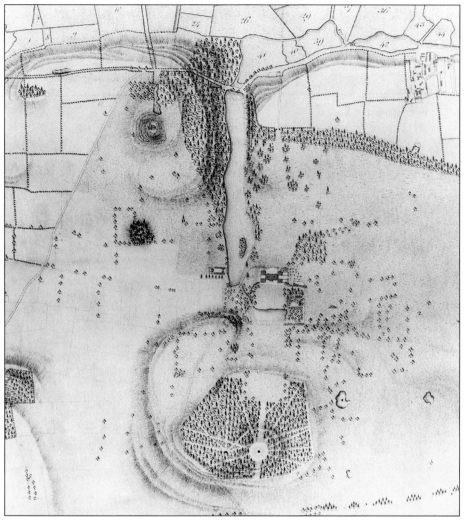

William Kent's drawing of his layout of the south lawn up to the Great Wood. (*By kind permission of the Trustees of the Holkham Estate*)

H   E   O

St Edmunds
Point   S   A   L   T   M
                Holme   Brancaſt
Hunstanton   Thornham
Lights   Tichwell
        Hunstanton

                Ringstead
                Mag
    Ringstead   Choſsett
        par   S M Y T H D O N
Hitcham   Ringstead

Burcham Haven   Sedgford   Docking
                                          Stan   hon
                                        H. HARE Eſqr

        I. STILEMAN Eſq   Fring   Bar
                                                in the
Lodge
    Snetſham   Be
        Ingalsthorp   Burcham Mag:

Homer End Creek   Shernbourn   Burcham   Bagtho
Bever   Burcham Newto
        Daſingham

        Sandringham   Anmer   R. H. Sr R. Wa
verton

        Newton   Houghton
        Hitcham   W Rudham
ngle
    Apleton   G
Bek   Riſeing   Hillington   Harple
    RISEING CASTLE
R   E   B   R   I   D   G   E   Maſſ
    Riſeing   Roydon
    Lodge   Congham

ynn
    Baudsey
YNN   Lezjate   Welen
            Grimeſton
                    Geyton
dleton Tower
iddleton   Aſh Wicking   Geytonthorp   R

A section of James Corbridge's 1730 map of Norfolk, showing Holkham's position relative to the great house of Sir Robert Walpole at Houghton and that of the Townshend family at Raynham. *(By kind permission of Mr Raymond Frostick)*

Thomas Coke shown in the procession of the new Knights of the Order of the Bath in 1725, engraved in John Pine's *The Procession and Ceremonies Observed at the Installation of the Companions of the Bath, London, 1726. (By kind permission of the Trustees of the Holkham Estate)*

Right: William Hogarth's cutting satire on the madness of the South Sea Bubble, engraved in that year but not published until 1724. *(© British Museum)*

Below: William Hogarth's engraving of a main of cocks being fought in the King's Cockpit in Whitehall, probably issued in the 1760s. *(© British Museum)*

Chief Justice Sir Edward Coke, painted by Cornelius Johnson in the reign of King James I. *(By kind permission of the Trustees of the Holkham Estate)*

Thomas Coke just returned from the Grand Tour in 1718, by Francesco Trevisani. *(By kind permission of the Trustees of the Holkham Estate)*

Holkham, an aerial view of the house and park. *(By kind permission of the Trustees of the Holkham Estate)*

both sexes with pleasure. These houses are well, and often richly furnished, and every device for exciting the senses is either at hand or can be provided. Girls do not live there but they are fetched in [sedan] chairs when required. None but those who are specially attractive in all ways are so honoured, and for this reason they often send their address to a hundred of these bagnios in order to make themselves known. The English retain their solemnity even as regards their pleasures, and consequently the business of such a house is conducted with a seriousness and propriety which is hard to credit. All noise and uproar is banned here; no loud footsteps are heard, every corner is carpeted and the numerous attendants speak quietly among themselves. These pleasures are very expensive, but in spite of this many houses of the kind are full every night.[26]

It was to be expected that when Giacomo Casanova visited London in mid-century he should make the acquaintance of such establishments: 'I also visited the bagnios, where a rich man can sup, bathe and sleep with a fashionable courtesan, of which species there are many in London. It makes a magnificent debauch and only costs six guineas.'[27]

Edward Coke was 19 when his elder brother arranged for his rites of passage to be conveniently and discreetly celebrated, and it was common practice that any minor expenses incurred would be dealt with by their body servants, while they themselves settled up with the reigning madam. Coke's friend Lord Chesterfield, who, in Dr Johnson's opinion, had the morals of a whore and the manners of a dancing master, would not have raised an eyebrow. He informed his son that liaisons were part of a young man's education and desirable as long as they were conducted with decorum.[28]

Sir Charles Hanbury Williams, who was later to become His Majesty's Minister to the Court of Frederick the Great, had an unenviable reputation as 'an odious man, a busybody and a gossip',[29] but he was an adept at summary character sketches, using them to point up his vignettes of contemporary society. In *Isabella: Or the Morning* the characters include Coke (Lord Lovel), General Charles Churchill and Philip Dormer Stanhope (Lord Chesterfield).[30] In the 'Argument': 'The whole company roused by Lord L[ove]l's coming into the room – His character – He talks of the Opera, of Ch[esterfie]ld and Fanny [Lady F.Sk-y] – Lady Fanny's looks awing to love.' Later, the two old roués Churchill and Chesterfield are paying court to the Duchess when:

Into the room see sweating L——l break,
The D[utches]s rises, and the Elders wake:
L——l, the oddest character in town;
A lover, statesman, connoisseur, buffoon:
Extract him well, this is his quintessence,
Much folly, but more cunning, and some sense;
To neither party is his heart inclin'd,
He steer'd through both, with politicks refin'd;
Voted with Walpole, and with Pultney din'd.
His lordship makes a bow, and takes his seat,
Then opens with preliminary chat;
'I am glad to see your Grace – the Gen'ral too –
Old Charles, how is it! Dicky! how d'ye do?
Madam, I hear that you was at the play,
You did not say one word on't yesterday;
I went, who'd no engagement, any share,
To th'opera – Were there many people there?'
The Dutchess cry'd:– 'Yes, Madam, a great many,'
Says Lovel – 'There was Ch[esterfiel]d and Fanny.
In that eternal whisper, which begun
Ten years ago, and never will be done;
For tho' you know he sees her evr'y day,
Still he has ever something new to say;
There's nothing upon earth so hard to me,
As keeping up discourse eternally;
He never lets the conversation fall,
And I'm sure Fanny can't keep up the the ball;
I saw that her replies were never long,
And with her eyes, she answer'd for her tongue,
Poor I, am forc'd to keep my distance now,
She won't ev'n curt'sy if I make a bow.'
'Why, things are strangely chang'd,' the Gen'ral cry'd;
'Ay, *Fortune de la guerre*,' my lord reply'd:
'But you and I, Charles hardly find things so,
As we both did some twenty years ago.'
'And take off twenty years,' reply'd her Grace,
'Twould do no harm to Lady Fanny's face;

My Lord, you never see her but at night,
By th' advantageous help of candle-light:
Drest out with every aid that is adorning,
Oh, if your Lordship saw her in a morning!
It is no more than Fanny once so fair;
No roses bloom, no lilies flourish there:
But hollow eyes, and pale and faded cheek,
Repentance, love and disappointment speak.'
The General found a lucky minute now
To speak – 'Ah, Ma'am you did not know Miss How'
I'll tell you all her history, he cry'd -
at this Charles S[tanhop]e gap'd extremely wide;
Poor Dicky sat on thorns; her Grace turn'd pale,
And L[ove]l trembl'd at th' impending tale.

The scene closes with:

Home to his dinner St[anho]pe goes alone:
Dicky to fast with her, her Grace invites,
and L[ove]l's coachman drives unbid to White's.

Allowing for artistic licence and the need to entertain, Hanbury Williams
sheds an interesting light on Thomas Coke and the company he kept. His
enthusiasm for opera needs no emphasis, but here it is caught up with his
liaison with Fanny, shared, it would seem, with Churchill for twenty years.
And then there is his fear that Churchill might embarrass them all with the
history of a Miss How. 'Sweating Lovel' charging into the room suggests both
energy and intemperance, and when at length the party breaks up, Coke's
coachman knows without asking that his master intends to gamble at
White's. His nature was to be loud and rumbustious in company, which
Hanbury Williams catches in these lines:[31]

Unless perchance Earl Leicester comes,
As noisy as a dozen drums.
An makes a horrid pother,
Else might we quiet sit and quaff,
And Gently chat, and gayly laugh
At this, at that, and t'other.

Much later in his life, Horace Walpole described him as 'a very cunning man but not a deep one. He affected frankness and a noisy kind of buffoonery, both to disguise his art, and his superficial understanding.'[32] But Walpole was often acidulous and, as a gossipy friend of Coke's estranged daughter-in-law Lady Mary, was not unbiased.

Coke's enthusiasm for Holkham is used as a peg on which to hang a political squib: *An Epistle from Lord L[ove]l to Lord C[hesterfiel]d. by Mr P[ulteney].*[33] (This is generally credited to Hanbury Williams, but the Cambridge University Library copy has the note: 'Said to be writ by Mr Pulteney'.)

I

O Holkham! blest, belov'd abode!
Productive of an Annual Ode,
If C[hesterfiel]d inspire:
Clio and I will club for Wit,
Beneath the spreading Oak we'll sit,
And thrumb the Lyrick Lyre.

II

How beauteous is this rural Scene!
With constant Verdure ever green,
How healthy, gay and pleasant!
A clean, tho' an ungrateful Soil,
Rewarding well the Sportsman's Toil;
With Partridges and Pheasant.

The fourth stanza comes to the point: his opposition to current government policy and, incidentally, his political neutrality:

IV

But hold! to Love I bid adieu,
A greater Theme is now in view,
I feel my Country's Ruin:
Next Winter I'll resign my Place,
No longer share the sad Disgrace,
And blush for what is doing.

V

The Cries of an insulted Land,
Redress of Injuries demand.
Let's out for *England's* Glory!
I'm ready to take part with you,
And am become a Patriot too,
But neither Wig nor Tory.

The final verse addresses Coke partiality for the Prime Minister but not his brother Horace's conduct of foreign affairs:

X

This Boon alone, my Lord, I crave,
Many will join us, do but save,
One single Sinner for us:
Grant for our sakes this only Job,
Some Mercy show our old Friend *B[o]b*,
Do what you will with *H[orac]e*.

This may not be an accurate assessment of Coke's political stance and he was, of course, much too aware of the value of 'place' to resign his Postmaster-Generalship. Nevertheless, as a contemporary thumbnail sketch it deepens our perception of this complicated character who 'steer'd through both [parties] with politicks refin'd'.

In the earlier piece it was, perhaps, an exaggeration to say that Coke inclined to neither party, for he was never less than an old-style Whig, and in any case Walpole and Pulteney were notorious for reviling each other across the floor of the Commons and then carousing together in the small hours. However, there is a passage in the Egmont diaries that has a bearing on Coke's approach to politics:

29th January, 1729–30.
This morning Mr Capel Moore came to see me, and made me smile at a story touching my Lord Lovel (Mr Cook [*sic*] of Norfolk that was made a Baron when this King came to the Crown). My Lord, coming up to town against the meeting of Parliament, told the Earl of Chesterfield that now he was come he did not know how to vote. 'Why, with the Court, to be

sure,' replied the Earl. 'Aye, but', said Lovel, 'the Court is so divided that I don't know which way it leans. There are', said he, 'in it a country party, a Spanish party, and a French party.' 'If you are under a difficulty', replied the Earl, 'go to Sir Robert Walpole; he will direct you.' Says Lovel, 'If I vote with the court, I expect to be paid for it.' 'How paid?' said Chesterfield. 'Why', the other replied, 'I have an estate sufficient for an Earl or a Viscount at least, and I shall expect to be made one of them.' 'That', replied Chesterfield, 'is impossible; it is asking a thing the King cannot do.' Lovel replied, 'He did not understand him, that the King had made him a Baron two year ago, and might make a Viscount if he pleased, for he was the fountain of honour and nothing tied up his hands. To say there that it was impossible implied something he did not comprehend, and he must insist to know his lordship's meaning.' 'Why, if you will have it,' replied the Earl, 'it is a maxim of our law that the King can do no wrong.' Which said, he left my Lord Lovel to digest it as well as he could.[34]

To evaluate this high-quality gossip (leaving aside its passage through a third party before reaching the page), one or two points should be borne in mind. Lord Egmont was no friend of Lord Lovel, and, apart from circulating a number of scandalous reports about his marriage, he entered into an acrimonious tussle with him in the 1730s over Harwich and its MP when Lovel, as Postmaster-General, controlled the packet service at the port. What it does do, however, is confirm Thomas Coke's ambivalent attitude to politics. Unlike his ancestor the Chief Justice, or Coke of Norfolk, his eventual successor at Holkham, he was not by nature a political animal. He might be said to be a fair example in this context of an eighteenth-century placeman, using the advantages that came his way through his political position to further his own particular interests.

A counter to that generalisation is perhaps to be found in his response to a political cause célèbre in 1722. Habeas Corpus had been suspended and Jacobite plots were again in the air. Christopher Layer, 'the only militant Jacobite whom Norfolk produced . . . [was] a broken-down lawyer who . . . thrust himself into the hesitating councils of the Jacobite leaders and planned a conspiracy of unexampled futility'.[35] There were several interlinking plots involving Francis Atterbury, Bishop of Rochester, among others, and Layer's contribution was a plan to assassinate the King at Kensington Palace.

Atterbury was arrested in August 1722, sentenced to deprivation and exile, and Layer was charged with high treason and came to trial at the Bar of the King's Bench in the following November. There was intense public interest, and, for that reason, it is not surprising to find an entry in the household accounts showing that an earnest of a guinea was paid for seven places at his trial. There was, however, a particular reason why Thomas Coke wished to follow the proceedings. Back in Norfolk, Layer's uncle, another Christopher Layer, who had chosen the young Jacobite as his heir and had seen to his education, was now in low circumstances and was lodging with Will Pickford the huntsman at Beck Hall, Billingford, the base for Coke's hunting activities. Renowned as a breeder of hounds, he had sold some of them to Coke and in 1719 was given a gratuity of £80 for his foxhounds. In London, his nephew stood trial on 21 November before the Lord Chief Justice, and the jury took but half an hour to find him guilty. After a week's adjournment, he was sentenced to be hung, drawn and quartered, and, despite further attempts to extract more information and harassed by seven postponements, he was executed at Tyburn and his head impaled at Temple Bar – the only one of the conspirators to lose his life.[36] Thomas Coke, however, continued to support the elder Christopher with board and lodging, gifts of a horse, a suit of clothes and even a perriwig, and finally saw that he was decently buried at Holkham when he died in 1726. This episode surely shows that Coke's nature, both in politics and religion, was extremely flexible. Despite the prevailing public hysteria over Jacobite plots, he was not afraid to support a man whose heir had been executed as an enemy of the state and who had consorted with papists.

A number of references have been made elsewhere in these pages to Thomas Coke's generosity, and it is worth considering this aspect of his character a little more closely as it is evidenced in the accounts. As a Bloomsbury resident he subscribed regularly to the Charity School of St Giles's, and, when the new church of St George's Hanover Square was consecrated within his parish in 1725, he responded to charitable appeals, such as the one made in 1728 for the relief of sufferers by fire. Overall charitable giving can be assessed by looking at summaries of expenditure in various places – for 1719 the total was £351 6s 2d, and for the Michaelmas quarter of 1720 it was £60 1s 6d, but the human interest lies in the dozens of individual cases scattered through the pages. For example, a group of poor people in a neighbouring London parish were helped:

	s	d
A Charity Gift to Abigail Reed of St Andrews	10	6
Do. to Eliz. Quinter and her Children, of Ditto	10	6
Do. to Mary Lightfoot of the same	5	0
Do. to Eliz. Williams of the same Parish	5	0
Do. to Eliz. Wilkinson and her two children in Mark Lane at the Bell and Castle	10	6

The individual acts of charity continue with Mr Burgis, who was burned out of the Swan Inn, Holborn Ditch and was given three guineas; Mr Foxton, 'who is poor and in trouble', received £10; Betty Dean was given a guinea and then two more 'because she was ill of a Rheumatis'; £3 6s went to 'Mr Whimprey's poor family at the Mint'; 'A poor man that had his tongue cut out' was given a guinea, and at the same time 'Old Bridget' had half a guinea; en route to Hothfield, Coke paused at Southwark to give money to prisoners, and many times on the road the poor people at the coach door benefited.

The pattern when Coke was at Holkham was not dissimilar. In 1727 'To Mr Summerscales his Honour's Charity for instructing Poor Children at Castleacre £5'. In 1719 £20 had been given 'to poor people in distress this year', and £14 11s 'was left to be distributed to ye poor when my Master went away'; in addition, during the Christmas season, five bushels of wheat and over thirty stone of beef were distributed to the Holkham poor. In 1725 'a poor Spanier' (possibly a shipwrecked sailor) was presented with two new shirts and a pair of breeches, and two years later half a guinea was given to 'two poor slaves', who were probably seamen who had been captured by the Moors and held in slavery. At that time, when the majority of cottages were thatched, fire was a constant menace, and the only relief available to the poor who were made homeless thereby was either through a brief distributed to churches in the county and read from the pulpit, or by personal appeal to local gentry. Ralph Diggs of Burnham chose the latter course and was given a guinea in charity. Thomas was often over at Holt on business or pleasure and one would have expected him to contribute to the rebuilding of the church with a handsome twenty guineas – the only surprise is that it was fifteen years after the disastrous town fire of 1708. A few old family servants were in receipt of annuities in the 1720s: Longstreth had £20 a year, Richard Pullin £15 a year, and at Holkham James Palmer received £1 6s a quarter 'charity money' in 1727. Fourteen years after his father's death, Coke thought it right to give a guinea each to Edward Coke's old coachman and groom.

There is often no way of telling whether payments were made as a result of personal contact or suggestions from senior servants, but many entries embody the phrase 'by His Honour's (or my Master's) order'. On one occasion a gift of two guineas went by way of the Revd Mr Batchelor 'to a very poor man, a housekeeper in St Giles'. Occasionally, servants are named as the contact: 'To a poor man by Aram (the Holkham gardener) 2s.6d.'; 'To a poor man att Krick [Creake] by Robert Webster (a groom) 1s.'. During the years following his return from the Grand Tour, Coke sent presents on a number of occasions to friends in Italy, and in 1720 he spent £80 on watches and snuffboxes for this purpose.

Set against the totality of his wealth, the sums may appear insignificant, but for most of the 1720s Coke was desperately short of ready money and deep in debt. Nevertheless, the picture emerges of a man whose benevolence prompted him to forgive debts (as he did with his former steward, Humphrey Smith), to soften hard bargains, and to have a care for those on the fringes of society, to whom a shilling and a shirt meant food in place of hunger and warmth instead of cold.

Georgian England was 'a society in which disagreements over how best to worship God and seek salvation, how to organise the Church and the relationship between church and state, were matters of urgent concern'.[37] It was an age in which religion was a social obligation as well as a personal experience, and, at all levels, a key determinant in social identification; throughout the 1720s there is ample evidence that Thomas Coke conformed to the expected norms of a practising member of the Established Church. He had the patronage of a number of Anglican livings; the Holkham vicar the Revd Springall received ten guineas a quarter for reading prayers at the house, while Mr Batchelor had twelve guineas for a similar service in town, and Coke attended his parish church regularly both in town and in the country. Once again, however, his personal behaviour was by no means typical. Some of his close friends were Roman Catholics, and, in particular, he maintained a lifelong connection with the Bedingfeld family in Norfolk who had suffered grievously as recusants in the seventeenth century. This could, however, be seen merely as a continuation of a familial link, in that Sir Edward Coke the Chief Justice's wife Bridget was the daughter of Ann

Bedingfeld by her first husband, John Paston. At the opposite end of the sectarian spectrum, there is no evidence that he evinced any animus towards the strong nonconformist element in the county, and the Whig party that he stoutly supported had always been traditionally associated with Dissenters. Throughout his whole character there ran a thread of difference and of the unexpected, and in his reactions to the conventions of his time he might well have adopted the injunction so often proclaimed by his successor, Coke of Norfolk, 'Live and let live.'

Later in life Thomas admitted that Holkham could be depressing. Writing a largely sympathetic letter to his estranged daughter-in-law, Lady Mary Coke, in 1747 he concluded: 'I wish I could say any thing entertaining from this lonely place . . . but I only converse with trees.'[38] Not long before he died he was seen by an acquaintance gloomily surveying the scene at Holkham and complaining that he had 'eaten up all his neighbours' so that the nearest was the King of Denmark. Having by that time lost his only son and not enjoying the best of health, he had, perhaps, reason to be cast down, but it should not be taken as a measure of his character. Ketton-Cremer's thumbnail sketch lists his qualities: 'His geniality, his love of sport, his hospitable and convivial manner of life blended agreeably with an enthusiasm for classical learning and a devotion to the most rigid standards of Palladian architecture.'[39] Towards the end of his life, however, Coke described himself to George Townshend as 'grown quite unwieldy and unfit . . . by a long, lazy and inactive life . . . an old fellow retired from the world who cannot even without great fatigue visit his friends': in view of the fact that he was politely declining to accept a duelling challenge, there was more than an ounce of special pleading in this statement, but in 1757, just two years before he died, to his guest Admiral Boscowen he was still 'the fat, laughing, joking peer' whose hospitality delighted all his friends, to whom he was known as 'Trot'. A dispassionate assessment might see him as a man of his time as far as venial faults were concerned, gregarious and enlivened by a measure of eccentricity, and blessed with a generous nature. But overriding any other quality, here was a man of taste amounting to genius.

Chapter 8

THE ARTS, CULTURE AND TASTE

he first half of the eighteenth century was a time when the arts (and music in particular) flourished in Europe. Taking their lead from Versailles and aiming to emulate its splendours, princely courts established music as an important indicator of taste, and most of them had their own orchestras, or at least groups of musicians under the leadership of professionals. From 1717 to 1723, before moving to Leipzig, Johann Sebastian Bach was Kapellmeister to Prince Leopold of Anhalt-Cöthen (who was himself a gifted musician). Handel had beeen Kapellmeister to George I in Hanover before coming to England in 1711, and many of the royal or noble families enjoyed making music themselves, commonly assisted by professionals.

There was, however, a significant difference between the European situation and the position in England. In the former, all the initiatives stemmed from the various courts, and musical life was concentrated within very small coteries, whereas in England, royal patronage was nominal and it was upper- and middle-class society that encouraged and sustained musical life. Lord Burlington, for example, invited Handel to live in his house within

two years of the composer's arrival in London. A determining factor in this
was the relative size of capital cities. With its population of half a million in
1700, London was five times the size of Vienna (at that time the largest city
on the Continent) and it was ten times bigger than all the rest. Its character,
too, was markedly different in that it had a public sphere that was much
larger and more powerful than that of other cities; it had very little
bureaucracy, and enjoyed a relative social and political stability that was a
matter of envy and remark.[1] In provincial England, society at large took its
lead from London. Norwich, with its 26,000 inhabitants, was the second city
in the kingdom and had begun to be active musically. The City Waits had
been giving monthly concerts since 1714, and ten years later there was
sufficient interest to warrant weekly musical meetings, even though the scale
was more modest, the musicians less eminent and the audience less
sophisticated than in the metropolis. A little later, works by Corelli, Alberti
and Vivaldi were being performed by 'the best masters from Norwich' in the
Great Hall at Yarmouth, and Henry Crossgrove, printer of the *Norwich
Gazette*, had been advertising music for sale in his paper for some time.[2]

Thomas Coke's musical interests and ability blossomed early, as evidenced
by entries in his servant Edward Jarrett's accounts kept on the Grand Tour.
They show that he went often to the opera, and, in a letter to his governors
from Aix in September 1713,[3] his tutor Dr Hobart told them that the boy
took lessons twice a day on the flute. He often bought or hired musical
instruments, and on 30 April 1716 in an excess of enthusiasm three
harpsichords were acquired in the one day. Apart from his own appreciation
he will have seen, through his continuing contacts with royal and noble
society, the social kudos earned by musical activity, and soon after his return
to England he became directly involved in the musical life of fashionable
London. As one of a group of prominent noblemen, politicians and leaders of
London society, Coke was one of the first subscribers to the Royal Academy of
Music, established to create a suitably staged annual season of opera at the
King's Theatre in the Haymarket, which had been designed by Vanbrugh and
opened in 1705. The Academy was founded in 1719 specifically to support
Italian opera, and, although royal support was not on a European scale, the
venture attracted an annual subsidy of £1,000 for its first five years and was
granted a royal charter. It was financed as a joint-stock company, each
subscriber funding at least £200 of stock. The Duke of Newcastle as Lord
Chamberlain, the Duke of Chandos and Lord Burlington led with £1,000

each, and the initial proposal claimed that 'Opera's [sic] are the most harmless of all publick Diversions. They are an Encouragement and Support to an Art that has been cherished by all Polite Nations.' Heidigger, the Swiss impresario, imported the principal singers and staged masquerades at the Haymarket when as many as 700 members of the public came in costume (including the Cokes).[4] It was a neat demonstration of the mixed nature of London's cultural scene, partly royal, partly aristocratic and partly commercial – a couple of dozen peers combining with the gentry, intent on turning in a profit for the venture's shareholders. It came to dominate the capital's social life during the reign of George I and the first years of George II, although, given the cost of admission and the limited capacity of the theatre, its effect on the general public's aesthetic awareness must have been marginal. Most support came from the gentry in the 'season' (roughly October to March), with lower-class audiences adding support at Christmas and Easter. During most of the eighteenth century Tuesdays and Saturdays were 'opera nights'.[5]

Nevertheless, the contemporary view is nicely illustrated in John Gay's letter to Jonathan Swift of 1723:

> As for the reigning amusement of the town, it is entirely music . . . Everybody is grown now as great a judge of music, as they were in your time of poetry, and folks, that could not distinguish one tune from another, now daily dispute about the different styles of Handel, Bononcini, and Attilio. People have now forgot Homer and Virgil and Cæsar, or at least, they have lost their ranks: for, in London and Westminster, in all polite conversations, Senesino [the leading Italian castrato] is daily voted to be the greatest man that ever lived.[6]

The craze for guest singers, particularly from Italy, had encouraged them to make exorbitant demands, for, while a named actor's average salary was under £100, the castrato Cassani secured a three-year contract of £800 a year in the early days.[7]

Opera in the Italian style was the current overriding enthusiasm; accordingly, the Academy's first production in 1720 was Giovannis Porta's *Numitore*, followed swiftly by Handel's *Radamisto*, dedicated to the King and received with tremendous enthusiasm, with a joint appearance in the royal box signifying the end of the rift between the King and the Prince of Wales.

Within a year the King's Theatre had Handel and Bononcini as resident composers, and the virtuoso cellist Filippo Amadei was playing in the orchestra.[8] For most of the 1720s London was the operatic capital of Europe, with the finest artistes, composers and designers of sets and costumes. Increasingly, virtuoso solo singing, usually in the soprano and alto voice ranges, together with colourful costumes and elaborate scenery, became the chief attraction for visitors to the opera. The Academy did, however, enter troubled waters in 1726. In the production of Handel's new opera *Alessandro*, the patrons decided to challenge the reigning prima donna Francesca Cuzzoni with a rival, the Venetian soprano Faustina Bordoni. This led to the two divas eventually coming to blows on the stage in the presence of the Prince of Wales in the following year – a diversion that delighted the audience, but that brought the season to a close, attracting general ridicule.

The fracas heralded the end of a chapter in London's musical history. A contemporary comment ran, 'The subscription is expired and nobody will renew it', and the Royal Academy of Music closed on 1 June 1728. Towards the end there was a general reluctance to meet mounting production costs, and the outstanding success in 1728 of Gay's *Beggar's Opera* in the ballad-opera form confirmed a decisive change in public taste and, indeed, in the character of the audience itself, which had broadened its social base. A letter Coke wrote to Lord Burlington in 1736 shows that, while public taste had changed to opera's detriment, his enthusiasm was undiminished: 'I am sorry to hear operas do so badly – you know as a virtuoso I encourage both, and have subscribed to Hendell [Handel's success in the oratorio medium was in the ascendant] for which I have been severely reprimanded by my brethren.'[9] Throughout its short existence, he regularly paid his dues to the Academy's deputy treasurer, Mr Kipling (the first of 5 per cent for £300 and later at 10 per cent), and he was a steady patron of the opera, paying half a guinea a ticket. He sometimes treated his servants to a performance, as when Mrs Thompson and three companions went by coach to see the opera *Narcissus* in June 1720, having been given 3s 3d tickets. On his first visit to London as land steward in May 1722, George Appleyard went to a performance with John Casey, the house steward, using 6s 6d tickets. By the end of the Academy's life prices had risen significantly, with patrons' seats costing £1 6s and servants' places half a guinea. Handbills advertising coming productions were delivered to Thanet House, and John Tompkins, the bill-sticker, found a place on the Christmas box list in company with the opera house box-keepers.

In 1720 one of Signor Castrucci's performances was obviously appreciated by Coke, who ordered him to be given five guineas.

The accounts provide plenty of evidence to show that there was sustained musical activity within the family setting. Harpsichords and spinets were tuned and repaired regularly by Mr Locton and Mr Colson [or Coston], and Mr Rosincroft [or Roseingrave], 'the Spinet Master', received a six-guinea gratuity in 1719. Mr Cortivril, a music master, was paid a guinea for tuition during the same year, and another music master was a Mr Smith, who was paid £9 10s for 'writing the singers and instrument parts of an opera'. It was probably for this work that four violins, a lute, a bass and two tenors were hired 'for an opera rehearsal' soon after, and 'Mrs Robinson the singing woman' who received two guineas may have taken part as well. The following year Monsieur Siris earned £7 1s for three months' tuition in dancing and the hautboy: the combination suggests that it was either Thomas or Lady Margaret who was under instruction.

Two things can be suggested as evidence that there was corporate music making in the household. First are the entries in the accounts for the purchase of instruments. In 1719, soon after they had established themselves at Thanet House, the Cokes bought six violins, three hautboys, a bassoon, a base, a lute and two tenor horns for a total of twenty-two guineas. The following year a French horn came from Mr Harris, and in 1722 three more French horns with silver mouthpieces costing £9 were bought from Christian Bennet (who mended two others); four guineas were spent on two more violins and a dance book, another hautboy and a curtall (an early form of bassoon). The second clue that points to chamber music being played at home is the fact that in 1723 and 1724 five guineas were spent on the footman Philip Bender being taught to play the French horn. Similarly, Jerry Somering, a fellow footman, had a violin bought for him in 1727. Few were able to match the Duke of Chandos's resident orchestra, but it was not uncommon for fashionable households to enrol servants in forming musical ensembles, and the ability to play an instrument was sometimes a factor in selecting staff. The genteel enjoyment of music was very much in fashion, and in 1721 Coke chose to pay a Mr Liniker 7s 6d for writing three songs 'out of ye Saranatta' so that he might present them to Lady Cartwright, and a Mr Smith was paid for writing out an overture. Even when at Holkham there was music-making where Mr Barlow, the spinet master, was employed, and 'the Linn music' were given two guineas when they visited at Christmas

1719. Corby, the Norfolk fiddler, received half a guinea in 1721, and in 1728 an itinerant German got the same for entertaining the company on the French horn. The chamber music that the family will have enjoyed in town would still attract an audience today. Francesco Germiniani, the Italian composer and virtuoso violinist, came to England in 1714 and was an immediate success, staying until his death in 1726. His earliest concertos were arrangements of Arcangelo Corelli's celebrated sonatas, which were printed in 1726, and, with Vivaldi's music being published and sold across Europe, the Italians led in both style and form. Germiniani performed more in the houses of the wealthy than in public, often taking the difficult solo parts in concert with amateurs, and, remembering that Coke's close friend Lady Burlington was his patron, it is at least possible that Thomas played in his company.

Coke's parents had been keen theatregoers and his mother had collected a fine series of seventeenth-century plays, which are now in the Bodleian Library. It is no surprise, therefore, to find him patronising the two London theatres. During the 1720s there was constant rivalry between Drury Lane and the Lincolns-Inn-Fields theatre (commonly called the New House) – the latter was facing bankruptcy in 1722 when it took on *Marianne*, a tragedy by Elijah Fenton, which Drury Lane had rejected. The play was a huge success, and the ploy was repeated when John Rich, the manager, chose to produce *The London Cuckolds* for the Lord Mayor's Show day. Drury Lane had dropped 'that scandalous piece and the roughest piece of bawdy going', but the apprentices were delighted to see it on their main holiday of the year, and it was repeated for decades. Unlike their approach to opera, the playgoing tastes of the nobility in general were not noticeably different from those of the lower classes, whose sports and diversions they often shared; but their motives often differed. In 1741 a playgoer said that 'he always took it that people only came there to see and be seen – for as to what was said, he owned, he never understood anything of the matter, and no fashionable people dare shew their faces until they have seen it [the latest play]'.[10] During the mid-1720s both theatres relished the new craze for pantomime, starting with *The Necromancer* at Lincolns-Inn-Fields, a piece that was elaborate, expensive and spectacular and appeared on forty-six of sixty-six bills between November 1723 and March 1724. At Drury Lane, *Harlequin Dr Faustus* was played thirty-five times in the same season, and a comment in *Mist's Weekly Journal* confirmed the public's reaction: 'It is of the nature of pantomime, partly grotesque and partly vocal, but far exceeds all ever yet shewn, in the magnificence and beauty of the scenes, the number and richness of the habits, as well as the fable, which is purely poetical, as the Italian opera ought to be.' The mid-1720s represented a kind of watershed in taste in that two changes were taking place: the appeal to the intellect was being overtaken by spectacle – eyes and ears rather than brain – and there was a sharp increase in the number of theatregoers.[11] Here is John Rich defending pantomime against opera:

> But look at recent attempts to establish grand opera. The subscription system is at best a temporary expedient and has proved ineffective since, with all available funds going to imported singers, it does not provide support for the requisite scenic display. At the critical juncture pantomime comes forward with the missing ingredients, to offer a more nearly balanced diet of drama, music and scenery and, incidentally, to solve the financial problem left by the failure of the device of subscription.[12]

The success of the new form culminated in Rich's production of John Gay's *The Beggar's Opera* at Lincolns-Inn-Fields in 1728. The Duke of Argyll was at the first night, and, before the first act was over, Pope and Swift heard him say 'It will do! It must do!' The Duke, they said, had an infallible knack of knowing, better than anyone living, the taste of the public. Even the aristocracy deserted the Old House and the opera for it.

In discussing Thomas Coke's enthusiasm for the stage there is some danger of confusion over names. A contemporary of his was Sir Thomas Coke, a Derbyshire MP who was the Lord Chamberlain, and as such was responsible for licensing all plays.[13] He was not related to our Thomas and neither was Thomas Cooke, a dramatist of the day and author of *Mournful Nuptuals* (1739).

Handbills from both theatres were delivered to Thanet House, and the way in which Coke distributed his vails shows that he patronised both theatres equally, with the recipients being named in the accounts. The Drury Lane box-keepers were Messrs Nayler, King and Mills, with Trot, Wilmer, Lovelace and Taylor at Lincolns-Inn-Fields. The average gift was a guinea, but Thomas Naylor was given five guineas on one occasion in 1720 and two guineas in 1722. Plays seldom achieved a run of more than a few days, and so individual actors depended heavily on benefit nights. Average ticket prices in the 1720s were five shillings for boxes, three for the Pit, two for the Middle Gallery, and one for the Upper Gallery. Coke usually paid eight shillings for his box, but there was a two-shilling surcharge for special productions and for benefits. He was sometimes minded to give more, as in May 1721, when he gave an extra half guinea 'to a French Comedian on his Benefit night'. Punks and whores figure casually in many dramatic prologues, and the late-seventeenth-century 'ladies of Drury' were still part of the theatrical experience. Nor was there always a good example set by their betters, with young bloods often insisting on sitting on the stage; in 1718 three gentlemen were denied access behind the scenes, 'whereupon they went into the pit & pelted the cast with apples and went on stage with drawn swords & broke down the sconces which put the house in an uproar'.[14] A contemporary description gives the normal audience distribution: 'Boxes – royals & persons of quality; Pit – wits, censors, squires, beaus, bullies, whores; Middle Gallery – citizens' wives & daughters, serving-men, journeymen, apprentices; Upper Gallery – footmen, coachmen & the like'. From about 1700 footmen were admitted free to the Upper Gallery for the fifth act, and later the Drury Lane manager let them in for the whole play. This was swiftly taken as a right rather than a privilege, and violence followed. A 1720s comment was: 'Almost every night this winter [the footmen] have made such an intolerable disturbance that the players could not be heard and their masters forc'd to hiss 'em into silence.' When Coke treated his servants, however, they would have used the Middle Gallery. Unlike the contemporary musical fare, most of the plays that Coke went to see are unlikely to be staged again, with the exception perhaps of some of the better Restoration comedies; but the hit of the eighteenth century, *The Beggar's Opera*, has lived on in popularity and has been revived in a variety of forms.

Much of Thomas Coke's time on his Grand Tour must have been concerned, however unconsciously, with the acquisition of beautiful and interesting things to grace the house he hoped to build. It may be assumed that from the very beginning he envisaged a mansion in Palladian style in which statuary, pictures, Old Master drawings and books would all find a place. In contrast with other young men of means who were touring Europe at that time, Coke was allowed an extremely generous allowance. Because he was a minor under the control of guardians, its level was determined in Chancery by the Master of the Rolls, who set the amount at £1,000 a year. That worthy's own grandson was allowed £400, and a few years earlier Ashe

Windham of Felbrigg had £600.[15] Despite that, two of the boy's letters to his grandfather in 1714 show that, in his delight and enthusiasm for all that he found and saw, he stretched his resources beyond their limit. From Rome in May he wrote:

> I am become since my stay at Rome a perfect virtuoso, & a great lover of pictures, even so far as to venture to incroach on the kindness of my guardians in having bought some few. I wrote last post to Sir Edw. and Mr Coke [his two other guardians] to desire a separate allowance for that purpose, but it would be too much taking upon me to trouble you with any such demand.

Four months later he was in Padua:

> In my last to you from Rome, I told you of my great love for pictures, I fear I have a little outrun in those I have bespoke, but being myself at Rome & seeing such a number of fine things, I must confess I trusted so much to my own life that I could not hinder myself from making free with more money than my allowance, & am afraid incroaching too much upon the good nature & kindness of my guardians. I wrote to Sir Ed. & Mr Coke to desire them if possible to gett the Chancery to indemnify my guardians for that & the other ill managements that I have made . . . I have left several pictures tho' marked down in my pockett book in case of conveniences of getting them when I come to age.

In the following January, when he was in Turin, he confesses to having the same difficulty over books, but the letter shows significantly that, even at 18, he had firm ideas about what he wanted and that he was making the selection himself:

> During my voiage round Italy I have bought several of the most valuable authors that have write [sic] in Italian or about the country, the reason that I incroach so far on your kindness to me & venter to put my guardians to that risk is, that if I miss'd the occasion of buying books while I am travelling, I should not be able to find several of the best of them, & it's impossible to buy them to my mind unless I myself am present, & certainly one of the greatest ornaments to a gentleman or his family is a fine library.[16]

During his six years abroad, with the help of Dr Hobart, his tutor, his friend William Kent, and Domenico Ferrari, who was to become his librarian, Coke steadily accumulated the beautiful, precious and deliciously exciting objets d'art that were to form one of England's finest collections. It was during his second visit to Rome in 1716 that he showed a particular interest in antique sculpture, and it was then that he drew particularly on the advice of Kent, who had many useful contacts among the artistic fraternity. Two of the most important acquisitions at this time were the statues of Diana and Lucius Antonius formerly belonging to the Congregazione dell'Arciconfraternità della Santa Annunziata.[17] When he eventually returned to England, the immediate concerns were his marriage and the settlement of the estate, but soon after, consignments began to arrive at the London docks from Italy and the Low Countries. For the next ten years the need was for a holding operation, and another twenty years passed before part of his great house was fit to receive the treasures he had garnered so enthusiastically.

The household accounts of the 1720s have many entries that deal with the Grand Tour acquisitions, and some are more illuminating than others. Individual pieces, paintings and books can occasionally be identified, but more often the references are in general terms – so many drawings or a bale of books being seen through customs, and there were a number of enquiries made at the Customs House about ships coming in with pictures and books. Decisions had to be made concerning storage, and, in the first instance, books, statuary and pictures were consigned to Thanet House in Bloomsbury or warehoused for the time being. The amount over a lengthy period was considerable, for Mr Gibson, who owned a convenient yard and storage facilities, was paid £20 a year, and later Gibson & Co. were allowed £105 'for their trouble in Mr Coke's affairs'. Thomas's personal case and other freight came home in the ship *Sea Nymph* from Leghorn (Livorno) and there was £23 2s to pay in clearing it through customs; another large consignment was shipped in the *Junior*, on which an even heavier charge was levied. There is one instance, in 1718, where a Mr Kinsey charged a fee of nine guineas for valuing three parcels of books and pictures, and this may have been a case where there was disagreement about the correct level of customs dues. Consignments sometimes went astray, and in 1720 Abraham Thomas, the valet-de-chambre, spent a great deal of time and 13 shillings in expenses before he was able to track down the ship that had a box of books on board destined for Thanet House. Mr Hays was paid for 'bringing home a Statue and two Heads' in June 1719, and in the following January the especially fine statue of Diana together with unidentified pictures was shipped to England by courtesy of the Royal Navy in HMS *Superb* under the care of Captain Masters; this was an example of the facilities that serving officers were prepared to offer to rich and influential travellers with the tacit approval of the Admiralty. The expenses of unloading from Woolwich and transport back to Thanet House came to £7 18s 6d, while customs duties and officers' fees came to another £12 8s. What became known as 'the Great Jupiter [or Jubiter] statue' had been purchased from Antonio Borioni in 1717. Exactly which deity it was designed to represent is not at all clear because the style was used indiscriminately for Zeus, Asculepius, Aries and Poseidon. Mrs Angelicoussis describes it as a deity of the Dresden Zeus type.[18] Be that as it may, it caused a certain amount of difficulty on arrival in London, possibly because of its size. In 1721 it was stored in Mr Badham's yard for 187 weeks at a cost of £21 14s 6d. Landing, wharfage and carpenter's work cost another ten guineas, with the carpenters having to strengthen the case, which was so rotten it would not bear being hoisted over the wharf. At the beginning of May, with the help of a Mr Palmer (and having treated him to dinner), the house steward had it brought to Thanet House on a cart. Mrs Angelicoussis believes that it was never displayed at Thanet House,[19] but an account entry for 16 May 1721 in Casey's book has: 'To Palmers men at ye rearing ye Statues upon end. 5s.', so the great statue was at least inspected, perhaps in the garden, if not placed on permanent show. Seven years later a sailcloth was purchased 'to cover Jubiter', reinforcing the suggestion that it was housed temporarily in the open air. It remained in London for at least a decade before being transferred to Holkham. The initial design for the Marble Hall envisaged it standing within the curves of a divided staircase leading up to the Saloon, but this plan was discarded in favour of the existing layout, so that the great statue never stood within the house and currently lies in pieces in the unroofed nineteenth-century orangery. In 1954 the head was removed and taken to the Conservation Department of the British Museum for restoration, and is now displayed in the Smoking Room below the South Portico. In 1728 the sculptor Baptist Guelfi was employed to repair statues, and in the following year a Mr Woodall made a pedestal and repaired another piece, but the accounts do not unfortunately give any idea which they were. Guelfi was at work for some time, being paid £20 initially, followed by a further £20 a month later, and received a final payment of £30.

The same situation obtains concerning pictures, with tantalising snippets of detail intermixed among vague descriptions. Some entries concern paintings that had been brought on the Grand Tour, while others obviously relate to London commissions, and yet others to pictures already in the possession of various members of the family. On 16 January 1719 there is an entry: 'Paid to Mr Hay[s] for the Large Claud Lorain. Charges Duties &c. on ye great Vandike Albano &c. £200'. The Claude bought from Mr Hays is likely to have been his celebrated *Apollo flaying Marsyas*, which now hangs by the fireplace in the South Drawing Room, and the Van Dyke is the equestrian portrait of the Duc d'Arenberg now in the Saloon, which was bought by Thomas Coke in Paris in 1718; 'the Albano' referred to a painting of the Holy Family by Francesco Albani, which is no longer in the house. At the same time, two animal pictures by Francisco Imperiale (now hung on the Chapel Wing landing) are mentioned, and a fruit piece by Gerard David came from Mr Hays for £30, together with an unidentified picture by Jo. Francisco Bulouis, which cost £52. Mr Walton of Somerset House was given two guineas for his care of 'the Great Picture' in March 1719, it having been brought from there to Thanet House in the previous April with a straining frame. There are sound reasons for believing that this entry refers to *The Vision of Aeneas in the Elysian Fields* by Sebastiano Conca, which now hangs above the stairs leading to the South Tribune in the Family Wing. 'It was in 1717, soon after he had seen Lake Avernus that the nineteen-year-old Thomas Coke commissioned a huge canvas of the Vision of Aeneas in the Elysian Fields, with himself as Virgil holding a lyre. This was evidently the choice of a classicist, but such scholars were quick to become connoisseurs.'[20] The picture measures some 10ft by 8ft, justifying its name as 'The Great Picture'. To the left-hand side, Virgil with his lyre sits surrounded by philosophers and astrologers, shepherds and maidens, all singing his bucolic poems. Although the canvas is dark with varnish, the face of Virgil strongly resembles Thomas Coke as he was portrayed by Francesco Trevisani. It was hung in the London house throughout the rest of Coke's life and came down to Holkham only in 1760. The young collector may well have acquired four drawings by Sebastiano Conca when he sat for the artist in Rome in 1717; they are all of classical subjects and are to be found in the Old Master Drawings Collection.[21] At the sale after his grandmother's death in 1722, Thomas bought in a number of things, including Sir Godfrey Kneller's portraits of his great-grandparents the Duke and Duchess of Leeds, which now hang in the State Sitting Room (the Duke is perhaps better known and remembered as 'the Great Danby', the powerful Tory earl who flourished under Charles II and fell from grace only to rise again and play a key role in the Revolution of 1688 and the reign of William and Mary). During 1722 a Signor Ignatius was commissioned to paint a portrait of Lady Margaret, which she gave to her sister Lady Harold, and, although this has not been traced, the portrait of her with her son Edward painted in 1727 by Jonathan Richardson hangs in the North State Bedroom. In the following year a packing case was made 'for his honr.s pictures & Lady's for Norf.' – an indication that pictures from both sides of the family were included in the collection that eventually graced the great house. Even in the first year of their marriage, pictures were being moved from Sir John Newton's house in Soho Square to Thanet House, so that it was an ongoing process of consolidation.

With a collection of pictures assembled over a period of a few years, there was a good deal to be done by way of restoration and framing. Apart from the work involved in receiving and forwarding pictures shipped in from the Continent, Mr Hays was paid for lining, mending and straining a number of them on to new frames. Additional straining frames were bought from Mr Howard, and a Mr Newbolt was paid ten guineas for mending and cleaning several pictures. There was a bill of £35 15s from Jackson, the frame maker, and Matthew Gosset [or Gloset] in the same trade made two large gilt frames for £35. Mr Vanstretton was paid for cleaning a number of pictures, and Mr Green presented a bill of four guineas for mending and cleaning others.[22]

During the time he was abroad Thomas Coke bought a great many Old Master drawings, of which 328 remain at Holkham.[23] Several were purchased directly from the artists themselves, notably Benedici Luti, Guiseppe Chiari, Andrea Procaccini and Francesco Trevisani. Many relate to buildings and pictures that Coke himself had seen, and in some cases they are linked directly to pictures he had purchased, such as the preliminary sketch in black ink and chalk on blue paper for Luigi Garzi's *Cincinattus recalled from the Plough*, hung now in the Chapel Wing first floor drawing room;[24] another example, which is inscribed 'Claudio fecit Roma 1671', is the study, in ink and brown wash over black chalk, for the nymphs at the centre of Claude's *Coast view with Perseus and the Origin of Coral*, which now hangs on the east wall of the Landscape Room.[25] Although its artistic ranking is not high, one of the most interesting drawings has two tiny figures gazing up at the immense reredos behind the high altar in the church of the Gesù in Rome – they are young Thomas with his tutor Dr Hobart.[26]

Coke was very active in this field on the Grand Tour between 1714 and 1716 in all the major Italian cities, making good use of William Kent and Andrew Hay as his agents. Ten years after the return to England, drawings were still arriving, although they are likely to have been selected by agents in Italy or elsewhere rather than the residue of his own selections. In the late 1740s more examples were obtained from the painter-cum-dealer Gavin Hamilton in Rome, where he was one of a coterie that included Matthew Brettingham (senior), Coke's master builder at Holkham. The collection was still growing in the Earl's last years and a few drawings were even added by the Dowager after his death in 1759. In our period, the accounts refer briefly to the drawings in a few places, as in 1721, when it was noted that customs dues of 11s 6d and freightage of 16s 8d had been paid to John Oxenford the Customs House Officer when a case of books and prints arrived on the ship *Ruby*. Oxenford was slipped a further guinea for his trouble and continued to be sweetened with tips over the next few years as more goods came in. In 1728 £1 5s 6d was paid in duty on 307 drawings on paper, plus half-a-crown for the land waiter, another for the Customs Officer Mr Emerson, a shilling for the warehouse keeper and three shillings for porters and the house steward's expenses. Some of the drawings had been mounted in Rome, but the majority, once they had been unpacked, had to be mounted and stored. It was not long before a Monsieur Pellitere (Pelletier, Palletire, Pellitiers) was spending a lot of time 'pasting drawings'; in 1719 he mounted well over a hundred drawings – and it was an expensive business, a typical charge being four guineas for mounting fourteen drawings. He appears to have been a dealer as well, selling some to Coke and also providing three portfolios in which to house them; in 1722 he charged £25 for 'designs', but there is no clue as to their subject.

A few of the manuscripts that arrived in these early years are easily recognised, such as the Leonardo manuscript that was to become known as the 'Codex Leicester' and that became the property of Mr William (Bill) Gates. One of the early arrivals in 1719 was William Dempster's *Etruria Regale*; it was the first serious attempt to explore the history of the Etruscans and had been bought in Florence for eleven guineas in 1717 from Professor Salvini. It is now Holkham MS 501, and with it may be found not only the subsequent printed edition dedicated to Coke but also the original drawings for many of the illustrations with their copper plates. In that same year a consignment of manuscripts arrived from Hamburg on the *Golden Hart*, but, like the majority of shipments, no details are given concerning the contents.

Books came in bales, boxes and parcels from a number of north European and Italian ports – Calais, Hamburg, Amsterdam, Leghorn – and an example of the routine at the wharf is worth quoting from the steward's account book of 1728:

	£	s	d
My passage by water to ye ship twice to make an entry of ye books	0	1	0
The freight and primage [the customary allowance to the master and crew for the loading and care of the cargo]	0	13	0
The office and a boat	0	3	0
Entry and Duty in ye Long Room	0	9	6
The Land Waiter	0	2	6
Porterage to and fro the warehouse	0	2	0
Mr Emerson ye Searcher	0	1	0
The warehouse keeper	0	1	0
A coach home with Do.	0	2	0
	£1	14	0
The Entry and Duty of 307 Drawings on paper	1	5	6
The Land Waiter	0	2	6
Mr Emerson ye Searcher	0	2	6
The Warehouse keeper	0	1	0
Porters and my passage and expenses	0	3	0
	£1	14	6

The impression is surely one of a long succession of hands held out for the customary rewards, without which delays, negligence and pure dumb insolence were no doubt inevitable. Most of the entries during the decade for books concern those that were being bought steadily in considerable quantity from London booksellers, but by 1723 John Brindley was steadily at work binding the foreign acquisitions to Thomas Coke's specification and impressing the family arms on the covers. Once again, a number of books that are still on Holkham's shelves can be identified, but they are all examples of titles that were bought in London after the return to this country. They include Eleazar Albin's *A Natural History of English Insects* bought on subscription in 1719, the Duke of Buckingham's works in three volumes in 1724, and Thomas Madox's *Firma Burgi* of 1726.

A more typical entry, however, details Dr Ferrari's week's purchases in
1728:

Paid Dr Ferrari the following bills	£	s	d
Mr Giles for books	2	8	0
Mr Vanderhoeck for D.o	2	14	6
Mr Proevost & Co. for D.o	2	10	0
Mr Lymassey for D.o	6	0	0
Dr Ferrari as by bill	3	15	0
	£17	7	6

The library was continually enlarged throughout the 1720s, mainly using
London booksellers, but even when he was on tour elsewhere in the country
Coke was buying books. On early visits to Minster Lovell and Longford he
found things either to his taste or for necessary reading on his journey in
bookshops in Oxford, Banbury and Market Harborough.[27]

In all these activities the 1720s were years in which the various collections
that the young man planned for his great house of the future were being
brought together and consolidated. Some of the paintings could be hung
straight away at Thanet House in London or at Holkham, and many of the
books were housed initially in the extended library of the town house; for the
manuscripts, the statuary and much else, it was a time for conservation and
safe storage while he forged ahead with what was to be his life's work.

Chapter 9

SPORT

rom his youth, Thomas Coke's character was an intriguing mixture
of the intellectual and the active. In 1711, when he left his school in
Isleworth to go to live with his kinsman at Longford in Derbyshire,
Sir Edward found that 'he learns his book, and plays with an equall good
spiritt'. He felt, however, that there was need for a carefully chosen tutor, and
the Revd David Wilkins, a pedagogue of German extraction and of some
standing, was appointed. Wilkins was impressed by his new charge and wrote
to Sir John Newton, one of the boy's guardians:

As for my young Gentleman, he is of extraordinary good natural parts, of a
great capacity, who has applyed himself extremely much in reading some
of the best classical authors, and Latin as well as English Poets, and is
nothing at all wanting but a continuance of the same studies . . . This only
gives me a little uneasiness, that his delight is so much in Cock fighting,
and although I tried to dissuade him quite from it, yet seeing that this
diversion does not hinder his course of studies, I've reduced this pleasure to
once a Week, since it is impossible to take him quite off from it.[1]

An extract from the tutor's accounts of 1711 give some idea of what was involved:[2]

		£	s	d
April	To Mr Coke for his pockitt & for Cocks & Cockmatches	3	8	6
	Pd. for 3 pr. pf silver Gaffles [spurs] for ye Cocks	0	0	10
April 28	Paid by Mr Cokes Order to severall people for keeping his cocks	0	5	0
May 19	To Francis Burton for Cloath, thread, needles, Ribon & Makeing of Cocke bagges	0	10	2
June 15	Paid at Longford for his Cockfighting	0	2	3
" 18	To Sir Nathaniel's man for bringing a Cock to Mr Coke	0	2	6
" 19	for bags for his Cocks	0	6	0
" 22	for gaffles for his Cocks	0	10	0
" 23	paid at Yeaveley [Derbys] where we dined & to his Cock feeders	0	2	6
" 24	At Church	0	1	0
	At Bentley [Fenny Bentley, Derbys] Cocking	0	10	0
	For a Cock bought at Bentley	0	5	0
	To bet with the Cockers 3 guineas	3	4	6
	More to bet	0	13	0
	For feeding his Cocks	2	0	0
		£12	11	3
Of this he gave me back		0	8	6

On 9 June the young man had complained to his grandfather: 'I have no sport here now, cock fighting is out,' and again in the following month:

Now I have no diversions but shooting which is at this time of year very dull, and Sir Ed: don't much care if I should shoot and I [am] forc'd to shoot sparrows & such little birds of which there are most about the house, & I must not shoot here because it frights Mrs Chaney & I am forc'd to go a mile or two to kill 5 or 6 little birds.[3]

During the summer of the following year Thomas was staying at Holkham and, in a letter to Sir John Newton, the land agent Humphrey Smith reported: 'Coming this day from Holkham to wate upon my Master Coke, found him at Elmham Parke where hee had chose a Buck and helped kill the same.'

On his return from the Grand Tour his passion for sport was unabated and centred initially on Longford. In a letter to his grandfather he wrote: 'In the country one's whole time is employ'd either in entertainment at home or in field sports; since I have been here I have retriev'd my old facultys of hallowing the hounds as well as ever.'[4] But his passion was still for cockfighting. In the year of his marriage he attended a cocking at the Blackamoor's Head in Ashbourne that lasted four days. Having bought nine one-shilling tickets he went on to lose seven guineas at the match. While there, he bought more cocks at an average of five shillings each, and paid board wages for his coachman and postilion, as well as keep for seven cocks. Soon after, 'The Charge & expense of ye Great cock match against Mr Meynel in Derbyshire' added £123 13s 0½d to the grand total of £130 17s 8½d on the cocking account for 1718. In the following year, he spent just over £140 on cocking at Longford, having cockpens made there for use at Holkham, and servants travelled to and fro on that account, hiring horses at Leicester on the way. Longford Wakes fair was held in July, and the cocking there meant giving the fiddlers half-a-crown, while the ringers 'and a poor man' shared 16s 8d between them. Having been to Bath, Coke stayed again at Longford in 1721 from June until October and only then paid for some cockpens that he had ordered in 1718.

It was obviously his intention to indulge in the sport in Norfolk, but, apart from the references just given, nothing shows in the accounts until 1727, when Edward Sadler is named as 'the fighting cock handler' on £5 a year and listed as a cottage tenant in Holkham village. He went over to Longford twice, once with three men in November, and again with a companion in the following March to bring back cocks and hens, and was paid for 'getting up cocks and feeding them'; thirteen shillings were allowed for 'The old Derbyshire man and young Sadler for their care and trouble with cocks' (after a few years in the post, Sadler was clever enough to sell off four cocks to the kitchen – flavoursome possibly, but they must have been mighty tough). In the following year, the two stable odd-job men, John Topleys and Will Gazeley, were away for a fortnight on a trip to Derby for cocks, and birds were bought locally, probably at Holt. Sadler was paid board wages and expenses at cockings held at Wells, and at Lynn in 1728 Coke put up at the Duke's Head, taking with him George Appleyard, the steward, a coachman, a postilion and Jerry Somering, one of his footmen (and possibly his favourite). Appleyard claimed a guinea's expenses for 'going in ye pit', there were wigs to be powdered, and the borough's waits and bell-ringers were rewarded. The house bill was £5 6s 8d and stabling for six coach horses and two saddle horses for four nights cost £3 7s 4d. In all, the cocking account was debited £13 13s 6d as a result of the outing. In the same year there was a four-day event at Holt, and Jerry Somering was given an extra three shillings for going three days 'into ye cockpit', possibly as a handling assistant to Sadler. Again, Coke took his coach and three saddle horses to the cocking and stayed at the Feathers. At Holkham that year, John Topley drew 18s 8d expenses 'in putting out Cocks to walks', and their food was mainly supplied by Thomas Beeston, the miller, as part of the regular consignments for the farmyard fowls. The fighting birds' diet was wheat and barley, some of which was ground as coarse flour 'for ye cocks' bread', and a quantity of 'great oatmeal', and tenant farmer Henry Knott provided seventy-six quarts of milk for them during the year. The birds were carried to matches in cock bags, and cotton worsted and thread were bought from Markant the local draper so that Margaret Pickford, the hare huntsman's wife, could make twenty-seven of them for seven shillings. Her husband sometimes took a hand in the arrangements and drew board wages and expenses for attendance at cockings. There is no mention of it in our decade, but the household accounts for 1747 include an entry referring to repairs being made to the cockpit, which may have been built before 1730. A faint echo of the young man's enthusiasm occurred in Coke of Norfolk's time. The 2nd Earl remembered that, when bad weather prevented the house party from enjoying sport outside, his father amused his guests by staging cockfights under the portico, beyond the saloon doors, which were viewed 'with the keenest interest by all, including the Duke of Sussex'. Thomas, Baron Lovel, as he stood poised to begin his life's work in creating the finest Palladian mansion in England, would have understood the attraction of the sport and loathed the setting chosen by his successor.

Sir Edward Coke remarked on Thomas's appetite for the chase when he first stayed at Longford in 1711. Writing to Sir John Newton, he was worried about 'his going too often abroad an hunting with the Gentlemen about us, which I find makes him grow more cool in his studyes and less tractable' (which was one of the reasons why he supported the idea of the Grand Tour). By the time the young man had returned from the Continent he had become a skilled horseman, and within a year he was riding to hounds regularly. Making Longford his base from early autumn until the New Year in 1719, he hunted at Hilton, staying overnight at Sutton and Burton in Staffordshire, and at Hollington and Draycott in Derbyshire. It was in Norfolk, however, that most development took place. He lost no time in acquiring a pack of hounds and a pack of harriers. At least to begin with, hounds were boarded out, and Pickford the hare huntsman kept thirty couple for the Michaelmas quarter of 1719 for thirty shillings a week. Hugh Prescod similarly boarded thirty-six couple of hare hounds for a fortnight at one shilling a couple. Because it transpired that Pickford was the loser in keeping seventeen couple of hare hounds for the spring quarter for £9 7s, 'my Master is pleas'd to allow the same but not to be a presedent' [sic]. However, the practice of keeping his pack of sixty couple of hounds and ten couple of greyhounds at Beckhall near Billingford was soon established. The house, which still stands some way back from the road between Bawdswell and Billingford, was used on occasion by Coke and his friends when hunting, but the farm was held on a twenty-one-year lease by Osbert Wetherell from the mid-1720s, supplying the hunt establishment with grass and oats on occasion.

The distinction is not always made, but the hare huntsman used a combination of harriers and greyhounds. The strength of the packs fluctuated. In the last quarter of 1719 there were only thirty couple of foxhounds on the books, but the number of hare hounds had risen to thirty-six couple. A further variation in that year was that Christopher Layer, the Booton dog-breeder, was paid a gratuity of £80 for his 'fox hounds' and was boarded at 'Mr Bell's of Beck Hall'. The fox huntsman was Thomas Groom (joined or assisted by John Bailey in 1722), and the first whippers-in were Tom Robinson, Walter Gardiner and John Morrish successively. As hare huntsman, William Pickford earned only £5 a year against Groom's £20, but his duties were clearly less onerous and he doubled as a gamekeeper. He and his wife had a Holkham cottage and were fortunate that a rent arrear equal to a year's wages was 'forgiven by Sir Thomas' in 1727. All the hunt staff wore fustian livery (more about their clothing can be found in Chapter 12). During the hunting season the hunt staff slept at Beckhall, but the huntsman had his bed carried back to Holkham for the rest of the year and the horses were housed in the hunting groom's stable out of season, where John Large helped out on three shillings a week. Stephen Mann served as dog-boy or dog-feeder until his early death in 1727, when he was succeeded by the young John Mountain. They worked mainly at the Beckhall kennels, which were fully equipped with a copper boiler (which was replaced in 1727) and storage facilities. The feed bill for the dogs was considerable. In the Michaelmas quarter of 1719 it came to £68 9s 9d, and they ate forty-nine comb of meal, eighty-two 'fleshes' (probably mutton), a quantity of kitchen swill, an unspecified quantity of 'offles' from Narborough the local butcher, and fifty-five 'dog horses'. The latter continued to figure largely in the hounds' diet, and in 1728 eighty-six of them were bought along with six old cows. Horses past their useful working life were bought, either 'on the hoof' and kept at pasture, or as deadstock from the knackers; their boiled flesh was the first choice for most huntsmen, and, at five or six shillings each, they were good value. Like the fighting cocks, whelps were given plenty of milk. By 1726 the annual food bill was stable at about £170. When necessary, Mr Jones, the Fakenham apothecary, supplied drugs for the hounds' ailments, charging £13 for his services in 1726. The huntsman was equipped with scissors and fleams (veterinary lancets), and for both hounds and horses the efficacy of bleeding was unquestioned, following the standard medical practice of the day. Village women gathered 'longwort' for the hounds. This may have been the common Lungwort (*pulmonaria officinalis*), but it is more likely that this was the local name for one of the Stachys family of herbs – the Betonys and the Woundworts that were widely used by country folk for their healing properties. The cost of the hounds themselves varied: six couple of harriers were bought from Lord Thanet's huntsman Mr Mansell for eight guineas soon after Thomas Coke's wedding, while Sir Ralph Hare's huntsman at Stow Bardolph was given ten guineas as 'a gratification' for fifteen couple of dogs, although their price is not quoted. Four of the hunt staff journeyed into Lincolnshire for a few days in 1725 and may have gone in search of suitable stock, but no details of any purchases survive.

Coke ranged quite widely over the county in his pursuit of the fox. He was often at Oxborough, the home of his friend Sir Harry Bedingfeld, when the drastic rebuilding of the south side of the moated mansion was still in the future. Apart from the pleasures of hunting he was able to enjoy Bedingfeld's hospitality in the Great Hall, which was 50ft long and as high, under a roof that rivalled Westminster's, and which was recognised as the finest hall of any country mansion in the land.[5] Over the Christmas and New Year of 1722/3, they were joined by Lord Lichfield, Lord Gower, Mr Levison Gower and one of Coke's Newton relations. Sir Harry was often at Holkham, and in 1722 he had a hunting cap bought for him, having perhaps lost his in the chase. Holt was often used as a hunt rendezvous, and the Holkham party always put up at the Feathers Inn and were looked after by Martin Ayers, the landlord, normally from Tuesday to Saturday. The arrangements were supervised by Andrew Griffiths, the upper butler, and John Gundaymore, the chef, saw to his master's meals; all the hunt staff were there on board wages, with hounds being taken to the meet in the dog cart. There was hunting too from Bayfield, where in 1798 Jackson Pratt in his *Gleanings in England* confessed that 'at times he stood charm-bound' as he explored that delectable tract of countryside. Bayfield Hall was the country seat of William Jermy; Coke's hunt servants were lodged and entertained and the horses stabled and bated at the house while he was there in 1727. Meets were frequently at Swaffham, and before he was fully established at Holkham, Thomas travelled down to stay there for ten days in February 1720, taking with him Marmaduke Wyvel, his sister Cary's husband and his Uncle Newton. The costs on the road were carefully apportioned so that his meat and drink cost him only £2 13s 9d, but stabling at £17 4s 3d, plus £21 2s 0½d for feed, and the four servants' travelling expenses and board wages adding another £18 17s 3d meant a total of £57 3s 6½d. At about £5 10s a day, it would hardly have raised an eyebrow. Sir Harry Bedingfeld joined them there, and 'the boy Shepherd' fell ill, and had to be nursed for two days, which probably mortified him. Closer to home Coke hunted in the Burnhams, and he had scarcely arrived at Holkham on 15 September 1722 intent on doing just that when his coach overturned and he injured his shoulder. The accident was bad enough for him to call on the services of Mr Tubbing, the Burnham surgeon, but it was not long before he was fit enough to ride again. Some thought was naturally given to refreshment in the field, and in December 1720 a Mr Cockey provided 'Cantines with knives and forks [in] 'em & Glass Bottles for wine Complete to carry on Horse back when Hunting or Shooting'.

To establish good hunting conditions there were a number of things that needed attention and improvement. At least six fox coverts were established within the decade in the Holkham area by improving suitable woodland. In 1720 over £50 was spent on enclosing the coverts in the Holkham and Dunton parishes, and in the mid-1720s a new covert was established in the latter, which was fenced about with hurdles to allow it to mature. In 1722 George Gardiner earned £11 3s 6d for 120 rods of ditching round an unnamed covert and for sowing whins within it. Fir Close at Creake Abbey was rented from Mr Powditch for a covert, and a riding and a road were cut through it to improve access; an Egmere tenant was paid to preserve a covert there, and the one at Brazenhall was hedged in 1724, with gates added and a ride cut through it.

The work of burrow stopping went on throughout the period, from Holt in the east, across to the Creakes and Burnhams in the west, and south to the Fakenham and Walsingham areas, giving work to William Wegg and Thomas Palmer, who were both gamekeepers, and Tom Mallet among others. In 1726 the £70 entered against 'incidental expenses of the hunt' was largely spent on burrow stopping. It was work that combined conveniently with gamekeeping duties; Thomas Palmer was tipped two guineas for 'taking a snarer' while burrow stopping, and the warrant involved cost half a guinea. There was an established reward system on the estate for informers who could point the finger at fox killers and poachers – two Creake men were taken before the Justice in 1721, and search warrants were obtained from Mr Walpole and Mr Life for use against poachers at Castle Acre and elsewhere. The keepers were invested with special police powers under the terms of an Act of 1671 that granted every landowner who was also lord of the manor the right to appoint a gamekeeper and authorised him to confiscate dogs, firearms and other equipment from persons suspected of being unqualified to hunt, and to bring before magistrates any poachers caught. A man called Jarvis (possibly a gamekeeper) claimed 15s 1d in expenses for carrying poachers before the Justices at Walsingham, and the Egmere shepherd's page (his boy helper) was rewarded for informing on his master's son for snaring – a scenario that bears thinking about. A local bricklayer was paid for the same sort of thing, and in 1727 four Holkham youngsters, 'young Mallet', Dow, Palmer and Sam Leader, were all rewarded for catching snarers.

The stock of foxes was increased in a number of ways. Between two and four shillings were paid for foxes brought from Martham, the Fleggs and the Creakes, while a warrener was given half a guinea for three large cubs. Coke's friend Mr Archer presented him with two big fox bitches in London, Mr Wortley's servant was given five shillings for bringing a fox, and a Mr Curtis's man had half a crown when he came on a similar errand. A keeper was given half a guinea for saving two litters at Holt Wood, and the two Holkham shepherds had a guinea each to encourage them to preserve foxes, with £3 2s 6d more for 'laying in the earths'. Hunting across farming country inevitably means some damage, although in the eighteenth century there would be little inclination to criticise one's landlord or neighbour. Fair reparation seems to have been made, and Thomas Newbegin, for example, was given five shillings for damage done on his land when digging out a fox.

The emphasis was obviously on foxes, but there are three references in the 1720s that show that Coke went deer hunting from time to time. In 1721, accompanied by his usual retinue of servants, he stayed at the Duke's Head at Lynn 'for the Doe chase', and the previous year William Pigg, the Waterden tenant, was tipped 'when hunting the doe'. Coke stayed for a few days at his Oxfordshire manor of Minster Lovell in the autumn of 1723 and took the opportunity to go 'buck hunting'. The expenses entered were minimal, so it was probably within his own deer park.

Having established a pack of harriers with its own staff, Coke undoubtedly chased the hare, but there are few clues in the accounts to establish the frequency of meets. They would have been seasonal, and the costs involved were much less than those for fox hunting. In the Midsummer quarter of 1719 'several people' were tipped a total of £3 14s for 'the finding of 74 hares', and gamekeeper Thomas Palmer was also paid extra for finding hares.

The huntsmen's control of hounds and riders has always been traditionally associated with the use of the hunting horn. Thomas Groom, Coke's fox huntsman, had his own French horn with a box to keep it in. Among his master's first purchases were six horns, which cost £1 3s, with three sheets of 'hunting notes' thrown in. A year later, 'the boy Robinson', one of the whippers-in, was taught to blow 'the streight horn' by a Mr Cowper, and his instrument with its 'sheet of notes' was priced at 4s 6d. One or two incidental costs are of interest, such as the canteens mentioned previously and 'a chair for my Master to hunt in' (an adaptation of a normal hacking saddle), for which Coke paid £9.

Many years later in his old age, in an emollient letter to George, Viscount Townshend, who had foolishly challenged him to a duel, Thomas Coke confessed that he was not a good shot: 'and as for a pistol I could never hit a barn door with a gun'.[6] Nevertheless, there is plenty of evidence of shooting activity, and when he stayed at Holt Feathers for the hunting in the 1720s he hired a nag 'to go a shooting'. Few archive entries deal specifically with guns, although there is a record that Maskall the London gunsmith charged nine shillings for cleaning and mending a fowling piece in 1719. Powder and shot were purchased regularly, and a typical entry reads: '7lbs of Jersey unglaiz'd gunpowder @ 16s.4d., 28lb of shot @ 3s.6d., a cask & 2 bags of flints @ 1s.10d.'. French flints were judged superior to the local Brandon variety but were expensive at twenty-five for a shilling. The local supplier for powder and shot was James Thompson of Walsingham, who stocked the necessary powder horns and bags. In 1728 a Philip Bender had his gun repaired, and, having been furnished with shooting boots, he reported the killing of nineteen assorted hawks, herons and weasels at Fulmodeston and was paid for them together with his expenses. This was all gamekeeper's work, and the fact that a footman on the house staff shared the same name is probably a happenstance, but Coke may have enrolled one of his footmen as a loader or guide if he was a Norfolkman and had the necessary skills.

The kennels housed a couple of spaniels, and Tom Mallet, the kennelman, earned £1 11s 6d for 'teaching the spaniel called Lady to set'. Coke 'went a seting' [sic] with a Mr Dering in the autumn of 1720, and may well have taken the spaniels with him. Will Pickford, the hare huntsman-cum-gamekeeper, supplied some wild duck to put in the flight ponds in the mid-1720s and fed them with barley, but there is no way of knowing where the ponds were. The two most likely locations were south of the Clint (there were ponds of some sort there) or north of the marsh road. Coke certainly went out to shoot duck in the winter.

Game birds, especially partridges, were reared on the manor, and, although the scale is unlikely to have been large, it is notable that wheat was bought specifically to feed them. Netting can hardly be classed as sport, but it was undoubtedly popular, and indeed vital for supplying small birds for the table. London purchases from Thomas Brown's shop included an 18 by 7yd partridge net, a lark net, and an 8 by 4yd fly net 'to lay over hares', and from Thomas Guintham came two 'brace birds', which were live decoy birds secured with bandages.

Coke hunted the badger, in common with most eighteenth-century sportsmen, and his gamekeeper, Thomas Palmer, was paid for catching them, in combination again with stopping burrows. Otter hunting provided another diversion, and Robert Breese, who is named as the official otter hunter, drew a couple of guineas a year and will have used the two otter poles purchased in 1720.

While he was staying at Hothfield for his wedding with Lady Margaret, Coke went fishing at 'Rumney', with Will Holland, his personal footman, to carry things and be generally useful; soon after he is found buying 'angle rods and fishing tackle' in London. One would have expected that the sensible place to buy a boat would have been on the Norfolk coast, but, as so often with the very rich, the homely was not to be compared with metropolitan quality, and in 1727 a fishing boat, complete with rigging, was bought from a

Mr Tiley in London for £15. It was then shipped to Holkham, where a tarpaulin was made for it. Another craft came from Mr Apps's yard in town, with oars and sail for twelve guineas, and more fishing tackle was bought at the same time. Local opportunities were not, however, to be despised, and Parson Springall's boat and oars were had very reasonably the year before. About that time, one of the boats was 'graved' for 9s 2d by John Baker – that is, it had its bottom scraped and coated with tar. For supplying the house a fisherman called Wortley was hired with two assistants for fishing and for mending nets, and there were fish traps installed in the marshes. In 1727 coarse fish were bought for stocking the lake, 200 perch from Mr Ayscough and 200 jack pike from Mr Peckover, in order to provide convenient sport for the owner and for those of his friends such as Mr Bedingfeld who lived at nearby Warham. One of the sailing boats from London was in use on the Clint by 1730.

Thomas Coke does not seem to have been particularly attracted by horse racing, despite the popularity and relative proximity of Newmarket. However, when he stayed at Minster Lovell in 1723 he went to the Oxford races for a week, putting up at the Angel with two servants. The Bicester meeting followed, and there was a bill for eatables, fire and the use of linen at the Blue Boar. In common with one or two other places in Norfolk, race meetings were held annually at Holt each summer in the early eighteenth century, and they were the great social events of the year for the area, with Assemblies held on the Tuesday and Thursday. The three-day meeting in July 1728 was one in which Coke seems to have taken a particular interest. He was apparently one of the group called 'the contributors' or sponsors, and was involved in the promotion of the event to the extent of placing an advertisement in nine consecutive issues of the *Whitehall Evening Post*. This was a Whig London paper, one of the eight periodicals run by the ageing Daniel Defoe in the 1720s and where the Newmarket programmes could be found. No copies of the paper have survived, but luckily the *Norwich Mercury* carried a local notice in three issues in June and early July 1728:

At Holt in Norfolk, on Tuesday the 23d of July next, a Purse, Value 20 Guineas, will be run for on the Course there, 3 Heats, 4 Miles each Heat, by any Horse, Mare, or Gelding, which never won at any one Time in Plate or Stakes above the Value of 30 Guineas, carrying Ten Stone, Bridle and Sadle included, paying for Entrance two Guineas, if a Contributor one

Guinea. On Wednesday the 24th of the same Instant, the Town Plate, Value 10 Guineas, will be run for on the same Course by Galloways, not exceeding 14 Hands, carrying Nine Stone, Bridle and Sadle included . . . paying one Guinea Entrance, if a Contributor half a Guinea. On Thursday the 25th of the same Instant, a Purse Value 30 Guineas will be run for on the same Course, 3 Heats, 4 Miles at each Heat, by any Horse, Mare or Gelding that never won at any one time above the value of 50 Guineas in Plate or Stakes, to carry 11 Stone, Bridle and Sadle included, paying Entrance 3 Guineas, if a Contributor 2 Guineas. No less than 3 Horses &c. to enter and start for the Plate and Purses abovesaid. Every Horse . . . which enters for either Plate or Purses must stand at a Publick House in the said Town which subscribes no less than 5 Shillings at least 10 Days before running, to give notice to John Brooke Clerk of the Course, at their coming to Town, to be entered and measured at the Kings-Arms in Holt on Wednesday the 17th of July 1728.

The advertisement ends on a minatory note: 'A Mare commonly known by the Name of the *Weazel*, now or late in the possession of a Man going by the Name of John Onthank, alias Allthank, alias Unthank, living in or near the City of Norwich is utterly excluded from entring or running for the aforesaid Plate or Purses.' Of more interest to Coke was the concluding 'NB': 'There will be a Main of Cocks fought 21 of a-side; also there will be an Assembly on Thursday Night at the Town-Hall, and the Comedians will attend the whole Meeting.' It turned out that the whole thing was 'put off for a week by reason of the Sessions', and Coke stayed as usual at the Feathers, paying two guineas for his lodging, accompanied by his coachman, Will Holland, and the three footmen, Philip Bender, William Heriot and Jerry Somering.

There is no mention of the game of bowls at Holkham, but, when he stayed at Longford, Coke was often at the green, laying out a little money and tipping the boy. He may well have played himself or merely laid bets on the skill of others, and the same applies to the one mention of tennis (that is, real tennis) in the decade's accounts. On 14 January 1721 John Casey advanced his master 15 shillings 'for the pocket' when he visited the Earl of Buckingham 'and at the Tenis Court'. Using the term 'sport' a little loosely, one might mention that Coke could claim to be reasonably proficient in self-defence. At least, in 1722, he paid the necessary 'earnest' to the fencing master, Mr Figg, and bought two light swords. Lessons followed shortly after at two guineas for a month's 'Teaching my Master to play at Sword and Quarter Staff'.

Sport was hugely important to Thomas Coke, from the time as a boy when he was obsessed with cockfighting, to when his enthusiasm in later years focused on hunting the fox, and it formed the basis for a wide range of social alliances, particularly in Norfolk. It buttressed his position as one of the premier landowners, and was the more remarkable because, as part of his character, it lay alongside his reputation as a man of the arts. They did not impinge on each other but were two sides of a single coin.

Chapter 10

FOOD, DRINK AND HOUSEHOLD SUPPLIES

*I*n the eighteenth century food was a major preoccupation, which was natural enough in those who could never be sure where their next meal was coming from, but also for those in better circumstances. To eat handsomely was a measure of social standing, and hospitality demanded a lavish table. Corpulence was fashionable and Samuel Johnson declared: 'I mind my belly very well, for I look upon it that he who does not mind his belly will hardly mind anything else.'[1] At the coronation of George II in October 1727 the celebrations included a vast banquet laid out in Westminster Hall featuring seventy-five different dishes and fifty plates of garnishes. A characteristic combination of sweets and savouries was cunningly displayed to tempt the eyes and stimulate the palates of hundreds of guests; multi-coloured jellies, collared veal, bombards, geese à la daube, fricandos, cheesecakes, venison pasties and grand pyramids of sweetmeats were continually replenished during the three whole days that the gargantuan feast lasted. Charles Carter, a chef with long experience in catering for the nobility, was the mastermind behind this extravaganza and published his *The Complete Practical Cook* in 1730.[2] More perhaps than on any other subject, the household accounts provide a mass of detailed information on food and drink. There is so much to remark and ponder over, to analyse and dissect, that it is extremely difficult not to be so engulfed in the torrent of minutiæ that any overall assessment is hampered by the temptation to digress.

During the eighteenth and, indeed, the nineteenth centuries, employment of servants, particularly on a large scale, posed a continuing problem in any household's economy. The kitchen, still room and brewhouse were breeding grounds for fraud and straightforward theft. All tradesmen dealt with the senior servants – the house steward, the chef or cook, the butler – the personal livery servants and even with the doorkeeper. The number of tradesmen supplying the family regularly, especially in London, was considerable, and competition was fierce. Unless the master or mistress kept a close eye on purchasing and had an awareness of current costs, private deals between shopkeepers and staff were a constant threat, and the percentage that could be creamed off was a temptation.

Over-ordering could be balanced against private trading in meat and drink especially, and the large amounts ordered of virtually everything in a household such as that of the Cokes inevitably resulted in surplus. In an age when refrigeration was unknown (except for the use of ice in summer) food rapidly became stale or uneatable, a fact that encouraged over-ordering to forestall complaints at the table. The feeling that they were in danger of being cheated caused the masters of wealthier households to set up elaborate accounting mechanisms, in our case involving a series of day-books, house steward's, butler's and chef's ledgers, together with records of purchases by the porter and other servants. By conning them over, the master or mistress could keep a running check on expenditure, or at least feel that they were doing so. In the same way that modern millionaires seem sometimes to be more concerned with the milk bill than with weightier matters, so their predecessors became peremptory over trifles.

In the Holkham accounts, expenditure is always divided into main categories, and here we are concerned with the kitchen, still room and cellar. The first and last are self-explanatory; the second dealt with all those commodities that were used to make liqueurs and cordials, preserves, puddings, cakes and biscuits, sweetmeats and confectionery. Ingredients that were the basis for some medicines were also entered under the still room heading. Although there were variations, the family generally moved to Norfolk in July and returned to London in late February. As a result, there were two culinary regimes, with some significant differences, and two groups of suppliers. In addition, there were certain items that were sometimes, and in some cases always, bought in London for the country, while others were sent up to town from Holkham.

When considering the range and volume of foodstuff consumed it is important to bear in mind the numbers sitting at table on an average day, both at Holkham and at Thanet House. Of these, the family was the smallest part. Thomas, Lady Margaret, his two younger brothers, his sister and, in time, his baby son constituted the basis; the librarian, Dr Ferrari, always dined with the family. To these might perhaps be added an average of three guests, although that number rose, on occasion, to many more. In town there were always between twenty-five and forty servants, a number that fluctuated as staff came and went, and that dropped to small numbers on board wages when the family was elsewhere. At Holkham the family number would be the same, with the addition of the Holkham parson, Richard Springall; the average number at the steward's table was seven and at the servants' table thirty-five, plus three footmen and anyone working in the house at the time – a total of about fifty. The servants of any visitors were boarded during their stay.

The cost of the household's food may be gauged by considering the bill for a sample of three separate weeks during the period under review. In London the total for a week in May 1721 was £11 17s 3½d, for a week in March 1724 it was £13 14s 0½d, and for a week in February 1727 it was £10 2s 7d – an average of £11 18s. Three Holkham examples may be compared: for a week in October 1719 the bill was £20 3s 6d, for a week in October 1721 the bill was £18 0s 10d, and for the week immediately following it was £14 5s 0½d – an average of £17 9s 9d. A much lower average figure of £8 5s 1d is obtained from the Holkham bills for six weeks in 1726, and the weekly food bills for the whole of that particular quarter average £8 7s 8d; these reductions may reflect a certain amount of belt-tightening at a time when Coke's resources were under pressure.

The summaries drawn up in the house steward's accounts for the years 1723, 1724 and 1725 provide a useful breakdown of expenses into common categories:

	1723			1724			1725		
	£	s	d	£	s	d	£	s	d
Butcher	238	19	4¼	279	5	7	392	5	0
Poulterer	113	9	4	70	19	10½	94	18	0
Baker	56	2	6½	73	5	4	108	7	3½
Fishmonger	55	17	7	43	17	6	50	2	0
Butter, Eggs, &c.	45	14	0	57	14	0	83	0	2
Herbs, Fruit &c.	18	2	0	10	6	2½	8	17	4
Grocer	29	2	3	43	9	9	49	16	6
Confectioner	19	5	6	12	5	3	14	12	4
Cheesemonger	9	9	6½	8	9	6	26	13	7
Pastry Cook	1	18	0	12	5	3	0	5	2½
	£588	0	1¼	£611	16	3	£828	17	5½

An average of these yearly figures yields a weekly cost of £13 0s 1d.

The Englishman's passion for meat was notorious, and it is noticeable that expenditure on meat was far higher than on any other commodity, averaging 44.5 per cent of the whole over the three years. It is worth examining in more detail how the money was laid out.

In the London week of February 1727 previously quoted, 38 stone 1¼lb of beef was bought from Mr Chamberlain, the butcher, for £4 9s, and about 3 stone 8lb of veal and lamb for 12s 6d. The poulterer's bill of 16s 6d would have paid for about twenty-five fowls or their equivalent; in addition, a 23lb ham cost 11s 6d, and two rabbits, a pound of bacon and a 'set' of cowheel added another 3s 6d. Using a median figure of thirty-five as the number at table in the house, the amount of meat available per head was at least 17lb or 2½lb a day. During that week, the bill of Fortescue, the fishmonger, of a shilling was unusually low – the average was in the region of twelve to fifteen shillings; the varieties available included plaice, flounders, crayfish, trout, skate and oysters. Anchovies were normally bought from 'the herb woman' in London or from a high-class provision merchant such as Heathfield.

At Holkham, the figures for the Michaelmas quarter of 1726 provide a more detailed breakdown, and the weekly averages were: beef 31 stone 9lb; mutton 3 stone 8½lb; pork 2 stone 8lb; veal 1 stone 3lb, with the addition of five sucking pigs, a bullock's head and a calf's head; the average amount of butcher's meat available per person each week would have been about 11lb. This is much less than the London figure, but there is a big difference in the amount of poultry bought, although the cost is comparable at an average of fourteen shillings a week. It is to be expected that there was a greater variety available, and during that quarter the house was supplied with 12 geese (two of them wild), 2 turkeys, 203 wildfowl, 47 game birds, 40 chickens, 32 tame pigeons, 27 rabbits and some larks. If the whole decade is scanned in this context, the variety of wildlife consumed is extraordinary, and includes bitterns, curlews, redshanks, grey plovers, bustards, larks in multiples of up to thirteen dozen, teal, mallard, widgeon, gnats (the local name for sandpipers) and even a heron. The game birds were nearly all partridges – 169 in a quarter in 1719 against only nine pheasants – and, although Thomas Pigg, the Waterden tenant, could sell the Hall thirty-three woodcock, they came with only seven pheasants. This apparent scarcity of pheasants may account for the curious entry in 1728 that records that a dozen pheasants were bought live in London with 'coops and cages to carry down' to Holkham, although they could conceivably have been tame birds that were bought for their decorative qualities rather than for food. George Appleyard provided over half the beef, all the mutton and most of the pork from the home farm, with the rest being supplied by three local butchers.

Other meat products of various sorts occur here and there. At Holkham, Dame Sarah Lawson was employed in cleaning tripe, calves' feet and hog bellies, and, although they are not mentioned in Norfolk, both black and white puddings were bought in London, together with sweetbreads. A fat pig was bought there 'to make a marqueseen', and another specifically to barbecue. At Holkham, Gazeley, the butcher, was paid half a guinea for killing and collaring a brawn (a boar), and two collars (rolled and tied) were bought from Morell for £2 8s. One of the more unusual items in the 1720 London accounts is the 1s 6d spent on 'Coxe Combs', which came with a goose, four dozen larks and five tame pigeons from the poulterer – the only suggestion that comes to mind is that they were used as decoration on a dish.

During the quarter the Holkham weekly bill for fish averaged fifteen shillings, much as it did in London, but again the variety available reflected local conditions, with cod, smelts (small fish of the salmon family), whiting, dabs, sole, herring, trout, breadcock (or bretts, the Norfolk name for turbot), ling, lobsters, oysters and shrimps on the menu. Most of the fish came from a Mr Wortley, but Richard Porter, the Newdigates tenant, provided some, as did another tenant, Henry May. There is an instance of forty smelts being bought at Lynn for 1s 6d, and a basket of them for 3s 8d. Sturgeon was not found locally, but in 1721 a keg of it was supplied by the London fishmonger Mr Truelove for a guinea and sent down to the country. Oysters were eaten in great quantities, both in town and at Holkham. They were bought by the pint, the quart and the barrel (the equivalent of two quarts), or by the score or the hundred. The finest were 'the large Burnham Ground oysters', which cost 3s 6d to four shillings a hundred against 2s 6d for the small variety. The only mention of cockles occurs in 1728, when a peck of them came from John Clark the local butcher, and Markant, the Wells grocer, supplied anchovies now and then. There were two instances in 1728 of fish being fetched from Denver and Wiggenhall St Mary Magdalen in West Norfolk, and, as three-day outings were involved, the likelihood is that they were trips to stock one or more fish-ponds. The gudgeon is a small freshwater fish that is often used as bait but seldom, if ever, eaten nowadays. Nonetheless, it was on the menu when the family stayed at Bath in 1721, and Izaak Walton considered it an excellent fish to eat.

In London, virtually all the household's bread came from one baker, William King, for most of the period, who was occasionally used for the 'baking of things' – that is food that it was more convenient to cook away from the house. He supplied an average of sixteen 'half-peck' and quartern loaves a week at 1s 1d, 'small bread', anything from fifty to a hundred halfpenny rolls a week, 'raspins'[3] and sometimes flour. King's place as the regular family baker was taken by Mr Tomlin in 1728, and a Mr Seignadier occurs briefly at that time supplying what was possibly specialist or fancy bread. At Holkham the Hall bakehouse provided most of the bread that was needed, although sometimes it was bought in, with flour and oatmeal being purchased in bulk. Mrs Herman was a London pastry cook who produced apple pies, tarts and cheesecakes, and she was called upon now and then to provide specialities like 'a great cake wt. 25¼lb', priced at a shilling a pound. 'Old Mary Allen' (often called 'Goody Allen') and 'Mother Dow' were Holkham's casual charwomen who also turned their hands to baking biscuits for the house. Confectionery as such is hardly mentioned there, although some Shrewsbury cakes were bought in 1727.

In town, dairy products were bought at the door, specifically from Mrs Wetherall, 'the butter woman', and Mrs David, 'the milk woman', although many account entries do not specify a source, and some supplies probably came from itinerants. A typical example reads: 'Paid for ½lb butter 5d., for 41 q[uar]ts milk 5s.1¼d., 5 p[in]ts cream 2s.6d.'. Butter was sold by the firkin, the pint and the pound, and at Holkham it was nearly all supplied either by Nicholas Anger, the Neals' tenant, or by Richard Porter of Newdigates, both of whom provided milk and cream as well. Salt butter was occasionally bought from Mr Tidd of Wells, a 56lb firkin at a time. At 4½d a pound it was, on average, 1½d cheaper than fresh butter, and was stored at the Hall in iron-bound wooden tubs made specially by Robert Wood, the village cooper, and painted by Loades 'the dauber'.

In London, eggs were bought at the door from Mrs Wetherall, and also at Clare market, sometimes as many as a hundred at a time. On one occasion Will Holland, the coachman, was paid for some new-laid eggs, which he had perhaps come across while out with his master. At Holkham, the Hall was obviously a target for anyone with eggs to sell. A number of the tenant farmers were regular suppliers, and even Mrs Appleyard, the steward's wife, joined in. Quantities ranged from over 200 down to a few from cottagers such as the Widow Fishpoole; one entry reads: '30 eggs from a stranger' and another: 'To sev'rall people 100 eggs'; 'A lad from Creak' came with forty-six, and a man from Burnham was paid 5d for eleven. Remembering that a labourer's day wage was no more than a shilling, it is no surprise to find a man walking the 8 miles from Morston to sell 1s 6d worth of oysters; the chance to sell a few eggs or shellfish at the Hall was not to be sneezed at.

Cheese was normally bought in bulk. Haycock, the Norfolk cheesemonger, supplied 1cwt of Warwickshire at 2d per pound, 37 stone of Cheshire, and over 1cwt of an unspecified variety at 3d per pound. In London the range included cream cheeses from Mrs David, the milk woman, who also sold a 'Jackdaw' cheese for 1s 2d; quantities of Warwickshire, Old Cheshire (including one order for 4cwt, 27lb) and Gloucester came from a number of cheesemongers, at prices slightly higher than in the country. It is noticeable that Cheddar cheese, the commonest variety on the market now, is not mentioned at all in the 1720 accounts. The only foreign cheese bought was Parmesan, in quantities varying from ½lb to 16lb at 2s 6d a pound from Lyde the cheesemonger.

In London, the vegetables were bought mainly from the basket woman at the door, and from Mrs McDougall, the herb woman, who also supplied greens and 'sallets'. In their season, cauliflowers, artichokes, cucumbers, 'roots', peas, mushrooms, garden beans and asparagus all feature, and the last-named was bought by the basket or by the hundred for making soup. There is also an instance of a basket of asparagus being bought for seven shillings in February, which must have been a forced product from a greenhouse. Peas were bought by the sieve when new and then by the peck or bushel. Truffles were a luxury supplied by Rawlinson, who also dealt in wine and cheese, and a Mr Buisont, whose 'wet [white?] trofles' were very expensive at seventeen shillings per pound. In the Holkham sections of the accounts there are very few entries for vegetables, but it so happens that the single reference in ten years to today's most common vegetable is a payment there of 2s 2d to Mr Sherringham for 'a pig & pettitoes'. Samphire was then, as now, a peculiarly Norfolk delicacy, and the Holkham fisherman Richard Wortley sold quantities to the Hall.

Soft fruit was sometimes bought from Mrs McDougall and sometimes direct from Covent Garden market. Most of it was destined for the still room for desserts and for the preserves that were made there, although Sarah Newton, another fruiterer, was paid for preserving fruit. Thanet House was close enough to Clare market and Covent Garden to ensure that a wide choice was available. The apple varieties included golden pippins, golden runnets, Kentish and Holland pippins, all of which were bought by the hundred; cooking apples feature specifically for the making of apple dumplings. There were oranges, lemons and the more unusual tamarinds; the soft fruit included morells, Kentish cherries (bought by the dozen not by the pound), apricots, strawberries, peaches and gooseberries (bought by the quart), which were used to make gooseberry fool; pears were bought principally for dessert, and choice Boncritons cost a surprising 1s 6d each, although Nonpareils were a lot cheaper and were bought by the hundred. Down at Holkham, a great many quinces were used to make quince jelly, and most of them came from Parson Springall's garden.

The still room must have been an enticing place, judging by the range of its products. Treacle, honey and caraway seeds were bought 'for gingerbread &c.' so that Mrs Thompson the housekeeper could exercise her skills, and sugar came as single or double-refined in loaf form from Peckover, the grocer. The very light, thin, crisp cakes called wafers that were often eaten with wine were baked between wafer irons in the still room, where comfits or sugar plums were also made. By 1728 a 'confectioner' had joined the staff; he would have worked in the still room rather than the kitchen. The chocolate that was bought from Knowles in 6lb- and 7lb-packs was used to make the increasingly popular alternative drink to coffee rather than for eating as a sweet. Home-made wine was also a still-room responsibility, and in 1721 seventeen pecks of cowslips, four pecks of rose petals and a quantity of elderflowers were bought for the purpose. Calves' feet were rendered down and used with lemon and eggs in the making of jellies, and cream was often bought specifically for the still room rather than the kitchen for making puddings and desserts; in one instance artificial flowers were bought, which may have been used for decorating a particular dish. In the summer, ice cream, sold by the pot, came from a Mr Arthur, and, as porterage was charged, he must have been some distance away. Flummery, the name given to a variety of sweet dishes made with milk and eggs, was another summer dish that was bought in, featuring on the menu when the family stayed at Bath in 1721. Mrs McDougall kept the house supplied with herbs, having bargained for them on 'Primrose Hill', Covent Garden, where the 'simplers' from the country sold their herbs. Although she was the chosen vendor, a man was paid separately for distilling herb essences for use in the house in cookery and for medicinal purposes. There are many examples of goods bought in bulk, but the fifty coconuts bought from Mr Serracold at one go in 1719 seem remarkably lavish, and at £13 per hundred they were not cheap. Salt, as an everyday commodity, was bought in bulk, and there are one or two Holkham instances where it is specifically described as 'bay salt'. Will Pickford the hare huntsman sold the house two stones' worth in 1727, and Mrs Hayden supplied a stone the following year. The quality of this particular salt caught the eye of Daniel Defoe: 'From Weyburn west lyes Clye, where there are large salt-works, and very good salt made, which is sold all over the county, and sometimes sent to Holland, and to the Baltic.'[4]

Before Thomas Coke's visit in October 1720, Humphrey Smith made sure that Hill Hall was well provisioned by ordering these supplies during the preceding fortnight:

		£	s	d
Meat	72st 1lb of beef [2s 8d per st]	9	12	2
	11st 7lb of mutton [3s 6d per st]	2	3	9
Poultry	3 geese, 2 turkeys, 69 fowls, 10 chickens	2	5	10
Fish	150 oysters	0	6	0
	salt & fresh fish	0	3	6
Eggs &c.		0	1	11
Cheese	5st 11lb [c. 2½d per lb]	0	17	4
Butter	65lb [6d per lb]	1	12	6

Milk	27 quarts [1*d* per quart]	0	2	3
Cream	6 quarts [4*d* per quart]	0	2	0
Flour	6 sacks of wheat meal [1*s* 2*d* per stone]	4	4	0
	2 sacks of fine flour [2*s* per stone]	2	8	0
	2 combs of bran	0	8	0
	1 comb of barley meal	0	8	0
	oatmeal	0	0	5
Sundries	2lb sugar	0	1	0
	2½lb treacle	0	0	5
	1lb currants	0	0	7
	yeast	0	4	0
	cinnamon	0	0	2½
Fruit	(unspecified but from John Creed the gardener)	5	2 10
		£31	4	4½

The list contains no surprises and confirms the major role of butcher's meat in the household's diet.

As the routine became established of spending a large part of the year at Holkham, so too did the practice of sending supplies down from London, both before and during that time. Lightweight items may have gone by carrier or coach, but the majority were shipped to Wells from Brown's wharf. In some cases it was probably a question of rarity or quality that governed the choice of supplier – a gallon of olives, with bottles and baskets to pack them in, from Godwin, the oilman; nine cheeses weighing 2cwt 14lb from Garlick, the cheesemonger; in 1728, 60lb of Gloucester from Mr Dawson and 4cwt of Cheshire cheese from Mr Green were sent down together. Both Bohea and green tea were sometimes sent, although both were on sale in Norfolk. A recurring item was lemons, which were dispatched by fifties, hundreds and two hundreds, almost certainly for making arrack punch; they were not unobtainable in Norfolk, seeing that the butler once bought 462 for the still room there, paying a good deal more than London prices, but perhaps that was panic buying to cope with an unexpected party. In contrast, pistachio nuts were not to be had in Norfolk and 2lb were sent down now and then, as were quantities of truffles and morello cherries.[5] Spa water was fashionable and often prescribed, so plentiful supplies were sent up from town. The high quality of London-cured bacon might have been the reason for buying four sides from Edwards in 1727, but the half-hogshead of vinegar that went with

them could surely have been bought locally. The same thought occurs over
the 5 bushels and 1½ pecks of fine flour that Edward Jarrett ordered from
William King, the London Baker, to be sent to Holkham, when Beeston the
local miller regularly provided the Hall with both fine and household-grade
flour. The strangest example in all this traffic was the 100 eggs bought in
Holborn from a Mr Elland in May 1727 for 9s 8d 'to send to Holkham'.

Sometimes the flow was reversed, and country specialities went up to
London, as the 25lb of brawn and 6¾ pints of honey in 1721, and 4 turkeys
with 3 neats' tongues the following year. Saltfish were obtainable in London,
but when John Aram, the Holkham gardener, went up to town in May 1728,
he took a couple of dozen with him that had been bought in Wells. Mention
has been made of the apparent scarcity of pheasants, and this may explain
the sending of a brace and a partridge by the Lynn coach in 1721, even
though it cost more than the birds were worth in carriage.

Food prices remained stable throughout the period, but a comprehensive
comparison between town and country is hampered by seasonal variations
and other factors. Despite that, variations in some staple commodities are
worth noting:

	London	Norfolk
Butcher's meat [per stone]	2s 8d–4s 0d	2s 11d–3s 2d
Milk [per quart]	1½d	1¼d
Cream [per quart]	1s	6½d
Butter [per lb]	8½d	5d
Eggs [per 100]	6s	4s 2d
Flour – Fine [per stone]	1s 8d	2s 4d
Flour – Household [per stone]	1s 6d	2s

There were considerable variations in the Norfolk unit prices where the
amounts were small, and it is understandable that a leveret, which could be
had for 4d at Holkham, cost 6s 6d in St James's market.

As for drink, the effect of an abundance of cheap raw spirit so graphically
illustrated in Hogarth's *Gin Lane* had already begun to affect the people of
London in the 1720s, and heavy drinking, particularly among the well-to-do,
was well established as a social habit in the early part of the century. G.M.
Trevelyan's assessment was characteristically trenchant: 'Drunkedness [*sic*]
was the acknowledged national vice of Englishmen of all classes . . . It is hard

to say whether the men of fashion or the rural gentry were the worst soakers.'[6] To be fashionable it was expected of gentlemen that they would keep well-stocked cellars and drink themselves under the table on occasion without loss of face.

In London alone, over 11 million gallons of spirits were being drunk in a year; Prime Minister Robert Walpole's household consumed over 1,000 bottles of white Lisbon wine in 1733.[7] The latter was one of the results of the Methuen Port Wine Treaty of 1713 that gave Portuguese wines a significant advantage over French. 'Portugal wines neat and natural' could be bought at 1s 4d a quart in any tavern. The bulk of the port, however, was immature – hence the widespread incidence of gout among English gentlemen.[8] Contraband smuggling was endemic and prompted Dudley North's steward to complain in 1721 of the 'incredible quantity of French brandy' brought illegally into the country 'which doth not only Impoverish the Nation but procures an Ill habit amongst the meaner Sort of people and not only makes them sottish and lazey but will Qualifie them for Robbing, Pilfering, Housebreaking or what not'.[9]

Spirits, wine, ale and beer were bought and brewed for the Coke household in large quantities, and even as a young man Thomas Coke matched the social habits of his contemporaries in the matter of drink. At that time it was not usual to lay down wine for maturing over a number of years, since most was drunk young in the present-day fashion. The favourite spirit was brandy, and, judging by the vendors, the family's supplies were nearly all smuggled ashore on the Norfolk coast. Amounts and frequency of delivery varied, but it normally came in gill or quart 'stoups', 'ankers' (eight gallons) and 'half-ankers'. Being contraband, the quantities were never larger than this, and Parson Springall was often the go-between, along with John Clark, the local butcher, and one or two villagers. When it was bought legally in London, having been through customs, it cost eight or nine shillings a gallon, and at that price it sometimes featured in the still-room account as a base for liqueurs and for preserving; the smugglers' price seems to have been about half that. The first mention of whisky occurs in 1722, when six bottles of 'usquebaugh' were bought from Thomas Coot for £2 8s, and the only other specific mention is in 1727, when another dozen pints came from Mr Collings at £3 18s. Rum is not mentioned very often, but in 1727 ten gallons came from Mr Crosfield in Norfolk for £4, and the following year thirty gallons were bought from Mr Thomason, a London vintner, at seven shillings a gallon. The only reference to gin is when Richard Wortley, the Holkham fisherman, was given two shillings for a bottle of contraband Geneva in 1728. The spirit that was bought in the largest quantities was arrack, used as the basis for making 'rack punch', one of the most popular drinks for large parties. A whole series of purchases are noted, the largest being in 1721, when sixty gallons at sixteen shillings per gallon were supplied by Messrs Thomason and Pomfrett. On that occasion it went through customs before being packed in hampers and sent by sea to Wells.

The wine intake was very broad-based, including varieties from France, Spain, Hungary and Portugal, and it came in a number of quantities. Some was bottled or sold by the flask, but most was bought by the 22¼ gallon barrel, the 52½ gallon hogshead and the 105 gallon pipe. The heaviest purchases were of 'Mountain', a variety of Malaga that was probably nothing like the wine produced there now. Eighty gallons were bought in 1719, forty-five gallons and a half-hogshead in 1724, sixty-one gallons and a half-hogshead in 1727 and a series of smaller lots in between. Claret featured widely and came through customs in bulk by the hogshead (one in 1721, four in 1723, one in 1724, two in 1727 at around £40 each) and also by the bottle and by the flask; of the latter, at least forty-two were smuggled into Norfolk. The temptation to patronise the smugglers is understandable when the charges on lawful traffic are considered; in 1720, sixty-one gallons of Burgundy carried a customs duty of £13 15s, on top of the £1 11s for freightage and other charges. In 1727, two pipes and forty-three gallons of red port, and a hogshead and six gallons of white port came in, plus over forty gallons of Canary. Mr Schaart was a London vintner who specialised in Rhenish wine, supplying it in small quantities throughout the period. Towards the end of the century when Thomas Jefferson was near Tain he found that the eastern slopes of the Côte Rotie produced a wine 'of the first quality' called Hermitage. It was a blend of grapes in a ratio of eight red for one white, which, he noted, 'cannot be drunk under four years'. Coke may have received the same advice when he bought two hogsheads from Monsieur More in 1721 for £73 10s. That is fourteen shillings a gallon, which, with the duty and freightage, would have made it unusually expensive. Champagne was not inexpensive at four to five shillings a bottle and was bought in small quantities, ranging from a few bottles a year to over fifty in 1727 and again in 1728.

The cellars at Thanet House and Hill Hall were obviously kept well supplied, but there were one or two occasions when special provision was made. When Coke came down to Norfolk to be elected a Knight of the Shire in 1722, sixteen hampers of wine were shipped by Oxbrough of Wells from London, and a pipe, two half-hogsheads and two hampers were brought over from Lynn. Coke's entry into the Court circle gave him (and his senior servants) the opportunity to taste the contents of the royal cellars. In 1722 Andrew Griffiths paid Mr Allen the Duke of Kent's steward £13 4s for a parcel of Burgundy, and he secured a dozen bottles of Rhenish from the King's cellar at about the same time. The cellar of Montague House next door in Great Russell Street was another source, and two casks were bought specifically to fill with wine there. Dr Hobart, who had been Coke's tutor on the Grand Tour, was reimbursed for some Moselle that he had brought back from a European trip, and also for a mixed bag of champagne, Bordeaux and Hermitage, which came 'as a trial' from Calais. There is also one instance of five bottles being bought from Simson, the vintner, 'for a taste', and most suppliers would surely be persuasive in inviting their clients to sample before buying. There is evidence that Coke sometimes subscribed for consignments of claret in advance and paid for it by the hogshead as it came in to Rawlinson's cellars – in 1727 he took delivery of two hogsheads, which were the remainder of an order worth £66. There were times when he chose wine as a present: he sent 150 bottles in two hampers to his old guardian Sir Edward Coke at Longford in 1720, and six gallons of brandy for Christmas in 1727. He was assiduous in keeping up his Italian contacts, and in 1722 he sent a present of thirty-five gallons of Canary to Sir Thomas Derham in Leghorn. Sometimes he was the recipient: there was a gift of Tokay from a Mr Discow, and the Florentine envoy's servant was tipped half a guinea for bringing a present of wine from his master in April 1719. All this trafficking and consumption meant that the amount of wine to be racked and bottled was considerable; a wine cooper was paid £7 for work in the cellar, for which isinglass, cotton and mustard seed were apparently necessary, and eggs were used to 'force' wine. The wine cooper's bill for wine forcing and racking several hogsheads amounted to £7 9s. The amount of adulteration and use of additives that went on in the trade generally was notorious, with green vitriol, copperas, catechu and similar substances commonly used,[10] but there is no evidence that anything of that nature was used in the Coke cellars. The butler ordered corks in quantity (up to seventeen gross at a time) and bottles by the gross, and there is one instance of shot being bought 'to wash bottles', presumably as a scouring agent in the rinsing water.

The only time that the servants legitimately tasted the contents of the wine cellars was on special occasions such as audit feasts, when ample supplies of punch were served. The butler and other senior house staff would have had plenty of opportunity to sample their master's wine and would, indeed, need to do so on occasion. By and large, however, the servants drank beer, and in London most of the ale came from Mann's brewery and the small beer from Mr Buckland, who supplied twenty-five barrels of it in 1727. In 1719 beer was freighted to town from Burton on Trent (passing through customs in the process), and, when Coke was staying at Longford soon after his return from the Continent, he placed an order with a Burton brewer for ale to be sent overseas, no doubt to an acquaintance or contact made during his tour. When he was at Holkham in the autumn and winter of that year, ale and beer were bought locally, but for the rest of the period it was brewed in-house by a number of different servants. John Creed, the gardener, brewed a supply in 1721, and in 1724 William Fellows was brought in to brew ninety-eight combs of malt, the house having its own malt mill. He boarded with Catherine Loynes, the maid-cum-housekeeper, for four weeks, and once he stayed for a month with John Aram, the under-gardener, being helped by Richard Gay for nineteen days and nine nights. In the main, however, it was the casual helpers such as Henry Walker, Robert Mays, William Dow and Will Medcalf who did the work. An indication of the brewhouse's capacity is the fact that the last-named brewed four hogsheads of ale and seven of small beer there in 1728. In the previous January, at the servants' New Year feast, the home-brew ran out and they were given five shillings to buy in extra supplies. The Holkham product was evidently of good enough quality to travel, and hampers of it were sometimes sent up to Thanet House.

A summary of the household expenses for the year ending 25 March 1726 includes an informative tabulation of the cellar expenses when the family were in London for the first quarter, at Holkham for the second and third quarters and nine weeks of the final quarter:

Wine	Hhds	Gals	Qts	£ s d
To Mr Miles for Burgundy	0	3	0	02 15 0
To Mrs Maimon Burgundy & Champagne	0	15	0	18 15 0
To Mr Schoart for Rhenish wine	0	3	0	01 11 0
To Do. for Do.	0	3	0	01 13 2
To Mr Porter for French wine	0	1	2	00 10 0

To Mr Rawlinson for French wine	1	0	0	45 04 0	
To Richd. Porter for Do. in the Countrey	0	25	2	07 13 0	
John Varditt for Do. [both contraband]	0	27	0	08 02 0	
James Bordman white port wine	1	0	0		
Do. Mountain	0	31	2	21 14 0	
Nicholas Stairs for Mountain & Canary	0	33	0	12 03 0	
James Smith for Mountain	0	15	0	04 15 0	
James Berney on Acct. of French Port	5	0	0	80 00 0	
Batson for Mountain wine	0	40	2	14 10 0	
Nichs. Stairs at 6s. pr. Gallon	0	20	0	06 04 8	
For Brandy bo.t of Fra. Harrison [contraband]	0	0	5	01 00 0	
For Arrack of John Cowper	0	10	0	08 01 6	
For Rum by Wm. Tomley [porter]	0	6	0	02 14 0	
	10	46	1	£237 05 4	

Ale & Beer in London	Barrells	£ s d	£ s d
Mrs Sanders Beer Brewer to Mar 25 1725			
a bill not brot. into the last Account		18 00 0	
Do. her bill of this year for a Quarter of a			
yr. in full to Jan. 1 1725	31	13 19 0	
Mann Ale Brewer	15½	34 02 0	
Buckland Small Beer Brewer at 10s. p. Bar.	17	08 10 0	£74 11 0

Malt [at Holkham]	Combs	Bushells	£ s d	£ s d
Of Richd. Porter [tenant]	51	2	31 09 6	
Of Catherine Lyons [Loines] [laundry-maid]	2	2	01 10 0	
Of Woodcraft	23	0	13 16 0	
Of Ditto	58	0	35 08 0	
Of Blyford	68	0	47 12 0	
Of Richard Porter	25	0	16 12 0	
Do. Grinding & Carriage			02 07 8	
To Blyford for Beans Sacks &c.			02 03 9	£150 18 11

Hopps	Qr	lb	£ s d	£ s d
Of Catherine Lyons		3	00 03 0	
Of Robert Haylet [tenant]		60	03 00 0	
Of Ditto		30	03 00 0	

			£ s d	£ s d
In Nich. Stairs bill		12	01 04 0	
Of Woodcraft	1	8	06 00 0	
Of Gladish	2	80	21 16 0	
Of Thomson	1	20	14 04 2	£49 07 2
	5	101		

Brewing	*Coombs*	£ s d	£ s d
To Nat. Wilkinson for brewing	19	00 19 0	
To Wm. Fellows	74 Do.	03 14 0	
To Do.	84	05 12 2	
	177		
To Benjamin Naylor do. Assisting		01 03 6	
To Henry May for do.		02 08 2	£13 16 10
			£525 19 3

This figure may be compared with £962 11s 2d, which was the total cost of all food and groceries for that year.

As an alternative to strong drink, tea and coffee became increasingly important in the household budgets of the day, and the beverages prompted a whole series of social conventions – the coffee houses in the city and 'the dish of tay' at home. The first green China tea was imported into England in the 1660s as a medicine and *digestif* and was very expensive at about £2 5s a pound. Its popularity had grown by the beginning of the eighteenth century, but the first quantum leap in demand came in the 1720s. The East India Company sold 200,000lb in 1720, but by the end of the decade its annual sales had topped a million pounds in weight.[11]

Entries in the accounts for tea purchases do not follow a regular pattern and are not particularly helpful in trying to establish a level of consumption in the household. Typical early entries read:

1719 April 24th   Paid Mrs Lewin's bill for tea and glasses £16.
1719 September 12th Paid to Mrs Lewin for tea from April 20th to 12th
                     August £14.
1720 March 7th   Tea for My Lady £1.4.0d.

It would seem likely that much of the buying was hidden within non-itemised bills that were presented by grocers such as the Lewins, and a number of entries show that individual servants bought small amounts on demand. However, some information can be gleaned about prices. In 1722, in London, one pound of Imperial green tea cost nineteen shillings, and, according to Keay, the price of the cheaper bohea tea dropped during the 1720s to around seven shillings a pound.

With a high tax level, the East India Company's increased trade was matched by rival companies importing into Europe and then smuggling tea across the Channel and the North Sea. At Holkham between 1726 and 1728 we find the parson Springall supplying tea to the house, and this was undoubtedly smuggled. That, however, does not seem to have made it any cheaper. He charged eighteen shillings a pound for Imperial green tea and ten shillings for bohea in 1726, and £1 a pound for Imperial in 1728.

The popularity of tea brought with it a market for porcelain from which to drink it, and this was met by importing cups from China as ballast along with the tea. In November 1721 an account entry reads: 'For China and tea £15.14.0d.'. Canisters were bought for use as storage, and the value of the commodity was emphasised in 1720 by buying a canister padlock for two shillings.

According to the antiquary Anthony Wood (1632–95) the first English coffee house was opened in Oxford in 1650 by one of the Jews readmitted into England by Cromwell. A few years later the owner transferred his business to Holborn in London. By the end of the century there were over seven thousand coffee houses in the City, and more than 100 tons of beans were being imported annually.[12] The record of coffee buying in the Coke household matches that of tea in its lack of clarity, and there seems to have been no set pattern. This may have been because of the well-established trade of the city coffee houses and the possibility, again, that purchases were embedded within large grocery orders. Judging by the entries, the amounts varied considerably: in the first quarter of 1723, three pounds were bought, plus 'coffee and spice, as per bill £1 4s 6d', but in the third quarter only one entry can be found and that for a single pound. Over the decade the price varied between 5s and 5s 8d per pound, and, as with tea, small amounts were bought by the hall porter and other servants.

Another social stimulant with its own conventions was tobacco. Since the seventeenth century tobacco, as one of the pleasures or vices of life, has been inextricably linked with drink. Enjoyed in the same social situations, often procured from a common supplier, considered by government as a natural source of revenue, and attracting opprobrium in equal measure, it was a common addiction in the eighteenth century until it fell for a while from favour under George III. The taking of snuff became general during the first year of Queen Anne's reign as a result of the immense quantities thrown onto the London market after the capture of Spanish ships loaded with snuff in the action of Vigo Bay. Thomas Coke bought 'Barcelony' at ten shillings, 'Brazeil' at £1 and Havana at £1 10s per pound. By today's standards the amounts were immense, multiple pounds rather than ounces, and this was partly because the eighteenth-century snuffbox was a fashion accessory and, to allow the goldsmith or jeweller scope, it was generously proportioned; three- or four-ounce capacity was not unusual, and, because snuff (like tobacco) will go stale if not kept in an airtight container, a great deal will have gone to waste. It has also to be said that contemporary comments point to generous amounts being stuffed up the nostrils and even more soiling the addicts' waistcoats. More was spent on tobacco for smoking than on snuff. The cost was much lower, ranging from one shilling to 1s 6d per pound; 14lb were sent down to Holkham in 1724, and the following year the tobacconists Tompson and Williams supplied an impressive 60lb between them at a cost of £5 12s 8d. Clay pipes, the long 'churchwardens' variety, were not expected to last very long and were bought by the gross or half-gross; the superior glazed pipes cost twelve shillings a gross against the 'common' variety at 2s 6d. When they were required in Norfolk, Markant, a local grocer, could supply tobacco and pipes, and a gross of pipes once came from Edward Peckover, who traded mainly as a corn merchant and draper. The tobacco was shipped in hogsheads to the retailers and Markant sold them on to Holkham with a quantity of red lead for caulking so that they could be re-used for storage purposes.

It is not until our own day that tobacco has achieved such a bad reputation. For over three hundred years in varying forms it was the consolation of both rich and poor, both men and women; addiction blended easily with national habits of drinking particularly, and its effect on health was not one that concerned the majority, including the medical profession.

Thomas Coke's parents had died leaving considerable debts, and, in consequence, the heir's guardians were obliged to sell the household effects, including the silver. It was to put this right that, soon after his marriage, Coke commissioned Paul de Lamerie, London's leading silversmith, to supply a full range of tableware at a cost of nearly £3,000. To underline the significance of this lavish provision, it should be set alongside the £2,917 that was the cost of all the works of art purchased on the Grand Tour. Contemporary information on de Lamerie's work is scarce, and it is fortunate that the household accounts give a detailed listing of what was supplied. A transcript of the entries and the silver's subsequent history has been published separately;[13] suffice it to say here that unfortunately none of de Lamerie's work remains at Holkham or has been traced elsewhere. The financial crisis that followed Coke's heavy losses in the South Sea Bubble entailed mortgaging the plate in 1727:

> Received of Mr Waller on mortgage of Sir Thos. Coke's
>   Plate to him at a £5 per Cent from this day June 16th   £1600
> Deduct being paid to Mr Waller 6 weeks interest of the
>   £1600 to this Day which he kept in his hands for
>   Sir Thos. Coke's use   £8 12 6
> Paid to the Officer at the Bank   £1 1 0
> Paid for the Writings and Trouble on this occasion   £3 3 0

When things returned to normal, the silver was used both in town and in the country, and two 'Large Strong Trunks with Iron Barrs for to hold the Plate' and in which to transport it were ordered, with additional cases for two of the larger items.

Pewter was used for everyday, and in 1720 Mr Ridding, the pewterer, was paid for twelve guineas' worth to be sent down to Holkham. In 1727 another pewterer, Mr Audley, supplied the following:

> 4 water dishes at 2s per lb.; 12 plates   £7 3 0
> 16 dishes and 4 doz. plates, 2 doz. spoons, a
>   hoop stand and engraving   £6 7 0

In the following year there was a second order: 10 dishes and 24 plates and engraving £4.19.0. During the same quarter the cutler Mr Savigny supplied two dozen horn-handled knives and two dozen forks for £1 2s to be sent to Holkham, and a Norfolk pewterer, Mr Hingham, supplied six saucepans with covers and four small dishes at the same price per pound. China and glass figure frequently among the purchases, but in nearly every case merely as 'chinaware' or 'glassware'. All the pewter currently displayed in the Old Kitchen was bought for servant use in the 1820s.

Most of the lighting was provided by candles, which were bought for town and country from London tallow chandlers. There were three types, the cheapest of which were the common tallow candles at 5s 8d a dozen. Of better quality were the mould candles at seven shillings a dozen, and the best were the wax candles, which were sold at 2s 8d per pound. A typical order from tallow chandler Mr Francis would be for twenty dozen of common and three dozen of mould, with 10lb of wax candles from Mr Taylor. Kitchen waste provided a useful source of income, and a 1724 entry records 44 stone 3lb of tallow being sold to the chandler for £7 4s 3d. In their way, wax candles were an eighteenth-century class indicator. Emily, Duchess of Leinster, in a letter to Lady Leitrim in 1767, was not sure what status William Ogilvie should have as a tutor. Should he be given tallow candles for his room, which would indicate that, like previous companions to her sons, he was first and foremost a servant? Or should he have wax candles, as befitted a gentleman employee or friend of the family? Her friend said: 'Oh moulds will do, till we see a little.' (William subsequently became Emily's lover and eventually her second husband, creating on the way rather larger social problems, but providing a happy ending.[14]) The houses were not entirely dependent on candles but the use of lamps was limited, and in one case the phrase 'for My Lady's lamp' is used against a purchase of colza oil. This was extracted from cole-seed; the alternative was train oil, which came from whale blubber. All was supplied by oilmen such as Mark Bennett in Norfolk and Mr Godwin in London, who also sold olive oil, scouring sand and salt to the kitchen.

Among the more esoteric commodities listed occasionally are lampblack for the butler so that he could make ink, and a strainer made of tammy (a fine worsted cloth) so that the cook could make 'coolee' (cullis), a strong broth of meat or fowl that had to be strained. Fowl wings were bought from poulterers for use as hearth brushes, a usage both economic and effective that lingered on in some Suffolk farmhouses until the 1930s.

Using the 1728 entries, it is possible to compare fuel costs for Holkham and Thanet House, although the figures do not take into account any stocks in hand:

		£ s d	£ s d
London. 1st quarter	4 chaldrons* of coal	18 2 0	18 2 0
Holkham. 2nd quarter	600 whins†	1 0 9	
	66 sacks of charcoal	6 6 0	
	8 bushels of charcoal	0 10 8	7 17 5
Holkham. 3rd quarter	3 bushels of charcoal	0 4 0	
	1800 whins	3 4 6	
	80 sacks of charcoal	7 16 0	
	63 chaldrons of coal	59 17 0	
	loading cost	1 14 0	72 15 6
London. 4th quarter	31 sacks of charcoal	3 0 0	
	4 bushels of charcoal	0 5 4	
	25 chaldrons of coal 4 tons of Scotch coal	2 5 0	
	billets, brushes, roots‡	12 11 0	
	72 sacks of charcoal	6 9 0	61 5 0

* A chaldron of coal was a dry measure equal to 36 bushels.

† Whins were furze or gorse cuttings used to heat ovens for baking.

‡ Billets were kindling; brushes were the city equivalent of whins; roots were logs.

It will be seen that the London price for a chaldron of coal was 9s 6d against a Norfolk price of nineteen shillings, to which a loading cost was added at Wells quayside. Some coal was landed at Burnham Overy Staithe, and in 1727 forty-two cart loads from there cost £42 10s 6d. In contrast with these figures, one authority quotes £2 to £4 as the eighteenth-century London cost of a chaldron, but the Holkham accounts do not support this, at least in the 1720s.[15] A bushel of charcoal cost 1s 4d both in London and in Holkham. With the autumn/winter quarter at Holkham using sixty-three chaldrons of coal against the winter/spring quarter in town using twenty-five chaldrons, a reasonable assumption is that the venerable and rambling Elizabethan Hill Hall was a good deal more difficult to heat than the compact, soundly built Thanet House in Bloomsbury. The stock held at Holkham proved attractive to the local thieves, and two village boys were given sixpence for detecting a coal stealer.

No doubt Thanet House and Hill Hall were both adequately furnished when Thomas Coke assumed control, but throughout the 1720s a good deal of furniture was purchased and much of it shipped to Holkham. A few items were bought in at his grandmother Lady Ann Walpole's sale in 1722, but the only piece of furniture mentioned is an India chest for £20. A good deal, however, was spent on fabrics – 128 yards in eight pieces of red flowered damask for £48, three pieces of 'ell-wide red silk' for £7 10s, and 81½ yards of black velvet for £6 15s. In 1719 eight black Dutch chairs from Mr Old cost £2 15s, having been inspected by Mrs Johnson, the housekeeper, who went to and fro by coach. The following year, eighteen walnut chairs upholstered in leather costing £19 11s 6d were bought specifically for Holkham, along with eighteen others in cane. Mrs Tooms was paid £52 10s for 'a Chinie Bed', and the blue taffeta used to line it was supplied by Mrs Frombten for £30 17s 6d; to complete this expensive item, 70 yards of blue and white holland were used to make an outside case for it. In 1722 more items were sent down to the country – two dozen chairs from Mr Van Ruyen, three walnut chests of drawers from Mr Stroad, together with quilts, blankets, mattresses, assorted fire irons and colours to paint some of the rooms. A stove grate, fire irons and fender were destined for 'ye Lodge Chamber at Holkham', and 34 yards of 'blue stuff' for the Counting Room bed means that a servant slept there on guard duty. The majority of these things were taken by cart down to Brown's wharf on the Thames, corded up in boxes and crates for shipment to Wells by Oxbrough the Norfolk shipowner. Benjamin Smith was another ship-master who was employed, and, although his home port is not given, it is likely to have been Wells, Cley or Burnham; in 1725 he was reimbursed £1 14s 6d 'for carrying goods from London'. Nevertheless, a number of the less bulky items went down by road, and James Large the Swaffham carrier was used regularly on this account, submitting bills of up to £40 in some years.

It would seem that the Cokes commissioned at least one carpet to a particular design in that, in 1722, Mr George Sanderson received eight guineas for drawing the design of a carpet on paper. At Holkham in 1727, Mr Leworthy 'painted a carpet', which was probably a canvas floor cloth such as was used later in the Long Library. To do so he was supplied by Markant, the local grocer, with 'Brown Despain' (Spanish Brown), an earth with a reddish colour used as a pigment. Pyramids of minerals were a very fashionable form of table decoration at the time, and Thomas must have acquired a pair on the Continent, for a 1719 entry shows that customs fees were paid on 'the two pirramids'. They were then taken by chairmen to

Myers' Coffee House, where the proprietor charged four guineas for putting them together.

Of the many things that were sent down to Holkham throughout the decade, only two can tentatively be identified in the house today. In 1729 a dumb waiter was bought from Mr Birtle for £1 8s, and it could be the only one now in the house, a simple three-tier model in mahogany of the right period. The second candidate is the pair of large leather 'jacks' bought in 1719 for £1 3s. Sometimes called bombards, they are cumbrous water jugs for kitchen use, and of the three that now stand by the range in the Old Kitchen, two might well be that particular pair.

Chapter 11

TRAVEL AND STABLE MATTERS

*T*he eighteenth century has rightly been called the 'age of the horse'. With the steady growth of commerce, a burgeoning population, particularly in London, and the increase in travel for both business and pleasure, the roads and streets were thick with horse traffic. In London especially there was a heavy concentration, with commercial concerns like the larger breweries each stabling hundreds of dray horses. Wherever possible, even small rivers such as the Lark, which was navigable up to Bury St Edmunds, carried barges, and coastwise traffic was heavy, but in the main transit by road was 'Hobson's choice', using heavy wagons or strings of packhorses; the latter could carry up to half a ton each and far outnumbered mounted travellers. In many places, paved causeways wide enough for one horse were built by the side of the dirt roads specifically for the pack trains, but individual horsemen naturally chose to use them too, so that a certain amount of conflict was inevitable. In 1739 there was still no hard road beyond Grantham going north, only the causeways. Nothing moved faster than the horse throughout the century, but, although the first turnpike act had been passed in 1662 and turnpike trusts began to be established in growing numbers after 1706, the condition of the roads got steadily worse as traffic increased. The situation was exacerbated by the vast numbers of beasts that were herded on main roads: in one year 20,000 cattle passed along the Wisbech highway, 40,000 Highland cattle were driven down to fatten on Norfolk marshes, and droves of up to 2,000 Norfolk geese and turkeys at a time began to move toward London immediately after harvest; by mid-century 100,000 cattle and 75,000 sheep made their way to the Smithfield market annually.[1] The concentration of all this traffic on the metropolis made the environs particularly vulnerable. In 1736 Lord Hervey complained: 'The road between Kensington and London is so infamously bad that we live here in the same solitude as we should do if cast on a rock in the middle of the ocean, and all the Londoners tell us that there is between them and us a great impassable gulf of mud.'[2] As late as the middle of the century, the Mile End road 'resembled a stagnant lake of deep mud from Whitechapel to Stratford, with some deep and dangerous sloughs; in many places it was hard work for the horses to go faster than a foot pace, on level ground, with a light four-wheel post-chaise'. Not only were there bad roads to contend with, but travellers often lost their way. Things had not improved a great deal since Samuel Pepys's coachman managed to get lost in broad daylight between Newbury and Reading in the 1660s. Even in Norfolk, the accounts show that guides were paid to find the way to Oxborough and Melton Constable in 1719, and two were hired when crossing Brandon heath in 1721. The most bizarre example occurs in the same year when a guide was apparently needed to chart the route from Warham to Holkham, a journey of no more than 5 or 6 miles.

In this world in which the horse dominated nearly all movement, Thomas Coke's establishment needed to be well equipped. Apart from the practical concerns of regular travel between London and Holkham, and the need to visit outlying parts of the Great Estate, there was the matter of his position in society. The possession of a coach and six that could be properly accompanied by a retinue of coachman, postilion and outriders was a most potent status symbol. This, again, was a continuation of the perception current in the previous century. When Pepys used his 'chariot' for the first time on May Day 1669 it was the culmination of a long-standing ambition to establish his status in society.[3]

Stable establishments were maintained both in London and at Holkham. In town, eight coach horses and four saddle horses were the average numbers; the vehicles were a travelling coach, a town chariot (the 'fine chariot'), a travelling chariot, a chaise-marine (a chaise whose body rested on suspension straps) and the two berlins, which had been bought in Paris in 1717. Thanet House did not have sufficient accommodation for so many, and two stables together with two coach houses and a chamber were rented from Mr Morton's livery stables nearby, where some of the horses were kept standing at livery and Lady Margaret's sedan chair was stored. The latter was taken in hand for alteration and repair in 1725 by Mr Vaughan, who charged £25 for his work. In all, this extra stabling cost between £50 and £60 a quarter. Mr Budworth was the London coachmaker chosen to carry out work for the household, and in 1725 he charged £218 18s 6d for augmenting the fleet with a new travelling coach and a new one-horse chaise, and for painting them. He was also under contract to maintain the vehicles, and in that same quarter he drew £50 for keeping the coach in repair. After Coke had been raised to the peerage in 1728, there was a little flurry of activity to raise the standard of the harness and accoutrements or 'furniture'. Mr Vanbushell was paid £10 for four sets of tapestry furniture, and Mr Addison had a guinea for painting a pattern design to be used on them. Mrs Bignell received £12 3s for four livery saddles and for making up the tapestry furniture complete with bridles. She had a further fifteen guineas for three saddles in blue cloth and silver lace embellished with the letter 'L' and coronet. A little sidelight on the care that was taken to improve the appearance of the turnout is provided by the note that, in 1719 at least, two 'long tails' were bought for the coach horses from a Mr Waring for £1 8s. Mr Dark was the London farrier, and an example of his quarterly bills shows that he supplied 161 shoes for the carriage horses at 8d a shoe, 106 shoes for the saddle horses at 6d a shoe, and added £10 11s for the farriery – a total of £18 12s 6d. When shoes were cast on the road, the coachman had to pay a little more and claimed accordingly. Without furnishing a reason, an entry of August 1722 in the accounts records that Coke made journeys to Tetsworth in Oxfordshire and to Rochester using a hired coach, coachman and postilion, but the fact that men were hired to watch the house suggests that Lady Margaret was also away and had probably commandeered the family coach. At a time when he was journeying regularly to her family home at Hothfield in Kent he kept horses stabled at Dartford, Rochester and Bearsted so that he would have no need to hire post horses.

The Holkham establishment was naturally larger than that in London, and in 1719 the stables housed thirty-five horses, and the number increased with the establishment of the hunt in the years that followed. Such estate maps as survive give little evidence as to the whereabouts of the Hill Hall stable block, but it will have been to the east of the house, and there were separate carriage and saddle horse sections and a pad groom's stable; breeding mares and wintering foals were kept at Godwick, the old family house a few miles away. With this number of horses there was naturally a fairly heavy turnover, and animals were bought steadily throughout the period at Holkham, in London, and quite often on visits elsewhere – eight coach and saddle horses were bought at Longford on one occasion, for example. Nevertheless, most if not all were named, and the choice varied between the place where they had been bought, the vendor's name or a particular characteristic of the horse. Here is a list of those named in 1719: Gretton's Ridgel, Suckling, Eggleton, Clarke, Paurkin's Cropp, Longford, Hulton, Walpole, Pye Bald, Cripple, Mansel, Barton, Farnham Royal, Wyvill's Clumsy, Huntingfield, Ashborne Black, Royalton, Pigg, Manag'd Crop, Perkins, Ashborne Bay, Yorkshire Black, Chatsworth, Sympsons Skew and Smock Face.

The stable fare varied little and was a standard mixture of hay, oats, bran and beans, and the ubiquitous bracken of the neighbouring heaths was mowed for use as litter. Horse doctoring was an in-house matter, and the coachman had a case of fleams (lancets) bought for him in 1727 so that his horses could be bled in the same way as his fellow humans. Jones, the family's apothecary, supplied powdered antimony, sulphur, Tolu balsam and the ingredients to make Tilsit ointment for stable use. A pound of quicksilver and four gallons of aquavit bought in the same year may have been the basis for making mercury ointment; the record is silent on just how and to what effect 'herrings for ye horses' feet' were used. As one would expect, all farriery in Norfolk was in the hands of Henry Knott, the Holkham blacksmith, with James Kendall being responsible at Beck Hall for hunt horses stabled there. Occasionally, the services of a Captain Bedford were called on in London to train horses and riders. In 1727 he was paid 1½ guineas for 'schooling a horse to the bit', and in the same year he charged 12 guineas for teaching young Edward Coke to ride over a period of four months. The overall cost of maintaining the stables (not including staff costs) varied a good deal from year to year: in 1719 it totalled £1,683, in 1720 £1,015, but was no more than £253 in 1727. Horse prices were very variable; an average saddle horse could be had for £7 to £10, and 'a Little Poney for Master Coke' cost two guineas. However, Sir Thomas Greasley charged £29 18s 6d for a chestnut mare in 1719, and a grey stone horse (a stallion) from Mr Mansell, Lord

Thanet's huntsman, cost £52 10s. Hotspur the grey gelding was sold to Sir Philip Parker in the following year for thirty-five guineas, and in 1723 Mr Newton paid £40 19s for one of Coke's mares, which indicates that bloodstock was changing hands at between £30 and £60.

Slow and sometimes arduous journeys were an accepted part of the family's lifestyle, and the seasonal moves between London and Norfolk were planned and carried out with care and a certain amount of style. A typical example is the transfer that was made in September 1720. They set out for the country on the 22nd in the coach and the chaise-marine, and, although Lady Margaret's brother-in-law Lord Harold was a guest, he paid for his own horses and met half of the house bills en route. The first overnight stop was at Hockerill, where the bill was £5 19s, including £2 4s for the horses, plus vails of 7s 6d. The next day they journeyed as far as Newmarket, where the horses were baited, and then went on to spend the night at the Bull at Barton Mills at a cheaper rate overall of £3 17s 8d. The last day on the road was broken at Swaffham to bait the horses, and Holkham was reached in the evening. Four turnpike charges and the toll at Barton Mills' bridge came to 8s 11d. Coke planned to stay in the country for a few months and so a dozen servants were included in the party, headed by James Davis, the under-butler and 1st footman. With him were the footman James Mason, Lady Margaret's 2nd footman William Shadbolt, Coke's footman William Holland, the junior coachman Thomas Johnson, John Walker the 2nd groom, one of the postilions, Jack Large the stable helper, 'the Boy Tom', Lady Margaret's maid Mrs Jenny, and Jane Love the upper-laundry-maid. The chef John Gundaymore made up the round dozen and had the distinction of having his drinks on the road itemised separately. The incidental expenses included payment to a landowner for going through his grounds, for guarding the chaise-marine at night, for 'walnuts &c' for those in the coach, and 6d for poor people on the road. Allowing for Lord Harold's contribution, and for the servants' board wages, the journey cost £15 15s in all. When the family returned to London in December, they took four days over the journey, and, because Coke's sister Cary and her husband went with them, a second chaise was brought into use, with the servants travelling in a waggon. Mrs Jenny had been ill during their stay and was spared the rigours of the waggon by taking a place in the Lynn stagecoach. Lord Harold rounded off his Holkham visit by shooting at Godwick and was provided with horses and a groom as far as Swaffham on his way home.

When the servants travelled back to London without the family in January 1722, they used the coach, the chaise and some of the Holkham horses, but hired another couple for the footmen. It was on that journey that they enrolled the services of two guides to see them across Brandon Heath, and they varied the route by diverting to Epping and Leytonstone. At other times, stopovers were made at Newport Pagnell, Bourn Bridge and Hoddesdon. The cost of the Holkham to London trip in 1728 when the Cokes travelled with the same number of servants was £22 14s 11d, a rise of nearly 50 per cent. At that time, to 'ride post', as George Appleyard, the steward, did (that is to hire fresh horses at each stage), cost £3 4s 3d for the 106 miles. In July 1728 Lord Lovel (as he was by then) made his way home through Essex and Suffolk, and, although no details are given of stopping places, the journey took five days. With him were a dozen servants headed by Appleyard, who dispensed £4 19s to 'the ringers on the road'. Once, in 1725, it was 'the ringers and musicians' at Thetford who benefited, and at those places where travellers stopped regularly, the local band obviously held themselves ready to make for the church and raise the bells in the expectation of a worthwhile reward.

In September 1718 Thomas journeyed to Longford in Derbyshire to introduce his bride to his old guardian Sir Edward Coke, taking care to send a considerable quantity of wine in advance as a present. Their progress was leisurely, taking in Hampton Court, Farnham Royal (a family manor), Windsor, Stoke Poges (which had been a family property), Reading, Oxford, Woodstock (to view Blenheim which was nearly finished), Minster Lovell (another family manor), Banbury, Daventry, Market Harborough, Burley-on-the-hill (where they stayed three nights with Lord Nottingham), Nottingham and Derby. There they were met by Longford people to the sound of welcoming church bells before being escorted to Longford. They were made much of while they were there, and Thomas must have enjoyed showing Lady Margaret all those things he had enjoyed as a boy. It may have been in this context that he rewarded 'ye men that danced Fadden at Longford' – a traditional Derbyshire country dance.

Horses were not always the order of the day, for during their stay a boy was sent forty-two times to Derby on foot between October and Christmas, and twenty-six more times before the end of February. His pay was 6d for each 18-mile round trip, but at least he was allowed a horse on the three occasions 'when the waters were out'. The family's return journey to London was a little more straightforward, via Swarkstone, Loughborough, Leicester, Market Harborough, Lamport, Northampton, Newport Pagnell, St Albans and Barnet, with four overnight stops at inns. Longford servants, coaches and horses were used for this journey, and four manorial pinders* were paid en route to mind the company's horses rather than impound them. The eight days' board wages that were paid would have covered the servants' expenses returning to Derbyshire. Abraham Thomas, the valet-de-chambre recorded his travelling expenses in some detail when he went with his master down to Bristol in 1724. There were house and stable bills at Maidenhead, Marlborough and Bath, and the horses were baited at Speenhamland and Sandy Lane. Five turnpike charges were levied on the journey and a shilling was given for coming through a farmer's ground at Laycock. Coke was shaved at Marlborough and Bath, where he lodged with Lord Salisbury. What with the three servants' board wages, drink upon the road, and the odd shilling for having the dog Chance sent back to London, the expenses for the journey came to £36 4s ½d.

Details concerned with horses and travel are scattered throughout the accounts and help to complete a rounded picture of life in the age of the horse. When Mrs Thompson, the housekeeper, used the Lynn coach for her journeys between Holkham and London, as she did occasionally, a place was booked for her with ten shillings left at the agent's as 'an earnest' of her intention to travel, and she was always escorted from Holkham to catch the coach at Lynn. It could not be said that the stagecoach was a comfortable alternative at that time. The vehicles were not much more than unsprung waggons without proper windows and could average only about 40 miles a day.[4] Horses are known for their stamina and reliability, but they occasionally failed their riders; Steward Humphrey Smith's bay gelding died when he was on his way to Farnham Royal, and as it was his own he claimed £10 in compensation; one night in 1722, Robert Coke's man lost the horse Eggleton in Epping Forest and a Mr Lincoln was tipped 5s 6d for finding and stabling it at an inn. It was a place in which to be wary, as George Appleyard, the land steward, found to his cost: in that same year an account entry reads: 'By order of my Maister, he's please to allow me 3 Guyneas which was taken from me by a Highwayman.'

---

* A pinder was a manorial officer whose duty it was to impound stray animals.

Chapter 12

SERVANTS

*T*he eighteenth century brought a number of economic developments that carried in their train a whole variety of social changes; they, in their turn, created a steadily increasing demand for domestic servants throughout the period. If, by whatever means, an attempt were made to identify the relative sizes of occupational groups, the servant class would without doubt rank with the largest. A number of contemporary analyses give some indication of the position: in 1767 Jonas Hanway calculated that one person in every thirteen living in London was a domestic, giving a total of 50,000.[1]

By the end of the century a London Magistrate's estimate was 200,000 servants, based on the calculation that 100,000 of the 241,000 families in London kept an average of two servants.[2] The surge was largely accounted for by the rapid growth of the middle class and the increasing wealth generated by manufacturing industry and entrepreneurial commerce. That in itself had a knock-on effect as it related to the nobility and gentry. For them, the importance of maintaining a numerous train of servants was greatly intensified by this challenge from below. Their requirement moved from that which a gentleman's status demanded to what he could afford. It was particularly important in their judgement to have a large retinue in London, where, owing to the impersonality of urban society, the visible marks of social position assumed a greater consequence than in the country – members of the upper class were acutely conscious of how their households compared with those of their neighbours. This will certainly have been so for the Cokes in Great Russell Street.

The Duke of Somerset's household ran to over a hundred in the 1690s, and in the first twenty years of the eighteenth century he employed twenty-six menservants, so that the total was probably in the region of fifty;[3] in mid-century the Duke of Bedford's London establishment alone was forty all told.[4] However, a corrective was applied by the Duchess of Marlborough, who made do with a mere thirteen in the vastness of Blenheim.[5]

The metropolis was a constant lure for all those who sought advancement, better living and adventure, not least among domestics. A move there was often seen as a solution by those who, under the laws of Settlement, did not qualify for a place in their own country parish and were driven to move away. Pregnant unmarried women were particularly vulnerable: Defoe remarks that a common joke was to ask 'if they had been church'd before they came home'.[6] To be 'in service' was both a refuge and a means whereby improved social status could be obtained. It demanded little or no financial outlay and had the virtue of ensuring a sheltered existence.[7] As a piece of Irish advice to servants had it: 'Whatever Changes happen in public Affairs, your Circumstances are unaffected by them. Whether Provisions are dear or cheap is the same Thing to you. Secure of having all your real Necessities supplied, you rise without Anxiety, and go to Bed without danger of having your Repose disturbed.'[8]

The chief sources of supply were the families of small farmers and farm labourers, with employers showing a strong preference for the former:

small farmers were the people that used to stock the country with the best of servants: these were the nurseries for breeding up industrious and virtuous young men and women; whereas the generality of servants, now-a-days, are such as have had but little opportunity of learning how to do business so as to be fit to make good servants; for the labourer cannot be expected to be able to give his children that learning which is proper to fit them for good places; whilst those who rent small farms have generally the where-withal to give their children learning sufficient to qualify them to read virtuous books, and to know how to behave in a proper and decent manner. Besides, the girls have opportunities of learning at home how to brew, bake, cook, knit, sew, and get up linnen, &c., whereas poor people's children have no such advantages.[9]

Selection continued to be a problem throughout the eighteenth century. In 1790 the cantankerous De Trusler, in his *London Advisor and Guide*, stressed that caution was needed when developing 'attachments' to servants. He recommended country persons of simple tastes and manners in order to avoid the problems associated with employing 'persons who had aspirations to ape the status of their employers'. Trusler was, by his own admission, confirmed in his opinions by an embarrassing incident when visiting a nobleman, in that he mistakenly introduced himself to a finely dressed servant, believing him to be his master. Remarks on the capacity of servants to assume fine dress and coiffures were central to the moral and critical discourse of the period on the serving classes. Typically, there were commentaries on the means whereby such menials were able to afford luxuries, and laments on the decline of 'subordination', the indulgence of masters, and the vices of profiteering and pilfering that were assumed to be endemic in the lower orders.

Thomas Coke enjoyed the inestimable benefit of a very large estate on which he could call for suitable servants recommended by his own steward, bailiffs or tenants. That this was a happy state of affairs is confirmed by a correspondent in a contemporary newspaper:

I have often thought of the great interest a nobleman, or gentleman of large estate, might always secure by only the proper choice of his *domestics*. Such an one cannot be without a great number of tenants, who might think their children honoured in the *service* of his lord-ship, and whose tenures would be a sort of *security* for the honesty and good behaviour of the servant.[10]

At a time of heightened commercial expansion, there was strong competition in London, where most servants were hired, and there was a heavy turnover, caused partly by the city's high mortality rates. London-bred servants were said to be wanton in habit and unscrupulous in practice, qualities not unexpected, particularly in areas such as Holborn and the parish of St Giles. Moreover, urban living was supposed to have given them a sophistication characterised by a highly insubordinate spirit and an exceptionally self-interested attitude.[11] Later in the century a newspaper correspondent showed that the same view was still current: 'In the remote parts of the kingdom, which have little connection with the capital, servants are tractable and industrious, at least they are infinitely more so that those to be met with in London and its environs.'[12] Contemporary comments on rudeness, extravagence and insolence were numerous. Nevertheless, the demand was so intense that during the first third of the eighteenth century the charity schools of London and Westminster provided the market with 3,873 girls and 3,366 boys as domestics.[13] Wages were as much as 100 per cent higher than in the country, and the interaction between heavy demand and a higher standard of living, with a much more varied diet, prompted higher wage demands and their satisfaction.[14]

In the case of the Coke household it may be assumed that the majority of the servants were recruited from Norfolk and Suffolk; and, when the size and composition of the staff are examined, it is clear that its master was typical of his rank and class. Although the accounts books furnish a great deal of detail about servants, their names, occupations, wages and conditions, there are difficulties in determining the whole picture with certainty. Accounts were kept at three levels at least, and only the main series has survived. Servants were, moreover, maintained both in London and at Holkham, and some staff were employed in both places. Payment was normally quarterly, but there were exceptions, when wages were paid in arrears or in advance, and there were many overlaps caused by changes in staff and summary dismissals. The analysis that follows, therefore, can be no more than a careful approximation of the actual situation.

There was an accepted servant hierarchy in families such as the Cokes, and the main division was between upper and lower servants. The former were administrative, supervisory or skilled, and normally wore their own clothes; the latter were controlled and directed, being divided into those who wore livery and those who did not but were provided with clothing. These distinctions were of considerable importance throughout the century. An upper servant's protest in John O'Keefe's play *Tony Lumpkin in Town* makes the point: 'Do you make no difference between a servant in livery, and a gentleman's gentleman? In the country, I suppose it's "hail fellow well met"; but here, Sir, we are delicate, nice in our distinctions; for a valet moves in a sphere, and lives in a stile as superior to a footman, as a Pall-Mall groom porter to the marker of a tennis-court.'[15]

In the 1720s Thomas Coke's London household comprised the following upper servants:

Name	Position	Wages p.a.
John Casey	house steward	£30
Edward Jarrett	assistant house steward	£20
Abraham Thomas	valet-de-chambre	£20
Andrew Griffiths	upper butler	£12
John Gundaymore	cook	£40
Mrs Johnson (later Mrs Shaw)	housekeeper	£20

John Casey was in overall charge of the household and kept the main accounts until his early death in 1723 (he was succeeded by David Williams, on £40, who was discharged in 1726). All departmental and individual accounts went to Casey for collation, and he prepared the quarterly and annual summaries. He was also called on by Coke and Lady Margaret to provide them with ready cash when necessary. Apart from the duties of his office, Casey was close to the family. After Edward and Cary Coke had died in 1707, he and his wife cared for 'Neddy' and 'Bobby', Thomas's younger brothers, together with their nurse, for an additional £60 a quarter. He taught them their 'three 'R's', and they stayed with the Caseys until they were in their teens.

Edward Jarrett's position is less easy to determine, and the title accorded him is notional. He had been Coke's valet-de-chambre on the Grand Tour, keeping the day-to-day accounts of expenditure that are an invaluable mine of information for students almost 300 years later. From 1718 until 1722 he maintained a separate account book itemising Coke's personal expenditure and also household expenses both in London and at Holkham, being reimbursed by Casey at the end of each week. It details purchases over a wide range of goods – food, beer, candles, dry goods, clothing, linen, brushes and other equipment – and he paid casual staff their wages. It is unlikely, however, that he initiated orders, but rather that he was responsible for carrying them out.

Andrew Griffiths's duties were carried out with very little variation over the next two centuries by generations of butlers who became in the public imagination the very essence of the superior servant, as seen on the stage or found in countless novels. From his pantry he presided over the silver, glass, china and tableware, and the security of the plate was his responsibility. 'As all the Plate is committed to your care, never suffer strangers to come into the place where it is kept, nor let the place be ever left open.'[16] He was required to be knowledgeable in matters of wine vintages and the technical aspects of cellarage: 'Take great care of your wine and other liquors, not only to keep them in good order, but likewise to prevent their being embezzled, or given away to any person besides those who have a right to them according to your instructions.'[17] In conjunction with the house steward, he superintended the service at table. Perhaps more than any other, the post required 'a man of known integrity', and 'a becoming carriage'.[18]

The valet-de-chambre's chief concern was his master's appearance. Having brought him his morning draught, or a dish of tea, he assisted Coke in the process of dressing, selecting suitable apparel for the day ahead and then literally helping him on with his clothes. 'The more care you take in dressing your master in a fashionable manner, the more respect you show for him, and you will be much taken notice of for your fidelity.'[19] He would be expected to be competent to dress his master's hair and service his wigs – a matter requiring considerable skill, using hair powder supplied by Mr Wintle the perfumier. Twenty or so pounds of it, in three grades, was used every month, the finest for the master and the cheapest for the liveried servants. John Macdonald, a contemporary valet, went to the lengths of staying with a hairdresser in order 'to bring my hand into hairdressing again'.[20] A knowledge of French was accounted an advantage, and the valet normally attended his master everywhere, although it will be seen that Thomas Coke had two personal footmen as well.

John Gundaymore, the cook, was the highest paid of all the upper house servants, and this reflected the importance that English high society of the time placed on cuisine. When he was discharged at Michaelmas 1725, he was replaced by Monsieur Noireaux (or Norreaux), who had been recruited in Paris and drew £22 10s in travelling expenses on his arrival. His salary was set at sixty guineas a year, and Jean Baptiste (dubbed 'French Jack'), an erstwhile groom, was appointed 2nd French cook. Noireaux left the following year, and his replacement, with Baptiste and an under-cook, went to

Holkham with the family; another indication of the preferential treatment accorded to the cooks is the fact that their washing was always itemised separately. During the ten years covered by this survey, the household had a number of male cooks, some of whom lasted only a few weeks. The first requirement was always familiarity with French practice, particularly over the manner of sauces; the upper classes were very attracted by Parisian cuisine and the reputation of *les officiers de bouche* in the houses of the French nobility. In the 1780s the situation had not changed; La Rochefoucauld noted: 'English cooks are not very clever folk, and even in the best houses one fares very ill. The height of luxury is to have a Frenchman, but few people can afford the expense.'[21]

Mrs Johnson, the housekeeper, controlled all the maids, dealt with the stores of household necessaries, ran the laundry and at least some of the affairs of the still room, and was responsible for all cleaning. Oil lamps and candles were probably in her care, although the butler may have looked after them.

The liveried servant's greatest asset was the ability to display his master's wealth and importance. This was best achieved by securing a place in a large establishment, which not only impressed the world by its size but also ensured that the quality of the livery would be above criticism. Of all servants, the liveried staff were the target of most adverse comment and the sharpest satire. Men of good physique were much sought after, and their looks, coupled with a lifestyle that required very little hard work sustained by good living, made them the subject of envy by their peers and barely suppressed irritation for their betters. It was said that 'their sole office is fatuously to wait upon the person of their owner, and so to put in evidence his ability unproductively to consume a large amount of service'.[22]

Livery was an expression of status. Magnificent and deliberately archaic, based as it was on court dress of the early years of the century, it suggested grandeur, and its highly expensive ornamentation showed that its wearers were engaged solely in ceremonial activities. In the Coke household the chosen livery was dark blue set off by red facings and revers. The cloth was purchased in bulk and made up by William Haines or another of Coke's tailors. In 1725, for example, 33 yards of blue broadcloth at seven shillings per yard, and 15 yards of red at 11s 6d per yard, costing £18 11s in all, came from the draper Samuel Cook. A much larger amount was expended on applied decoration – the laceman Alexander Lawman's bill for liveries that year was £61, and the coachmen's hats were trimmed with lace costing about sixteen shillings, showing that the working dress was anything but plain; the postilions were tricked out in white buckskin breeches, and perukes, stockings, boots and shoes were provided to complete the ensemble. The terms of service normally laid down a routine of annual replacement of livery, but, if they preferred, servants sometimes took a cash equivalent instead – Robert Webster, the 1st Groom, was paid £7 in 1726 on that score.

Although he had a limited seniority, the footman had perhaps the highest profile of the liveried servants.

Name	Position	Wages p.a.
James Davis	under-butler and 1st footman	£8
Abraham Blauner	2nd footman (the 'Germain')	£8
William Holland	Thomas Coke's footman	£7
John Mason	footman	£7
William Shadbolt	lady's 2nd footman	£7

A footman had a range of duties both inside and outside the house: he waited at table, served tea and was always available to answer the call of his master or mistress to snuff candles, draw curtains, open doors or do any of the plenitude of things that served to ease their path through life. A mahogany dumb waiter stands in the passage outside the audit room in Holkham Hall today and is possibly the same one that was bought from Mr Birtle in 1729; its significance might well relate to one of James Boswell's asides made half a century later: 'We dined in all the elegance of two courses, and a desert, with dumb waiters, except when the second course and the desert were served. We talked with unreserved freedom, as we had nothing to fear' (the footman's ability to eavesdrop accounted for his reputation as a great one for gossip).[23] Outside, the footman ran errands, took messages to other houses, and rode on the back of the family coach with one or sometimes two of his fellows. Lady Margaret used her sedan chair a great deal, and a footman walked in front to clear the way; she was often out six nights in a week and William Holland and James Davis received regular bonus payments for 'lighting my lady' when they acted as linkmen on the way to the theatre or elsewhere, using flambeaux bought for a guinea a dozen. To venture out at night without a servant was to invite robbery or worse, and, like their master, the footmen carried light swords called 'hangers': 'August 1719. £1 7s for Mending and Cleaning Serv.ts Hangers, and a new Hanger, Girdles and Froggs.' This was despite the fact that *The Gazette* in 1701 had noted that 'the wearing of swords when attending any of the nobility and gentry was forbidden' because 'many mischiefs and dangerous accidents had occurred'. Four of the servants were equipped with a brace of pistols apiece, to be carried when travelling with the family by coach.

There was always a substantial stable staff, as shown by this selection from the 1720s:

Name	Position	Wages p.a.
Francis Riggs	1st coachman	£8
Frank Richard	2nd coachman	£6
Thomas Johnson	coachman/undergroom/farrier	£5
Samuel Skegg	postilion	£6
Edmund Gittos	postilion	£6
Charles House	postilion	£6
Robert Webster	1st groom	£6
John Walker	2nd groom	£6
Jean Baptiste	groom	£5
John Redfern	stable-boy	£5
Edward 'the Boy' Sadler	stable-boy	5s
'Old John' Greer	helper	irregular payments
Cord Rolston	stable labourer	1s per day

The coachman was recognised as the senior livery servant, and, apart from his driving skills, he was responsible for the management of the stables, control of the stable staff, maintenance of the vehicles and the ordering of fodder. When Johnson died in 1722, the St Giles's burial register described him as a farrier, and all shoeing was under his superintendence, if not carried out by him. Richard Chaplain was his successor and was paid extra for doubling as a farrier. The coachmen, postilions and three of the footmen (those who rode with the coach) were issued with boots fitted with white metal spurs, though why Will Holland and James Davis, the under-butler, should also have boots with white spurs at fourteen shillings a pair is not clear.

The postilions rode one of the near-side horses in the team of six that drew the coach and helped to guide them from that position. They wore standard riding livery, except that they were issued with silk bags for their hair, showing that they wore bag wigs rather than the bob wigs of the coachmen. It is difficult to be certain of the establishment number in their case because there were a great many changes. During the decade under review at least sixteen postilions were employed, some for very short periods.

The grooms and lower stable staff did not wear livery. The grooms had the care of the horses in stables; they fed and watered them and dosed them when necessary. The coachman was issued with a set of fleams, but the grooms are more likely to have used them. Jean Baptiste was in all probability recruited on Coke's return journey from the Continent and was transformed into the '2nd French Cook' in 1725, thereby trebling his wages. John Redfern was followed after six months by Samuel Goodacres. Edward Sadler's wages soon rose to £2 10s, but he was then discharged. He was appointed 'cocker' at Holkham later. 'Old John' had clothing bought for him occasionally, and Tom Robinson, the Holkham hunt's whipper-in, was in town at times, having handkerchiefs and neckcloths given him.

Within the house, the lower servants did not wear livery.

Name	Position	Wages p.a.
William Tomley	porter	£10
John Macklin	watchman	£10
Thomas Davis	houseman	£10

The porter's was a responsible position, and the duties, in this household at least, were a trifle idiosyncratic. Will Tomley naturally kept watch on the front door and, following his master's directions, received or discouraged callers accordingly, and shared the security duties with the butler. He was always at hand to carry out small services for Coke and, perhaps because his service was of long standing, he acted in a personal capacity, buying things like a couple of quarts of whisky, ice cream and bottles of aniseed water. He paid for coach and chair hire, posted letters, even shaving his master and furnishing him with small change on occasion. This all-round usefulness was reflected in his salary.

Davis's wage is high for a general handyman to deal with fuel, rubbish and similar tasks, and may reflect a security responsibility, although there are no clues as to Davis's actual duties; he does not seem to have been replaced when he was discharged in 1722.

There were also several female servants in the house:

Name	Position	Wages p.a.
Mrs Jenny	lady's maid?	£–?
Mrs Key	nurse	£–?
Mrs Smith	nurse	£10
Ann Baker	cook's maid	£6
Mary Dorham	housekeeper's maid	£5
Ann Brown	housemaid	£5
Elizabeth Lish	housemaid	£5
Jane Love	upper-laundry-maid	£6
Catherine Loines	under-laundry-maid	£5
Frances Lucas	nursery-maid	£5

It is likely that Mrs Jenny was a Hothfield servant who came with Lady Margaret on her marriage. Mrs Smith was an old family servant already in receipt of a £10 annuity who was brought back to nurse 'little Master' Edward Coke. Frances Lucas was appointed on the birth of 'little Master'.

Then, there were various casual staff employed in London:

Name	Position	Wages
William Edwin	nightwatchman	1s per night
Thomas Etherington	nightwatchman	1s per night
Samuel Grinston	nightwatchman	1s per night
William Griffith	chairman	
Richard Idle	chairman	
Ann Blinkhorn	charwoman	£1 5s 6d, 8s and 18s 6d
Mary Macdonnell	charwoman	7s and 9s
Gazeley	slaughterman	£1 2s 2d
Ann Palmer	charwoman	£2 14s 0d
Eliza Davies	charwoman	£1 13s 0d
Jane Sylis	charwoman	6s
The widow Carter	charwoman	10s

The nightwatchmen were employed either as assistants to John Macklin or as replacements, particularly when the family were in the country. The chairmen were not on the establishment but were paid by the journey for carrying Lady Margaret in her own sedan chair.

As for the other casual staff, in the last quarter's accounts for Thanet House of 1725, these are described as 'chairwomen & assistance in the house and offices'.

At £10 12s 2d, the cost of the casual labour was an appreciable addition to the main wages bill. Mrs Blinkhorn was drafted in as an emergency cook for over three months in 1721 on a shilling a day plus board and lodging; she occasionally helped out in the laundry and was sometimes taken down to Holkham. Mary Macdonnell called regularly at the house as 'Mrs McDoull the herb woman'.

At the Holkham establishment there was a different senior staff;

Name	Position	Wages p.a.
Humphrey Smith	land steward	£30
Edward Smith	gentleman of the horse	£30
Thomas Morecroft	master carpenter/clerk of works	£30
John Halsey	surveyor	£12 rising to £30
Johannes Wildebald	apprentice	

Humphrey Smith was succeeded in 1722 by George Appleyard on £200 p.a. There is no clue as to the trade or profession to which the German boy Johannes Wildebald was apprenticed, but he was paid £8 in advance 'on completion'. In the early 1720s Coke laid out £20 on binding apprentices at Holkham, and in 1725 Thomas Robinson is listed as 'the apprenticed stable-boy', with his mother Martha receiving £20 'consideration money' the following year.

Holkham had a coachman's stable, a groom's stable for saddle horses, and a pad-groom's stable for easy-paced horses. The coachmen, grooms and postilions served at Holkham as well as in London, and a number of other men are named in these posts through the 1720s. As with the higher servants, there were a number of other men who served as stable helpers at Holkham during the decade, and some of the stable-boys progressed through their hierarchy and on to be grooms. The lower stable staff included:

Name	Position	Wages
John Fowler	1st stable-boy	£2 10s 0d p.a.
Henry Palmer	2nd stable-boy	£2 10s 0d p.a.
Thomas Porter	3rd stable-boy	£2 10s 0d p.a.
Thomas Barefoot	4th stable-boy	£2 10s 0d p.a.

Edward Bernard	stable-boy	£2 10s 0d p.a.
Robert Kitchen	stable-boy	£2 10s 0d p.a.
Gamaliel Gregory	coachman's stable helper	3s per week
Thomas Pickworth	coachman's stable helper	3s per week
John Wilkins	coachman's stable helper	3s per week
Alexander Clay	pad-groom's stable helper	3s per week
John Clare	pad-groom's stable helper	2s 6d per week

There was also a hunt staff:

Name	Position	Wages
Thomas Groom	fox huntsman	£20 p.a
John Bailey	fox huntsman's assistant	£8 p.a. [from 1722]
William Pickford	hare huntsman	£5 p.a.
Thomas Robinson	whipper-in	£2 10s 0d p.a.
Stephen Mann	dog-boy	£3 p.a.
John Large	helper	3s per week
John Halley	gamekeeper	£12 p.a.

Thomas Robinson was followed by Walter Gardiner and John Morrish successively. After Stephen Mann's early death in 1727 he was replaced by the boy John Mountain.

The grooms, stable-boys, huntsmen and their boys all wore livery made of fustian (a thick twilled short-napped cloth) over buckskin breeches and stockings, although Tom Robinson as a new whipper-in needed to be kitted out with the basic four shirts, stockings and shoes (plus a knife and fork) in 1719, and his working dress was a linen 'frock' or smock, as was the dog-boy's. The livery allowance for a stable-boy's boots, shoes and stockings was seventeen shillings. In 1727 Thomas Groom, the fox huntsman, had a coat specially made for him by John Stoakes, the Norfolk tailor, using shagg, a cloth having a velvet nap on one side.

Meanwhile, the following staff worked in the garden:

Name	Position	Wages p.a.
John Creed	head gardener	£7
John Wade	under-gardener	£8
John [?] Pennington [or Peniston]	gardener	£6

When work began on the 'great lawn' John Creed was followed by John Aram (who had been under-gardener) at £20 p.a. John Wade was followed by Andrew Parker at £12 p.a.

There were separate lower servants at Hill Hall:

Name	Position	Wages p.a.
Ann Bulmer	housemaid	£5
Sophia Garrouch	housemaid	£5
Mary Rogers	laundry-maid	?
Elizabeth Stephens	laundry-maid	£6 10s 0d

Other Holkham servants without specified duties included:

Name	Wages p.a.
W. Clark	£12
John Martin	£10
Samuel Staple	£8
Susannah Bakeman	£6
Ann Coates	£6
Mary Pim	£6
Ann Leech	£5
Elizabeth Simson	£5

The wage levels indicate that most of these would have been lower servants.

One of the major differences between the establishments of Thanet House and Hill Hall is that the latter employed (and no doubt attracted) much more casual help, as the following list gathered from several years shows:

Name	Position/task	Wages
Dame Brand	nursing the sick	lump sum (no period given)
Dame Ann England	sick nursing and kitchen help	lump sum (no period given)
Ann England jun.	helping housemaids	3s per week
Margaret Dow	kitchen help	3s per week approx.
Mary Jolly	kitchen help	3s per week approx.
Ann Lewis	kitchen help	3s per week approx.

Dame King	washing	8*d* per day
Dame Leather	washing	7*d* per day
Elizabeth Walker	washing	7*d* per day
Dame Amy Sheltram	laundry help	8*d* per day
Dame Sarah Lawson	washing & scouring	2*s* 6*d* per week
Mary Walker	'help when the family came down'	1*s*
Henry Walker	in-house brewing	?
Robin Mays	in-house brewing	?
John [?] Dow	brewing assistant	4*s*
Frank Harrison	brewing assistant	4*s*
Richard Wortley	looking after fowls	?
Thomas Waller	cutting wood	?
William Medcalf	cutting wood & brewing	?

On the basis of this analysis it can be concluded that the Thanet House establishment was in the region of thirty-eight, plus a dozen or so casual workers, and the annual wages bill was about £335. The Holkham total was roughly the same, with an annual cost of just over £300, which rose to £472 by 1723. Overall, in the mid-1720s Thomas Coke's retinue numbered between seventy and eighty, costing about £800 a year. This takes no account of the payments made to bailiffs and woodreeves on the various manors, or to miscellaneous staff such as Thomas Pigg, the keeper of the North Elmham deer park, or William England, the Holkham ratcatcher.[24]

There were innumerable changes in staff during the 1720s, not all of them satisfactorily documented in the surviving accounts, and there was considerable fluidity in the market, which was a matter of contemporary remark, at least as far as footmen were concerned:

tho' you had taken him from the Dunghill, out of an Hospital, or a Prison, you shall never keep him longer than he can make his Place what his Estimation of himself thinks he deserves; nay the best and most civiliz'd, that never were Saucy and Impertinent, will leave the most indulgent Master, and to get handsomely away, frame fifty Excuses, and tell downright Lies as soon as they can mend themselves.[25]

Hecht took the view that long service was exceptional,[26] and newspaper advertisements show that the average tenure of a place was three or four years. In his career as a footman, John Macdonald served twenty-seven masters in thirty-nine years.[27]

Nevertheless, in the Coke household, the following servants who had been taken on in 1719 were still with the family in 1728: James Davis, who had been under-butler and footman in 1718, had been promoted to butler; Andrew Griffiths, the 1st footman-cum-under-butler, had become the house steward; Abraham Thomas was still the valet-de-chambre, and Will Holland continued as Thomas's personal footman; William Tomley remained as the porter at Thanet House, while Robert Webster, who had been a common groom in 1718, had been promoted to 1st groom, although John Large had risen no further and remained a helper; 'French Jack' Baptiste had become the 2nd French cook, and faithful Ann Blinkhorn, the charwoman, was ferried to Holkham on occasion and still helped out as an emergency cook if required.

Servants were normally hired on the basis of 'a month's wages or a month's warning' if they were to be dismissed, and the initial annual wage was sometimes raised within a short time if they proved to be satisfactory. One steady source of additional income, at least for the upper and liveried servants, was gratuities or vails. These were collected from guests as they left, and from others as 'considerations' in the course of business. A servant would often be given some idea of the amount that he could expect before he was hired; a coachman's place, for example, was advertised in 1760 at '£10 per annum with £6 in vails'.[28] The amount given each time depended on his rank and on that of the guest. Queen Caroline once remarked that 'she had found it a pretty large expense . . . to visit her friends even in town' because of the vails expected.[29] The nobility and gentry became more and more aggrieved over the convention as the century wore on, but the practice did not disappear until the 1780s. It is noticeable that, when Thomas Coke himself gave the vails, they were in large amounts – nine guineas to Lord Hobart's servants, ten guineas to the Duke of Grafton's staff. On family visits, he often left a lump sum with a senior servant to be distributed among the rest; his departure from Longford in 1721 was marked by a gift of thirty guineas for the servants. He made a point of varying the gratuities according to the rank of the employer rather than the employee in question, twice tipping a royal groom two guineas. He obviously felt that his own servants had been under-appreciated by Lady Salisbury when she paid a visit in 1720 and augmented the vails himself by ten guineas.

The familiar tradition of Christmas boxes was well established by this time, and a sample from the December accounts of 1722 gives an idea of the length of the list waiting on the generosity of the Thanet House establishment:

The Turn Cock	2s 6d
To the Old Woman yt Sweeps	2s
To the Coal and Woodmongers men	2s 6d
To the Beer Bruers Men	2s 6d
To the Ale Brewers Men	2s 6d
To the Butchers Apprentices	2s 6d
To the Locksmiths Apprentices	2s
To the Bakers Apprentice	2s
To the Sadlers Apprentice	2s
To the Carpenters Men	2s
To the Dustman	2s 6d
To the Braziers Man	1s
To the Glaziers Apprentice	1s
To the Taylers Men	2s 6d
To the Pewkeeper in the Church	5s
To the Postman	5s
To the Man that brings the Bills from Drury Lane Play House	2s 6d
To the Mans [sic] that bring Do. from the Opera House	2s 6d
To the Man that brings Do. from Lincolns Inn [Playhouse]	2s 6d
To the Watchman	5s
To the Book Binders Apprentice	1s 6d
To the Tallow Chandlers Boy	1s
To the Coach and Harnis Apprentice	2s
To the House Smiths Man	2s
To the Bricklayers Men	2s 6d
To the Farriers Man	2s 6d
To the two Gerls that Sweeps the Street	2s
To the Door Keeeper at the Stairs in the Church	2s 6d
To the Chimney Sweepers	2s
To the Waits	5s

The total of £3 17s was not excessive (although it did equal six months' wages for a London labourer), and, perhaps as a side effect of the Christmas spirit, when the auditor marked the entry as having been undercast by 4s 6d, he got it wrong too.

When the family went away, either on a visit or down to the country, some servants were retained on board wages while they were away. These were money payments, calculated on a weekly basis in place of meals, with the object of reducing extravagance and the level of pilfering. Many employers felt that it was more economical than having servants fed in the house when there was no one to supervise the catering. At the same time, others resented the fact that the allowances gave 'a constant excuse to loiter at public houses', where the servants squandered their money 'in gaming, drunkenness, and extravagence' and where it was suspected they discussed the idiosyncracies and private lives of their employers.[30] Be that as it may, board wages were graded according to status, and the following servants were left in town when the Cokes 'with several servants' went to stay with Sir Edward Coke at Longford, Derbyshire in 1719:

John Gundaymore	cook	19 weeks	@10s p.w.
Andrew Griffith	butler	"	@10s p.w.
William Tomley	porter	"	@ 7s p.w.
William Shadbolt	footman	"	@ 7s p.w.
Jane Love	laundry-maid	"	@ 6s p.w.
Catherine Loines	under-laundry-maid	"	@ 6s p.w.
Betty Lish	housemaid	"	@ 6s p.w.
Ann Baker	cook's maid	"	@ 6s p.w.
Sarah Young	housekeeper's maid	17 weeks	@ 6s p.w.
'Old John' Grayer	helper	19 weeks	@ 3s p.w.

Later in the century, the rate quoted for an upper servant was 10s 6d a week with fire and candle and seven shillings for an under-servant, so the Thanet House staff may have been paid at the top end of the scale for their time.[31]

When the family stayed at Hothfield for eleven days in February 1721, they took with them only a coachman and postilion, Thomas Coke's footman, two other footmen and Lady Margaret's maid.

For those servants out of livery, all clothing was provided with the exception (in most cases) of shirts, neckcloths, stockings and shoes. Sometimes an extra payment would be made to a servant 'for wearing his own clothes' for all or part of the year. The livery and stable servants were issued with new boots every Lady Day, and one year Will Shadbolt the footman drew twelve shillings in lieu shortly after. By and large, servants of both sexes were well dressed throughout the period, whether in livery or in mufti; in 1719 the two coachmen were given a guinea each towards the cost of their periwigs, and in 1724 even Tom Robinson, the groom's boy, had a horse-hair peruke. It was important to them and to their employer that their appearance should reflect the tone and standing of the family. This was made easier in many cases by having clothing passed on to them by their masters and mistresses. In general, servants tended to ape their employers in dress habits, and the burgeoning popularity of cotton over wool made this easier and less expensive. When a member of the family or a close relative died, the servants were put into mourning. John Casey, the house steward, was allowed £10 for mourning when Lady Ann Walpole, Thomas Coke's grandmother, died, and two housemaids, two laundry-maids and the cook's maid received dresses, shoes, stockings, headcloths, gloves, fans, girdles, knots and buckles; the coachman and the postilion had gloves and buckles.

Thomas Coke's parents had always been good to their servants when they lived in St James's Square, where there was a household of fourteen men and eleven women. His mother, Cary Coke, paid for the footmen to be taught the three 'R's,[32] and old servants were still being paid annuities in her son's time: Longstreath, who was a veteran family retainer, having served both Thomas's father and grandfather, received £20 a year, Richard Pullin £15 a year, and Nurse Smith (who probably had nursed Thomas himself) had £10 a year. Coke stood godfather for Longstreth's son Thomas and gave him a present of two guineas when he met him at Longford, and Nurse Smith's son and grandson both received gratuities when they called at Thanet House. In the country there were similar cases: James Palmer was a Holkham pensioner who drew two shillings a week, besides his fee as parish clerk of five shillings a year, and John Curtis was an old servant drawing a pension of two shillings a week.

That the family tradition was maintained is shown by the way in which Thomas's servants were cared for. In 1718 a nurse was paid £3 7s 2½d for dieting and attending Sarah Young, the housekeeper's maid, when she lay ill with smallpox for three weeks. There was an extra shilling for scouring the blankets, and three weeks' lodging were paid for Sarah while she recovered. In the following year a nurse attended one of the postilions when he was ill, and, when housemaid Betty Lish succumbed to smallpox, Nurse Foster was paid £4 18s for attending her, and a sedan chair was hired to take the girl to her to lodgings; she was discharged when she was moved out of the house but was reinstated when she recovered. In 1721 Jack Large, the stable helper, was badly bitten by a dog, and a surgeon was fetched to attend him; he then contracted what was thought to be chickenpox and was nursed for a fortnight; Thomas Johnson, the coachman, was nursed for three weeks before he died. The master carpenter Thomas Morecroft fractured his leg and Mr Tubbing, the Burnham surgeon, received £1 10s for setting it; in Holkham village, Frances Kemp was paid half-a-crown for lodging and looking after 'Old Wegg' for three weeks, while Goody Palmer had ten shillings for nursing estate dependants for five weeks. When Stephen Mann, the young dog-feeder, died in 1726, his wages and board wages were duly paid to his sister, and the funeral expenses of £2 6s 9d were handled by the huntsman.

Having given instances of contemporary appeals to employers to treat their servants as they would members of their own families, Jean Hecht went on record as believing 'that no such harmony as characterised the relationship in theory existed in fact'.[33] This is directly contradicted by the evidence in these ledgers, at least as far as the Coke ménage was concerned. Apart from the annuities and continuing medical and nursing care already mentioned, there were gifts of clothing: 'Nov. 12, 1720, Paid Mr Lane ye Taylor for making a Cloth Suit for John Greer ['Old John', the stable helper] & all Materials (given as Charity) £4.12.0d.'. All servants were provided with bedding, and at Holkham Goody Allen was paid five shillings for making and marking twelve pairs of sheets out of hempen cloth that were certainly not for the family.

The Coke tradition of encouraging book learning was continued when Mr Flavel was paid sixteen shillings for teaching the whipper-in Tom Robinson to read and write, and in 1720 the stablemen were given a Bible, an Aesop, a spelling book and a copy of Richard Allestree's enormously popular *The Whole Duty of Man*. Thomas Johnson, the coachman, was helped in his work by having to hand copies of *The Complete Horseman* and *The Perfect Farrier*.

Virtue was rewarded on occasion too, as when a stable-boy was given half-a-crown for handing in two guineas that he had found in the stables, and misfortune did not go unnoticed either, for, when Abraham Thomas, the valet, was robbed of three guineas by a highwayman near Epping, Coke reimbursed it as a reasonable expense.

It has to be said that Coke was not alone in treating servants well. Among his contemporaries, the Duke of Chandos at Cannons had a doctor to attend staff regularly in the 1720s,[34] and the Duke of Bedford was similarly concerned.[35] By way of recreation in town, upper servants were sometimes given the price of theatre tickets: in May 1720 four servants were treated to the opera, and again in the following month to see *Narcissus*, while in 1722 Messrs Casey, Appleyard and Thomas went to see the opera *Griselda*. It was not all 'noses to the grindstone' in the Coke household.

Chapter 13

WHAT OF THE FUTURE?

W̶e have seen how Thomas Coke entered his inheritance, newly married, well travelled, full of confidence and knowing what it was that he wanted. He lost no time in taking his proper place in society, becoming one of the first holders of the Order of the Bath and progressing three years later to the peerage as Baron Lovel. By that time he had assumed firm control of his widespread estates and, with the assistance and advice of George Appleyard, his new land steward, was establishing forward-looking and innovative policies in their management. Like many of his generation he was drawn by the lure of easy money and vast profit into the South Sea Company adventure, and lost heavily in consequence. Driven by the need for ready money, he even resorted to pawning his Bath jewel and the family silver for a time, while borrowing expensively and trying his luck at the card table – it must be said with some success. While he does not seem to have allowed these circumstances to lower his standards or change his way of life (the immense value of his land and properties as security allowed him to borrow with ease), the decade of the 1720s was not a time when he could commit himself to the long-term building project on which he was determined. In the present day, when completion of even a large building project is expected within a year or so, it is often forgotten how long it took to build a new country mansion in the eighteenth century. Many were never completed by those who began them, and it was sometimes a grandson who carried the project through to the end. An extreme example was Castle Howard in Yorkshire, which was begun by the 3rd Earl of Carlisle in 1700 but was finally completed only in the early nineteenth century. Holkham was thirty years in the building: the family wing was completed in 1740, but a start was not made on the main block until after William Kent's death in 1748, with the southern half completed by 1753 and the northern half by 1759, the year in which Lord Leicester (as he had become) died. He continued to respond to new architectural ideas and to make changes in the interior right up to the end, but had to leave the house to be completed by the dowager countess, which she achieved in 1764.

Nevertheless, I have shown in Chapter 3 how, even if he could not plunge straight into the project that was to be his life's work, the young man made good use of the waiting time. He identified his chosen site, and by the mid-1720s he was discussing the form the building should take with Lord Burlington and William Kent, and having tentative plans drawn up. As has been shown, a great deal of work was done to prepare the site in advance of building, and it wanted only the impetus supplied by an improvement in the family fortunes for the next stage to begin.

That came about through Coke's marriage to Lady Margaret Tufton. In 1680 Charles II presented her father, the Earl of Thanet, with a grant of the lighthouse at Dungeness. Such grants were a characteristic product of the seventeenth century, when monarchs, always short of ready money, rewarded servants and repaid debts by delegating to the recipients the right to levy tolls and receive the revenue. As part of his daughter's dowry the Earl assigned the grant to Lord Lovel (as Coke had become). On the Earl's death in 1729, Lord Lovel was able to take it up, the only requirements being that he should pay a yearly rent of £6 13s 4d and promise to maintain a light 'for the safety and direction of mariners'. In return, he was given power to take one penny per ton of cargo from the masters of all ships, British and foreign alike, both inward and outward bound, who passed the light. Orders were given to all 'Customers, Collectors, Comptrollers, Surveyors, Searchers and Waiters' at all English ports that 'they should not permit any goods to be discharged or clear any ship without a ticket or note under the handwriting of Lord Lovel's deputies'. There were two lightkeepers and a supervisor at Lydd, and the whole business was controlled by a chief agent in London. The grant was to run until 1737, when Lord Lovel managed to have it renewed for another thirty-one years, to last until 1768. In 1740, however, he secured yet another grant for sixty years to run consecutively, and so it was not until 1828 that his successor, Coke of Norfolk, relinquished it. Meanwhile, it proved a very profitable concern, more and more so as time went by. From Christmas 1730 until Christmas 1732, gross receipts coming in to the chief agent in London, after deduction of commission at the ports, were £3,298. After all necessary expenses had been met, the average annual income was about £1,375. As shipping traffic in the Channel increased over the years so did the return from the light, until it was over £2,000 in 1760. It is likely that the promise of a steady source of additional income was a factor in Lovel's decision to begin building the new house in 1734. Until the Family Wing was completed, he and his wife lived in the old Hill Hall, which stood very close by and was connected by a passage so that the kitchens could be used and guests accommodated; it remained in use until it was demolished in 1757.

It takes an effort of imagination to visualise what it must have been like to live under such circumstances. Today, the door at the head of the Family Wing stairs opens into the South Tribune, giving a vista of the succession of state rooms that lie beyond; in the 1740s it would have opened on an enormous void wherein the main structure of the house was taking shape. The whole area around the house was for years on end one huge building site, and the noise, dust and general confusion must, at times, have been intolerable. It was perhaps as well that the family spent much of their time in London and elsewhere, particularly during the season, and that Thanet House in Bloomsbury was available to house the growing collection of antique statues, paintings and books. Lord Lovel was raised to the Earldom of Leicester in 1744 and continued to collect fine things for his great house. In the early 1750s the younger Matthew Brettingham, son of Holkham's architect, acted as his agent in buying statuary, paintings and drawings in Rome.[1]

Until the main house was completed, entertainment was necessarily confined to the Family Wing, and, in a letter to Ashe Windham, Patrick St Clair, the young cleric from Felbrigg, gave a spirited description of Lord Lovel's son Edward's coming-of-age party in 1740:

The splendour of the birth day at Holkham was wonderfully great. There was not many people at the dinner, but most came after. The Ball began at 8 a clock, in the Room that is design'd for My Lord's library, which is a little too strait. They went to supper at 12, ninety and odd covers were laid in the green house, the dishes all cold, with high pyramids of sweet meats. About 80 Ladies only sat down at first; and were succeeded by others who stood, with a greater quantity of Gentlemen. A bottle of red and another of white wine were set at every Mess, with bottles, that every body might help themselves, there being few or no servants admitted. There was an admirable fire work play'd off upon the water, which is very large, and the company all went away about 4 a clock. The orangery was illuminated far beyond Vaux-Hall.[2]

Another guest remarked on 'the beautiful illumination in the Wilderness, in a most exquisite taste . . . The concourse of people was so great on this occasion that upwards of 40 hogsheads of ale were given to the populace.' Musicians were imported from Norwich, Lynn and Thetford, guns were fired, and nearly 2,000 little lamps were lit – a splendid occasion.

Not only did the house take many years to complete, but the slow growth of hardwood trees meant that it was a long while before the surrounding park assumed the character that Coke had in mind. Some of the early visitors were distinctly unimpressed, and when John, Lord Hervey, came in 1731 with Sir Thomas Robinson of Rokeby to dine, he wrote: 'It is at present a most unpleasant place; but he [Lord Lovel] comforts himself with a park in embryo, and a Burlington house with four pavilions on paper.' At about the same time Sir Thomas Robertson was taken to see Lord Lovel in his 'exceeding bad old house' and was pessimistic about 'so much to be compassed only by art, time and expense'.

Thomas Coke's only surviving son, Edward, whose coming-of-age party has just been mentioned, was a sickly youth on whom all his father's hopes rested. It was for him and his posterity that the great house was planned, and he showed early promise both at Westminster School and at Oxford. In 1738 he duly followed Thomas in taking the Grand Tour under the tutelage of George Shelvocke, who, it has to be said, had neither Dr Hobart's grace nor his erudition and was known for his 'rough air and rougher voice'. The young man took in the Carnival at Venice, where he sat for Rosalba Carriera, and he flirted with the Princess Elenora Borghese in Rome. Edward was elected as an MP for Norwich in 1741, and went again to the Continent the following year, this time in company with the intriguing combination of Horace Walpole, the poet Gray and Sir Francis Dashwood. By now a viscount, following his father's elevation to the Earldom of Leicester, he contracted a disastrous marriage in 1747 with Lady Mary Campbell, youngest daughter of the 2nd Duke of Argyll – known with her sisters by their contemporaries as the 'screaming sisterhood'. She was undoubtedly eccentric, but the young lord treated her very badly and, according to Lady Louisa Stuart, on the wedding night he was 'determined to mortify the fair bride by every means in his power . . . and she prepared to become the wretched victim of abhorred compulsion. Therefore, coolly assuring her she was quite mistaken in apprehending any violence from him, he begged she would make herself quite easy, and wished her a very good night.' It is unlikely that the marriage was ever consummated (Lady Mary was known by some as 'the Virgin of Holkham' thereafter), and things went from bad to worse. She complained of being held against her will at Holkham, and her mother obtained a writ of Habeas Corpus, which led to a court appearance of all the parties and eventually to a legal separation.

Lord Edward, having been accused of ill-treating Lady Mary, is recorded in the Chatsworth papers as fighting an inconclusive duel with Sir Harry Ballenden. He had by this time become a notorious rake, leading the most dissolute of lives. Having given him over completely, Horace Walpole commented: 'He is always drunk and has lost immense sums at play, and is least an out-pensioner of Bedlam, his mother's family have many of them been mad.' His poor health and profligate lifestyle led to an early grave: he died aged 34 in 1753; in doing so he shattered the hopes of his father of seeing a worthy heir come into the inheritance he was spending his life creating.

In 1755, in an action off Newfoundland, Edward Boscawan triggered the outbreak of the Seven Years War by sinking two French men-of-war, and two years later the Admiral described his friend Coke as the 'fat, laughing, joking peer' – a fair description of someone who had mellowed and spread with the years. He was without doubt a heavyweight, for, when he stayed at Boughton House in 1749 with the Duke of Montagu, the party indulged in the fashionable pastime of weighing themselves, with Leicester tipping the scales at 19 stone 8lb (121kg). It was perhaps one of the reasons why he did not live to see Boscawan take command in the Mediterranean and trounce the

French again in 1759. The lack of an heir undoubtedly clouded his days, at least on occasion, and he once complained that he 'had swallowed up all his neighbours and the nearest now was the King of Denmark'. By the time of his death in 1759 he had long since withdrawn from active politics and spent most of his time and probably all his energies in striving to complete the great house and entertaining his friends in it, even though it was incomplete and largely unfurnished. The popular enthusiasm for Palladianism was fading and was shortly overtaken by the new styles introduced by the Adam brothers; but Lord Leicester's personal vision was not to be laid aside. Even so, there must have been times when he looked back nostalgically to the 1720s when he was planning to create the finest house of his generation and fill it with delectable things selected and arranged with intelligence and taste.

Happily for his descendants, Holkham has survived virtually intact, with its contents largely undisturbed and its beauty enhanced by the patina of age and the full maturity of the surrounding park. The house is still lived in by the family, and the thousands who visit it each year appreciate the contrast with some other stately homes that are museums in all but name. Coke might look askance at the heritage industry that glibly markets iconic buildings such as his, but the decade we have had under review in this book was for him truly a time of promise.

A List of Manors and Properties Purchased by Sir Edward Coke[1]

Pitsea Hall, Essex

Crustwich Hall, Essex

Buries [sic] Markes, London

Thorington Hall, Tiliardes &c., Suffolk

Westons, Suffolk

Thorington Wimples with Wenhaston, Suffolk

Thorington Burwards, Suffolk

Thorington, Grayes, Suffolk

Hinton Hall, Suffolk

Tittleshall Austens, Norfolk

Tittleshall, Skippons

Tittleshall, Peakehall

Tittleshall, Towneshends

Tittleshall, Yelvertons

Tittleshall, Coxforde

Tittleshall, Baxters

Tittleshall, Greinston, Calys, Nortons &c.

Tittleshall, Mileham, Davies &c.

Tittleshall, Newhall

Newton Close, Norfolk

Longham, Hall & Guntons, Norfolk

Godwicke, Norfolk

Panworth Hall, Norfolk

Wellingham, Wesenham & Tofttrees, Norfolk

Wesenham, Northall, Kipton &c., Norfolk

Wesenham Belles and Skippons, Dunton & Doughton, Norfolk

Westleham [?], Norfolk

Little Dunham, Norfolk

Kempstone, Norfolk

Thorneham and Pannington, Norfolk

Massingham and Feltham Monkes, Norfolk

South Creake Roseys, Norfolk

North Elmham, Norfolk

Flitcham Priory, Cockfield, Barnedestons & Poyninge, Norfolk

Burghall by Aylesham, Norfolk

Waxham, Norfolk

Huntingfield Cokes olim Wyvills, Suffolk

Fulmerston, Norfolk

Stoke Pogeis, Buckinghamshire

Cippenham, Buckinghamshire

Blithing Hundred, Suffolk

Hastings and Bintry, Norfolk

Laxfield, Suffolk

Beck & Beckhall, Norfolk

Mynster Lovell (including the Free Chase), Oxfordshire

Wisdomes Woods, Oxfordshire

South Creake Skymans, Norfolk
Wherstead, Suffolk
Wherstead Hall, Suffolk
Baddingham, Suffolk
Huntingfield Hall & Newhawe & park,
    Suffolk
Norwich, Conisforth Street, Paston
    House, Norfolk
Wesenham Rectory, Norfolk
Donyatt, Somerset
Castle Acre, honour & castle, Norfolk
Waterden, Norfolk
Longford, Derbyshire
Wherstead Wagstaves, Suffolk
Appleton, Norfolk
Cokely, Suffolk
Swaffham Bulbeck, Cambridgeshire
Ditton, Cambridgeshire
Lambsholme (Mildenhall), Suffolk
Okeford Shilling (alias Shillington),
    Dorset
Durweston & Knighton, Dorset
Billingford, Norfolk

Bilaugh Rectory, Norfolk
Baylies alias Whitemershe,
    Buckinghamshire
Bournehall, Suffolk
Wood Ditton Rectory, Cambridgeshire
Bishops Cleve advowson, Gloucestershire
Flitcham Mights, Norfolk
Horham Jernegans, Suffolk
Aldham Hall, Suffolk
Knightleyes, Staffordshire
Horham Thorhall & Wootton, Suffolk
Sparham Stewkhall & Beston, Norfolk
Thorington Hall, Weneston, Suffolk
Farnham Mill, Buckinghamshire
Billingford Cokes nuper Hartestange,
    Norfolk
Holkham Neales, Lucas &c., Norfolk
Flitcham Hovelle, Norfolk
Longham Priors, Watlington (in
    Longham), Norfolk
Morgrave Knightleyes, Norfolk
Sparham Cokes late Poleys, Norfolk
Candolent olim Campdolent, Suffolk[2]

INDIVIDUAL MANORS OF THE GREAT ESTATE IN THE 1720S[1]

ARRANGED BY COUNTY

Norfolk

Billingford

Acreage: 1,004	Surveyed by John Halsey (?) *c.* 1718–24 (Holkham Archives Map No. 4)	
Bailiff	Christopher Andrews (followed by John Halsey)	
Principal tenants	William and Thomas Bell	farm
	Michael Bloomfield	farm
	Thomas Edwards	Bylaugh impropriation
	Thomas Meck	Beck Hall, Foxley foldcourse, etc.
	(followed by Widow Meck; followed by Osborn Wetherall)	
	Simon Springold	farm
Other tenants	Anne Baily	
	Thomas Bulman	
	John Church	
	Ann Clayton	
	Widow Gage	
	Richard Hardingham (followed by Robert Leeds)	
	Richard Pitts	
	John Sadler	
	Alice Terry	
	John Wright, Court keeper	
	Samuel Wilson	
	Revd Hardy	Bylaugh Curate

Bintree

Acreage: 339	Surveyed *c.* 1718–26 (Holkham Archives Map No. 10)
Bailiff	Christopher Andrews, followed by John Halsey
Principal tenants	Christopher Andrews — farm and foldcourse
	(followed by William and
	Thomas Bell)
Other tenants	Ann Clayton
	Elias Brett
	Richard Bulman
	John and Mary Ellis

Castle Acre

Acreage: 2,152	Surveyed *c.* 17--? (Holkham Archives Map No. 30)	
Bailiff	John Halsey	
Principal tenants	Francis Anderson	Abbey farm, Newton Mill
	George Archer	Blanches
	(followed by John Archer)	
	William Hall	Wicken farm
	(followed by John Dalton)	
	Isaac Poley	Beckhams
	Thomas Sizeland	Steads
	William Stead	Masons
Other tenants	Jeffery Brown	lands in Narford
	John Burdon	lands in Palgrave
	John Goodbody	
	Frances Mason, widow	
	Revd Abraham Pimlow	Vicar
	John Tinkler	
Craftsmen and suppliers	John Baker	carpenter
	Jeffery Brown	for lime
	John Edge	mason (bricklayer)
	Mr Hall	blacksmith
	William Wiskers	dauber
The Ostrich Inn	Tenanted by John Tinkler	repairs and improvements
(formerly The Crown)		1727
The Swan alehouse	Bought from Baily Mariner 1717	

Dunton and Doughton

Acreage: 1,457	Surveyed *c.* 1724 (Holkham Archives Map No. 44)
Bailiff	John Halsey

Principal tenants	Joshua Flight	South Mill and land there
	(followed by William Darby)	
	Peter Tubbing	demesne lands and rectory
	(followed by Henry Mallett)	
Craftsmen and suppliers	John Baker	carpenter
	Thomas Byard	millwright (for new wheel at South Mill)
	Richard Elliott	blacksmith
	Robert Gardener	carpenter
	Mr Glover	for lime
	John Layton	mason (bricklayer)
	Robert Loads	for nails
	John Sharp	blacksmith

North Elmham

Acreage: 345	Surveyed by Humphrey Smith 1708	
	(Holkham Archives Map No. 50)	
Principal tenant	Andrew Pigg	park keeper and
	(followed by Thomas Pigg)	swan-upper

Summary of bucks given in 1717:

1 Sir Edward Coke	1 Marmaduke Wyvill Esq.	1 Bishop of Norwich
1 Mr Lamb	1 Mr Casey	1 Sir John Newton
1 Philip Roberts Esq.	1 R. Harding Esq.	1 John Coke Esq.
1 Sir John Rouse	1 Christopher Bedingfeld Esq.	1 Lady Anne Walpole
1 Richard Freston Esq.	1 Thomas Gibson Esq.	1 Edward Coke Esq.
1 Roger North Esq.	1 Mr Jacomb	17 in all

Flitcham

Acreage: 2,799	Surveyed by John Halsey 1724	
	Acreages quoted in 1717, 1723	
Bailiff	John Rogers Gent.	
	(followed by John Halsey)	
Principal tenants	Thomas Bastard	Flitcham Hall
	John Frankland	Flitcham Abbey, Snowering foldcourse
	Henry Pigg	Little Appleton
	(followed by John Chamberlain)	
Other tenant	John Sporne	
Craftsmen and suppliers	John Baker	carpenter
	Richard Branton	for tiles

	Ann Dates	for bricks
	Clare Leverington	for mason's work
	Richard Seamor	blacksmith
	Mr Whall	for pantiles and rooftiles
	John Wright	for lime
Curate	Revd Rice	
	(followed by Revd Money)	

Fulmodeston

Acreage: 1,095	Surveyed by John Halsey *c.* 1725–8	
	(Holkham Archives Maps Nos 56, 57)	
Bailiff	John Back	
	(followed by John Halsey)	
Principal tenants	John Back	Little Severall
	Jacob Cook	Manor House and
		demesne lands
	Francis Etteridge	Clipston
	(followed by John Money;	
	followed by Jacob Cook)	
	John Gold	
	and William Mitchell	the woods
	James Lee and	
	John Langwood	grazing ground
Other tenant	Charles Black	
Craftsmen and suppliers	Thomas Haylett	carpenter

Great Massingham

Acreage: 807	Surveyed by John Halsey 1720s	
	(Holkham Archives Map No. 100)	
Bailiff	John Rogers Gent.	
Principal tenant	John Carr	farm and foldcourse
Other tenants	John Gill	
	John Walker	

Holkham

Acreage: 3,911	Listed in 1717	
Principal tenants	Edward Carter	Thoroughgoods
	(followed by James Bircham)	
	Roger Cooper and	
	Nicholas Anger	Newdigates

(followed by Richard Porter)

Edward Creamer	Lushers, marshes
Nathaniel Kendarly	The Clint and marshes
Thomas Magnus	Honclecrondale, Dalehole Marsh

(followed by William Leeds)

Elizabeth Narborough	Neals

(followed by Nicholas Anger)

Ann Nichols, widow	Peterston
Richard Porter	Nettletons, the Malt House
Humphrey Smith	Hill Hall farm, Wellands,

(followed by Thomas Coke)   marshes

Other tenants	Widow Allen	
	John Cillis	cottage
	John Curtis	cottage
	Richard Faircloth	Thackers
	George Flood	
	James Fremingham	cottage

(followed by his widow)

William Gazeley	
Gamaliel Gregory	cottage
Stephen Harrison	cottage
William Jervis	
William Jolly	Dows Yard
John Kemp	Warren and Coney Hall, cottage
Henry Knotts	Mansers, the old dog kennel yard with house and smithy
Robert Knotts	
Robert Leech	cottage
Mary Lewis	
Sarah Lewis	Marum Hills
William Manser	cottage

(followed by his widow)

William Mellenton	brick kiln

(followed by his widow then taken in hand)

William Metcalf	cottage
Thomas Palmer	cottage
William Pickford	cottage

	Francis Rutley	cottage
	Thomas Sadler	cottage
	Edmund Schulthram	cottage
	(followed by his widow)	
	William Wegg	
Craftsmen and suppliers	John Baker	sawyer
	William Jolly	carpenter
	John Layton	bricklayer
	Robert Loads	for nails
	Richard Porter	for bricks and lime
	Robert Wood	cooper
	Nicholas Woodrow	for tiles

Kempstone

Acreage: 162	Surveyed by John Halsey *c.* 1725–8	
	(Holkham Archives Map No. 9)	
Principal tenant	William Heard	The manor, foldcourse and
		impropriation

Longham and Wendling

Acreage: 984	Surveyed *c.* 1718–25 (Holkham Archives Map No. 96)	
Bailiff	John Rogers Gent. (followed by John Halsey)	
Principal tenants	Revd John Lane	Wendling Rectory
	(followed by Revd John Francis)	
	Thomas Pigg	Hall farm
	(followed by William Pigg;	
	followed by Thomas Pigg)	
	Nicholas Sayer	farm
	John Watson	farm
	(followed by Thomas Pigg;	
	followed by William Pigg;	
	followed by Thomas Pigg)	
	Richard Pilch	farm
	(followed by Samuel Mosby)	
Other tenants	Richard Farrer	cottage and croft
	(followed by John Madder)	
	John Hearne	cottage and croft
	Widow Herring	cottage and croft
	Richard Turner	cottage
	Elizabeth Twydney	cottage and rood of land

	Edward Wasey	rood of land
Curate	Revd Lane	serving the cure at
	(followed by Revd John Francis;	Longham and
	followed by Revd Leech)	Wendling

Martham

Acreage: 188	No survey. Acreage calculated on 5s per acre	
Bailiff	John Christmas	
Principal tenant	John Christmas	farm
Craftsmen and suppliers	Charles Annison	carpenter
	Samuel Bridgwell	for timber
	John Brown	a ladder
	Mr Ginnis	for plank
	William Harmer	for nails and spikes
	Martin Mumford	dauber

The estate paid a causeway rate of 6s 10½d a year.

Panworth Hall

Acreage: 616	No survey. Acreage calculated on 5s per acre	
Bailiff	Anthony Cotton (on behalf of the Duke of Grafton)	
Principal tenant	The Duke of Grafton	Panworth Hall farm and foldcourse
	(followed by Anthony Cotton;	
	followed by Robert Wightman)	
Other tenants	Judith Bell	
	Mr and Mrs Womack	

One end of the Hall was converted into a brewhouse and malthouse in 1727

Quarles

Acreage: 586	Surveyed early 18th century?	
	(Holkham Archives Maps Nos 105 and 106)	
Principal tenant	James Feverall	the farm (A Wells poor tax paid on behalf of this tenant)
	Thomas Powditch	part of the Quarles farm
Other tenants	Thomas Barker	
	Richard Child	
	John Skippon	
	—— Sparks	

| Craftsmen and suppliers | Mr Curtis | for tiles |
| | John Keney (or Kerey) | bricklayer |

South Creake

Acreage: 1,001	Surveyed by James Corbridge (?) *c.* 1728–44	
Bailiff	Robert Rice	
	(followed by William Dewsing)	
Principal tenant	Robert Rice	Manor of Roses, fold
	(followed by William Dewsing)	courses and common in
		Creake and Syderstone,
		a limekiln and a
		tenement
Craftsmen and suppliers	John Layton	mason (bricklayer)
	Robert May	for hurdles
	Richard Porter	for deals (Holkham tenant/
		timber merchant)
	Robert Rice	for lime
	Miles Rust	carpenter
	Peter Tubbing	for bricks (Dunton tenant)
	William Sherwood	for tiles

Sparham

Acreage: 1,299	1722 entry headed 'Old Survey'	
	(Enclosure map 1809; Holkham Archives Map No. 110)	
Bailiff	Christopher Andrews	
	(followed by John Halsey)	
Principal tenants	William Coddenham	farm
	Edward Fisher	farm
	Edmund Hudson	Hutchinson's tenement
		with 110 acres etc.
	John Hudson	Hunts or Townshends etc.
	Henry Mallett	Giggs (Diggs?) or
	(followed by Edward Copeman)	Blakeneys
	William Murrell	Sparham Hall and liberty
		of sheepwalk (*see below*)
Other tenants	Rayner Dobbs	
	Jeffrey Flood	
	(followed by Widow Flood)	
	William Flood	
	Edmund Kent	

	Robert Munsey	lands in Whitwell
	(followed by Robert Tills)	
Craftsmen and suppliers	John Baker	carpenter
	Charles Bannard	glazier
	Richard Brown	for paviours
	William Coddenham	thatcher
	George Curryson	dauber
	John Edge	mason (bricklayer)
	Robert Loads	for nails
	Thomas Morecroft	estate master carpenter

Blacksmith's house and shop, which had been blown down in the 'Great Wind' of 1714, repaired in 1717.

Holkham Archive F/G2(2) fos 399–400

A letter from Humphrey Smith the Estate Agent to Sir John Newton, one of Thomas Coke's Trustees:

Holkham Aug. 29th 1709

Most Hond. Sir,

I received a letter about 10 days agoe from Mr John Coke [another Trustee] being a bout Lord Yarmouth's Estate at Sparham. Vizt.

1st The value of ye Estate

2d. The Sheep Walk not mentioned my account

3d Whether ye Rents was advanced

4th Whether ye Tenants would take leases

5 A Bout Repairs

6 A Bout Improvemts p. marle

In Answer	£ s. d.
1st That the psent Farme Rent are parnd[?] no more then	118:11:00
And ye Mannor Rents no more then	03:12:09½
In all	122:03:09½

2d. The Sheep Walk as my Lord Calls it is no more than Murrells Farme has the Shack or Winter Feedage of 3 Bridg Field; wch will keep a bout 150 sheep, and Considering the Charge of a Servant to keep so small a Trip, its not worth over and a bove his Wages 20 shillings, and has so been lett and for no more.

3d The Rents are advanced as I menconed in my Survey, for I saw their old Leases in Lady Doughers time; however I think that ye psent Rents (tho high enough) will be kept up,

4th and ye Tenants are willing to take Leases for 11 or 21 years.

5 That Murrells house and out housingeings in reasonable repair except one part of

ye Roofe of ye head house; wch will cost at least what I menconed in my acct. as also ye other two houses, but if yr Honr. buy ye Estate thay may be lett down, and the Ground layd to other Farmes.

It is highly Conveniant that yr. Honr. buys this Estate to make Mr Cokes ye more intire. It is from this Town that my Lord Coke begins his Family in King Edw. Ye 2d Raign, there=fore one would Covit to have ye whole, and I doe recomend to yr. Honr. ye giving his Lordship 18 years Purchase reather than lett another person in.

Note: Archive F/G 2 (2) fol. 408 (Estate Accts 1708–10) lists under Purchases: Estate of my Ld Yarmouth at Sparham £2260.

Tittleshall manors (Tittleshall, Godwick, Mileham and Beeston)

Acreage: 2,797	Surveyed *c.* 1725–8 (Holkham Archives Map No. 114)	
Bailiff	John Baker	
	(followed by John Halsey)	
Principal tenants	John Baker	Little Wicken farm,
	(followed by Thomas Morecroft)	Tittleshall woods
	William Bayfield	Nortons, Tittleshall
	James Carington	Burwood farm in Mileham
	Pomfret Flaxmore	Peakhall Closes
	(followed by Thomas Haylet jun.)	
	Thomas Haylet	Wicken farm
	Edward Pettiver	Grainstone (or Grimstone) Hall farm
	Richard Porter	Part of the East Field
	John Rudd	Beeston farm
	Humphrey Smith	Godwick, Peakhall and Burwood Hall farm
	(followed by Thomas Coke; Thomas Haylet and Thomas Morecroft (parts of Godwick))	
	William Smith	Walters, Peakhall foldcourse
	(followed by Pomfret Flaxmore; followed by Thomas Haylet jun.)	
	Col. Walpole (Coke's grandmother's second husband) leased Godwick, Peakhall and Burwood Hall in Mileham in 1717 and was in arrears	
Other tenants	Revd Budworth	part of Fishers tenement
	James Pilch	farm and tenement
	William Whitby	part of Fishers tenement

The brick kiln was thrown into Thomas Haylet's farm in 1725 having been managed
by Morecroft.

Waterden

Acreage: 770	Surveyed by John Halsey 1713–14	
	(Holkham Archives Map No. 125)	
Principal tenant	William Pigg	farm and foldcourse
	(followed by Thomas Pigg)	
Suppliers	Richard Porter	for deals
	(Holkham tenant)	
	Mr Woodcraft	for battens and pales

Weasenham

Acreage: 2,123	Enclosure map 1809 (Holkham Archives Map No. 128)	
Bailiff	John Rogers Gent.	
Principal tenants	John Kent	farm
	(followed by William Kent)	
	John Tubbing	Portlands (or Purlands) farm and foldcourse
	Peter Tubbing	Tythe farm
	(followed by William Kent; followed by John Tubbing)	
Other tenants	John Alcock	
	John Baily	
	John Berney	
	Thomas Carr	
	Robert Child	
	Revd Samuel Cushion	
	Robert Johnson	
	Joseph Moulton	
	William Moulton	
	John Rogers	
	James Safely	
	William Safely	
	Richard Wick	
	Richard Wright	

Wellingham

Acreage: 587	Enclosure Map 1809 (Holkham Archives Map No. 134)
Bailiff	John Baker

	(followed by John Halsey)	
Principal tenant	Nathaniel Page	farm and foldcourse

West Lexham

Acreage: 963	Surveyed by H. Renmer, Dereham 1774	
Bailiff	John Halsey	
Principal tenant	John Laws	farm and foldcourse
	(followed by Matthew Tennant)	
Other tenants	William Green	

Suffolk

Aldham Hall and Woods

Acreage: 546	Acreage listed	
Principal tenant	John Newman	
Other tenants	Mary Bacon	
	Mary Bury	
	Ann Cole	
	Mr Martin	
	Richard Powis Esq.	
	Ann Spurling	
	Isaac Steward	
Craftsmen and suppliers	John Bendall	carpenter
	Joseph Dunnegham	for tiles
	Samuel Fenning	thatcher
	Thomas Johnson	for nails

Hall farm blacksmith's shop rebuilt 1727.

Cratfield

Acreage: 250	Estimated
Bailiff	Charles Hutchinson
Tenants (all small rents)	Alice Barrow, widow
	Robert Collyer
	John Crompton
	Robert Draine
	Samuel Dresser
	Charles Fox
	John Fox
	Benjamin Hatcher
	Robert Lemon
	Henry Mounser, Gent.

William Newson
John Tallent
Richard Waynforth
Elizabeth and Alice Williams

Horham Thorphall and Thorpehall wood

Acreage: 196	Acreage listed	
Bailiff	Richard Adams	
Principal tenant	Amos Alexander	Manor farm
	(followed by John Philpott;	
	followed by Samuel Pulham)	
Other tenants	Thomas Brereton	
	Henry Carver	
	Edward Frere, Esq.	
	Thomas Gowing	
	James Green	
	Robert Hudson	
	James Watling	

Horham Jernegans

Acreage: 114	Acreage listed	
Bailiff	Richard Adams	
Principal tenants	George Brooke	Red House farm (part)
	John Moulton	"
	(followed by Samuel Pulham)	
Other tenants	Richard Adams	
	Mr Booke	
	Henry Carver	
	Mary Catchpole	
	Mr Hudson	
	Mr Lowde	

Samuel Pulham was paid fees for looking after the woods and for keeping the Court.

Huntingfield Park

Acreage: 733	Estimated	
Bailiff	Charles Hutchinson	
Principal tenants	John Baldry	Newhaugh farm (part)
	Thomas Borret	
	Robert Goodall	Badingham farm
	Ann Hodgkinson	Newhaugh farm (part)

	Charles Hutchinson	Newhaugh farm (part)
	Peter Pullen	The Hundred and Liberty of Blithing
	Richard Somers (followed by William Nicholls; followed by George Appleyard)	Park farm
	William Spalding	Newhaugh farm (part)
Other tenants	William Freston	
	Thomas Grey	
	William Nicholls	
	Richard Nunn	
	Mr Okeover	
	Thomas Pooley	
	Robert Woolnough	
Craftsmen and suppliers	James Cunningham	drainage
	William Kettle	drainage
	Michael Moulton	carpenter
	William Pepper	for bricks
	John Smith	for nails and ironwork
	John Smith	thatcher

Huntingfield Manor

Acreage: 1,248	Estimated	
Bailiff	Charles Hutchinson	
Principal tenants	Thomas Borret	farm
	Richard Somers	farm
	William Nicholls	farm
Other tenants	Stephen Aldous	
	Sarah Baldry, widow	
	Robert Booth	
	Reginald Collet	
	Mr Cremer	
	George Dashwood, Esq.	
	Revd Thomas Freeston	
	Thomas Grey	
	Robert Lemon	
	John Meadows	
	Mark Snelling	
	James Ward, Gent.	
Craftsmen and suppliers	George Burrows	ditching

John Harmon	dauber
Henry Lacey	ditching
James Legget	thatcher
Michael Moulton	carpenter
Thomas Newson	for nails
Elias Richards	ditching
Augustine Smith	thatcher
John Smith	blacksmith
William Spalding	carpenter's work, thatching and nails

Laxfield
Acreage: 30
Bailiff
Small tenants only

Estimated
Charles Hutchinson
Henry Beazant
Henry Bicker
John Borret, Esq.
William Brampton
Thomas King
John Copland
John Dresser
Lucy Haws
John Lee
William Legate
John Murton
Henry North
Mary Smith
James Spurling
Margaret Taylor
William Woods

Some rents taken from 'the old shops'.

Laxfield Rectory
Acreage: 327
Bailiff
Principal tenants

Estimated	
Charles Hutchinson	
Edward Booth	Mansion House and
(followed by John Aldous)	demesne
Charles Hutchinson	Clarks pightle
*Daniel Jessop	messuage and 14 closes in Chediston

Other tenants	Mary Burdwood
	John Butcher
	John Coldham, Gent.
	Robert Corneby
	Edmund Folcard
	Charles Fox
	Thomas Girling
	Thomas Green
	Elizabeth Hinchloe
	Nicholas Jacob
	Mary Meers, widow
	Sarah Rabdy
	Richard Randle
	William Short
	John Smith
	Ann, Elizabeth and Mary Thredgall

* Jessop's Chediston farm sold to Mr Plummer for £525 in 1725.

Laxfield Roadstreet

Acreage: 20	Estimated
Bailiff	Charles Hutchinson
Small tenants	

Mildenhall, Lambsholme

| Acreage: 66 acres | Acreage listed |
| Tenant | Mrs Jane Howlett |

Within Sir Thomas Hanmer's manor of Mildenhall. Sold to him in 1725.

Scotshall and Westleton

Acreage: 2,709	Acreage listed	
Bailiff	Charles Hutchinson	
Principal tenant	Richard Chediston	Scotshall demesne
Other tenants	John Hacon	
	Thomas Ingham	marshland
	John and Robert Mollet	
	Joseph Pooley	the windmill
	Thomas Tedman	copyhold in Westelton Street
	Thomas Tuthill	Newmans tenement
	John Wilson	Bensteads marshes

Thorington

Acreage: 77	Acreage listed	
Bailiff	Charles Hutchinson	
Tenants	William Burwood	
	Samuel Cotton	Haugh Wood
	William Harvey	
	Richard Searle	

Kent

Kingsdown (Kingsdown, Brawnshatch, Maplescombe and Aishe)

Acreage: 2,153	Calculated on 1725 revised rents @ 6s per acre	
Bailiff	Samuel Hill	
Woodward	John Richardson	
	(followed by John Gladdish)	
Principal tenants	William Baker	farm
	James Burrows	Barons Hatch
	(followed by his widow)	(Brawnshatch) and woods
	Henry Chapman	Mapplescombe farm and woods
	John Gladdish	farm in Aishe
	Samuel and Richard Hill	Heverplace farm, Clarks farm and the woods
	Thomas Marshall	farm and blacksmith's
	(followed by William Perryer)	shop
	Nicholas Middleton	Feilders
	John Rawlins	farm
	(followed by Thomas Rawlins)	
	Robert Richardson	farm and woods
Other tenants	Revd Atwood	
	Thomas Chapman	
	William Johnson	
	William Marshall	
Suppliers	Mr Pope	for deals

Dorset

Durweston

Acreage: 150	Estimated
Bailiff	John Burt (followed by Henry King)
Small tenants	Henry Aplin

Richard Aplin
John Burt   Sulcomb Copps
Nicholas Coward
John Grey
Roger Hart
Benjamin Johnson
Richard King
Phebe Pelly
Robert Polden
John Prower
John Rabbits
Richard Roberts
Widow Sommers
Widow Vine
Mr Wind

Royalty of the river rented to William Dominey (arrested for non-payment 1726).

Shillington

Acreage: 190	Estimated
Bailiff	John Burt
	(followed by Henry King)
Small tenants	Thomas Bissen
	Thomas Burt
	Richard Cole
	Richard Cox
	William Dominey
	John Ford
	Robert Ford
	Thomas Gillingham
	Rebecca Gosney
	James Hallet
	John Lodder
	Mr Melmoth
	John Pope
	John Rabbits
	Richard Rabbits
	William Ridout
	Robert Rogers
	John Sampson
	John Simms

Mrs West

Walter White

William White

A brick kiln was rented by Allen Lawrence.

Somerset

Donyatt

Acreage: 172	Somerset Archives Ref. DD/X/PTM
Bailiff	John Marks (followed by Henry King)
Principal tenants	William Banfield
	Peter Drower
	John Marks
	Samuel Marks
	John Morley
Other tenants	Richard Adams
	William Battin
	Joan Burridge
	Stephen Burridge
	George Clavelshaw
	James Comb
	William Crocker
	May Denman
	George Dinham
	Ambrose Drake
	John England
	John French
	Widow Gillet
	Thomas Gummer
	Widow Hart
	Avise Haynes, widow
	James Haynes
	John Holmes
	John Horder
	Thomas Horsey
	James Hull
	John Hunt
	John Jackson
	Reynold Lessey
	Mary Mandry
	William Marks

Thomas Osborne
Robert Porter
Thomas Roper
John Rutter
May Single
Thomas Smith
Hugh Spiller
Richard Trott
James Vincent
George Warmouth
John Wheby
John Woodward

The mill was leased to John Baker.
William Stuckey had a brick kiln – probably rented.

Portbury

Acreage: 1,610	Somerset Archives Ref. DD/PN 49
Bailiff	George Collet
	(followed by Mr Atherton and Humphrey King)
Small tenants	John Atherton
	Mr Berkins
	John Bond
	John Booke
	James Brooke
	Robert Browne
	George Collet
	Joseph Dandy
	Robert Davis
	Widow Delamore
	Joseph Edwards
	Thomas Fry
	Thomas Hardy
	Widow Higgins
	Charles Hodsby
	John Jennings
	Widow Morris
	Sir George Norton (for Portbury Hill)
	Joseph Purnell
	Widow Sparks
	John Stretch

                    John Thomas
                    Richard White   Portbury Hill Warren
                    Absalom Williams
                    Ann Wilmott
                    James Worm
                    Robert Yates
                    James Yeeles

Water Grist Mill rented by John Jackson followed by Thomas Bryant, who also rented
a windmill, and 'leased a spot of ground to erect a windmill on ye common'.
The Bailiff of the Hundred was Richard Tuckey.

Staffordshire
Knightley

Acreage: 1,982	Staffordshire Archives. Undated map of the Manor of Knightley (*c.* 1728–44) D615/M/4/39 (cottages and crofts in the Waste accounting for 13 acres)
Bailiff	John Bayly (followed by Thomas Wilkins)
Woodward	Edward Moore

Principal tenants	Richard Ash	farm
	Widow Ash	farm
	(followed by Robert Bayly)	
	Thomas Blakeman	farm
	William Davenhill	farm
	Richard Jordain	farm
	Edward Moore	half Park farm
	John Oakley	farm
	George Slin	farm
	James Smart	farm and two tenements
	Francis Smith	farm
	John Tomkinson	half Park farm
	(followed by John Meeson)	
	John Tomkinson	farm
	Richard Venables	farm
	(followed by Widow Hadderton)	
	Jane Walters, widow	farm
	(followed by John Walters)	
Other tenants	Elias Bradshaw	
	Thomas Bradshaw	
	George Fernihaugh	

Mrs Haynes

Mrs Hull

Widow Latham

John Lee

Edward Millington

Richard North

Thomas Roden

Thomas Selman

William Willington

Richard Wright

Oxfordshire

Minster Lovell

Acreage: 1,447	Figure supplied from *VCH Oxfordshire*	
Bailiff	Thomas Wheeler, Gent. (followed by John Dubber)	
Gamekeeper	Robert Parker (liveried)	
Principal tenants	Widow Coppin (followed by John Coppin)	The Hall (part)
	Richard Harris	The Mill
	Robert Parker	Piercies tenement
	Mr Peacock's assigns (followed by Paul Smith)	Little Minster farm
	William Smith	two tenements
	Thomas Wheeler (followed by John Mallam)	The Hall (part)
Other tenants	Mrs Arnold	
	Moses Brooks	
	Widow Clack	
	Widow Clanvil	
	Charles Clark	
	Deodatis Collis	
	John Collis	
	John Coppin	
	Widow Coppin	
	Herbert Fletcher	
	George Fuller	
	Richard Harris	
	Widow Harris	
	William Lay	

John Lewis

Robert Palmer

Edward Rigins

Thomas Simons

Paul Smith

William Smith

Jonathan Thomas

John Whiters

John Williams

Royalty of the river let to Dr Wheeler followed by Mr Peacock.

Craftsmen and suppliers	Mr Blagrave	for locks
	Henry Carter	thatcher
	Richard Cook	blacksmith
	John Harwood	for bricks and lime
	William Lock	carpenter and mason work
	Mr Scriven	glazier
	Mr Willet	for red lead and oil

Buckinghamshire

Farnham Royal

Acreage: 494	Surveyed 1727 (Holkham Archives Map No. M/173)	
Bailiff and woodward	Joseph Hearne	
Principal tenants	Widow Hearne	farm
	Robert Ives	the Warren House
	Robert Kingham	the Mill and lands
	John Langton	Farnham Court farm, the
	(followed by Joseph Langton)	Warren House, Shasbrook Lands
	Widow Wilkinson	farm and Seer Green
	(followed by Joseph Wilkinson)	woods
Other tenants	William Boddington	
	Elizabeth Bodys	
	George Courant	
	Joseph Hearne	
Craftsmen and suppliers	John Edgeson	for bricks
	Mr Griffiths	for ironmongery
	Joseph Hearne	carpenter
	Robert Ives	mason
	William Norman	carpenter

Thomas Webb   glazier
Mr Wise   for tiles

London

Bevis Marks, Coke's Court and Camomile Street in the Parish of All Hallows in the Wall.

		£	s	d
1724				
Tenants	Mr Beane, paid by Mr Nicols at the Bank	6	0	0
	Mrs Dashwood of Spittle Field Market, Collier	12	0	0
	Mr Charles Highmore of Peckham in Surrey	17	10	0
	Mr John Highmore, at the Blackamoor's Head in Cheapside	5	10	0
	Mr/Mrs Walford, at the Hand & Pen in Houndsditch	18	0	0
	Mr Needham, at the Dolphin in Cheapside for 3 Houses,			
	Vizt. for his own £7, Mr Alvarius's £6 & Mr Glover's £7	20	0	0
	Mrs Proctor, paid by Mr Lamego in Coke's Court	10	0	0
	Mrs Sanders	6	0	0
	Mrs Woodward, paid by Mr Mulford in Cursitor's Alley	6	0	0
	Mrs Whitwich [or Whitwick] for the Saracen's Head Inn,	100	0	0
	paid by Mr Nicols at the Bank			
1725	Mrs Hendrick [or Kenderick/ Kenrick] (late Procters)	10	0	0
	Mr Orbell	5	10	0
1728	Mr Mulford in Curstors Alley, Chancery Lane (late John			
	Highmore)	6	0	0
	Mr Hilliard at the Cross Keys in Bishop Gate Street (late			
	Mrs Sanders)	6	0	0

ADVOWSONS IN THE GIFT OF THOMAS COKE[1]

	£ p.a.	
Bishops Cleeve a peculiar [Glos.]	700	[listed on p. 3 @ £500]
Donyett Rectory [Donyatt, Som.]	80	
Shillingston Rectory [Shillington, Dorset]	170	let at £200
Durweston Rectory [Dorset]	70	let at £105 and house kept in hand
Huntingfield Rectory [Suffolk]	170	
Cookly Rectory [Cookley, Suffolk]	70	
Horham Rectory [Suffolk]	120	
Laxfield & Cratfield Vicarage [Suffolk]	120	
Aldham Rectory [Suffolk]	70	
Holkham Vicarage [Norfolk]	50	
Waterden Rectory [Norfolk]	50	
Dunton Vicarage [Norfolk]	40	
Wellingham Rectory [Norfolk]	30	
Tittleshall & Godwick Rectory [Norfolk]	180	[listed on p. 3 @ £100]
Longham & Wendling Curacy [Norfolk]	60	
Castleacre Vicarage [Norfolk]	40	
Flitcham Curacy [Norfolk]	40	
Billingford Rectory [Norfolk]	80	
Bilaugh Curacy [Bylaugh, Norfolk]	30	
Kempstone Vicarage [Norfolk]	50	

Appendix 4

HOUSEHOLD AND OTHER ACCOUNT BOOKS CONSULTED

1. 'Mr Casey's Book 1718–1720' (House Steward John Casey)[1]
2. 'Mr Jarrett's Acct. 1718' (Valet/Assistant House Steward Edward Jarrett; covering 1718–22)[2]
3. 'Mr Casey's Cash Book 1721–23'[3]
4. 'This Journal book belonging to the Honble Thomas Coke Esq. Containing An Account of his Domestick Expences, Stable . . . Household Goods, and . . . May 13th 1718' (partly illegible; Master of the Horse Edward Smith)

   This volume also contains:
    (a) Domestic accounts, 1719–20 (Land Steward Humphrey Smith)
    (b) Domestic accounts, 1720 (Casey)
    (c) Domestic accounts, 1721 (Jarrett)
    (d) Domestic accounts, 1722–6 (H. Smith, Casey, Land Steward George Appleyard, House Steward David Williams)[4]
5. 'The Domestic Accounts of ye Honble Thomas Coke Esqr. posted quarterly for ye year 1719' (London and elsewhere; Casey)[5]
6. 'Household Accounts Jany 31st 1721 to Sept 30th 1723' (Valet Abraham Thomas)[6]
7. No cover title, accountant not identified

   This volume also contains:
    (a) 'Accounts of advowsons, rectories, vicaridges & curacys', 1718
    (b) (Marriage) jointure settlement
    (c) Grand Tour closing accounts, 1718–19
    (d) General accounts, 1721–2, 1723–5, 1726–7
    (e) South Sea Stock accounts
    (f) Statement of 1718 rents[7]
8. 'Leidger Book & Mr Coke's Accounts ending March 25th 1722' (accountant not identified)

This volume also contains:

    (a) Lady Walpole's estate (summary of the position after her death in 1722)

    (b) Profit and loss analysis for 1723

    (c) Interest payments, 1723–4[8]

9. 'Cash book & disbursements' (Covers 1723–6; Williams)[9]

10. 'Disbursements in Norfolk 1722 & 1723' (Appleyard)[10]
    'Holkham & Godwick Husbandry', 1722–3.

11. No cover title; accountant not identified; cash book, 1725–6[11]

12. 'Geo. Appleyard's Accot. of the Domestick Disbursements in Norfolk 1724–8'[12]

13. 'A General Daybook of Receipts & Payments 1727–8' (Appleyard)[13]

14. '1727–1729' (London weekly expenses; Williams and Upper Butler Andrew Griffiths)[14]

15. 'A.G. 1728 Journall Book' (Andrew Griffiths)[15]

16. 'An Accompt made up with the tenants at Holkham [for 1 year] ending Michas 1717' (Norfolk manors only; only 1717 entries transcribed; H. Smith)[16]

17. 'An Accompt made up with tenants at Holkham [for 1 year] ending Michas 1722' (continues to cover 1723–6; Appleyard)[17]

18. 'An Accompt made up with tenants at Holkham [for 1 year] ending at Michas. 1727' (only 1727–8 entries transcribed; Appleyard)[18]

NOTES

INTRODUCTION

1. James M. Rosenheim, *The Townshends of Raynham* (Middletown, CT: Wesleyan University Press, 1989), p. 136.
2. John Summerson, *Architecture in Britain 1530–1830*, rev. edn (London: Penguin, 1955), p. 194.
3. Christopher Hussey, *English Country Houses. Early Georgian 1715–1760*, rev. edn (London: Country Life, 1965).
4. Leo Schmidt *et al.*, *Holkham* (Munich, London and New York: Prestel, 2005), p. 18.
5. R.A.C. Parker, *Coke of Norfolk, a Financial and Agricultural Study, 1707–1842* (Oxford: Oxford University Press, 1975).
6. Arthur Young, *A Farmer's Tour through the East of England*, 4 vols (London: W. Strahan, 1771).
7. C.W. James, *Chief Justice Coke. His Family and Descendants at Holkham* (London: Country Life, 1929).
8. C.V. Wedgwood, *The Great Rebellion. The King's Peace 1637–1641* (London: Collins, 1955).

CHAPTER 1

1. Holkham Archives: A/7, previously MS 737.
2. Holkham Archives: F/TC8.
3. Today's equivalent would probably lie between £820,000 and £828,000.
4. Richard Holmes, *Redcoat. The British Soldier in the Age of Horse and Musket* (London: HarperCollins, 2001).

CHAPTER 2

1. Holkham Archives: E/G 17.
2. A skeleton list of all Sir Edward Coke's property is given in Appendix 1.

3. This is partly a speculative figure. The majority of Norfolk acreages, and the outlying manors of Knightley (Staffs.), Minster Lovell (Oxon.), Donyatt & Portbury (Somerset) have been confirmed by survey maps; about half the Suffolk manor entries quote acreages, but the rest have been calculated by using rental figures and average acreage values. Brief details of all the estate's manors, covering acreages, surveys, principal tenants, mills, kilns and smithies, county and other archive references, are tabulated in Appendix 2. After the sales of the outlying manors and the expansion and consolidation of the Norfolk estate in the nineteenth century, the total acreage was 43,025, making it more than twice the size of any other in the county. The figure today is 25,157 acres.

4. A.S. Turberville (ed.), *Johnson's England. An Account of the Life and Manners of his Age*, 2 vols, vol. 1 (Oxford: Oxford University Press, 1933), p. 265.

5. *Ibid.*, p. 266.

6. *Ibid.*, p. 268.

7. Holkham Archives: A/AV 1,5,7,9.

8. Holkham Archives: F/G2 (2) fo. 416.

9. Holkham Archives: F/G2 (3) fo.102.

10. G.E. Fussell, 'Norfolk Improvers': Their Farms and Methods', *Norfolk Archaeology*, 33 (1964).

11. Joan Thirsk (ed.), *The Agrarian History of England and Wales*, vol. 5 (Cambridge: Cambridge University Press, 1985).

12. William Marshall, *The Rural Economy of Norfolk*, 2nd edn, 2 vols (London: G. & W. Nichol, 1795).

13. M.E. Turner, J.V. Becket and B. Afton, *Agricultural Rent in England 1690–1914* (Cambridge: Cambridge University Press, 1997).

14. J. Caird, *English Agriculture 1850–1851* (London: Gregg International, 1968).

15. Walter Rose, *The Village Carpenter* (Cambridge: Cambridge University Press, 1937).

16. Naomi Riches, *The Agricultural Revolution in Norfolk* (Chapel Hill, NC: University of North Carolina Press, 1937), pp. 77 *passim*.

17. Young, *A Farmer's Tour*, vol. 4, p. 394.

18. Rosenheim, *The Townshends of Raynham*, pp. 155–6.

19. Thirsk, *The Agrarian History of England and Wales*, p. 576.

20. Estate maps known by him (or possibly his work) are listed in the notes on individual manors in Appendix 2.

21. Alienated Estates Box. P.G. Eden, 'Land Surveyors in Norfolk 1550–1850: Pt 1: The Estate Surveyors', *Norfolk Archaeology*, 35 (1973).

22. Names of local craftsmen will be found listed under each manor in Appendix 2.

23. Marshall, *The Rural Economy of Norfolk*.

24. John Robert Harvey, *Deer Hunting in Norfolk from Earliest Times* (Norwich: Norwich Mercury, 1910).

25. E.P. Thompson, *Whigs and Hunters* (London: Penguin, 1990), pp. 158–60.
26. Jonathan Swift, *Gulliver's Travels and Selected Writings in Prose and Verse*, ed. John Hayward (London: Nonesuch Press, 1946).
27. *Commons Journals*, 45 (1790), p. 169 (Alice Holt).
28. E.P. Shirley, *Some Accounts of English Deer Parks* (London: 1867), p. 50.
29. The family livings held in the 1720s are listed in Appendix 3.

CHAPTER 3

1. Lincoln Record Office: Monson Papers, 7/13/57, no. 1721.
2. British Museum: K Top XXXI, 42 b–h.
3. Leo Schmidt, *Thomas Coke, 1st Earl of Leicester. An Eighteeenth-Century Amateur Architect* (Freiburg: 1980), p. 5.
4. Lord Ilchester, *Lord Hervey and his Friends. 1726–1738* (London: John Murray, 1950).
5. It was common practice to butcher and sell off what were called 'dizzy', 'disordered' or 'casualty' sheep to the labourers for food at eight shillings each against the normal fourteen shillings for a healthy beast. The terms used suggest that these were cases of scrapie or something similar. Pigs 'killed by accident' were disposed of in the same way and a 'dizzy bullock' was sold for £1. A nineteenth-century Norfolk doctor found that many labourers contracted gangrene having eaten bad meat – the practice of buying up diseased animals may have been the root cause.
6. Holkham Archives: Map no. M/66.
7. By kind permission of Professor Leo Schmidt.
8. James Grigor, *The Eastern Arboretum* (London: Longman; Norwich: Stacey, 1841).

CHAPTER 4

1. Daniel Defoe, *A Tour through the Whole Island of Great Britain*, ed. D.N. Furbank and W.R. Owens (New Haven, CT: Yale University Press, 1991).
2. John Stow, *A Survey of the Cities of London and Westminster . . . Brought down from the Year 1633 . . . to the Present Time*, ed. John Strype (London: 1720).
3. Francis Place, *The Autobiography of Francis Place*, ed. Mary Thale (Cambridge: Cambridge University Press, 1972).
4. James Elmes, *Memoirs of the Life and Works of Sir Christopher Wren* (London: Priestly and Weale, 1823).
5. Woburn Abbey archives.
6. John Parton, *Some Account of the Hospital and Parish of St Giles in the Fields* (London: Luke Hansard & Son, 1822).
7. Jeremy Black, *An Illustrated History of Eighteenth-Century Britain, 1688–1793* (Manchester: Manchester University Press, 1996).

8. Defoe, *A Tour*, p. 153.

9. *Ibid.*, pp. 152–3.

10. Holkham Archives: F/G 2 (2) fo. 497.

11. David Mortier (Joseph Smith), *Nouveau théâtre de la Grande Bretagne (Britannia Illustrata)*, 4 vols (London: Joseph Smith, 1724–8).

12. Jenny Uglow, *Hogarth: A Life and a World* (London: Faber, 1997), pp. 495–7.

13. Dorothy George, *London Life in the Eighteenth Century*, rev. edn (London: Penguin, 1966), p. 53.

14. *Ibid.*, p. 54.

15. Paul Langford, *A Polite and Commercial People: England 1727–1783* (Oxford: Oxford University Press, 1989).

16. John Shebbeare, *Letters on the English Nation by Battista Angeloni*, vol. 2 (London: S. Crowder, H. Woodgate & J. Scott, 1756), p. 39.

17. Gordon Taylor, *St Giles-in-the-Fields: Its Part in History*, 8th edn (church guidebook, 1989).

18. Rowland Dobie, *The History of the United Parishes of St Giles-in-the-Fields and St George Bloomsbury* (London: the author, 1829).

CHAPTER 5

1. Helen MacFarlane and Paul Mortimer-Lee, 'Inflation over 300 Years', *Bank of England Quarterly Bulletin*, May 1994, p. 156.

2. *Ibid.*, p. 159.

3. *Ibid.*, p. 157.

4. Denis M. Devitt of the Office of National Statistics in a letter to Felix Pollak, 1996.

5. Lorna Weatherall, *Consumer Behaviour and Material Culture in Britain 1660–1760*, 2nd edn (London: Routledge, 1996), p. 99.

6. Roy Porter, *England in the Eighteenth Century*, rev. edn (London: Penguin Books, 1990), p. 202.

7. James, *Chief Justice Coke*, ch. 19.

8. J.V. Beckett, *The Aristocracy in England 1660–1914* (Oxford: Oxford University Press, 1986), pp. 8–9.

9. *Ibid.*, p. 311.

10. John Habakkuk, *Marriage, Debt and the Estates System* (Oxford: Oxford University Press, 1994), pp. 66, 447.

11. Richard Wilson and Alan Mackley, *Creating Paradise: The Building of the English Country House, 1660–1880* (London: Hambledon & London, 2000), pp. 297–8.

12. William Marshall, *On the Landed Property of England* (London: G. & W. Nichol, 1804), p. 1.

13. Parker, *Coke of Norfolk*, p. 13.

14. Plate 8 reproduces William Hogarth's scathing engraving; it was his first work in this medium, executed in 1721 but not published until 1724.

15. Charles Mackay, *Memoirs of Extraordinary Popular Delusions* (London: Richard Bentley, 1841), p. 46.

16. *A South-Sea Ballad; Or, Merry Remarks upon Exchange-Alley Bubbles* (1721).

17. Daniel Defoe, *London Journal*, 11 June 1720 (London).

18. John Carswell, *The South Sea Bubble* (London: Cresset Press, 1961).

19. Beckett, *The Aristocracy in England*, pp. 81–2.

20. Parker, *Coke of Norfolk*, ch.2.

21. Uglow, *Hogarth*, pp. 88–9.

22. J.H. Plumb, *Sir Robert Walpole*, 2 vols (London: Cresset Press, 1956).

23. Wilson and Mackley, *Creating Paradise*, p. 248.

24. *Ibid.*, pp. 307–8.

CHAPTER 6

1. Holkham Archives: F/G2(2) fo. 391.

2. Holkham Archives: F/G2 (2) fos 418, 442.

3. G.S. Thompson, *The Russells in Bloomsbury* (London: Cape, 1940).

4. Nurse Smith's family sometimes came to visit her at Thanet House; her son was a joiner and was given a guinea when he was there in 1719, and her grandson received half a guinea during the same week.

5. Nicholas Blundell, *Blundell's Diary and Letter Book*, ed. Margarett Blundell (Liverpool: Liverpool University Press, 1952), p. 26. Mrs Blundell's midwife was paid seven guineas in 1704, 'a high fee considering general values at that time'.

6. Holkham Archives: F/G2 (2).

7. Princess Anne to the Duchess of Marlborough in 1690 and 1695: 'I fancy ass's milk would do you good and that is what you might take morning or afternoon as it is most convenient.' 'For God's sake be persuaded to take some ass's milk that will not hinder you from anything but will cool and sweeten your blood.'

8. William Macmichael, *The Gold-Headed Cane* (London: Kimpton, 1923).

9. Sarah Markham, *John Loveday of Caversham: 1711–1789: The Life and Tours of an Eighteenth-Century Onlooker* (Wilton: Michael Russell, 1984).

10. Both portraits are still at Holkham, with the Richardson hung in the North State Bedroom.

11. Holkham Archives: F/G2 (2).

12. *Ibid.*

13. *Ibid.*

14. *Ibid.*

15. *Ibid.*

16. James Laver, *English Costume of the Eighteenth Century* (London: A. & C. Black, 1931).

17. James Woodforde, *The Diary of a Country Parson*, ed. John Berrisford, 5 vols (Oxford: Oxford University Press, 1926).

18. Holkham Archives: F/G 2 (2) fo. 393.

19. Historical Manuscripts Commission: *Diary of Viscount Percival, afterwards 1st Earl of Egmont*, 1920–3.

20. Lincoln Record Office: Monson Papers, Monson 7/13/64.

21. R.W. Ketton-Cremer, *Country Neighbourhood* (London: Faber, 1951).

CHAPTER 7

1. John Macky, *Memoirs of the Secret Services of John Macky Esq. during the Reigns of King William, Queen Anne and King George I, Published from his Original Manuscript. [containing] Characters of the Court of Great Britain* (London: 1733).

2. John Armstrong. *The Art of Preserving Health* (London: A. Millar, 1744).

3. James Anderson. *The Constitutions of the Ancient and Honourable Fraternity of Free and Accepted Masons*, rev. edn (London: J. Senex, 1723). pp. 210–11.

4. *Ibid.*

5. Hamon Le Strange, *History of Freemasonry in Norfolk* (Norwich: Agas H. Goose, 1896). p. 13.

6. Roy Porter, *Enlightenment* (London: Penguin, 2003), p. 37.

7. Bath Central Library: MS B914: 'Diary of a Tour by Three Students from Cambridge, 1725'.

8. C.H.C. Baker and M.I. Baker, *James Brydges 1st Duke of Chandos* (Oxford: Oxford University Press, 1949).

9. John Hervey, 1st Earl of Bristol, *The Letter-Books of John Hervey, First Earl of Bristol*, 3 vols (Wells: E. Jackson,1894).

10. Robert Halsband, *Lord Hervey. Eighteenth-century Courtier* (Oxford: Oxford University Press, 1973).

11. Sarah Osborn, *Political and Social Letters of a Lady of the Eighteenth Century, 1721–1771*, ed. E.F.D. Osborn (London: 1890).

12. Holkham Archives: F/G 2 (2).

13. *Statutes of the Most Honourable Order of the Bath* (Lord Lovel's personal copy is in the Holkham library).

14. John Pine, *The Procession and Ceremonies observed at the Time of the Installation of the Knights Companions of the most Honourable Military Order of the Bath* (Lord Lovel's subscription copy is in the Holkham library).

15. J.M. Beattie, *The English Court in the Reign of George I* (Cambridge: Cambridge University Press, 1967).

16. Osborn, *Political and Social Letters*.

17. Anthony Ashley Cooper, 3rd Earl of Shaftesbury, *Characteristics of Men, Manners, Opinions, Times*, ed. Lawrence E. Klein (Cambridge: Cambridge University Press, 1999), p. 206.

18. Holkham Archives: F/G2(2) fo. 422.

19. Holkham Archives: F/G2(4).

20. Holkham Archives: F/G2(2) fo. 442.

21. British Library (BL): Add. MS 38507, Townshend Papers vol. 16, Miscellaneous Papers 1707–83.

22. John Hervey, *Some Material towards Memoirs of the Reign of George II*, ed. Romney Sedgwick (London: Kimber, 1952).

23. Historical Manuscripts Commission (HMC): Diary of Viscount Percival afterwards 1st Earl of Egmont, 1920–3.

24. James, *Chief Justice Coke*.

25. Fernando Henriques, *Prostitution and Society*, vol. 2 (London: McKibbon & Kee, 1963).

26. Johann von d'Archenholz, *A Picture of England*, vol. 2 (London: P. Byrne, 1790), p. 75.

27. Giacomo Girolamo Casanova, *Giacomo Casanova: His Life and Memoirs* (London: Routledge, 1960).

28. Lord Chesterfield, Philip Dormer Stanhope, *The Letters of the Earl of Chesterfield to his Son*, ed. Charles Strachey (London: Methuen, 1901).

29. Nancy Mitford, *Frederick the Great* (London: Hamish Hamilton, 1970).

30. Charles Hanbury Williams, *The Odes of Sir Charles Hanbury Williams* (London: printed for S. Vandenburgh, 1775).

31. Charles Hanbury Williams, *The Works of Sir Charles Hanbury Williams . . . from the Originals in the Possession of his Grandson the Earl of Essex*, 3 vols, (London: 1822).

32. Horace Walpole, *Correspondence*, ed. Wilmarth S. Lewis (New Haven, CT, and London: Yale University Press, 1937).

33. William Pulteney, *An Epistle from Lord L[ove]l to Lord C[hesterfiel]d by Mr P[ulteney]* (London: printed for T. Cooper, 1740).

34. HMC: *Diary of the Earl of Egmont*.

35. R.W. Ketton-Cremer, *A Norfolk Gallery* (London: Faber, 1948).

36. *Ibid.*

37. Black, *Eighteenth-century Britain*.

38. Holkham Archives: F/G 2 (4) fo. 72.

39. R.W. Ketton-Cremer, *Norfolk Assembly* (London: Faber, 1957).

CHAPTER 8

1. T.W.C. Banning, *The Culture of Power and the Power of Culture*, Pt 3 (Oxford: Oxford University Press, 2002).

2. Michael Tilmouth, 'The Beginning of Provincial Concert Life', in Christopher Hogwood and Richard Luckett (eds), *Music in Eighteenth-century England* (Cambridge: Cambridge University Press, 1983).

3. Holkham Archives: F/G 2(2) 460.

4. Baker and Baker, *James Brydges 1st Duke of Chandos*.

5. Leo Hughes, *The Drama's Patrons* (Austin, TX: University of Texas Press, 1971).

6. Donald Burrows, *Handel* (Oxford: Oxford University Press, 1994).

7. J. Merrill Knapp, 'Handel, the Royal Academy of Music and its First Opera Season in London', *Musical Quarterly*, 45 (1959), pp. 145–67.

8. *Ibid.*

9. Michael Wilson, *William Kent* (London: Routledge & Kegan Paul, 1984).

10. Hughes, *The Drama's Patrons*.

11. *Ibid.*

12. Lewis Theobald, 'The Rape of Prosperine', in J.E. Galliard and L. Theobald, *The Sorcerer with the Loves of Pluto and Proserpine* (London: T. Wood, 1725), preface.

13. Judith Milhouse and Robert D.Hume, *Vice Chamberlain Coke's Theatrical Papers 1706–1715* (Carbondale, IL: Southern Illinois University Press, 1982).

14. Hughes, *The Drama's Patrons*.

15. Lincoln Record Office: Monson Papers, 7/12/196, letter from Peniston Lamb to Sir John Newton; and Ketton-Cremer, *Country Neighbourhood*, p. 24.

16. Holkham Archives: F/G2 (2).

17. Elizabeth Angelicoussis, *The Holkham Collection of Classical Sculptures* (Mainz: Verlag Philipp von Zabern, 2001).

18. *Ibid.*, p. 140.

19. *Ibid.*, p. 26 n. 36.

20. Andrew Wilton and Ilaria Bignamini, *Grand Tour: The Lure of Italy in the Eighteenth Century* (London: Tate Gallery Publishing, 1997).

21. A.E. Popham, *Old Master Drawings at Holkham Hall* ed. Christopher Lloyd (Chicago and London: Chicago University Press, 1986).

22. Details of all the paintings in the collection are now assembled on a database compiled by Frederick Jolly and held by the House Administrator.

23. Popham, *Old Master Drawings*.

24. *Ibid.*, no. 126.

25. *Ibid.*, no. 276.

26. *Ibid.*, no. 51.

27. D.P. Mortlock, *The Holkham Library. A History and Description* (London: The Roxburghe Club, 2006).

CHAPTER 9

1. Plate 9 reproduces William Hogarth's 1759 engraving of the Royal Cockpit in Birdcage Walk, which was built by Henry VIII and where, even as a young man, Coke is likely to have played.
2. Holkham Archives: MS 732B.
3. Holkham Archives: F/G2 (2)
4. Holkham Archives F/G2 (2) fo. 497.
5. E.M. Beloe, *Oxborough* (Norwich: Goose, 1898).
6. Ketton-Cremer, *Norfolk Assembly*.

CHAPTER 10

1. James Boswell, *Life of Samuel Johnson*, vol. 1, ed. G.B. Hill, rev. L.F. Powell (Oxford: Clarendon Press, 1934–50), p. 467.
2. Roy Porter and Marie Mulvey Roberts, *Pleasure in the Eighteenth Century* (London: Macmillan, 1996).
3. This may be a corruption of 'rastons' which were a cross between a brioche and a kind of vol-au-vent made with egg-enriched, sweetened and leavened dough. See Elizabeth David, *English Bread and Yeast Cookery* (London: Allen Lane, 1977).
4. Defoe, *A Tour through the Whole Island of Great Britain*.
5. It is notable that by the 1740s truffles were being obtained locally. 'The Boy Helsdon' was paid £1 for eight days 'trufiling', and in 1742 Philip Bender the footman drew £1 10s expenses for going into Northamptonshire with 'the Trufile Boy' and two horses.
6. G.M. Trevelyan. *The Illustrated English Social History*, vol.3 (London: Longmans, 1951).
7. Porter, *England in the Eighteenth Century*.
8. Edmund Pyle, *Memoirs of a Royal Chaplain 1729–63*, ed. E. Hartshorne (London: Bodley Head, 1905).
9. Suffolk Record Office: North MSS 331.
10. Elizabeth Burton, *The Georgians at Home* (London: Arrow Books, 1967).
11. John Keay, *The Honourable Company* (London: HarperCollins, 1991), pp. 348–9.
12. Aytoun Ellis, *The Penny Universities: A History of the Coffee Houses* (London: Secker & Warburg, 1956).
13. D.P. Mortlock, 'Thomas Coke and the Family Silver', *Silver Society Journal*, 9 (1997).
14. Stella Tillyard, *Aristocrats* (London: Weidenfeld and Nicolson, 1999).
15. Basil Williams, *The Whig Supremacy* (Oxford: Oxford University Press, 1939).

CHAPTER 11

1. Sydney and Beatrice Webb, *English Local Government*, vol. 5 (London: Longmans, 1913).
2. Hervey, *Memoirs of the Reign of George II*.
3. Samuel Pepys, *The Diary*, ed. Robert Latham and William Matthews, vol. 9 (London: Bell & Hyman, 1970–83).
4. Markham, *John Loveday of Caversham*.

CHAPTER 12

1. Jonas Hanway, *Letters on the Importance of Preserving the Rising Generation of the Labouring Part of our Fellow Subjects*, vol. 2 (London: 1767), p. 158.
2. Patrick Colquhoun, *A Treatise on the Police of the Metropolis* (London: Mawman, 1800), p. 151.
3. *The Gentleman's Magazine*, 61 (1791), p. 199.
4. Thompson, *The Russells in Bloomsbury*, p. 238.
5. Olivia Colville, *Duchess Sarah, Being the Social History and Times of Sarah Jennings, Duchess of Marlborough* (London: Longmans, Green & Co., 1904), p. 371.
6. Daniel Defoe, *The Great Law of Subordination Consider'd* (London: Samuel Harding, 1755), p. 86.
7. J. Jean Hecht, *The Domestic Servant Class in Eighteenth-century England* (London: Routledge & Kegan Paul, 1956), p. 19.
8. Eliza Haywood, *A New Present for a Servant-Maid* (London: G. Peach and H. Gardner, 1771), p. 32.
9. *Address to the P——t in Behalf of the Starving Multitude* (1766), p. 39.
10. *Westminster Journal*, 1745, reprinted in *The Gentleman's Magazine*, 15 (1745), pp. 544–5.
11. Hecht, *The Domestic Servant Class*, p. 11.
12. *London Packet*, 454, 18–21 September 1772, 4a.
13. Mary G. Jones, *The Charity School Movement* (Cambridge: Cambridge University Press, 1938), p. 51.
14. E.W. Gilboy. *Wages in Eighteenth-Century England* (Cambridge, MA: Harvard University Press, 1938).
15. John O'Keefe, *The Dramatic Works of John O'Keefe* (1798), p. 228.
16. Anthony Heasel, *Servants Book of Knowledge* (1773), p. 70, cited in Hecht, *The Domestic Servant Class*.
17. *Ibid.*
18. *Ibid.*, p. 70.
19. *Ibid.* p. 75.

20. John Macdonald, *Memoirs of an Eighteenth-century Footman* (London: Routledge & Sons, 1927), p. 93.

21. François Armand Frédéric de La Rochefoucauld, *A Frenchman's Year in Suffolk, 1784*, ed. and tr. Norman Scarfe (Woodbridge: Boydell Press; *Suffolk Records Society*, 30 (1988)), p. 19.

22. Thorstein Veblen, *The Theory of the Leisure Class* (London: Allen & Unwin, 1924), p. 63.

23. James Boswell, *The Letters of James Boswell*, ed. C.B. Tinker, vol. 1 (Oxford: Oxford University Press, 1924), pp. 225–6.

24. Details of manorial staff are to be found in Appendix 2.

25. Bernard Mandeville, *The Fable of the Bees* (London: Penguin, 1970), p. 347.

26. Hecht, *The Domestic Servant Class*, p. 82.

27. Macdonald, *Memoirs of an Eighteenth-century Footman*, xvi.

28. *Daily Advertiser*, 9288, 14 October 1760, 3a.

29. Hervey, *Memoirs of the Reign of George II*, vol. 2, p. 501.

30. G.M. Ditchfield and B. Keith-Lucas (eds), *A Kentish Parson: Selections from the Private Papers of the Revd Joseph Price, 1767–86* (Kent County Council, Arts and Libraries, 1991).

31. J. Trusler, *The London Adviser and Guide* (London: for the author, 1786).

32. James, *Chief Justice Coke*, p. 148.

33. Hecht, *The Domestic Servant Class*, p. 71.

34. Baker and Baker, *James Brydges First Duke of Chandos*, p. 182.

35. Thomson, *The Russells in Bloomsbury*.

CHAPTER 13

1. Popham, *Old Master Drawings*, p. 8.

2. Ketton-Cremer, *Country Neighbourhood*, pp. 212–13.

APPENDIX 1

1. Taken from the *Great Book of Conveyances*. Holkham Archive E/G 17 (formerly MS 764 and No. 342 in Sir Edward's Library Catalogue).

2. An alternative and variant list (with dates of acquisition) is to be found in Ralph Cauldwell, *The Holkham Estate from the time of Sir Edward Coke Lord Chief Justice of England in Queen Elizabeth's Reigne*. Holkham Archive E/G18. The marriage settlement of 1718 (Holkham Archives F/TC 8) also lists Portbury & Portishead, Somerset and, in addition, other Suffolk parishes in which land was held – Trimley St Mary & St Martin, Walton, Felixstowe, Kirton, Nacton, Fressingfield,

Stradbroke, Brundish, Wilby, Dennington, Badingham, Allington, Redlington, Denham, Eye, Hoxne, Hadleigh, Kersey, Whatfield, Elmsett, Hintlesham, Chattesham, Copdock, Darsham, Wingfield, Middleton, Feverton, Fordley, and Leyston.

APPENDIX 2

1. Lists of tenants are not necessarily complete – they include only those who happen to feature in the decade's accounts. In the small tenancies, names are not deleted where the property was taken by another tenant during the period.

APPENDIX 3

1. Holkham General Accounts 1718–29. Holkham Archives A/3 (formerly MS 741), 'The Several Advowsons, Rectories, Vicaridges & Curacys in the Gift of Thos. Coke Esqr. with their Annuall Value as they are Mentioned in a Deed of Settlement made by the said Thos. Coke in June 1718'.

APPENDIX 4

1. Holkham Archives A/5.
2. Holkham Archives A/4.
3. Holkham Archives A/6.
4. Holkham Archives A/7.
5. Holkham Archives A/8.
6. Holkham Archives A/9.
7. Holkham Archives A/3.
8. Holkham Archives A/7a.
9. Holkham Archives A/10.
10. Holkham Archives A/32.
11. Holkham Archives A/22.
12. Holkham Archives A/33.
13. Holkham Archives A/11.
14. Holkham Archives A/23.
15. Holkham Archives A/12.
16. Holkham Archives A/AU1.
17. Holkham Archives A/AU5.
18. Holkham Archives A/AU7.

BIBLIOGRAPHY

The place of publication is London unless indicated.

ARCHIVAL SOURCES

British Library
Bath Central Library
Historical Manuscripts Commission
Holkham Archives
Lincoln Record Office
Suffolk Record Office

SECONDARY SOURCES

An Address to the P——t in Behalf of the Starving Multitude, 1766

Anderson, James, *The Constitutions of the Ancient and Honourable Fraternity of Free and Accepted Masons*, rev. edn, J. Senex, 1723

Angelicoussis, Elizabeth, *The Holkham Collection of Classical Sculptures*, Mainz, Verlag Philipp von Zabern, 2001

Archenholz, Johann von d', *A Picture of England*, 3 vols, P. Byrne, 1790

Armstrong, John, *The Art of Preserving Health*, A. Millar, 1733

Baker, C.H.C. and M.I. Baker, *James Brydges 1st Duke of Chandos*, Oxford, Oxford University Press, 1949

Banning, T.W.C., *The Culture of Power and the Power of Culture*, Oxford, Oxford University Press, 2002

Beattie, J.M., *The English Court in the Reign of George I*, Cambridge, Cambridge University Press, 1967

Beckett, J.V., *The Aristocracy in England 1660–1914*, Oxford, Oxford University Press, 1986

Beloe, E.M., *Oxborough*, Norwich, Goose, 1898

Black, Jeremy, *An Illustrated History of Eighteenth-Century Britain, 1688–1793*, Manchester, Manchester University Press, 1996

——, (ed.), *Britain in the Age of Walpole*, Macmillan, 1984

Blomefield, Francis and Charles Parkin, *An Essay towards a Topographical History of the County of Norfolk*, 5 vols, Festfield/King's Lynn, F. Blomefield & C. Parkin, 1739–75

Blundell, Nicholas, *Blundell's Diary and Letter Book*, ed. Margaret Blundell, Liverpool, Liverpool University Press, 1952

Brettingham, Matthew, *The Plans, Elevations and Sections of Holkham in Norfolk*, J. Habercorn, 1761

Brewer, John, *The Pleasures of the Imagination. English Culture in the Eighteenth Century*, HarperCollins, 1997

Burnett, J., *A History of the Cost of Living*, Penguin, 1969

Burrows, Donald, *Handel*, Oxford, Oxford University Press, 1994

Burton, Elizabeth, *The Georgians at Home*, Arrow Books, 1967

Caird, J., *English Agriculture 1850–1851*, Gregg International, 1968

Cannon, J. *Aristocratic Century: The Peerage of Eighteenth-century England*, Cambridge, Cambridge University Press, 1984

Carswell, John, *The South Sea Bubble*, Cresset Press, 1961

Carthew, G.A., *The Hundred of Launditch and Deanery of Brisley in the County of Norfolk*, 3 vols, Norwich, Miller & Leavins, 1877–9

Colquhoun, Patrick, *A Treatise on the Police of the Metropolis*, Mawman, 1800

Colville, Olivia, *Duchess Sarah*, Longmans, Green & Co., 1904

Dawson, J., *The Stranger's Guide to Holkham*, Burnham, J. Dawson, 1817

Defoe, Daniel, *The Great Law of Subordination Consider'd*, Samuel Harding *et al.*, 1724

——, *A Tour through the Whole Island of Great Britain*, ed. D.N. Furbank and W.R. Owens, New Haven, CT, Yale University Press, 1991

'Diary of a Tour by Three Students from Cambridge', 1725, Bath Central Library, MS B914

The Diary of Viscount Percival afterwards 1st Earl of Egmont, 1920–3, Historical Manuscripts Commission

Dobie, Rowland, *The History of the United Parishes of St Giles-in-the-Fields and St George Bloomsbury*, R. Dobie, 1829

Earle, Peter, *The Making of the English Middle Class. Business, Society and Family Life in London 1660–1730*, Methuen, 1989

Eden, P.G. 'Land Surveyors in Norfolk 1550–1850. Part.1: The Estate Surveyors', *Norfolk Archaeology*, 35 (1973)

Egmont, 1st Earl, *see The Diary of Viscount Percival afterwards 1st Earl of Egmont.*

Elmes, James, *Memoirs of the Life and Works of Sir Christopher Wren*, Priestly and Weale, 1823

Fussell, G.E. 'Norfolk Improvers', *Norfolk Archaeology*, 33 (1964), 332–44

Gatrell, Vic, *City of Laughter: Sex and Satire in Eighteenth-Century London*. Atlantic Books, 2006

George, Dorothy, *London Life in the Eighteenth Century*, rev. edn, Penguin, 1966

Gilboy, E.W., *Wages in Eighteenth-Century England*, Cambridge, MA, Harvard University Press, 1934

Girouard, Mark, *Life in the English Country House*, New Haven, CT, Yale University Press, 1978

Grigor, James, *The Eastern Arboretum*, London, Longman; Norwich, Stacey, 1841

Habakkuk, John, 'English Landownership 1680–1740', *Economic History Review*, 10 (1940), 2–17

——, *Marriage, Debt and the Estates System*, Oxford, Oxford University Press, 1994

Halsband, Robert, *Lord Hervey. Eighteenth-Century Courtier*, Oxford, Oxford University Press, 1973

Hanbury Williams, Charles, *The Odes of Sir Charles Hanbury Williams*, S. Vandenburgh, 1775

——, *The Works of Sir Charles Hanbury Williams . . . from the Originals in the Possession of his Grandson the Earl of Essex*, 3 vols, 1822

Hanway, Jonas, *Letters on the Importance of Preserving the Rising Generation of the Labouring Part of our Fellow Subjects*, 1767

Harvey, John Robert, *Deer Hunting in Norfolk from Earliest Times*, Norwich, Norwich Mercury, 1910

Haywood, Eliza, *A New Present for a Servant-Maid*, London, Peach and Gardner, 1743

Heasel, Anthony, *Servants Book of Knowledge*, 1773

Hecht, J. Jean, *The Domestic Servant Class in Eighteenth-Century England*, Routledge & Kegan Paul, 1956

Henriques, Fernando, *Prostitution and Society*, 2 vols, McKibbon and Kee, 1963

Hervey, John, *The Letter-Books of John Hervey, First Earl of Bristol*, 3 vols, Wells: E. Jackson, 1894

——, *Some Material towards Memoirs of the Reign of George II*, ed. Romney Sedgwick, Kimber, 1952

Hill, Bridget, *Servants. English Domestics in the Eighteenth Century*, Oxford, Oxford University Press, 1996

Hogwood, Christopher and Richard Luckett (eds), *Music in Eighteenth-Century England*, Cambridge, Cambridge University Press, 1983

Holmes, Richard, *Redcoat. The British Soldier in the Age of Horse and Musket*, HarperCollins, 2001

Hughes, Leo, *The Drama's Patrons*, Austin, TX, Texas University Press, 1971

Hussey, Christopher, *English Country Houses. Early Georgian 1715–1760*, rev. edn, Country Life, 1965

Ingamells, John, *A Dictionary of British and Irish Travellers in Italy 1701–1800*, New Haven, CT, Yale University Press, 1997

James, C.W., *Chief Justice Coke. His Family and Descendants at Holkham*, Country Life, 1929

Jones, Mary G., *The Charity School Movement*, Cambridge, Cambridge University Press, 1938

Ketton-Cremer, R.W., *A Norfolk Gallery*, Faber, 1948

——, *Country Neighbourhood*, Faber, 1951

——, *Norfolk Assembly*, Faber, 1957

Knapp, J. Merrill, 'Handel, the Royal Academy of Music and its First Opera Season in London', *The Musical Quarterly*, 45 (1959)

Langford, Paul, *A Polite and Commercial People. England 1727–1783*, Oxford, Oxford University Press, 1989

Laver, James, *English Costume of the Eighteenth Century*, Black, 1931

Le Strange, Hamon, *History of Freemasonry in Norfolk*, Norwich, Goose, 1896

Lees-Milne, James, *The Earls of Creation*, Hamish Hamilton, 1962

Macdonald, John, *Memoirs of an Eighteenth-century Footman*, Routledge and Sons, 1927

MacFarlane, Helen and Paul Mortimer-Lee. 'Inflation over 300 years', *Bank of England Quarterly Bulletin*, May 1994

Mackay, Charles, *Memoirs of Extraordinary Popular Delusions*, Richard Bentley, 1841

Macky, John, *Memoirs of the Secret Services of John Macky Esq. during the Reigns of King William, Queen Anne and King George I, published from his original manuscript*, 1733

Mandeville, Bernard, *The Fable of the Bees*, Penguin, 1970

Markham, Sarah, *John Loveday of Caversham, 1711–1789: The Life and Tours of an Eighteenth-century Onlooker*, Wilton, Michael Russell, 1900

Marshall, William, *The Rural Economy of Norfolk*, 2nd edn, 2 vols, G. & W. Nichol, 1795

——, *On the Landed Property of England*, G. & W. Nichol, 1804.

Milhouse, Judith and Robert D. Hume, *Vice Chamberlain Coke's Theatrical Papers 1706–1715*, Carbondale, IL, Southern Illinois University Press, 1982

Mingay, G.E., *English Landed Society in the Eighteenth Century*, Routledge & Kegan Paul, 1963

Mortlock, D.P., *The Holkham Library. A History and Description*, Roxburghe Club, 2006

——, *Holkham Notes & Annals*, privately printed, 2002

——, 'Thomas Coke and the Family Silver', *Silver Society Journal*, 9 (1997)

Mui, Hoh-cheung and Lorna, *Shops and Shopkeeping in Eighteenth-century England*, Kingston, McGill-Queen's University Press, 1989

Mullan, John and Christopher Reid (eds), *Eighteenth-century Popular Culture. A Selection*, Oxford, Oxford University Press, 2000

'N'. 'The State of Husbandry in Norfolk', *Gentleman's Magazine*, 22 (1752)

Osborn, Sarah, *Political and Social Letters of a Lady of the Eighteenth Century, 1721–1771*, ed. E.F.D. Osborn, 1891

Parker, R.A.C., *Coke of Norfolk. A Financial and Agricultural Study, 1707–1842*, Oxford, Oxford University Press, 1975

——, 'Direct Taxation on the Coke Estates in the Eighteenth Century', *English Historical Review*, 71 (1956), 247–8

Pine, John, *The Procession and Ceremonies Observed at the Time of the Installation of the Knights Companions of the Most Honourable Military Order of the Bath*, 1730

Place, Francis, *The Autobiography of Francis Place*, ed. Mary Thale, Cambridge, Cambridge University Press, 1972

Plumb, J.H., *England in the Eighteenth Century*, Penguin, 1950

——, *Sir Robert Walpole*, 2 vols, Cresset Press, 1956

Popham, A.E., *Old Master Drawings at Holkham Hall*, ed. Christopher Lloyd, Chicago and London, Chicago University Press, 1986

Porter, Roy, *England in the Eighteenth Century*, rev. edn, Penguin, 1990

——, *Enlightenment*, Penguin, 2003

——, and Marie Mulvey Roberts, *Pleasure in the Eighteeenth Century*, Macmillan, 1996

Pyle, Edmund, *Memoirs of a Royal Chaplain 1729–63*, ed. E. Hartshorne, Bodley Head, 1905

Quinlan, Maurice J., *Victorian Prelude. A History of English Manners 1700–1830*, Hamden, CT, Archon Books, 1965

Reed, Michael, *The Georgian Triumph 1700–1830*, Routledge & Kegan Paul, 1983

Richardson, A.E., *Georgian England. A Survey of the Social Life, Trades, Industries and Art from 1700 to 1820*, Batsford, 1931

Riches, Naomi, *The Agricultural Revolution in Norfolk*, Chapel Hill, NC, University of North Carolina Press, 1937

Rochefoucauld, François de la, *A Frenchman's Year in Suffolk, 1784*, ed. and tr. Norman Scarfe, Woodbridge, Boydell Press; *Suffolk Records Society*, 30 (1988)

Rose, Walter, *The Village Carpenter*, Cambridge, Cambridge University Press, 1937

Rosenheim, James M., *The Townshends of Raynham*, Middletown, CT, Wesleyan University Press, 1989

Schmidt, Leo, *Thomas Coke, 1st Earl of Leicester: An Eighteenth-Century Amateur Architect* (Freiburg: 1980)

——, *et al.* (eds), *Holkham*, Munich, London & New York, Prestel, 2005

Shebbeare, John, *Letters on the English Nation by Battista Angeloni*, vol. 2, S. Crowder, H. Woodgate and J. Scott, 1756

Smith, A.H., *County and Court. Government and Politics in Norfolk 1558–1603*, Oxford, Oxford University Press, 1974

A South-Sea Ballad: or, Merry Remarks upon Exchange-Alley Bubbles, 1721

Steegman, John, *The Rule of Taste from George I to George IV*, Hutchinson, 1986

Stow, John, *A Survey of the Cities of London and Westminster . . . Brought down from the Year 1633 . . . to the Present Time*, ed. John Strype, 1720

Summerson, John, *Architecture in Britain 1530–1830*, rev. edn, Penguin History of Art, 1955

Swift, Jonathan, *Gulliver's Travels and Selected Writings in Prose and Verse*, ed. John Hayward, Nonesuch Press, 1946

Thirsk, J. (ed.). *The Agrarian History of England and Wales: 1640–1750*, vol. 5, Cambridge, Cambridge University Press, 1985

Thompson, Gladys Scott, *The Russells in Bloomsbury*, Cape, 1940

Tillyard, Stella, *Aristocrats*, Weidenfeld & Nicolson, 1994

Trevelyan, G.M., *The Illustrated English Social History*, Longmans, 1951

Turberville, A.S. (ed.), *Johnson's England. An Account of the Life and Manners of His Age*, 2 vols, Oxford, Oxford University Press, 1933

Turner, M.E., J.V. Becket and B. Afton, *Agricultural Rent in England. 1690–1914*, Cambridge, Cambridge University Press, 1997

Uglow, Jenny, *Hogarth. A Life and a World*, Faber, 1997

Veblen, Thorstein, *The Theory of the Leisure Class*, Allen & Unwin, 1924

Weatherall, Lorna, *Consumer Behaviour and Material Culture in Britain 1660–1760*, 2nd edn, Routledge & Kegan Paul, 1996

Webb, Sydney and Beatrice, *English Local Government*, Longmans, 1913

Williams, Basil, *The Whig Supremacy*, Oxford, Oxford University Press, 1939

Wilson, Michael, *William Kent*, Routledge & Kegan Paul, 1984

Wilson, Richard and Alan Mackley, *Creating Paradise. The Building of the English Country House 1660–1880*, Hambledon & London, 2000

Wilton, Andrew and Ilaria Bignamini, *Grand Tour: The Lure of Italy in the Eighteenth Century*, Tate Gallery Publishing, 1997

Woodforde, James, *The Diary of a Country Parson*, ed. John Berrisford, 5 vols, Oxford, Oxford University Press, 1926

Young, Arthur, *A Farmer's Tour through the East of England*, 4 vols, W. Strahan, 1771

INDEX

Abingdon, Lord, 107
accounting methods, 3, 17
Adams, Richard, Horham
    Thorpehall/Jernegans bailiff,
    232
Adams, Richard, Donyatt tenant,
    238
Addison, Mr, London coach-painter,
    186
*Address to the P——t in Behalf of the
    Starving Multitude, An*, 256,
    259
advowsons, *see* Church patronage
Aishe, *see* Kingsdown manors, Kent
Albani, Francesco, 142
Albin, Eleazar, 145
Alcock, John, Weasenham tenant,
    230
Aldham Hall, Suffolk, 231
Aldham Rectory, Suffolk, 244
Aldous, John, Laxfield Rectory
    tenant, 234
Aldous, Stephen, Huntingfield
    tenant, 22, 233
Alexander, Amos, Horham
    Thorpehall tenant, 232
Allen, Mary (Goody), Holkham
    charwoman, 165, 210, 224
All-Hallows-in-the-Wall Parish, *see*
    London, Bevis Marks
Allestree, Richard, 210
Alvarius, Mr, Bevis Marks tenant,
    243
Amadei, Filippo, cellist, 134
Amey, Mr, physician, 89
Amiance, Mr, surgeon, 101
Ampthill, Bedfordshire, 95
Anderson, Francis, Castle Acre
    tenant, 221
Anderson, James, 252, 259
Andrews, Christopher,
    Billingford/Bintree/Sparham
    bailiff, 220, 221, 227
Andrews, Laurence, London joiner,
    67
Angelicoussis, Elizabeth, 254, 259

Anger, Nicholas, Holkham tenant,
    38, 54, 55, 59, 166, 223, 224
Anne, Queen of England, 85, 86,
    110, 178, 251
Annison, Charles, Martham
    carpenter, 226
Aplin, Henry, Durweston tenant,
    236
Aplin, Richard, Durweston tenant,
    237
apothecaries, 101, 103
Appleton, Norfolk, 219
Appleyard, George, land steward, 18,
    20, 27, 31, 32, 113, 134, 149,
    164, 189, 190, 202, 211,
    212, 233
Appleyard, Mrs, 166
Apps, Mr, London boat-builder, 157
Aram, John, under/head gardener,
    45, 57, 129, 204
Archenholz, Johann von d', 259
Archer, George, Castle Acre tenant,
    27, 221
Archer, John, Castle Acre tenant,
    221
Arden, John, St Giles's vestry clerk,
    70
Armstrong, John, 109, 252
Arnold, Mrs, Minster Lovell tenant,
    241
Arslett, Mr, New Brentford
    nurseryman, 57
Arthur, Mr, London ice-cream seller,
    168
Ash, Richard, Knightley tenant, 240
Ash, widow, Knightley tenant, 240
Ashbourne, Derbyshire, 149
Ashcroft, Mrs, London haberdasher,
    86
asses' milk, 87, 91
assize rents, *see* rents
Astley, Jacob, Sir, 29, 110
Atherton, John, Portbury bailiff, 35,
    239
Athill, Nathaniel, Norfolk attorney,
    58

Atwood, Revd, Kingsdown tenant,
    236
Atwood, Mrs, Bath landlady, 111
Audley, Mr, pewterer, 90, 179
Austen, Robert, Norfolk yeoman, 15
Ayers, Martin, Feathers Inn landlord,
    152
Ayscough, Mr, London toyman, 100

Back, John, Fulmodeston bailiff, 223
Bacon, Edmund, Sir, 114
Bacon, Mary, Aldham tenant, 231
Bacon, R.N., 42, 54
badger hunting, 219
Badham, Mr, London storage factor,
    141
Badingham, Suffolk, 219
Badminton, Gloucestershire, 113
bagnios, 120ff.
Bailey, John, fox huntsman's
    assistant, 151, 203
Baily, Anne, Billingford tenant, 220
Baily, John, Weasenham tenant, 230
bailiffs, 30, 220ff.
Bakeman, Susannah, Holkham
    servant, 204
Baker, Ann, cook's maid, 201, 208
Baker, C.H.C. and M.I., 111, 133,
    252, 254, 257
Baker, John, Donyatt miller, 49, 239
Baker, John, Tittleshall bailiff, 229
Baker, John, Wellingham bailiff, 30,
    31, 32, 230
Baker, John, Norfolk
    carpenter/sawyer, 32, 221,
    222, 225, 228
Baker, William, Revd Dr, St Giles's
    rector, 69
Baker, William, Kingsdown tenant,
    236
Baker, Mrs, personal maid, 13
Baldry, John, Huntingfield Park
    tenant, 232
Baldry, Sarah, widow, Huntingfield
    Manor tenant, 233
Ballenden, Henry, Sir, 216

Banfield, William, Donyatt tenant, 238

Bannard, Charles, Norfolk glazier, 228

Banning, T.W.C., 253

Baptiste, Jean, groom/2nd French cook, 196, 199, 206

Barefoot, Thomas, 4th stable-boy, 202

Barker, Thomas, Quarles tenant, 226

Barlow, Mr, Norfolk spinet master, 135

Barnard, Mr, Ashford surgeon, 89

Barnet, Mr, London surgeon, 101

Barron, Mr, London undertaker, 70

Barrow, Alice, widow, Cratfield tenant, 231

Bastard, Thomas, Flitcham tenant, 222

Batchelor, Revd, London chaplain, 69, 129

Bateson, Mr, Norfolk surveyor, 39, 54

Bath, The Most Honourable Order of, 81, 82, 114ff., 252

Bath, Somerset, 89, 110ff., 165, 168

Batson, London vintner, 175

Battin, William, Donyatt tenant, 238

Bavand, Mr, London tax collector, 63

Bayfield, Norfolk, 153

Bayfield, William, Tittleshall tenant, 229

Bayly, John, Knightley bailiff, 240

Bayly, Robert, Knightley tenant, 240

Beane, Mr, Bevis Marks tenant, 243

beating the manor bounds, 25

Beattie, J.M., 252

Beazant, Henry, Laxfield tenant, 234

Beckett, J.V., 250, 251

Beck Hall, Billingford, Norfolk, 37, 88, 127, 151, 187, 218

Bedford, Wriothesley Russell, 6th Duke of, 39, 192, 211

Bedford, Capt., riding instructor, 90, 187

Bedingfeld, Christopher, 21, 29, 49, 157, 222

Bedingfeld, Henry, Sir, 60, 79, 110, 152, 153

Bedingfeld family, 129

beer, 174ff.

Beeston, Thomas, Norfolk miller, 150

Beeston-cum-Mileham manor, Norfolk, 26, 39, 229

Bell, Judith, Panworth Hall tenant, 226

Bell, William, Billingford tenant, 220

Bell, William and Thomas, Bintree tenants, 221

bell-ringers, 13, 14, 22, 70, 113, 149, 150, 189

Beloe, E.M., 255

Bendall, John, Suffolk carpenter, 231

Bender, Philip, footman, 135, 156, 158, 255

Bennet, Christian, musical instrument-maker, 135

Bennett, Mark, Norfolk oilman, 150

Bennett, Mr, Edward's tutor, 90, 91

Bentley, Mr, Uttoxeter perruqier, 100

Berkins, Mr, Portbury tenant, 239

Bernard, Edward, stable-boy, 203

Bernie, James, London vintner, 175

Bernie, John, Weasenham tenant, 230

Bertie, Charles, Thomas Coke's uncle, 84, 99

Bevis Marks, see London, Bevis Marks

Bicker, Henry, Laxfield tenant, 234

Bignamini, Ilaria, 254

Bignell, Mrs, London saddler, 186

Billingford manor, Norfolk, 25, 30, 35, 36, 37, 40, 219, 220, 244

Bingham, Mr, London draper, 96

Bintree manor, Norfolk, 21, 25, 29, 47, 218, 221

Bircham, James, Holkham tenant, 54, 59, 223

Birtle, Mr, London furniture dealer, 183, 198

Bishop of Norwich, see Trimnell, Charles, Bishop of Norwich

Bishops Cleve, Gloucestershire, 219, 244

Bissen, Thomas, Shillington tenant, 237

Black, Charles, Fulmodestan tenant, 223

Black, Jeremy, 249, 253

Blackamore's Head, Cheapside, see London, Bevis Marks

Blackheath, 108, 129

Blackman, Giles, aviary keeper, 103

Blagrave, Minster Lovell locksmith, 242

Blakeman, Thomas, Knightley tenant, 240

Blauner, Abraham, 2nd footman, 85, 198

Blickling, 60

Blinkhorn, Ann, London charwoman/cook, 201, 202, 206

Blithing Hundred, Suffolk, 27, 233

Blomfield, Michael, Billingford tenant, 220

Blue Boar inn, Holborn, 9, 64, 157

Blundell, Nicholas, 251

Blyford, John, Holkham draper etc., 97, 175

Boardman, James, London vintner, 175

board wages, 8, 208

Boddington, William, Farnham Royal tenant, 242

Bodys, Elizabeth, Farnham Royal tenant, 242

Bolton, Daniel, St Giles's vestry clerk, 70

Bond, John, Portbury tenant, 239

Bononcini, Giovanni, 133–4

Booke, John, Portbury tenant, 239

Booke, Horham Jernegans tenant, 232

Booth, Edward, Laxfield Rectory tenant, 234

Booth, Robert, Huntingfield Manor tenant, 233

Bordoni, Faustina, 134

Borghese, Elenora, Princess, 215

Borret, John, Laxfield tenant, 234

Borret, Thomas, Huntingfield Park/Manor tenant, 232, 233

Boscawen, Edward, Admiral (1711–61), 216

Bosen, John, London wood carver, 66

Bostwick, Mr, fencing and dancing master, 10

Boswell, James, 198, 255, 257

Bournehall, Suffolk, 219

bowls, 158

Bradshaw, Elias, Knightley tenant, 240

Bradshaw, Thomas, Knightley tenant, 240

Bramford, Suffolk, 28

Brampton, William, Laxfield tenant, 23, 234

Brand, Dame, Holkham casual worker, 204

Branton, Richard, Norfolk brick- and tile-maker, 222

Brawnshatch, see Kingsdown manors, Kent

Brazenhall, Norfolk, 153

Breese, Robert, otter hunter, 156

Brereton, James, schoolmaster, 89

Brereton, Thomas, Horham Thorpehall tenant, 232

Bretby, Derbyshire, 107

Brett, Elias, Bintree tenant, 221

Brettingham, Matthew, the Elder, 53, 144

Brettingham, Matthew, the Younger, 214

brick kilns, 31, 222, 224, 230, 231, 238, 239, 242

Bridget, 'Old', 128

Bridgewell, Samuel, Martham timber merchant, 226

Brindley, John, book-binder, 145

Bristol, Somerset, 89, 114, 190

Bristol, John Hervey, 1st Earl, 252

Bristol, Lady, 111
Bristol water, 91
Brooke, George, Horham Jernegans tenant, 232
Brooke, James, Portbury tenant, 239
Brooke, Mr, Holt Clerk of the Course, 158
Brooks, Moses, Minster Lovell tenant, 241
Brown, Ann, housemaid, 201
Brown, Jeffery, Castle Acre tenant/lime burner, 221
Brown, John, Martham ladder supplier, 226
Brown, Richard, Norfolk paviour, 228
Brown, Thomas, London net-maker, 156
Brown, Mr, Bath grocer, 112
Browne, Robert, Portbury tenant, 239
Brownlow St, Holborn, 67
Bryant, Thomas, Portbury miller, 240
Buckingham, John Sheffield, Duke of, 145
Buckingham, Earl of, 158
Buckinghamshire manor, 242
Buckland, Mr, London brewer, 174, 175
Budworth, Revd, Tittleshall rector, 48, 229
Budworth, Mr, London coachmaker, 82, 186
building maintenance and construction, 39ff.
Buisont, Mr, London truffle supplier, 167
Bulman, Richard, Bintree tenant, 221
Bulman, Thomas, Billingford tenant, 220
Bulmer, Ann, Holkham housemaid, 204
Burdon, John, Castle Acre tenant, 221
Burdwood, Mary, Laxfield tenant, 235
Burgh-by-Aylsham, Norfolk, 218
Burgis, Mr, Holborn innkeeper, 128
Burlington, Richard Boyle, 3rd Earl of (1694–1753), 4, 66, 69, 106, 131, 132, 134, 213
Burlington, Lady, 136
Burnett, J., 250
Burney, Charles, Dr, 102
Burnham Thorpe, Norfolk, 29
Burridge, Joan, Donyatt tenant, 238
Burridge, Stephen, Donyatt tenant, 25, 238
Burrows, Donald, 254
Burrows, George, Huntingfield ditcher, 233

Burrows, James, Kingsdown tenant, 236
burrow-stopping, 154
Burt, John, Durweston/Shillington bailiff, 236, 237
Burt, Thomas, Shillington tenant, 237
Burton, Elizabeth, 255
Burwood, William, Thorington tenant, 236
Bury, Mary, Aldham tenant, 231
Butcher, John, Laxfield tenant, 23, 235
Butt, James, Donyatt tenant, 23
Byard, Thomas, Norfolk millwright, 222
Bylaugh, Norfolk, 48, 219, 244

Caird, J., 248
Cauldwell, Ralph, land steward, 257
Camomile St, see London, Bevis Marks
Campbell, Colen, 52
Candelent Manor, Suffolk, 26, 219
Capper, Mr, London gardener, 67
Carlisle, Charles Howard, 3rd Earl of, 78
Carlton, Mr, Holkham landowner, 20
Caroline, Queen, 117, 206
Carr, John, Great Massingham tenant, 17, 223
Carr, Thomas, Weasenham tenant, 230
Carriera, Rosalba, 91, 99, 215
Carrington, James, Mileham tenant, 229
Carswell, John, 251
Carter, Bridget, Holkham tenant, 23
Carter, Charles, chef, 160
Carter, Edward, Holkham tenant, 223
Carter, Henry, Minster Lovell thatcher, 41, 242
Carter, 'Widow', Holkham tenant, 58
Carter, 'Widow', London charwoman, 201
Cartwright, Lady, 135
Carver, Henry, Horham Thorpehall/Horham Jernegans tenant, 232
Casanova, Giacomo, 123, 253
Casey, John, house steward, 12, 66, 78, 80, 87, 91, 93, 98, 113, 134, 141, 158, 195, 209, 222
Cassali, Andrea, 118
Cassani, Signor, castrato, 133
Castle Acre manor, Norfolk, 23, 27, 41, 48, 128, 154, 219, 244, 221
   Swan alehouse, 221
Castle Howard, Yorkshire, 213

Castrucci, Signor, opera singer, 135
Catchpole, Mary, Horham Jernegans tenant, 232
Chamberlain, Hugh, Dr, 80, 81, 87, 88
Chamberlain, John, Flitcham tenant, 222
Chamberlain, Mr, London butcher, 163
Chandler, Mrs, night nurse, 86
Chandos, James Brydges, Duke of, 78, 111, 132, 135, 211
Chaplain, Richard, coachman/farrier, 199
Chapman, Henry, Kingsdown tenant, 236
Chapman, Thomas, Kingsdown tenant, 236
charitable giving, 70
Charles II, King of England, 213
Chatsworth, Derbyshire, 45, 57
Chediston, Suffolk, 46, 234
Chediston, Richard, Scotshall tenant, 235
Cherriton, Mr, London glover, 90
Chesterfield, Derbyshire, 45, 57
Chesterfield, Philip Stanhope, Lord, 107, 121ff. 125, 253
Chiari, Guiseppe, 143
Child, Richard, Quarles tenant, 226
Child, Robert, Weasenham tenant, 230
Chippenham, Buckinghamshire, 218
Chiswick, 106
Christ's College, Cambridge, 29
Christmas, John, Martham, bailiff, 226
Christmas Boxes, 70, 104, 113, 134, 207
Church, John, Billingford tenant, 220
Church patronage, 47ff., 244, 258
Churchill, Charles, General, 121ff.
Cillis, John, Holkham tenant, 224
Civil List Tax, 117
Clack, widow, Minster Lovell tenant, 241
Clanvil, widow, Minster Lovell tenant, 241
Clare, His Majesty's Honour of, 47
Clare, John, pad-groom's helper, 203
Clark, Charles, Minster Lovell tenant, 241
Clark, James, Shepton Mallet cloth merchant, 96
Clark, John, Suffolk timber merchant, 34
Clark, John, Norfolk butcher, 165, 171
Clark, W., Holkham servant, 204
Claude Lorrain, 142, 143

Clavelshaw, George, Donyatt tenant, 238

Clay, Alexander, pad-groom's helper, 203

Clayton, Ann, Billingford/Bintree tenant, 220 221

Cleaver, John, London smith, 66

Clement, Mr, Bath baker, 112

Cliffords Inn, 15

clothing, 95ff.

coal mining, 35

Coates, Ann, Holkham servant, 204

Cockburn, John, 37

Cockey, Mr, cutler, 153

Cockfighting, 118, 147ff., 158

Coddenham, William, Sparham tenant/thatcher, 227

Codex Leicester, 144

Colquhoun, Patrick, 256

Colville, Olivia, 256

Conca, Seabstiano, 142

copyhold tenancies, 23

Coke, Anne, 91, 94

Coke, Bridget, 15, 129

Coke, Cary, 74, 209

Coke, Cary (Mrs Wyvil), 91, 188

Coke, Edward, Sir, Chief Justice (1552–1634), 15, 43, 46, 48, 51, 52, 113

Coke, Edward, Sir, Bart. (d. 1727), 8, 11, 18, 31, 51, 66, 85, 93, 113, 119, 147, 150, 173, 189, 208

Coke, Edward (1676–1707), 74

Coke, Edward (1702–33), 81, 91, 93, 107, 121, 222

Coke, Edward, Viscount (1719–53), 70, 85, 99, 101, 143, 187, 214
    establishment, 90
    schooling, 89ff.

Coke, John (1590–1661), 52

Coke, John (1636–71), 116

Coke, John, Thomas Coke's guardian, 8, 12, 20, 222, 228

Coke, Lady Mary, 124, 130, 216

Coke, Margaret, Countess of Leicester, Baroness Clifford (1700–75), 8, 85, 89, 100, 101, 106, 111, 119, 143, 180, 186, 198, 201, 213

Coke, Meriel, 52

Coke, Robert (1704–54), 10, 11, 13, 91, 93ff. 107, 113

Coke, Thomas, Baron Lovel, Earl of Leicester (1679–1759)
    advowsons, see Church patronage
    Burwood Hall farm, Mileham, 229
    Captain of the Band of Pensioners, 118

charities, 70, 127ff.
    collector and connoisseur, 138ff.
    design of Holkham Hall, 4, 57
    Earldom of Leicester, 214
    elevation to the peerage, 117
    farming practice and management,18ff., 27, 36, 55ff.
    financial affairs, 72ff.
    Freemasonry, 109
    Home farm, 224
    Justice of the Peace, 114
    Knight Companion of the Bath, 114ff.
    Knight of the Shire, 113, 173
    marriage, 7ff.; -jointure, 8; -presents, 11; -settlement, 258; -vails, 13; wedding clothes, 10ff.
    personality and character, 118ff.
    Serjeant-at-Arms in Ordinary, 116

Coke, Thomas, Sir, Lord Chamberlain, 137

Coke, Thomas William, 'Coke of Norfolk', 5, 42, 54, 130, 150, 214

Coke, Thomas William, 2nd Earl, 150

Coke's Court, see London, Bevis Marks

Coldham, John, Gent., Laxfield tenant, 235

Cole, Ann, Aldham tenant, 231

Cole, Richard, Shillington tenant, 237

Collet, George, Portbury surveyor/bailiff, 39, 239

Collet, Reginald, Huntingfield Manor tenant, 233

Collings, Mr, London vintner, 171

Collis, Deodatis, Minster Lovell tenant, 241

Collis, John, Minster Lovell tenant, 241

Collyer, Robert, Cratfield tenant, 231

Colquhoun, Patrick, 256

Colson [or Coston], Mr, London harpsichord-maker, 135

Colville, Olivia, 256

Comb, James, Donyatt tenant, 238

Commons Journals, 249

Conca, Sebastiano, 142

Conisbrough, Yorkshire, 45, 57

Cook, Samuel, London draper, 197

Cook, Jacob, Fulmodeston tenant, 223

Cook, Richard, Minster Lovell blacksmith, 242

Cooke, Henry, Holkham nurseryman, 57

Cooke, Thomas, dramatist, 137

Cookley, Suffolk, 219, 244

Cooley, Mr, toyman, 12

Cooley, Mrs, landlady, 8

Coote, Thomas, vintner, 171

Cooper, Roger, Holkham tenant, 223

Cope, William, Sir, 46

Copeman, Edward, Sparham tenant, 227

Copland, John, Laxfield tenant, 234

coppice wood, see forestry

Coppin, John, Minster Lovell tenant, 241

Coppin, 'Widow', Minster Lovell tenant, 241

Corbridge, James, cartographer, 227

Corby, Mr, Norfolk fiddler, 136

Corneby, Robert, Laxfield tenant, 235

Corelli, Archangelo, 136

Cortacelli, Mr and Mrs, London soap makers, 100

Cortivril, Mr, music master, 135

Coston, Mr, see Colson, Mr

Cotton, Anthony, Panworth Hall bailiff, 226

Cotton, Samuel, Thorington tenant, 236

Courant, George, Farnham Royal tenant, 242

Courts Leet, 21ff.

Covenant woods, 35

Coward, Nicholas, Durweston tenant, 237

Cowper, John, vintner, 175

Cowper, Norfolk music master, 155

Cox, Richard, Shillington tenant, 237

Cratfield manor, Suffolk, 22, 26, 28, 30, 49, 244, 231

Creake Abbey, Norfolk, 153

Creamer, Edward, Holkham tenant, 36, 48, 54, 59, 224

Creed, John, head gardener, 56, 57, 169, 174, 203

Cremer, Mr, Huntingfield Manor tenant, 233

Crocker, William, Donyatt tenant, 238

Crompton, John, Cratfield tenant, 231

Crosfield, Norfolk vintner, 171

Crossgrove, Henry, Norwich printer, 132

Cross Keys, Bishopgate, see London, Bevis Marks

Crustwich Hall, Essex, 218

clothing, see dress

Cun, Samuel, London surveyor, 66

Cunningham, Suffolk ditcher, 233

Cunningham, Mr, money-lender, 79

Curryson, George, Norfolk painter, 228

Curstor's Alley, Chancery Lane, *see* London, Bevis Marks
Curtis, John, pensioned servant, 209, 224
Curtis, Mr, Norfolk brick and tile supplier, 227
Curzon, Mr, 107
Cushion, Samuel, Revd, Weasenham tenant, 230
Cuzzoni, Francesca, diva, 134

Daily Advertiser, 257
Dalton, John, 221
Danby, Thomas Osborne, Earl of, *see* Leeds, Thomas Osborne, Duke of
Dandy, Joseph, Portbury tenant, 239
Darby, William, Dunton tenant, 221
Dark, Mr, London farrier, 186
Darsham-cum-Yoxford, Suffolk, 28
Dashwood, Francis, Sir, 216
Dashwood, George, Esq., Huntingfield Manor tenant, 233
Dashwood, Mrs, London tenant, 45, 243
Dates, Ann, Norfolk brickmaker, 223
Davenhill, William, Knightley tenant 240
David, Elizabeth, 255
David, Mrs, London milk and cheese woman, 165, 166
Davies, Eliza, London charwoman, 201
Davis, James, under-butler/1st footman, 188, 198, 199, 206
Davis, Robert, Portbury tenant, 239
Davis, Thomas, London houseman, 200
Davis, Mr, London carpenter, 66
Dawson, Mr, London cheesemonger, 169
Dean, Betty, 128
Deards, Mr, London jeweller, 100
deer parks and deer hunting, 43, 155
Defoe, Daniel, 64, 77, 157, 168, 192, 249, 250, 251, 255, 256
De Lamerie, Paul, 76
Delamore, 'Widow', Portbury tenant, 25, 49, 239
Delaplace, Dennis, schoolmaster, 89
Delescourt, Mr, dentist, 91
Dempster, William, 144
Denham, William, shipmaster, 57
Denman, May, Donyatt tenant, 238
dentistry, 91
Denver, Norfolk, 165
Derham, Thomas, Sir, 173
Devil Tavern, 173
Devitt, Denis M., 250

Dewsing, William, South Creake bailiff, 36, 227
Dickens, Sgt, surgeon, 89
Diggs, Ralph, Burnham resident, 128
Dinham, George, Donyatt tenant, 238
Disbrowe, Mr, tutor, 89
Disraeli, Benjamin, 76
Ditchfield, G.M. 257
ditching work, 42
Ditton, Cambridgeshire, 219
Dobbs, Rayner, Sparham tenant, 227
Dobie, Rowland, 250
dogs, 65, 103
Dolphin Inn, Cheapside, *see* London, Bevis Marks
Dominey, William, Durweston tenant 23, 237
Donyatt manor, Somerset, 18, 23, 24, 25, 28, 34, 38, 39, 41, 43, 46, 49, 50, 219, 238ff., 244
Dorham, Mary, housekeeper's maid, 201
Dorset manors, 236
Dotchen, Mrs, midwife, 85, 87
Doughton, *see* Dunton-cum-Doughton, manor, Norfolk
Douglas, Mother, *see* bagnios
Dow, John, Holkham casual worker, 174, 205
Dow, Margaret, 'Mother', Holkham charwoman, 165, 204
Dow, William, Holkham casual worker, 154, 174
Draine, Robert, Cratfield tenant, 231
Drake, Ambrose, Donyatt tenant, 238
drama and the stage, 136ff.
Drax, Mr, broker, 79
Draycott, Derbyshire, 151
dress, 95ff.
Dresser, John, Laxfield tenant, 23, 234
Dresser, Samuel, Cratfield tenant, 231
Dreury family, 15
drink, 112, 170ff.
Drower, Peter, Donyatt tenant, 238
drugs, 101ff.
Drury Lane theatre, 136ff.
  box-keepers, 137
Drut, Mr, Lord Thanet's house steward, 13
Dubber, John, Minster Lovell bailiff, 241
Dungeness Light, 82, 213ff.
Dunnegham, Joseph, Suffolk brick-and tile-maker, 231
Dunton-cum-Doughton manor, Norfolk, 29, 32, 38, 39, 49, 153, 218, 221, 244

Durweston manor, Dorset, 23, 24, 28, 29, 34, 38, 219, 244, 236ff.

Eden, P.G., 248
Edge, John, Norfolk bricklayer, 221, 228
Edgeson, John, Farnham Royal brickmaker, 242
Edwards, Joseph, Portbury Court foreman, 22, 239
Edwards, Mr, London grocer, 169
Edwards, Mrs, London milliner, 97
Edwin, William, nightwatchman, 201
Egmere, Norfolk, 154
Egmont, John Perceval, 1st Earl, 80, 101, 119, 125, 252, 253
Elliott, Richard, Norfolk blacksmith, 222
Elliott, Mr, drawing master, 90
Ellis, Aytoun, 255
Ellis, John and Mary, Bintree tenants, 221
Ellis, Mr, Isleworth schoolmaster, 85
Elmes, James, 62, 249
Elmham manor, *see* North Elmham manor, Norfolk
Emerson, Mr, Customs House Officer 144, 145
enclosures, 16
England, Ann, 'Dame', Holkham kitchen help, 204
England, Ann, jun., Holkham casual, 204
England, John, Donyatt tenant, 238
England, William, ratcatcher, 205
entertainers, 103
Essex, William Capell, Earl of, 117
Estate, the Great, *see* Great Estate
Etherington, Thomas, nightwatchman, 201
Etteridge, Francis, Fulmodeston tenant, 223
Euston, Suffolk, 110
Eye, Suffolk Castleguard and Chantry rents, 29

Faircloth, Richard, Holkham tenant, 224
Fairfax, Catherine, Lady, 14
fairs, 23
fancy dress, 108
Farnham Royal manor, Buckinghamshire, 26, 30, 32, 33, 49, 60, 189, 219, 242
Farrer, Richard, Longham/Wendling tenant, 225
fashions, *see* dress
fee farms, 28
Felbrigg, Norfolk, 60

Fellows, William, Norfolk brewing man, 174, 176
Fenny Bentley, Derbyshire, 148
Fenton, Elijah, 136
fencing, 158
Fenning, Samuel, Suffolk thatcher, 231
Fernihaugh, George, Knightley tenant, 240
Ferrari, Domenico Antonio, Dr, 67, 82, 92, 140, 146, 162
fertilisers, 30
Feverall, James, Quarles tenant, 226
Figg, Mr, fencing master, 158
Finch, Daniel, Lord, 80, 83
firearms, 11
fire engine, 65
fire insurance, 64
Fisher, Edward, Sparham tenant, 227
fishing, 156ff.
Fishpoole, 'Widow', Holkham cottager, 166
Flavel, Mr, Holkham teacher, 210
Flaxmore, Pomfret, Godwick tenant, 54, 229
Fletcher, Herbert, Minster Lovell tenant, 241
Flight, Joshua, Dunton tenant, 222
Flitcham manor, Norfolk, 28, 32, 39, 48, 218, 219, 222, 244
Flitcroft, Henry, 69
Flood, George, Holkham tenant, 224
Flood, Jeffery, Sparham tenant, 227
Flood, 'Widow', Sparham tenant, 227
Flood, William, Sparham tenant, 227
Folcard, Edmund, Laxfield tenant, 235
food, 112, 115, 160ff.
Ford, John, Shillington tenant, 237
Ford, Robert, Shillington tenant, 237
forestry, 30ff., 33
  see also timber supplies; Covenant woods
Forster, Nurse, 101, 210
Fortescue, Mr, London fishmonger, 163
Fountaine, Sir Andrew, 110, 116, 118
Fowler, John, 1st stable-boy, 202
Fox, Charles, Cratfield tenant, 231
Fox, Charles, Laxfield tenant, 235
Fox, John, Cratfield tenant, 231
foxes, 154
Foxton, Holborn pauper, 128
Framing, Mr, Swaffham apothecary, 103
Framingham, James, Holkham tenant, 57

Francis, John, Revd, Wendling curate, 225, 226
Francis, Mr, London tallow chandler, 180
Frankland, John, Flitcham tenant, 222
Frary, —, Holkham 'pump doctor', 34
Freemasonry, 59, 108ff.
Freeston, Thomas, Revd, Huntingfield Manor tenant, 233
free suit money, 28
Freke, Mr, publisher, 80
Fremingham, James, Holkham tenant, 224
French, John, Donyatt tenant, 238
Frere, Edward, Esq., Horham Thorpehall tenant, 232
Freston, Richard, 222
Freston, William, Huntingfield Park tenant, 233
Frombten, Mrs, London draper, 182
Fry, Thomas, Portbury tenant, 239
fuel, 180ff.
Fuller, George, Minster Lovell tenant, 241
Fuller, Mr, seedsman, 57
Fulmodeston manor, Norfolk, 30, 34, 39, 49, 57, 59, 156, 218, 223
Furnish, Robert, Sir, 14
furniture, 182ff.
Fussell, G.E., 248
Futter, Thomas, Holkham teamsman, 59

Gage, 'Widow', Billingford tenant, 220
gambling, 83
game birds, 156, 164, 170
Gameron, Mary, embroideress, 10, 101
games, 103
Gardener, Robert, Norfolk carpenter, 222
Gardiner, George, Holkham ditcher, 153
Gardiner, Walter, whipper-in, 151
Garlick, Mr, London cheesemonger, 169
Garrard, Mr, London apothecary, 86
Garrard, Mr, London jeweller, 87
Garrouch, Sophia, Holkham housemaid, 204
Garzi, Luigi, 143
Gates, William, 144
Gay, John, 133, 134, 137
Gay, Richard, Holkham helper, 174
Gayer, John, Stoke Poges owner, 52
Gayer, Robert, Stoke Poges owner, 52

Gazeley, William, Holkham tenant, 224
Gazeley, William, London stable-hand, 149
Gazeley, Mr, Norfolk butcher, 164
Gazeley, Mr, London slaughterman, 201
Geminiani, Francesco, 136
Gentleman's Magazine, The, 256
George I, King of England, 14, 105, 106, 114, 131, 133, 178
George II, King of England, 85, 117, 133, 160
George, Dorothy, 68, 250
Gibbs, James, architect, 66
Gibson, Thomas, 222
Gibson, Mr, jeweller, 116
Gibson & Co., storage factors, 14, 140
Gidney, Samuel, Holkham labourer, 59
Gilboy, E.W., 256
Gilkes, Mr, apothecary (?), 88
Gill, Mrs Bathsheba, London milliner, 86, 88, 97
Gill, John, Great Massingham tenant, 223
Gillet, widow, Donyatt tenant, 238
Gillingham, Thomas, Shillington bailiff, 50, 237
Ginnis, Martham (sawn plank supplied), 225
Girling, Thomas, Laxfield tenant, 235
Gittos, Edmund, postilion, 199
Gladdish, John, Kingsdown woodward, 236
Gladish, Holkham hops supplier, 176
Glover, Mr, Bevis Marks tenant, 243
Glover, Mr, Castle Acre builder, 48
Glover, Mr, lime burner, 222
Gobbet, Mr, Norwich householder, 46
Godwick manor, Norfolk, 15, 18, 27, 31, 54, 55, 187, 188, 218, 244, 229
Godwin, Mr, London oil man, 169, 180
Goff, Solomon, surveyor, 39
Gold, John, Fulmodeston tenant, 223
Goldsmith, Oliver, 110
Goodacres, Samuel, London stable-boy, 200
Goodall, Robert, Huntingfield Park tenant, 232
Goodbody, John, Castle Acre tenant, 221
Goodwood, 107
Goose & Gridiron alehouse, 108
Gosney, Widow, Shillington tenant, 50, 237

Gosset, Matthew, frame-maker, 143
Gould, Mrs, *see* bagnios
Gow, Mr London hatter, 90
Gower, Levison, 110
Gower, Lord, 110, 118, 152
Gowing, Richard, Huntingfield
    tenant, 22
Gowing, Thomas, Horham
    Thorpehall tenant, 232
Grafton, Charles Fitzroy, 2nd Duke
    of, 110, 116, 206, 226
Graham, George, London jeweller,
    10
Graham, Mr, London apothecary, 88
Grand Tour, 1, 7, 51, 75, 91, 92,
    118, 132, 138ff., 150, 173,
    179
gratuities, *see* vails
Gray, Thomas, 216
Gray, William, Huntingfield tenant,
    50
Greasley, Sir Thomas, 187
Great Book of Conveyances, The,
    15
Great Estate, The, 15ff., 257
Great Jupiter statue, The, 141
Great Lawn, The, 58ff.
Great Massingham manor, Norfolk,
    17, 27, 37, 39, 218, 223
Great Picture, The, 142
Great Wood, The, 58ff.
Great Yarmouth, Norfolk, 132
Green, James, Horham Thorpehall
    tenant, 232
Green, Thomas, Laxfield tenant, 235
Green, William, West Lexham
    tenant, 231
Green, Mr, picture restorer, 143
Green, Mr, London cheesemonger,
    169
Greenland Company, 79
Greer, John ('Old'), London helper,
    200, 208, 210
Gregory, Gamaliel, coachman's stable
    helper, 203, 224
Grey, John, Durweston tenant, 237
Grey, Thomas, Huntingfield
    Park/Manor tenant, 233
Griffin, Absalon, Holkham
    molecatcher, 60
Griffith, William, sedan-chair-man,
    201
Griffiths, Andrew, upper
    butler/house steward 35, 82,
    108, 153, 173, 195, 196,
    206, 208
Griffiths, Mr Farnham Royal
    blacksmith, 242
Griffiths, Mr, shoemaker, 90
Grigor, James, 249
Grinston, Samuel, nightwatchman,
    201

Groom, Thomas, fox huntsman,
    151, 155, 203
Guelfi, Baptist, sculptor, 141
Gullman, Mr Frankfort Resident,
    119
Gummer, Thomas, Donyatt tenant,
    238
Gundaymore, John, chef, 108, 112,
    153, 188, 195, 196, 208

Habakkuk, John, 250
Hacon, John, Scotshall tenant, 235
Hadderton, widow, Knightley tenant,
    240
Haines (Haynes/Hains), William,
    London tailor, 10, 12, 82, 90,
    96, 197
hair powder, 196
Halborow, Mr, London tailor and
    breeches-maker, 96
Hall, William, Castle Acre
    blacksmith, 221
Hallet, James, Shillington tenant,
    237
Halley, John, Norfolk gamekeeper,
    203
Halsband, Robert, 252
Halsey, Edmund, Stoke Poges owner,
    52
Halsey, John, surveyor; Castle
    Acre/Dunton/Flitcham/Fulmod
    eston/Sparham/Tittleshall/Well
    ingham/West Lexham bailiff,
    30, 38, 202, 220, 221, 222,
    223, 225, 227, 229, 230, 231
Hamilton, Sir David, obstetrician, 86
Hamilton, Gavin, 144
Hampton Court, 106, 189
Handel, George Frederic, 133, 134
Hanmer, Thomas, Sir, 46, 235
Hanway, Jonas, 168, 256
Harbord, Col., 114
Harding, R., 222
Hardingham, Richard, Billingford
    tenant, 220
Hardy, Thomas, Portbury tenant,
    239
Hardy, Revd, Bylaugh curate, 48,
    220
Hare, Sir Ralph, 110, 152
hare coursing, 151, 155
Harmer, Willliam, Martham
    ironmonger, 225
Harmon, John, Suffolk painter, 234
Harris, Richard, Minster Lovell
    miller, 241
Harris, 'Widow', Minster Lovell
    tenant, 241
Harris, Mr, London musical
    instrument-maker, 135
Harrison, Frank, Holkham casual,
    175, 205

Harrison, Stephen, Holkham tenant,
    224
Harrison, Mr, Bath Assembly Rooms
    owner, 112
Harold, Mary, Lady, 112
Harold, Lord, 108, 188
Hart, Roger, Durweston tenant, 237
Hart, 'Widow', Donyatt tenant, 238
harvest work, 42, 56
Harvey, John Robert, 43, 248
Harvey, William, Thorington tenant,
    236
Harwood, John, Minster Lovell
    brickmaker, 242
Hatcher, Benjamin, Cratfield tenant,
    231
Hatfield House, 106
Hawgood (or Hogwood) Mr, Edward
    (Little Master) Coke's writing-
    master, 89
Hawksmoor, Nicholas, 69
Haws, Lucy, Laxfield tenant, 234
Hay, Andrew, art agent, 144
Hayball, 'Widow', Donyatt tenant,
    24
Haycock, Mr, Norfolk cheesemonger
    166
Hayden, Mr, broker, 79, 80
Haylett, Thomas, Godwick
    tenant/farm bailiff, 37, 54, 55,
    175, 229
Haylett, Thomas, Norfolk carpenter,
    223
haymaking, 42
Haymarket Opera House, 115
Haynes, Avise, widow, Donyatt
    tenant, 238
Haynes, James, Donyatt tenant, 238
Haynes, Mr, Derby attorney, 50
Haynes, Mrs, Knightley tenant, 241
Hays, Mr, picture dealer and restorer,
    142, 143
Hays, Mr, London carter, 140
Haywood, Eliza, 256
health and personal medicine, 85,
    110
Heard, William, Kempstone tenant,
    225
Hearne, John, Longham/Wendling
    tenant, 225
Hearne, Joseph, Farnham Royal
    bailiff, woodward and
    carpenter, 49, 242
Hearne, widow, Farnham Royal
    tenant, 242
Heasel, Anthony, 256
Heathfield, Mr, London provision
    merchant, 163
Hecht, J. Jean, 205, 210, 256, 257
Heidigger, Monsieur, impresario, 133
Helsdon, —, the Holkham 'Trufile
    [*sic*] boy', 255

Hemmings, Mr, London glover, 97
Hendrick (or Kenderick/Kenrick)
    (late Proctors), Mr, Bevis Hall
    tenant, 243
Henriques, Fernando, 253
Hepburn, George, Dr, Kings Lynn
    physician, 102, 103
Heriot, William, footman, 158
heriots, 23
Herman, Mrs, London pastrycook,
    165
Herring, 'Widow',
    Longham/Wendling tenant,
    225
Hervey, John, Lord, 53, 117, 119,
    185, 215, 252, 253, 256, 257
Heydigger, Mr, Haymarket Opera
    House manager, 115
Hicks, Henry, lacemaker, 10
Higgins, widow, Portbury tenant,
    239
Highmore, Charles, Bevis Marks
    tenant, 45, 243
Highmore, John, artist, 115
Highmore, John, Bevis Marks tenant,
    45, 243
Hill, Samuel, Kingsdown bailiff, 236
Hill, Samuel and Richard,
    Kingsdown tenants, 20, 236
Hill, Mrs, London draper, 86, 88
Hilliard, Mr, Bevis Marks tenant,
    243
Hilton, Staffordshire, 150
Hinchloe, Elizabeth, Laxfield tenant,
    235
Hingham, Mr, Norfolk pewterer, 179
Hinton, Suffolk, 28, 218
Hobart, John, Sir, 60, 114
Hobart, Thomas, Dr, 118, 119, 132,
    140, 143, 173
Hodgkinson, Ann, Huntingfield Park
    tenant, 232
Hodgson, Mr, London apothecary, 88
Hodsby, Charles, Portbury tenant,
    24, 239
Hogarth, William, 170, 251, 255
Hogwood, Mr, see Hawgood, Mr
Holkham manor, Norfolk, 223
    aviary, see menagerie
    brick kiln, 224
    the Clint, 49, 54, 55, 157
    Coney Hall, 224
    Dalehole marsh, 224
    Dows yard, 224
    Hall, 4, 218
    Hill Hall, 35, 52ff., 181, 214
    Home farm, 18, 224
    Honclecronkdale, 37, 54
    Longlands, 32, 38, 41
    Lushers, 36, 48, 54
    marshes, 224
    malt house, 224

Mansors, 16, 54
Marum Hills, 224
menagerie (aviary), 103
Neals, 54, 59, 219
Nettletons, 32, 54
Newdigates, 30, 35, 54
Peterston, 48, 54
Thackers, 224
Thoroughgoods, 54, 59
Vicarage, 244
warren, 224
Wellands, 18
Wheatley manor, 52
Withersbys, 16
Holland, William, coachman, 158
Holland, William, Thomas Coke's
    footman, 156, 158, 166, 188,
    198, 199, 206
Holland, Dr Norfolk physician, 102
Hollington, Derbyshire, 151
Holmes, John, Donyatt tenant, 238
Holmes, Richard, 247
Holt, Norfolk, 114, 128, 150, 152,
    157
    Feathers Inn, 150, 152, 155, 158
    King's Arms, 158
Hopkins, George, St Giles's sexton,
    70
Horder, John, Donyatt tenant, 238
Horham manors, Suffolk, 26, 34,
    39, 49, 219, 244, 232ff.
Horham Jernegans, see Horham
    manors, Suffolk
Horham Thorpehall and Thorpehall
    wood, see Horham manors,
    Suffolk
horse racing, 157ff.
horses' names, 187
Horsey, Thomas, Donyatt tenant,
    238
Hoskins, Mr, Bath butcher, 112
Hothfield Place, Kent, 9, 85, 86,
    87ff., 89, 93, 156, 186
Hothfield, St Margaret's church, 12
Houghton, Norfolk, 52, 60
House, Charles, postilion, 199
How, John, St Giles's pew keeper,
    470
Howard, Mr, picture restorer, 143
Howlett, Jane, widow, Mildenhall
    Lambsholme tenant, 27, 235
Howman, John, Holkham labourer,
    58
Huddleston & Co., London drapers,
    96
Hudson, Edmund, Sparham tenant,
    227
Hudson, John, Sparham tenant, 227
Hudson, Robert, Horham Thorpehall
    tenant, 232
Hudson, Mr, Horham Jernegans
    tenant, 232

Hughes, Leo, 254
Hull, James, Donyatt tenant, 238
Hull, Mrs, Knightley tenant, 241
Hunt, John, Donyatt tenant, 24, 238
hunting, 149ff.
Huntingdon, Katherine, Countess of,
    15, 52
Huntingfield manors, Suffolk, 18,
    20ff., 30, 32, 39, 45, 50, 51,
    60, 218, 219, 244, 232ff.
Huntingfield Park, see Huntingfield
    manors, Suffolk
Huntingfield Manor, see Huntingfield
    manors, Suffolk
Hussey, Christopher, 4, 247
Hutchinson, Charles,
    Cratfield/Huntingfield/Laxfield/
    Scotshall and Westleton/
    Thorington bailiff, 30, 49,
    231ff.
Hutchinson, Mr, surveyor, 35

ilex trees, 59
Idle, Richard, sedan-chair-man, 201
Ilchester, Stephen Fox, Lord, 249
Imperiale, Francisco, 142
Impropriators, see Church patronage
inflation, 73
Ingham, Thomas, Scotshall tenant,
    235
Inner Temple, 15
insurance, fire, 64
Ireland, Mrs, landlady, 8
Isleworth, 92, 147
Ives, Robert, Farnham Royal
    bricklayer, 242

Jackson, John, Donyatt tenant, 238
Jackson, John, Portbury miller, 240
Jackson, Mr, frame-maker, 143
Jacob, Nicholas, Laxfield tenant, 235
Jacomb, Mr, 222
James, Charles Warburton, 1, 75,
    120, 247, 250, 253, 257
Jarrett, Edward, valet/assistant
    house steward, 10, 79, 83,
    118, 132, 170, 195
Jefferson, Thomas, US President,
    172
Jennings, John, Portbury tenant,
    239
Jenny, Mrs, Lady Margaret's maid,
    113, 188, 201
Jermy, William, 153
Jervis, William, Holkham tenant,
    224
Jessop, Daniel, Laxfield Rectory
    tenant, 234
Johnson, Benjamin, Durweston
    tenant, 237
Johnson, Robert, Weasenham
    tenant, 230

Johnson, Samuel, 88, 121, 160
Johnson, Thomas,
    coachman/groom/farrier, 70,
    188, 199, 210
Johnson, Thomas, Suffolk
    ironmonger, 231
Johnson, William, Kingsdown
    tenant, 236
Johnson, Mrs (later Shaw)
    housekeeper, 182, 195, 197
Jolly, Frederick, 254
Jolly, Mary, Holkham kitchen help,
    204
Jolly, William, Holkham carpenter,
    55, 224, 225
Jones, Mary G., 256
Jones, Mr, Fakenham apothecary,
    103, 152, 187
Jones, Mr, Norfolk horsedealer (?),
    87
Jones, —, Holkham asses' milk
    supplier, 87
Jordain, Richard, Knightley tenant,
    240
Jupiter statue, see Great Jupiter
    statue

Keay, John, 255
Kedleston, Derbyshire, 107
Keith-Lucas, B., 257
Kelsale, Suffolk, 28
Kemp, Francis, nurse, 210
Kemp, John, Holkham tenant, 224
Kempstone manor, Norfolk, 28, 39,
    218, 244, 225
Kemsing and Seele manors, Kent, 28
Kendall, James, Beck Hall
    blacksmith, 187
Kenderick, Mr, see Hendrick, Mr,
    Bevis Hall tenant
Keney (or Kerey), John, Norfolk
    bricklayer, 227
Kendarly, Nathaniel, Holkham
    tenant, 49, 54, 55, 224
Kenrick, Mr, see Hendrick, Mr, Bevis
    Hall tenant
Kensington Palace, 106
Kent manors, 236
Kent, Edmund, Sparham tenant, 227
Kent, John, Weasenham tenant, 230
Kent, William (1685–1748), 4, 52,
    57, 115, 140, 144, 213
Kent, William, Sparham tenant,
    227
Kent, William, Weasenham tenant,
    39, 230
Kerey, John, see Keney, John
Kettle, William, Suffolk ditcher, 233
Ketton Cremer, Robert Windham,
    130, 252, 253, 255, 257
Key, Mrs, 'Nurse', 87, 201
kilns, see brick kilns

Kindersley, Nathaniel, see Kendarly,
    Nathaniel
King, Henry, Dorset/Somerset bailiff,
    25, 30, 39, 236ff.
King, Humphrey, Portbury bailiff,
    239
King, Molly, see bagnios
King, Richard, Durweston tenant,
    237
King, Thomas, Laxfield tenant, 234
King, William, London baker, 165,
    170
King, Mr, London draper, 96
King, 'Dame', Holkham
    washerwoman, 205
Kingham, Robert, Farnham Royal
    miller, 242
Kingsdown manor, Kent, 17, 20, 26,
    28, 34, 236
Kings Lynn, Norfolk, 149, 155
King's Tax, 63
King's Theatre, Haymarket, 132
Kingston, Evelyn Pierrepoint, 5th
    Earl of, 107
Kinsey, Mr, valuer, 140
Kipling, Mr, Academy of Music
    treasurer, 134
Kitchen, Robert, stable-boy, 203
kitchen garden, 56
Knags, Revd Dr, St Giles's lecturer,
    69
Knapp, J. Merrill, 254
Kneller, Sir Godfrey, 142
Knightley manor, Staffordshire, 17,
    22, 24, 25, 28, 30, 34, 36, 37,
    50, 240
Knott (or Knotts), Henry, Holkham
    tenant/blacksmith, 37, 46, 54,
    150, 187, 224
Knott (or Knotts), Robert, Holkham
    tenant, 224
Knowles, Mr, London grocer, 167
Kubleston, Mr, London draper, 101

Lacey, Henry, Suffolk painter, 234
Lamb, Peniston, attorney, 3, 12, 20,
    75, 81, 82, 222
Lamego, Mr, see London, Bevis Marks
Lamerie, Paul de, silversmith, 179
land management, 18ff., 27, 36
Land Tax, 20ff., 29, 117
Lane, John, Revd, Wendling curate,
    48, 225, 226
Lane, Mr, London tailor, 210
Langford, Paul, 250
Langton, John, Farnham Royal
    tenant, 242
Langton, Joseph, Farnham Court
    tenant, 60, 242
Langwood, Fulmodeston tenant, 223
Large, John, stable helper, 101, 188,
    206, 210

Large, James, Swaffham carrier, 182
Large, John, huntsman's helper, 151,
    203
La Rochefoucauld, François de, 197,
    257
Latham, widow, Knightley tenant,
    241
Laurence, Edward, 3
Laver, James, 252
Lawman, Alexander, London
    laceman, 197
Lawrence, Allen, Shillington tenant,
    238
Laws, John, West Lexham tenant,
    231
Lawson, Sarah, Holkham kitchen
    helper, 164, 205
Lawson, Wilfrid, Sir, 78
Laxfield manors, Suffolk, 21ff., 26,
    30, 48, 218, 244, 234
Laxfield Rectory, see Laxfield manors,
    Suffolk
Laxfield Roadstreet, see Laxfield
    manors, Suffolk
Lay, William, Minster Lovell tenant,
    242
Layer, Christopher, 126ff.
Layer, Christopher (the elder), 127,
    151
Layer nursery, 38
Layton, John, Norfolk bricklayer, 32,
    222, 225, 227
Leach, Robert, Holkham tenant, 224
Leader, Samuel, Holkham boy, 154
leases, 19
Leather, Andrew, Holkham labourer,
    42
Leather, 'Dame', Holkham
    washerwoman, 205
Lee, James, Fulmodeston tenant, 57,
    223
Lee, John, Knightley tenant, 241
Lee, John, Laxfield tenant, 234
Lee, —, London roadman, 65
Leech, Ann, Holkham servant, 204
Leech, Revd, Longham curate, 225
Leeds, Robert, Billingford tenant,
    220
Leeds, Thomas Osborne, Duke of, 74,
    142
Leeds, William, Holkham tenant, 37,
    54, 224
Legate, William, Laxfield tenant,
    234
Leggett, James, Suffolk thatcher, 234
Leicester, John Sydney, 6th Earl of,
    28
Leicester, Margaret, Countess of, see
    Coke, Margaret, Countess of
    Leicester
Leeke, Mr, London hatter, 10, 97
Lemon, Robert, Cratfield tenant, 231

6
6
6
6
6
6
6
6
6

Lemon, Robert, Huntingfield manor tenant, 233
Le Neve, Mr, 114
Leonardo da Vinci, 144
Lessey, Reynold, Donyatt tenant, 238
Le Strange Hamon, 252
Le Strange, Sir Nicholas, 110
Leverington, Clare, Norfolk builder (?), 223
Lewin, Mrs, London grocer, 176
Lewis, Ann, Holkham casual, 204
Lewis, John, Minster Lovell tenant, 242
Lewis, Mary, Holkham tenant, 224
Lewis, Peter, Holkham wildfowler (?), 104
Lewis, Sarah, Holkham tenant, 224
Leworthy, Mr, Norfolk painter, 182
Lichfield, George Henry Lee, Earl of, 110, 152
Life Guards, Duke of Boloton's Regiment, 93
Lightfoot, Mary, Holborn pauper, 128
lighting, 107, 180
Lincolns-Inn-Fields theatre, 136ff.
  box-keepers, 137
Lindsey, William, Norwich tenant, 46
Lindsey, Dame, Bath hostess, 112
Liniker, Mr, music copyist, 135
Linnet, Revd, London chaplain, 70
Lish, Elizabeth, housemaid, 201, 208, 209
Little Appleton, Norfolk, see Flitcham manor, Norfolk
Little Dunham, Norfolk, 218
Littlejohn, Mr, shoemaker, 90
Little Wicken farm, 27, 54, 229
Livard, Mr, London perfumier, 100
liveried servants and livery, 151ff.
livestock, 55ff.
livings, see Church patronage
Lloyd, Betty, nurserymaid, 89
Loads, Robert, Norfolk ironmonger, 222, 225, 228
Loades, Mr, Holkham painter, 166
Lock, Edward, Minster Lovell builder, 39
Lock, William, Minster Lovell carpenter/bricklayer, 242
Locton, Mr, London harpsichord-maker, 135
Lodder, John, Shillington tenant, 237
Loines, Catherine, under-laundry-maid, 21, 174, 175, 201, 208
Lombard, Mr, Burnham landowner, 29

London
  Bevis Marks, 25, 45, 218, 243
  London Packet, 256
  Saracen's Head Inn, 45
Longford, Derbyshire, 18, 51, 66, 85, 93, 100, 107, 113, 146, 147, 149, 187, 189, 206, 219
Longham and Wendling manor, Norfolk, 21, 40, 48, 218, 219, 225, 244
Longstreth, —, pensioned servant, 128, 209
Lonsdale, Henry Lowther, Viscount, 78
Lorraine, Duke of, 92
Love, Jane, upper-laundry-maid, 188, 201, 208
Loveday, John, 89
Lovel Baronage, 117ff.
Lowde, Mr, Horham Jernegans tenant, 232
Lucas, Francis, nursery-maid, 98, 201
Luti, Benedici, 143
Luttrell, Ann, Portbury innkeeper (?), 22
Lyde, Mr, London cheesemonger, 166
Lynes, Mr, apothecary, 102
Lynn, see Kings Lynn

Macdonald, John, 196, 206, 257
McDonnell, Mary, Mrs, London herb woman, 166ff., 202, 209
MacFarlane, Helen, 72, 250
Machado, Joseph, broker, 79
Mackay, Charles, 251
Mackley, Alan, 250
Macklin, John, nightwatchman, 200ff.
Macky, John, 107, 252
Macmichael, William, 251
Madder, John, Longham/Wendling tenant, 225
Madox, Thomas, 145
Magnus, Thomas, Holkham tenant, 224
Maimon, Mrs, London vintner, 174
Mallam, John, Minster Lovell tenant 241
Mallet, Henry, Dunton tenant, 222
Mallet, Henry, Sparham tenant, 227
Mallet, Thomas, kennelman, 154, 156
Man & Day, drapers, 96
Mandeville, Bernard, 257
Mandry, Mary, Donyatt tenant, 24, 238
Mann, Stephen, dog-boy, 151, 203, 210
Manning, Thomas, Holkham boy, 59
Mann's Brewery, 174ff.

manorial customs, 21ff.
Mansell, Mr, Lord Thanet's huntsman, 152, 187
Mansor (or Manser), Robert, Holkham tenant, 16, 224
manure, 36
manuscripts, 144
Maplescombe, see Kingsdown manors, Kent
Marguerat, John, Edward Coke's footman, 90
Mariner, Baily, Castle Acre Swan owner, 221
Markant, Mr, Norfolk draper/grocer etc., 150, 165, 178, 182
Markham, Sarah, 251, 256
Marks, John, Donyatt bailiff, 50, 238
Marks, Samuel, Donyatt tenant, 238
Marks, Sarah, Donyatt tenant, 24
Marks, William, Donyatt tenant, 238
Marlborough, John Churchill, Duke of, 119
Marlborough, Sarah, Duchess of, 110, 192, 251
marling and marlpits, 19, 36, 56
Marriage, The, see Coke, Thomas, Baron Lovel, Earl of Leicester, 1679–1759
Marshall, Thomas, Kingsdown blacksmith, 236
Marshall, William, Kingsdown tenant, 236
Marshall, William, 40, 248, 250
Martham manor, Norfolk, 26, 29, 225
Martin, John, Holkham servant, 204
Martin, Aldham tenant, 231
Maskall, Mr, London gunsmith, 155
Mason, James (or John), footman, 188, 198
Mason, Francis, widow, Castle Acre tenant, 221
masquerades, see fancy dress
Massingham, Norfolk, see Great Massingham, Norfolk
Masters, Capt., RN, 141
Maurer, Mr, London costumier, 108
May, Henry, Holkham thatcher/labourer, 41, 58, 164, 176
May, Robert, Norfolk hurdle-maker, 227
Mays, Robert, Holkham in-house brewing, 174, 205
Mead, Richard, Dr, 88, 91, 103
Meadows, John, Huntingfield manor tenant, 233
Meck, Thomas, Billingford tenant, 220
Meck, 'Widow', Billingford tenant, 220

Medcalf, William, Holkham casual worker, 174, 205
medical expenses, 85, 88
Meers, Mary, widow, Laxfield tenant, 235
Meeson, John, Knightley tenant, 240
Mellenton,William, brickmaker, 55, 224
Melmoth, Mr, Shillington tenant, 237
Merrit, Ann, London sweep, 63
Metcalf, William, Holkham tenant, 224
Middleton, Hugh, London goldsmith, 63
Middleton, John, Wisbech church patron, 49
Middleton, Nicholas, Kingsdown tenant, 236
Might, William, Holkham horse-collar-maker, 55
Mildenhall manor, Suffolk, 27, 39, 46, 219, 235
Mileham manor, Norfolk, 26, 59, 229
Miles, Mr, London vintner, 172
Milhouse, Judith, 254
Millington, Edward, Knightley tenant, 241
Mills, Revd Dr, Holborn St Giles's curate, 69
Mills, Mr, Holborn St Giles's overseer, 63
Minster Lovell manor, Oxon, 23, 25, 28, 30, 32ff., 39, 41, 45, 46, 50, 51, 107, 146, 155, 189, 218, 241
Mitchell, William, Fulmodeston tenant, 223
Mitford, Nancy, 253
moles and molecatchers, 60
Mollet, John and Robert, Scotshall tenants, 235
Money, John, Fulmondeston tenant, 49, 223
Money, John, labourer, 36, 56
Money, Revd, Flitcham curate, 48, 223
Montagu, John Montagu, 2nd Duke of, 67
Montagu House, 62, 173
Moore, Capel, 125
Moore, Edward, Knightley woodward, 22, 24, 240
More, Monsieur, London vintner, 172
Morecroft, Thomas, estate master carpenter, 27, 31, 33, 35, 38, 39, 45, 48, 54, 55, 57, 202, 210, 228, 229
Moregrave, Norfolk, 219
Morell, Mr, Norfolk butcher, 164

Morgan, William, Sir, 115
Morley, John, Donyatt tenant, 238
Morn, Mr, London costumier, 108
Morrin, Mr, London perruquier, 99
Morris, widow, Portbury tenant, 239
Morrish, John, whipper-in, 151
Mortier, David, cartographer, 250
Mortimer-Lee, Paul, 250
Mortlock, D.P., 254, 255
Morton, Mr, Holborn livery stables, 186
Mosby, Samuel, Longham/Wendling tenant, 225
Moulton, Edward, Thorington landowner, 15
Moulton, John, Horham Jernegans tenant, 49, 232
Moulton, Joseph, Weasenham tenant, 230
Moulton, Michael, Suffolk carpenter, 233, 234
Moulton, William, Weasenham tenant 230
Mounser, Henry, Gent., Cratfield tenant, 231
Mountain, John, dog-boy/stable-boy, 114, 151
mourning customs; clothing, 97, 209
Mulford, Mr, Bevis Marks tenant, 243
Mumford, Martin, Martham painter, 226
Munsey, Robert, Sparham tenant, 228
Murrell, William, Sparham tenant, 227
Murton, John, Laxfield tenant, 234
music, 131ff.
musical instruments, 135
Myers' Coffee House, 183
Mynne, Sarah, Laxfield tenant, 23

Narborough, Elizabeth, Holkham tenant, 224
Narborough, Mr, Norfolk butcher, 152
Narford, Norfolk, 221
Nash, Richard (Beau), 111, 112
Naylor, Benjamin, Holkham casual, 176
Needham, Mr, Bevis Marks tenant, 45, 243
Newbegin, Thomas, Norfolk landowner, 154
Newbolt, Mr, picture restorer, 143
Newcastle, Thomas Pelham, Duke of 132
Newesham, Mrs, midwife, 87
Newman, John, Aldham tenant, 231
New River, The, 64

Newsham, Mr, London plumber (?), 65
Newson, Thomas, Suffolk ironmonger, 234
Newson, William, Cratfield tenant, 232
Newton, Isaac, Sir, 77
Newton, John, 110, 153, 188. 222
Newton, John, Sir, Thomas Coke's grandfather, 12, 18, 52, 67, 84, 91, 93, 99, 102, 143, 148, 150, 228
Newton, Sarah, London fruiterer, 167
Newton Close, Norfolk, 218
Newton Mill, Norfolk, 221
Nicholls, Anne, widow, Holkham tenant, 48, 54, 224
Nicholls, William, Huntingfield Park/Manor tenant, 233
Nicols, Mr, see London, Bevis Marks
Nobbs, John, Holkham labourer, 41
Norfolk manors, 220ff.
Norman, William, Farnham Royal carpenter, 243
Norreaux, Monsieur, chef, 196
North, Henry, Laxfield tenant, 234
North, Richard, Knightley tenant, 241
North, Roger, Sir, 222
North Elmham Deer Park, 33, 34, 43, 148, 218
North Elmham manor, 222
Norton, George, Sir, Portbury tenant, 239
Norwich
  Bishop of, see Trimnell, Charles, Bishop
  City Waits, 132
  Norwich Gazette, 132
  Norwich Mercury, 157
  Paston House, 15, 46, 219
  Pit Street, 46
  St Peter Parmentergate church, 15–16
Nottingham, Daniel Finch, Earl of, 189
Nunn, Richard, Huntingfield Park tenant, 233

Oakley, John, Knightley tenant, 240
Obelisk Wood, see Great Wood
O'Keefe, John, 194, 256
Okeover, Mr, Huntingfield Park tenant, 233
Old, Mr, London furniture dealer, 182
Old Master drawings, 143ff.
opera, 132ff.
Orbel, Mr, Bevis Hall tenant, 243
Osborn, Sarah, 117, 252

Osborne, Thomas, Donyatt tenant, 239
Osborne, Mr, London breeches-maker, 97
otter hunting, 156
Oxbrough, Mr, Wells shipowner, 173
Oxborough, Norfolk, 60, 152
Oxenford, John, Customs House Officer, 144
Oxford, Henrietta, Countess of, 110
Oxfordshire manor, 241

Page, Nathaniel, Wellingham tenant, 231
paintings, 142ff.
Palgrave, Norfolk, 221
Palmer, Ann, London charwoman, 201
Palmer, 'Goody', Holkham nurse, 210
Palmer, Henry, 2nd stable-boy, 154, 202
Palmer, James, Holkham pensioner, 128, 209
Palmer, Robert, Minster Lovell tenant, 242
Palmer, Thomas, gamekeeper, 154, 155, 224
Palmer, Mr, London carter, 141
pantomime, 136ff.
Panworth Hall manor, Norfolk, 17, 28, 39, 49, 218, 226
parish taxes, 25, 63
parish watch, 66
Parker, Andrew, under-gardener, 204
Parker, John, Norfolk brickmaker, 57
Parker, Sir Philip, 188
Parker, Robert, Minster Lovell gamekeeper, 41, 241
Parker, R.A.C., 4, 81, 247, 250, 251
Parker, Samuel, cartographer, 62
Parliament, Member of, see under Coke, Thomas, Baron Lovel, Earl of Leicester
Parton, John, 249
Paston, Bridget, see Coke, Bridget
Pattison, Mr, London smith, 66
Paulet, John, Earl of, 107
Peacock, Mr, Minster Lovell tenant, 23, 242
Peacock, Mr, assigns of, Minster Lovell tenant, 241
Peckover, Edward, Norfolk corn merchant, 178
Peckover, Mr, London grocer, 167
Peakhall, Norfolk, see Tittleshall manors, Norfolk
peerage, 105
Pellitere, Monsieur, art dealer, 144
Pelly, Phebe (sic), Durweston tenant, 237

Pennington, John, gardener, 203
Pennington, Joseph, 78
Pepper, William, Suffolk brickmaker, 233
Pepys, Samuel, 185, 256
Perkins, Mr, Chancery solicitor, 95
Perrin, Monsieur, mathematics teacher, 89
perukes, see wigs
Perryer, William, Kingsdown blacksmith tenant, 236
Peterborough, Charles Mordaunt, 3rd Earl of 67
pets, 103
Pettiver, Edward, Tittleshall tenant, 229
pewter, 179
Pharah, 'Nurse', 85
Philpott, John, Horham Thorpehall tenant, 232
Pickford, Margaret, 150
Pickford, William, hare huntsman, 21, 127, 151, 156, 165, 203, 224
Pickworth, Thomas, coachman's stable helper, 203
Pigg, Andrew, Deer Park keeper, 43ff., 222, 205
Pigg, Henry, Flitcham tenant, 222
Pigg, Thomas, Elmham tenant, 222
Pigg, Thomas, Longham/Wendling tenant, 225
Pigg, Thomas, Waterden tenant, 230
Pigg, William, Waterden tenant, 155, 164, 230
Pigg, William, Longham/Wendling tenant, 225
Pilch, James, Tittleshall tenant, 229
Pilch, Richard, Longham/Wendling tenant, 225
Pim, Mary, Holkham servant, 204
Pimlow, Abraham, Revd, Castle Acre vicar, 48, 221
Pine, John, 115, 252
pin money, 101
Pitsea Hall, Essex, 218
Pittone, Mr, South Sea Co. clerk, 80
Pitts, Richard, 220
Place, Francis, 62, 249
Plumb, J.H., 82, 251
Plummer, Mr, creditor, 82
poachers and poaching, 154
Polden, Robert, Durweston tenant, 237
Poley, Isaac, Castle Acre tenant, 221
Pomfret, Lord, 115
Pooley, Joseph, Scotshall miller, 235
Pooley, Thomas, Huntingfield Park tenant, 233
Pope, John, Shillington tenant, 237
Pope, Mr, Kent woodmerchant, 236
Popham, A.E., 254, 257

Porta, Giovanni, composer, 133
Portbury manor, Somerset, 21, 22, 24, 25, 28, 30, 39, 46, 49, 239
Porter, Richard, Holkham brick, tile and timber supplier, 21, 30, 35, 54, 164, 166, 175, 224, 225, 227, 229, 230
Porter, Robert, Donyatt tenant, 239
Porter, Roy, 250, 252, 255
Porter, Thomas, 3rd stable-boy, 202
Porter, Mr London vintner, 174
Portland, William Henry Bentinck, Duke of, 78
Portman, Henry, 80
postal services, 104
Pounds (village), 26
Powditch, Mr, Creake landowner, 153
Powditch, Thomas, Quarles tenant, 226
Powell, Thomas, St Giles's vestry clerk, 70
Powell, Mr, London draper, 96
Powis, Richard, Esq., Aldham tenant, 231
Pratt, Jackson, 153
Prescod, Hugh, boarding kennels, 151
Price, Mrs, Lord Thanet's housekeeper, 13
Prideaux, Humphrey, Dean of Norwich, 46
Procaccini, Andrea, 143
Proverb, Thomas, London nurseryman, 67
Prower, John, Durweston tenant, 237
Pugh, Mr, London glassman, 107
Pulham, Samuel, Horham Thorpehall/Jernegans tenant/woodward/court keeper, 39, 232
Pullen, Peter, Huntingfield Park (Hundred and Liberty of Blithing) tenant, 233
Pullin, Richard, pensioned servant, 128, 209
Pulteney, William, 1st Earl of Bath, 122, 124, 125, 253
pump trees, 34
Purden, John, nightwatchman, 65
Purden, Mr, London watchmaker, 90, 100
Purnell, Joseph, Portbury tenant, 239
Purvalent, Mrs, Bath brewer, 112
Pyle, Edmund, 255

Quarles manor, Norfolk, 29, 226
Queen of Hungary water, 102

Quinter, Elizabeth, Holkham pauper, 128
quit rents, 28ff.

Rabbits, John, Durweston tenant, 237
Rabbits, Richard, Durweston tenant, 237
Rabdy, Sarah, Laxfield tenant, 235
Ragland, Mr London tax collector, 63
Randby, Mr, surgeon, 91
Randle, Richard, Laxfield tenant, 23
Rawlins, John, Kingsdown tenant, 236
Rawlins, Thomas, Kingsdown tenant, 236
Rawlinson, Mr, London grocer/vintner, 167, 173, 175
Raworth, Jean, 115
Raynham, Norfolk, 57, 60
Redfern, John, London stable-boy, 200
Reece, Mrs, Bristol landlady, 113
Reed, Abigail, Holkham pauper, 128
Reeve, Mr, London hosier, 97
Renmer, E., Dereham surveyor, 231
rents, 26ff.
Rice, Robert, South Creake bailiff, lime burner, 227
Rice, William, glazier, 48
Rice, Revd, Flitcham curate, 48, 223
Rich, John, Drury Lane manager, 136, 137
Richard, Frank, 2nd coachman, 199
Richards, Elias, Suffolk ditcher, 234
Richardson, John, Kingsdown woodward, 236
Richardson, Jonathan, 91, 100, 143
Richardson, Robert, Kingsdown tenant, 236
Richmond, Charles Lennox, 2nd Duke of, 107, 108, 115
Richmond, Surrey, 106
Riches, Naomi, 248
Ridding, Mr, London pewterer, 179
Ridour, William, Durweston tenant, 237
Rigby, Edward, 54
Riggs, Francis, 1st coachman, 10, 111, 199
Rigins, Edward, Minster Lovell tenant, 242
ringers, see bell-ringers
riparian rights, 23
Rix, Edmund, Norfolk breeches maker, 56
Rix, George, Norfolk breeches maker, 56
road closures and replacements, 58
roads, 185ff.

Robe, Mr, broker, 79
Roberts, Gabriel, 'Governor', 81
Roberts, Philip, 94ff., 222
Roberts, Richard, Durweston tenant, 237
Roberts, Wenman, see Coke, Wenman
Robertson, Thomas, Sir, 53, 215
Robinson, Thomas, apprentice stable-boy, 202
Robinson, Thomas, whipper-in, 151, 155, 200, 203, 210
Robinson, Mrs, singing woman, 135
Rocques, John, cartographer, 67
Roden, Thomas, Knightley tenant, 241
Rogers, John, auditor, 31
Rogers, John, Gent., Flitcham/Great Massingham/Longham/Weasenham/ Wendling bailiff, 222, 223, 225, 230
Rogers, John, Weasenham tenant, 230
Rogers, Mary, Holkham laundry-maid, 204
Rogers, Robert, Durweston tenant, 237
Roper, Thomas, Donyatt tenant, 239
Rosalba, see Carriera, Rosalba
Rose, Walter, 248
Roseingrave, Mr, see Rosincroft, Mr
Rosenheim, James M., 4, 247, 248
Roses manor, Norfolk, see South Creake manor, Norfolk
Rosincroft, Mr, London spinet-master, 135
Roundiel, Mrs, London robe-maker, 118
Rous, John, Sir, 222
Royal Academy of Music, 108, 132ff.
Royal College of Physicians, 88
Rudd, John, Beeston tenant, 229
Russell, Rachel, Lady, 9, 61
Rust, Miles, Norfolk carpenter, 227
Ruth, —, Edward Coke's valet-de-chambre, 89
Rutley, Francis, Holkham tenant, 225
Rutter, John, Donyatt tenant, 239
Rutter, John, Portbury tenant, 24

Sadler, Edward, London stable-boy/cocker, 149, 200
Sadler, John, Billingford tenant, 220
Sadler, Thomas, Holkham tenant, 225
Safely, James, Weasenham tenant, 230
Safely, William, Weasenham tenant, 230
St Clair, Patrick, Revd, 214

St George's church, Hanover Square, 69
St Giles-in-the-Fields church, 69ff.
St Giles-in-the-Fields Parish, Holborn, 68ff.
St James's Square Nos 5 and 8: 74ff.
St John, Henry, 106
Salisbury, James Cecil, 19th Earl of, 29, 106, 190
Salisbury, Lady, 106, 206
Salvini, Prof., 144
samphire, 167
Sampson, John, Durweston tenant, 237
Sanders, Mrs, Bevis Marks tenant, 243
Sanders, Mrs, London brewer, 175
Sanderson, George, carpet designer, 182
Sandwich, Edward Montagu, 3rd Earl of, 28
Saracen's Head, see London, Bevis Marks
Savigny, Mr, London cutler, 179
Sayer, Nicholas, Longham/Wendling tenant, 225
Scarth, Mary, St Giles's parish 'raker', 63, 65
Schaart, Mr, London vintner, 172, 174
Scharf, George, lithographer, 62
Schmidt, Leo, Prof., 4, 53, 247, 249
Schulthram, Edmund, Holkham tenant, 225
Scotshall and Westleton manor, Suffolk, 26, 28, 32, 235
Scriven, Mr Minster Lovell glazier, 242
Seamor, Richard, Norfolk blacksmith, 223
Searle, Richard, Thorington tenant, 236
sedan chairs, 107, 112, 121, 198, 201
Seer Green Woods, see Farnham Royal manor, Bucks.
Seignadier, Mr, London baker, 165
Seller, John, cartographer, 12
Selman, Thomas, Knightley tenant, 241
Senesino, Signor, castrato, 133
Sergeant-at-Arms in Ordinary, see under Coke, Thomas, Lord Lovel
Seris, Monsieur, dancing master, 107
Serracold, Mr, London greengrocer, 168
servants' annuities, 209
servants' clothing, see clothing
servants, nursing, 209ff.
Seymour, Mr New River collector, 64
Shadbolt, William, lady's 2nd footman, 88, 198, 208, 209

Shaftsbury, Anthony Ashley Cooper, 3rd Earl, 118, 253
Sharp, John, Norfolk blacksmith, 222
Sharpe, Elizabeth, London plumber, 66
Shaw, Mrs, *see* Johnson, Mrs
Shebbeare, John, Dr, 68, 250
sheep shearing, 41, 56
Sheltram, Amy, 'Dame', Holkham washerwoman, 205
Shelvocke, George, 215
Sherringham, Norfolk butcher, 167
Sherwin, London bookseller, 80
Sherwood, William, Norfolk brick-and tile-maker, 227
Shillington manor, Dorset, 24, 29, 38, 50, 219, 237ff., 244
Shirley, E.P., 45, 249
shooting, 148, 155
Short, William, Laxfield tenant, 235
silver, 179ff.
Simkin, Mr, Bristol livery keeper, 113
Simms, John, Shillington tenant, 237
Simon, James, engraver, 67
Simons, Thomas, Minster Lovell tenant, 242
Simpson, Mr London vintner, 173
Simson, Elizabeth, Holkham servant, 204
Single, May, Donyatt tenant, 239
Siris, Monsieur, dancing/music master, 135
Sizeland, Thomas, Castle Acre tenant, 221
Skegg, Samuel, postilion, 199
Skenton, Mr, London toyman, 103
Skippon, John, Quarles tenant, 226
Slin, George, Knightley tenant, 240
Sloane, Hans, Sir, 85ff.
smallpox inoculation, 101
Smart, James, Knightley tenant, 240
Smith, Augustine, Suffolk thatcher, 234
Smith, Benjamin, Norfolk ship-master, 182
Smith, Edward, Master of the Horse, 7, 10, 18, 202
Smith, Francis, Knightley tenant, 240
Smith, Humphrey, Land Steward, 10, 12, 18, 31, 52, 54, 129, 148, 168, 190, 202, 222, 224, 228, 229
Smith, James, London vintner, 175
Smith, John, Laxfield tenant, 235
Smith, John, Suffolk blacksmith, 233, 234
Smith, John, Suffolk thatcher, 233
Smith, Mary, Laxfield tenant, 234

Smith, Paul, Minster Lovell tenant, 241, 242
Smith, Thomas, Donyatt tenant, 239
Smith, William, Minster Lovell tenant, 241, 242
Smith, William, Tittleshall tenant, 229
Smith, Mrs, nurse, 85ff., 98, 100, 201, 209
Smith, Mrs, London vintner, 90
smuggling, 171, 172, 177
Snelling, Bury, Huntingfield tenant, 22
Snelling, Mark, Huntingfield Manor tenant, 22, 233
Snow, Mr, money-lender, 80, 81
Snowering foldcourse, *see* Flitcham manor, Norfolk
snuff and snuffboxes, 10, 100, 129, 178
soil enrichment, *see* marl; manure
Somering, Jerry, footman, 135, 149, 150, 158
Somers, Richard, Huntingfield Park/Manor 233
Somerset manors, 238ff.
Somerset, Algernon Seymour, Duke of, 192
Sommers, widow, Durweston tenant, 237
Sondes, Catherine, Lady, 14, 98
Sondes, Edward Watson, Viscount, 14, 98
South-Sea Ballad, A, 251
Southampton House, 62
South Creake manor, Norfolk, 32, 35ff. 40, 218, 219, 227
South Sea Bubble, 76ff., 120
creditors, 81
Spalding, William, Huntingfield Park carpenter/thatcher/blacksmith, 233, 234
Sparks, —, Quarles tenant, 226
Sparks, widow, Portbury tenant, 239
Sparham manor, Norfolk, 25ff., 34ff. 219, 227–8
Spencer, Ann, milliner, 90
Spiller, Hugh, Donyatt tenant, 239
Sporne, John, Flitcham tenant, 222
Springall, Richard, Revd, Holkham vicar, 55, 87, 129, 157, 162, 167, 171, 177
Springold, Simon, Billingford tenant, 220
Spurling, Ann, Aldham tenant, 231
Spurling, James, Laxfield tenant, 234
squatters, 28
Staffordshire manor, 240
Stairs, Nicholas, vintner, 175, 176
Stallard, Mr, London glover, 97
Stanhope, Mrs 'Hellfire', *see* bagnios

Staple, Samuel, Holkham servant, 204
Starr, Webster, London jeweller, 116
Stead, William, Castle Acre tenant, 221
Stephens, Elizabeth, Holkham laundry-maid, 204
Steward, Isaac, Aldham tenant, 231
still room, 167ff.
Stoakes, John, Norfolk tailor, 97, 203
Stoke Poges, Buckinghamshire, 15, 52, 189, 218
Stow, John, 67, 249
Stow Bardolph, Norfolk, 152
street lighting, 65
Stretch, John, Portbury tenant, 239
Stroad, Mr, London furniture dealer, 182
Strype, John, 61, 67
Stuart, Louisa, Lady, 216
Stuckey, William, Donyatt brickmaker, 239
Suffolk manors, 231ff.
Summerscales, Mr, Castle Acre teacher, 128
Summerson, John, 4, 247
surveys and surveyors, 25, 27, 39, 220ff., 242
Swaffham, Norfolk, 153
Swaffham Bulbeck, Cambs., 219
Swanton, Richard, 55
swan-upper, 45
Swift, Jonathan, 44, 133, 249
swords, carried by servants, 198
Syderstone, Norfolk, *see* South Creake manor, Norfolk
Sylis, Jane, London charwoman, 201

Tallent, William, Cratfield tenant, 232
Talman, John, 52
Tankerville, Charles, Earl of, 107
Taylor, Gordon, 250
Taylor, Margaret, Laxfield tenant, 234
Taylor, Mr, London wax chandler, 180
taxes, *see* King's Tax; Land Tax; parish taxes; window tax
tea and coffee, 176ff.
Tedman, Thomas, Westleton tenant, 235
Tench, Mr, Lord Chancellor's Office, 117
Tennant, Matthew, West Lexham tenant, 231
tennis, 158
Terry, Alice, Billingford tenant, 220
Thackeray, William Makepeace, 62
Thanet, Thomas Tufton, 6th Earl of, 7, 61, 213

Thanet House, 61ff., 143, 167, 174
library, 67
Thatcher, John, Holkham yeoman, 16
thatching, 40
Theobald, Lewis, 254
Thirsk, Joan, 248
Thomas, Abraham, valet-de-chambre, 111, 140, 190, 195, 206, 210, 211
Thomas, John, Portbury tenant, 240
Thomas, Jonathan, Minster Lovell tenant, 242
Thomas, Mrs, milliner, 116
Thomason & Pomfret, London vintners, 171, 172
Thompson, E.P., 44, 249
Thompson, Gladys Scott, 251, 256, 257
Thompson, James, of Walsingham, 155
Thompson, Mrs, housekeeper, 111, 113, 134, 167, 190
Thorington manor, Suffolk, 15, 27, 218, 219, 236
Thornham, Norfolk, 218
Tid, Mr, Wells butter man, 166
Tiley, Mr, London boat-builder, 157
Tills, Robert, Sparham tenant, 228
Tillyard, Stella, 255
Tilmouth, Michael, 254
timber supplies, 35
see also forestry
Tinkler, John, Castle Acre Ostrich Inn (formerly The Crown) landlord/tenant, 221
tips see vails
Tittleshall manors, Norfolk, 15, 18, 21, 26, 31, 35, 37, 39, 47, 218, 244, 229
Tittleshall, St Mary's church, 47
tobacco, 177ff.
Tomkinson, John, Knightley tenant, 240
Tomley, William, Thanet House porter, 82, 175, 200, 206, 208
Tomlin, Mr, London baker, 165
Tompkins, John, bill-sticker, 134
Tompson, Mr, London tobacconist, 178
Tooms, Mrs, London furniture dealer, 182
toothpicks, 100
Topley, John, stable-hand, 149, 150
Tosier, Mrs, Blackheath landlady, 108
Towl, John, Holkham labourer, 58
Townshend, Benjamin, landscape gardener, 67
Townshend, Charles, Viscount, 28, 110

Townshend, George, Viscount, 130, 155
trainbands, 63
Trench, Mary, Donyatt tenant, 24
Trevelyan, G.M., 170, 255
Trevisani, Francesco, 142, 143
Trimnell, Charles, Bishop of Norwich, 222
trophy money, 25, 45
Trott, Richard, Donyatt tenant, 239
Truelove, Mr, London fishmonger, 165
truffles, 167, 255
Trusler, Dr, 193, 257
Tubbing, John, Weasenham tenant, 230
Tubbing, Peter, Dunton tenant, brick-kiln owner, 49, 222, 227
Tubbing, Peter, Weasenham tenant, 230
Tubbing, Mr, Burnham surgeon, 101ff., 153, 210
Tuckey, Richard, Somerset Hundred bailiff, 240
Tufton, Christian, Lady, 13
Tufton, Isabella, Lady, 111
Tufton, John, Sir, 12
Tufton, John, 81
Tufton, Margaret, Lady, see Coke, Margaret, Countess of Leicester
Tufton, Sackville, 80
Tufton, Thomas, 115
Turbeville, A.S., 248
Turbey, Richard, alehouse keeper, 108
Turner, Charles, Sir, 57
Turner, M.E., 248
Turner, Richard, Longham/Wendling tenant, 225
Tuthill, Thomas, Scotshall tenant, 235
Twamlow, Mrs, London hosier, 10
Tywdney, Elizabeth, Longham/Wendling tenant, 225

Uglow, Jennie, 250, 251
Uppark, 107

vails, 13, 70, 85, 89, 118, 137, 188, 206
Vanbushell, Mr, London coach furniture-maker, 186
Van Dyck, Sir Anthony, 142
Van Ruyen, Mr, London furniture dealer, 182
Van Stretton, Mr, London picture restorer, 143
Varditt, John, Holkham smuggler, 175
Vaston, John, surveyor, 25, 39

Vaughan, Mr, London sedan-chair-maker, 186
Veblen, Thorstein, 257
Venables, Richard, Knightley tenant, 240
venison, 44ff., 222
Verdon, John, London shoemaker, 10, 97
Vincent, James, Donyatt tenant, 239
Vine, 'Widow', Durweston tenant, 237
Vivaldi, Antonio, 136

Wade, John, under-gardener, 203
wage rates, 40ff.
Walford, Mr and Mrs, Bevis Marks tenants, 243
Walker, Elizabeth, Holkham casual, 205
Walker, Henry, Holkham in-house brewing, 58, 174, 205
Walker, John, 2nd groom, 188, 199
Walker, John, Great Massingham tenant, 223
Walker, Mary, Holkham casual, 205
Walker, Mr, London asses' milk supplier, 87
Waller, Thomas, Holkham casual, 205
Waller, Mr, creditor, 80, 82, 179
Walpole, Anne, Lady, 12, 45, 98, 103, 182, 209, 222
Walpole, Horace, 69, 114, 124, 216, 253
Walpole, Horatio, Colonel, d. 1717: 229
Walpole, Robert, Sir, 52, 60, 78, 82, 105, 110, 115, 117, 125, 126, 171
Walters, Jane, widow, Knightley tenant, 240
Walters, John, Knightley tenant, 240
Walters, Mrs, midwife, 88
Walton, Isaac, 165
Ward, James, Huntingfield Manor tenant, 233
Wardsilver Rents, 29
Warham, Norfolk, 57
Warmouth, George, Donyatt tenant, 239
Wasey, Edward, Longham/Wendling tenant, 225
watches, 100
Waterden manor, Norfolk, 40, 219, 244, 230
Watling, James, Horham Thorpehall tenant, 232
Watson, John, Longham /Wendling tenant, 225
Waxham, Norfolk, 218
Waynforth, Richard, Cratfield tenant, 232

Weasenham manor, Norfolk, 21, 36, 39, 48, 218, 219, 230

Weatherall, Lorna, 73, 250

Weatherall, Mrs, London butter woman, 165, 166

Webb, Sidney and Beatrice, 256

Webb, Thomas, Farnham Royal glazier, 243

Webster, Robert, 1st groom, 129, 198, 199, 206

Wedgewood, C.V., 5, 247

Wegg, William, warrener and gamekeeper, 54, 154, 225

Wellingham manor, Norfolk, 218, 230, 244

Wells, Mr, Norfolk brickmaker, 55

Wells-next-the-sea, Norfolk, 149, 169, 170, 172, 226

Wendling, Norfolk, see Longham and Wendling manor, Norfolk

Wensum Lodge, see Norwich, Paston House

West, Mrs, Shillington tenant, 238

Westleton, Suffolk, see Scotshall and Westleton manor, Suffolk

West Lexham manor, Norfolk, 22, 27, 37, 231

Westminster School, 90

Westminster Journal, 256

Wetherall, Osbert (Osborn), Beckhall tenant, 151, 220

Whall, Mr, Norfolk brick- and tile-maker, 223

Wheatley manor, see Holkham, Wheatley manor

Wheby, John, Donyatt tenant, 239

Wheeler, Thomas, Gent., Minster Lovell bailiff 241

Wheeler, Dr, Minster Lovell tenant, 23, 242

Wherstead, Suffolk, 219

Whimprey, Mr, 128

Whitby, William, Tittleshall tenant, 229

White, Richard, Portbury tenant, 240

White, Walter, Shillington tenant, 237

White, William, Shillington tenant, 238

White, Mr, Kensington landlord, 87

Whitehall Evening Post, 157

Whiteman, Robert, Panworth Hall tenant, 226

Whiters, John, Minster Lovell tenant, 242

White's Club, 123

Whitwell, Norfolk, see Sparham manor, Norfolk

Whitwich, Mrs, London innkeeper/Bevis Marks tenant, 45

Whitworth, Mr, broker, 80

Wick, Richard, Weasenham tenant, 230

Wicken farm, Norfolk, 221

Wiggenhall St Mary Magdalen, Norfolk, 165

Wighton, Norfolk, 21, 29

wigs, 10, 99ff. 199, 209

Wilbraham, Ralph, 115

Wildebald, Johannes, apprentice, 202

Wilkins, David, Revd, Thomas Coke's first tutor, 119, 147

Wilkins, John, coachman's stable helper, 203

Wilkins, Thomas, Knightley bailiff, 240

Wilkinson, Elizabeth, Holkham pauper, 128

Wilkinson, Joseph, Farnham Royal tenant, 242

Wilkinson, Nathanial, Holkham labourer, 58, 176

Wilkinson, 'Widow', Farnham Royal tenant, 242

Willet, Mr, Minster Lovell oilman, 242

Williams, Absalom, Portbury woodward, 39, 240

Williams, Basil, 255

Williams, Charles Hanbury, Sir, 121ff., 253

Williams, Elizabeth, Holborn pauper, 128

Williams, Elizabeth and Alice, Cratfield tenants, 232

Williams, John, Minster Lovell tenant, 242

Williams, Mr, London tobacconist, 178

Williams, Mr, surgeon, 91

Willington, William, Knightley tenant, 241

Wilmott, Ann, Portbury tenant, 240

Wilson, John, Scotshall tenant (Benstead marshes), 235

Wilson, Michael, 254

Wilson, Richard, 76, 83, 250, 251

Wilson, Samuel, Billingford tenant, 220

Wilson, Worcester, 115

Wilton, Andrew, 254

Wind, Mr, Durweston tenant, 237

window tax, 63

Windham, Ashe, 60, 110, 139

wine, 172ff.

Wintle, Mr, London perfumier, 196

Wisdom, Mr, London surgeon, 88

Wise, Mr, brick- and tile-maker, 243

Wiskers, William, Castle Acre painter, 221

Womack, Mr and Mrs, Panworth Hall tenants, 226

Wood, Anthony, 177

Wood, Robert, Holkham cooper, 166, 225

Woodall, Mr, sculptor, 141

Woodcraft, —, Holkham maltster, coppice timber, 175, 176, 230

Woodforde, James, Revd, 97, 252

woodland management, see forestry

Woodrow, Nicholas, Holkham tile supplier, 225

Woods, William, Laxfield tenant, 234

Woodward, John, Donyatt overseer, 25, 239

Woodward, John, Dr, 88

Woodward, Mrs, Bevis Marks tenant, 43

Woolnough, Robert, Huntingfield Park tenant, 233

Worm, James, Portbury tenant, 240

Wortley, Richard, Holkham fisherman, 157, 164, 167, 172, 205

Wren, Christopher, Sir, 62

Wright, Benjamin, Holkham labourer, 55

Wright, John, Billingford tenant, 220

Wright, John, Norfolk lime-burner, 223

Wright, Richard, Knightley tenant, 241

Wright, Richard, Weasenham tenant, 230

Wright, Mr, London corn chandler, 82

Wyse, Mrs, London milliner, 97

Wyvill, Marmaduke, 87, 153, 222

Yarmouth, Charles Paston, Lord, 228

Yeaveley, Derbyshire, 148

Yew, Mr, London hatter, 97

Young, Arthur, 5, 36, 247, 248

Young, Sarah, housekeeper's maid, 208, 209